CLARA VAUGHAN

BY

R. D. Blackmore

BOOK I.

CHAPTER I.

I do not mean to describe myself. Already I feel that the personal pronoun will appear too often in these pages. Knowing the faults of my character almost as well as my best friends know them, I shall attempt to hide them no more than would those beloved ones. Enough of this: the story I have to tell is strange, and short as my own its preamble.

The day when I was ten years old began my serious life. It was the 30th of December, 1842; and proud was the kiss my loving father gave me for spelling, writing, and pronouncing the date in English, French, and Italian. No very wonderful feat, it is true, for a clever child well-taught; but I was by no means a clever child; and no one except my father could teach me a single letter. When, after several years of wedlock, my parents found new joy in me, their bliss was soon overhung with care. They feared, but durst not own the fear, lest the wilful, passionate, loving creature, on whom their hearts were wholly set, should be torn from their love to a distance greater than the void of death; in a word, should prove insane. At length they could no longer hide this terror from each other. One look told it all; and I vaguely remember my hazy wonder at the scene that followed. Like a thief, I came from the corner behind the curtain-loops, and trembled at my father's knee, for him to say something to me. Then frightened at his silence--a thing unknown to me--I pulled his hands from before his eyes, and found hot tears upon them. I coaxed him then, and petted him, and felt his sorrows through me; then made believe to scold him for being so naughty as to cry. But I could not get his trouble from him, and he seemed to watch me through his kisses.

Before I had ceased to ponder dreamily over this great wonder, a vast event (for a child of seven) diverted me. Father, mother, and Tooty--for so I then was called--were drawn a long way by horses with yellow men upon them: from enlarged experience I infer that we must have posted to London. Here, among many marvels, I remember especially a long and mysterious interview with a kind, white-haired old gentleman, who wore most remarkable shoes. He took me upon his lap, which seemed to me rather a liberty; then he smoothed down my hair, and felt my head so much that I asked if he wanted to comb it, having made up my mind to kick if he dared to try such a thing. Then he put all sorts of baby questions to me which I was disposed to resent, having long discarded Cock Robin and Little Red-riding-hood. Unconsciously too, I was moved by Nature's strong hate of examination. But my father came up, and with tears in his eyes begged me to answer everything. Meanwhile my mother sat in a dark corner, as if her best doll was dying. With its innate pugnacity, my hazy intellect rose to the situation, and I narrowly heeded every thing.

"Now go, my dear," the old gentleman said at last; "you are a very good little girl indeed."

"That's a great lie," I cried; for I had learned bad words from a flighty girl, taken rashly as under-nurse.

The old gentleman seemed surprised, and my mother was dreadfully shocked. My father laughed first, then looked at me sadly; and I did what he expected, I jumped into his arms. At one word from him, I ran to the great physician, and humbly begged his pardon, and offered him my very dearest toy. He came up warmly, and shook my father's hand, and smiled from his heart at my mother.

"Allow me, Mrs. Vaughan--allow me, my dear sir--to congratulate you cordially. The head is a noble and honest one. It is the growth of the brain that causes these little commotions; but the congestion will not be permanent. The fits, that have so alarmed you, are at this age a good symptom; in fact, they are Nature's remedy. They may last for seven years, or even for ten; of course they will not depart at once. But the attacks will be milder, and the intervals longer, when she has turned fourteen. For the intellect you need have no fear whatever. Only keep her quiet, and never force her to learn. She must only learn when it comes as it were with the wind. She will never forget what she *does* learn."

Hereupon, unless I am much mistaken, my father and mother fell to and kissed and hugged one another, and I heard a sound like sobbing; then they caught me up, and devoured me, as if I were born anew; and staring round with great childish eyes, I could not catch the old gentleman's glance at all.

Henceforth I learned very little, the wind, perhaps, being unfavourable; and all the little I did learn came from my father's lips. His patience with me was wonderful; we spent most of the day together, and when he was forced to leave me, I took no food until he returned. Whenever his horse was ordered, Miss Clara's little grey pony began to neigh and to fidget, and Miss Clara was off in a moment to get her blue riding-skirt. Even when father went shooting or fishing, Tooty was sure to go too, except in the depth of winter; and then she was up at the top of the house, watching all round for the gun-smoke.

Ah, why do I linger so over these happy times--is it the pleasure of thinking how fondly we loved one another, or is it the pain of knowing that we can do so no more?

Now, the 30th of December was my parents' wedding-day, for I had been born six years exact after their affectionate union. And now that I was ten years old--a notable hinge on the door of life--how much they made, to be sure, of each other and of me! At dinner I sat in glory between them, upsetting all ceremony, pleasing my father, and teasing my mother, by many a childish sally. So genial a man my father was that he would talk to the servants, even on state occasions, quite as if they were human beings. Yet none of them ever took the smallest liberty with him, unless it were one to love him. Before dessert, I interred my queen doll, with much respect and some heartache, under a marble flag by the door, which had been prepared for the purpose. My father was chief-mourner, but did not cry to my liking, until I had pinched him well. After this typical good-bye to childhood, I rode him back to the dining-table, and helped him and my mother to the last of the West's St. Peter grapes, giving him all the fattest ones. Then we all drank health and love to one another, and I fell to in earnest at a child's delight. Dearest father kept supplying me with things much nicer than are now to be got, while my mother in vain pretended to guard the frontier. It was the first time I tasted Guava jelly; and now, even at the name, that scene is bright before me. The long high room oak-panelled, the lights and shadows flickering as on a dark bay horse, the crimson velvet curtains where the windows were gone to bed, the great black chairs with damask cushions, but hard and sharp at the edge, the mantel-piece all carved in stone which I was forbidden to kick, the massive lamp that never would let me eat without loose clouds of hair dancing all over my plate, and then the great fire, its rival, shuddering in blue flames at the thought of the frost outside; all these things, and even the ticking of the timepiece, are more palpable to me now than the desk on which I write. My father sat in his easy chair, laughing and joking, full of life and comfort, with his glass of old port beside him, his wife in front, and me, his "Claricrops," at his knee. More happy than a hundred kings, he wished for nothing better. At one time, perhaps, he had longed for a son to keep the ancient name, but now he was quite ashamed of the wish, as mutiny against me. After many an interchange, a drink for father, a sip for Tooty, he began to tell wondrous stories of the shots he had made that day; especially how he had killed a woodcock through a magpie's nest. My mother listened with playful admiration; I with breathless interest, and most profound belief.

Then we played at draughts, and fox and goose, and pretended even to play at chess, until it was nine o'clock, and my hour of grace expired. Three times Ann Maples came to fetch me, but I would not go. At last I went submissively at one kind word from my father. My mother obtained but a pouting kiss, for I wanted to wreak some vengeance; but my father I never kissed with less than all my heart and soul. I flung both arms around his neck, laid my little cheek to his, and whispered in his ear that I loved him more than all the world. Tenderly he clasped and kissed me, and now I am sure that through his smile he looked at me with sadness. Turning round at the doorway, I stretched my hands towards him, and met once more his loving, laughing eyes. Once more and only once. Next I saw him in his coffin, white and stark with death. By-and-by I will tell what I know; at present I can only feel. The emotions--away with long words--the passions which swept my little heart, with equal power rend it now. Long I lay dumb and stunned at the horror I could not grasp. Then with a scream, as in my fits, I flung upon his body. What to me were shroud and shell, the rigid look and the world of awe? Such things let step-children fear. Not I, when it was my father.

CHAPTER II.

How that deed was done, I learned at once, and will tell. By whom and why it was done, I have given my life to learn. The evidence laid before the coroner was a cloud and fog of mystery. For days and days my mother lay insensible. Then, for weeks and weeks, she would leap from her bed in fits of terror, stare, and shriek and faint. As for the servants, they knew very little, but imagined a great deal. The only other witnesses were a medical man, a shoemaker, and two London policemen. The servants said that, between one and two in the morning, a clear, wild shriek rang through the house. Large as the building was, this shriek unrepeated awoke nearly all but me. Rushing anyhow forth, they hurried and huddled together at the head of the great staircase, doubting what to do. Some said the cry came one way, some another. Meanwhile Ann Maples, who slept with me in an inner room at the end of a little passage, in the courage of terror went straight to her master and mistress. There, by the light of a dim night-lamp, used to visit me, she saw my mother upright in the bed, and pointing towards my father's breast. My father lay quite still; the bed-clothes were smooth upon him. My mother did not speak. Ann Maples took the lamp, and looked in her master's face. His eyes were open, wide open as in amazement, but the surprise was death. One arm was stiff around his wife, the other lax upon the pillow. As she described it in West-country phrase, "he looked all frore." The woman rushed from the room, and screamed along the passage. The servants ran to her, flurried and haggard, each afraid to be left behind. None except the butler dared to enter. Whispering and trembling they peered in after him, all ready to run away. Thomas Kenwood loved his master dearly, being his foster-brother. He at once removed the bedclothes, and found the fatal wound. So strongly and truly was it dealt, that it pierced the centre of my dear father's heart. One spot of blood and a small three-cornered hole was all that could be seen. The surgeon, who came soon after, said that the weapon must have been a very keen and finely-tempered dagger, probably of foreign make. The murderer must have been quite cool, and well acquainted with the human frame. Death followed the blow on the instant, without a motion or a groan. In my mother's left hand strongly clutched was a lock of long, black, shining hair. A curl very like it, but rather finer, lay on my father's bosom. In the room were no signs of disorder, no marks of forcible entrance.

One of the maids, a timid young thing, declared that soon after the stable-clock struck twelve, she had heard the front balusters creak; but as she was known to hear this every night, little importance was attached to it. The coroner paid more attention to the page (a sharp youth from London), who, being first in the main corridor, after the cry, saw, or thought he saw, a moving figure, where the faint starlight came in at the oriel window. He was the more believed, because he owned that he durst not follow it. But no way of escape could be discovered there, and the eastern window was strongly barred betwixt the mullions. No door, no window was anywhere found open.

Outside the house, the only trace was at one remarkable spot. The time had been chosen well. It was a hard black frost, without, as yet, any snow. The ground was like iron, and an Indian could have spied no trail. But at this one spot, twenty-five yards from the east end of the house, and on the verge of a dense shrubbery, a small spring, scarcely visible, oozed among the moss. Around its very head, it cleared, and kept, a narrow space quite free from green, and here its margin was a thin coat of black mineral mud, which never froze. This space, at the broadest, was but two feet and ten inches across from gravel to turf, yet now it held two distinct footprints, not of some one crossing and re-crossing, but of two successive steps leading from the house into the shrubbery. These footprints were remarkable; the one nearest the house was of the left foot, the other of the right. Each was the impression of a long, light, and pointed boot, very hollow at the instep. But they differed in this--the left footprint was plain and smooth, without mark of nail, or cue, or any other roughness; while the right one was clearly stamped in the centre of the sole with a small rectangular cross. This mark seemed to have been made by a cruciform piece of metal, or some other hard substance, inlaid into the sole. At least, so said a shoemaker, who was employed to examine it; and he added that the boots were not those of the present fashion, what he called "duck's bills" being then in vogue. This man being asked to account for the fact of the footprints being so close together, did so very easily, and with much simplicity. It was evident, he said, that a man of average stature, walking rapidly, would take nearly twice that distance in every stride; but here the verge of the shrubbery, and the branches striking him in the face, had suddenly curtailed the step. And to this, most likely, and not to any hurry or triumph, was to be ascribed the fact that one so wily and steadfast did not turn back and erase the dangerous tokens. Most likely, he did not feel what was beneath his feet, while he was battling with the tangle above.

Be that as it may, there the marks remained, like the blotting-paper of his crime. Casts of them were taken at once, and carefully have they been stored by me.

The shoemaker, a shrewd but talkative man, said unasked that he had never seen such boots as had left those marks, since the "Young Squire" (he meant Mr. Edgar Vaughan) went upon his travels. For this gratuitous statement, he was strongly rebuked by the coroner.

For the rest, all that could be found out, after close inquiry, was, that a stranger darkly clad had been seen by the gamekeepers, in a copse some half-mile from the house, while the men were beating for woodcocks on the previous day. He did not seem to be following my father, and they thought he had wandered out of the forest road. He glided quickly away, before they could see his features, but they knew that he was tall and swarthy. No footprints were found in that ride like those by the shrubbery spring.

I need not say what verdict the coroner's jury found.

CHAPTER III.

Thus far, I have written in sore haste, to tell, as plainly and as briefly as possible, that which has darkened all my life. Though it never leaves my waking thoughts, to dwell upon it before others is agony to me. Henceforth my tale will flow perhaps more easily, until I fall again into a grief almost as dark, and am struck by storms of passion which childhood's stature does not reach.

When the shock of the household, and the wonder of the county, and the hopes of constables (raised by a thousand pounds' reward) had subsided gradually, my mother continued to live in the old mansion, perhaps because none of her friends came forward to remove her. Under my father's will she was the sole executrix; but all the estates (including house and park) were left to my father's nearest relative, as trustee for myself, with a large annuity to my mother charged upon them. There were many other provisions and powers in the will, which are of no consequence to my story. The chief estate was large and rich, extending three or four miles from the house, which stood in a beautiful part of Gloucestershire. The entire rental was about 12,000*l.* a year. My father (whose name was Henry Valentine Vaughan), being a very active man in the prime of life, had employed no steward, but managed everything himself. The park, and two or three hundred acres round it, had always been kept in hand; the rest was let to thriving tenants, who loved (as they expressed it) "every hair on the head of a Vaughan." There was also a small farm near the sea, in a lonely part of Devonshire; but this was my mother's, having been left to her by her father, a clergyman in that neighbourhood.

My father's nearest relative was his half-brother, Edgar Vaughan, who had been educated for the Bar, and at one time seemed likely to become eminent; then suddenly he gave up his practice, and resided (or rather roved) abroad, during several years. Sinister rumours about him reached our neighbourhood, not long before my father's death. To these, however, the latter paid no attention, but always treated his brother Edgar with much cordiality and affection. But all admitted that Edgar Vaughan had far outrun his income as a younger son, which amounted to about 600*l.* a year. Of course, therefore, my father had often helped him.

On the third day after that night, my guardian came to Vaughan Park. He was said to have hurried from London, upon learning there what had happened.

The servants and others had vainly and foolishly tried to keep from me the nature of my loss. Soon I found out all they knew, and when the first tit and horror left me, I passed my whole time, light or dark, in roving from passage to passage, from room to room, from closet to closet, searching every chink and cranny for the murderer of my father. Though heretofore a timid child, while so engaged I knew not such a thing as fear; but peered, and groped, and listened, feeling every inch of wall and wainscot, crawling lest I should alarm my prey, spying through the slit of every door, and shaking every empty garment. Certain boards there were near the east window which sounded hollow; at these I scooped until I broke my nails. In vain nurse Maples locked me in her room, held me at her side, or even bound me to the bed. My ravings forced her soon to yield, and I would not allow her, or any one else, to follow me. The Gloucester physician said that since the disease of my mind had taken that shape, it would be more dangerous to thwart than to indulge it.

It was the evening of the third day, and weary with but never *of* my search, I was groping down the great oak-staircase in the dusk, hand after hand, and foot by foot, when suddenly the main door-bell rang. The snow was falling heavily, and had deadened the sound of wheels. At once I slid (as my father had taught me to do) down the broad balustrade, ran across the entrance-hall, and with my whole strength drew back the bolt of the lock. There I stood in the porch, unfrightened, but with a new kind of excitement on me. A tall dark man came up the steps, and shook the snow from his boots. The carriage-lamp shone in my face. I would not let him cross the threshold, but stood there and confronted him. He pretended to take me for some servant's child, and handed me a parcel covered with snow. I flung it down, and said, looking him full in the face, "I am Clara Vaughan, and you are the man who killed my father." "Carry her in, John," he said to the servant--"carry her in, or the poor little thing will die. What eyes!" and he used some foreign oath--"what wonderful eyes she has!"

That burst of passion was the last conscious act of the young and over-laboured brain. For three months I wandered outside the gates of sorrow. My guardian, as they told me, was most attentive throughout the whole course of the fever, and even in the press of business visited me three times every day. Meanwhile, my mother was slowly shaking off the stupor which lay upon her, and the new fear of losing me came through that thick heaviness, like the wind through a fog. Doubtless it helped to restore her senses, and awoke her to the work of life. Then, as time went on, her former beauty and gentleness came back, and her reason too, as regarded other subjects. But as to that which all so longed to know, not a spark of evidence could be had from her. The faintest allusion to that crime, the name of her loved husband, the mere word "murder" uttered in her presence--and the consciousness would leave her eyes, like a loan withdrawn. Upright she sat and rigid as when she was found that night, with the lines of her face as calm and cold as moonlight. Only two means there were by which her senses could be restored: one was low sweet music, the other profound sleep. She was never thrown into this cataleptic state by her own thoughts or words, nor even by those of others when in strict sequence upon her own. But any attempt to lead her to that one subject, no matter how craftily veiled, was sure to end in this. The skilful physician, who had known her many years, judged, after special study of this disease, in which he felt deep interest, that it was always present in her brain, but waited for external aid to master her. I need not say that she was now unfit for any stranger's converse, and even her most careful friends must touch sometimes the motive string.

As I recovered slowly from long illness, the loss of my best friend and the search for my worst enemy revived and reigned within me. Sometimes my guardian would deign to reason with me upon what he called "my monomania." When he did so, I would fix my eyes upon him, but never tried to answer. Now and then, those eyes seemed to cause him some uneasiness; at other times he would laugh and compare them pleasantly to the blue fire-damp in a coal-mine. His dislike of their scrutiny was well known to me, and incited me the more to urge it. But in spite of all, he was ever kind and gentle to me, and even tried some grimly playful overtures to my love, which fled from him with loathing, albeit a slow conviction formed that I had wronged him by suspicion.

Edgar Malins Vaughan, then about thirty-seven years old, was (I suppose) a very handsome man, and perhaps of a more striking presence than my dearest father. His face, when he was pleased, reminded me strongly of the glance and smile I had lost, but never could it convey that soft sweet look, which still came through the clouds to me, now and then in dreams. The outlines of my guardian's face were keener too and stronger, and his complexion far more swarthy. His eyes were of a hard steel-blue, and never seemed to change. A slight lameness, perceptible only at times, did not impair his activity, but served him as a pretext for declining all field-sports, for which (unlike my father) he had no real taste.

His enjoyments, if he had any--and I suppose all men have some--seemed to consist in the management of the estate (which he took entirely upon himself), in satiric literature and the news of the day, or in lonely rides and sails upon the lake. It was hinted too, by Thomas Kenwood, who disliked and feared him strangely, that he drank spirits or foreign cordials in his own room, late at night. There was nothing to confirm this charge; he was always up betimes, his hand was never tremulous, nor did his colour change.

CHAPTER IV.

My life--childhood I can scarcely call it--went quietly for several years. The eastern wing of the house was left unused, and rarely traversed by any but myself. Foolish tales, of course, were told about it; but my frequent visits found nothing to confirm them. At night, whenever I could slip from the care of good but matter-of-fact Ann Maples, I used to wander down the long corridor, and squeeze through the iron gate now set there, half in hope and half in fear of meeting my father's spirit. For such an occasion all my questions were prepared, and all the answers canvassed. My infant mind was struggling ever to pierce the mystery which so vaguely led its life. Years only quickened my resolve to be the due avenger, and hardened the set resolve into a fatalist's conviction. My mother, always full of religious feeling, taught me daily in the Scriptures, and tried to make me pray. But I could not take the mild teachings of the Gospel as a little child. To me the Psalms of David, and those books of the Old Testament which recount and seem to applaud revenge, were sweeter than all the balm of Gilead; they supplied a terse and vigorous form to my perpetual yearnings. With a child's impiety, I claimed for myself the mission of the Jews against the enemies of the Lord. The forms of prayer, which my mother taught me, I mumbled through, while looking in her gentle face, with anything but a prayerful gaze. For my own bedside I kept a widely different form, which even now I shudder to repeat. And yet I loved dear mother truly, and pitied her sometimes with tears; but the shadow-love was far the deeper.

My father's grave was in the churchyard of the little village which clustered and nestled beyond our lodge. It was a real grave. The thought of lying in a vault had always been loathsome to him, and he said that it struck him cold. So fond was he of air and light and freedom, the change of seasons and weather, and the shifting of the sun and stars, that he used to pray that they still might pass over his buried head; that he might lie, not in the dark lockers of death, but in the open hand of time. His friends used to think it strange that a man of so light and festive nature should ever talk of death; yet so he often did, not morbidly, but with good cheer. In pursuance, therefore, of his well-known wish, the vaults wherein there lay five centuries of Vaughan dust were not opened for him; neither was his grave built over with a hideous ash-bin; but lay narrow, fair, and humble, with a plain, low headstone of the whitest marble, bearing his initials deeply carved in grey. Through our warm love and pity, and that of all the village, and not in mere compliance with an old usage of the western counties, his simple bed was ever green and white with the fairest of low flowers. Though otherwise too moody and reckless to be a gardener, I loved to rear from seed his favourite plants, and keep them in my room until they blossomed; then I would set them carefully along his grave, and lie down beside it, and wonder whether his spirit took pleasure in them.

But more often, it must be owned, I laid a darker tribute there. The gloomy channel into which my young mind had been forced was overhung, as might be expected, by a sombre growth. The legends of midnight spirits, and the tales of blackest crime, shed their poison on me. From the dust of the library I exhumed all records of the most famous atrocities, and devoured them at my father's grave. As yet I was too young to know what grief it would cause to him who slept there, could he but learn what his only child was doing. That knowledge would at once have checked me, for his presence was ever with me, and his memory cast my thoughts, as moonlight shapes the shadows.

The view from the churchyard was a lovely English scene. What higher praise can I give than this? Long time a wanderer in foreign parts, nothing have I seen that comes from nature to the heart like a true English landscape.

The little church stood back on a quiet hill, which bent its wings in a gentle curve to shelter it from the north and east. These bending wings were feathered, soft as down, with, larches, hawthorn, and the lightly-pencilled birch, between which, here and there, the bluff rocks stood their ground. Southward, and beyond the glen, how fair a spread of waving country we could see! To the left, our pretty lake, all clear and calm, gave back the survey of the trees, until a bold gnoll, fringed with alders, led it out of sight. Far away upon the right, the Severn stole along its silver road, leaving many a reach and bend, which caught towards eventide the notice of the travelled sun. Upon the horizon might be seen at times, the blue distance of the Brecon hills.

Often when I sat here all alone, and the evening dusk came on, although I held those volumes on my lap, I could not but forget the murders and the revenge of men, the motives, form, and evidence of crime, and nurse a vague desire to dream my life away.

Sometimes also my mother would come here, to read her favourite Gospel of St. John. Then I would lay the dark records on the turf, and sit with my injury hot upon me, wondering at her peaceful face. While, for her sake, I rejoiced to see the tears of comfort and contentment dawning in her eyes, I never grieved that the soft chastenment was not shed on me. For her I loved and admired it; for myself I scorned it utterly.

The same clear sunshine was upon us both: we both were looking on the same fair scene--the gold of ripening corn, the emerald of woods and pastures, the crystal of the lake and stream; above us both the peaceful heaven was shed, and the late distress was but a night gone by--wherefore had it left to one the dew of life, to the other a thunderbolt? I knew not the reason then, but now I know it well.

Although my favourite style of literature was not likely to improve the mind, or yield that honeyed melancholy which some young ladies woo, to me it did but little harm. My will was so bent upon one object, and the whole substance and shape of my thoughts so stanch in their sole ductility thereto, that other things went idly by me, if they showed no power to promote my end. But upon palpable life, and the doings of nature I became observant beyond my age. Things in growth or motion round me impressed themselves on my senses, as if a nerve were touched. The uncoiling of a fern-frond, the shrinking of a bind-weed blossom, the escape of a cap-pinched bud, the projection of a seed, or the sparks from a fading tuberose, in short, the lighter prints of Nature's sandalled foot, were traced and counted by me. Not that I derived a maiden pleasure from them, as happy persons do, but that it seemed my business narrowly to heed them.

As for the proud phenomena of imperial man, so far as they yet survive the crucible of convention--the lines where cunning crouches, the smile that is but a brain-flash, the veil let down across the wide mouth of greed, the guilt they try to make volatile in charity,--all these I was not old and poor enough to learn. Yet I marked unconsciously the traits of individuals, the mannerism, the gesture, and the mode of speech, the complex motive, and the underflow of thought. So all I did, and all I dreamed, had one colour and one aim.

My education, it is just to say, was neglected by no one but myself. My father's love of air and heaven had descended to me, and nothing but my mother's prayers or my own dark quest could keep me in the house. Abstract principles and skeleton dogmas I could never grasp; but whatever was vivid and shrewd and native, whatever had point and purpose, was seized by me and made my own. My faculties were not large, but steadfast now, and concentrated.

Though several masters tried their best, and my governess did all she could, I chose to learn but little. Drawing and music (to soothe my mother) were my principal studies. Of poetry I took no heed, except in the fierce old drama.

Enough of this. I have said so much, not for my sake, but for my story.

CHAPTER V.

On the fifth anniversary of my father's death, when I was fifteen years of age, I went to visit (as I always did upon that day) the fatal room. Although this chamber had been so long unused, the furniture was allowed to remain; and I insisted passionately that it should be my charge. What had seemed the petulance of a child was now the strong will of a thoughtful girl.

I took the key from my bosom, where I always kept it, and turned it in the lock. No mortal had entered that door since I passed it in my last paroxysm, three weeks and a day before. I saw a cobweb reaching from the black finger-plate to the third mould of the beading. The weather had been damp, and the door stuck fast to the jamb, then yielded with a crack. Though I was bold that day, and in a mood of triumph, some awe fell on me as I entered. There hung the heavy curtain, last drawn by the murderer's hand; there lay the bed-clothes, raised for the blow, and replaced on death; and there was the pillow where sleep had been so prolonged. All these I saw with a forced and fearful glance, and my breath stood still as the wind in a grave.

Presently a light cloud floated off the sun, and a white glare from the snow of the morning burst across the room. My sight was not so dimmed with tears as it generally was when I stood there, for I had just read the history of a long-hidden crime detected, and my eyes were full of fierce hope. But stricken soon to the wonted depth of sadness, with the throbs of my heart falling like the avenger's step, I went minutely through my death-inspection. I felt all round the dusty wainscot, opened the wardrobes and cupboards, raised the lids of the deep-bayed window-seats, peered shuddering down the dark closet, where I believed the assassin had lurked, started and stared at myself in the mirror, to see how lone and wan I looked, and then approached the bed, to finish my search in the usual place, by lying and sobbing where my father died. I had glanced beneath it and round the pillars, and clutched the curtain as if to squeeze out the truth, and was just about to throw myself on the coverlet and indulge the fit so bitterly held at bay, when something on the hangings above the head-board stopped me suddenly. There I saw a narrow line of deep and glowing red. It grew so vivid on the faded damask, and in the white glare of the level sun, that I thought it was on fire. Hastily setting a chair by the pillar, for I would not tread on that bed, I leaped up, and closely examined the crimson vein.

Without thinking, I knew what it was--the heart-blood of my father. There were three distinct and several marks, traced by the reeking dagger. The first on the left, which had caught my glance, was the broadest and clearest to read. Two lines, meeting at a right angle, rudely formed a Roman L. Rudely I say, for the poniard had been too rich in red ink, which had clotted where the two strokes met. The second letter was a Roman D, formed also by two bold strokes, the upright very distinct, the curve less easily traced at the top, but the lower part deep and clear. The third letter was not so plain. It looked like C at first, but upon further examination I felt convinced that it was meant for an O, left incomplete through the want of more writing fluid; or was it then that my mother had seized the dark author by the hair, as he stooped to incline his pen that the last drop might trickle down?

Deciphering thus with fingers and eyes, I traced these letters of blood, one by one, over and over again, till they danced in my gaze like the northern lights. I stood upon tiptoe and kissed them; I cared not what I was doing: it was my own father's blood, and I thought of the heart it came from, not of the hand which shed it. When I turned away, the surprise, for which till then I had found no time, broke full upon me. How could these letters, in spite of all my vigilance, so long have remained unseen? Why did the murderer peril his life yet more by staying to write the record, and seal perhaps the conviction of his deed? And what did these characters mean? Of these three questions, the first was readily solved. The other two remained to me as new shadows of wonder. Several causes had conspired to defer so long this discovery. In the first place, the damask had been of rich lilac, shot with a pile of carmine, which, in the waving play of light, glossed at once and obscured the crimson stain, until the fading hues of art left in strong contrast nature's abiding paint. Secondly, my rapid growth and the clearness of my eyes that day lessened the distance and favoured perception. Again--and this was perhaps the paramount cause--the winter sun, with rays unabsorbed by the snow, threw his sheer dint upon that very spot, keen, level, and uncoloured--a thing which could happen on few days in the year, and for few minutes each day, and which never had happened during my previous search. Perhaps there was also some chemical action of the rays of light which evoked as well as showed the colour; but of this I do not know enough to speak. Suffice it that the letters were there, at first a great shock and terror, but soon a strong encouragement to me.

My course was at once to perpetuate the marks and speculate upon them at leisure, for I knew not how fleeting they might be. I hurried downstairs, and speaking to no one procured some clear tissue paper. Applying this to the damask, and holding a card behind, I carefully traced with a pencil so much of the letters as could be perceived through the medium, and completed the sketch by copying most carefully the rest; It was, however, beyond my power to keep my hand from trembling. A shade flitted over my drawing--oh, how my heart leaped!

When I had finished the pencil-sketch, and before it was inked over (for I could not bring myself to paint it red), I knelt where my father died and thanked God for this guidance to me. By the time I had dried my eyes the sun was passed and the lines of blood were gone, even though I knew where to seek them, having left a pin in the damask. By measuring I found that the letters were just three feet and a quarter above the spot where my father's head had been. The largest of them, the L, was three inches long and an eighth of an inch in width; the others were nearly as long, but nothing like so wide.

Trembling now, for the rush of passion which stills the body was past, and stepping silently on the long silent floor, I went to the deep dark-mullioned window and tried to look forth. After all my lone tumult, perhaps I wanted to see the world. But my jaded eyes and brain showed only the same three letters burning on the snow and sky. Evening, a winter evening, was fluttering down. The sun was spent and stopped by a grey mist, and the landscape full of dreariness and cold. For miles, the earth lay white and wan, with nothing to part life from death. No step was on the snow, no wind among the trees; fences, shrubs, and hillocks were as wrinkles in a winding-sheet, and every stark branch had like me its own cold load to carry.

But on the left, just in sight from the gable-window, was a spot, black as midnight, in the billowy snow. It was the spring which had stored for me the footprints. Perhaps I was superstitious then; the omen was accepted. Suddenly a last gleam from the dauntless sun came through the ancient glass, and flung a crimson spot upon my breast. It was the red heart, centre of our shield, won with Coeur de Lion.

Oh scutcheons, blazonments, and other gewgaws, by which men think to ennoble daylight murders, how long shall fools account it honour to be tattooed with you? Mercy, fellow-feeling, truth, humility, virtues that never flap their wings, but shrink lest they should know they stoop, what have these won? Gaze sinister, and their crest a pillory.

With that red pride upon my breast, and that black heart within, and my young form stately with revenge, I was a true descendant of Crusaders.

CHAPTER VI.

To no one, not even to Thomas Kenwood (in whom I confided most), did I impart the discovery just described. Again and again I went to examine those letters, jealous at once of my secret, and fearful lest they should vanish. But though they remained perhaps unaltered, they never appeared so vivid as on that day.

With keener interest I began once more to track, from page to page, from volume to volume, the chronicled steps of limping but sure-footed justice.

Not long after this I was provided with a companion. "Clara," said my guardian one day at breakfast, "you live too much alone. Have you any friends in the neighbourhood?"

"None in the world, except my mother."

"Well, I must try to survive the exclusion. I have done my best. But your mother has succeeded in finding a colleague. There's a cousin of yours coming here very soon."

"Mother dear," I cried in some surprise, "you never told me that you had any nieces."

"Neither have I, my darling," she replied, "nor any nephews either; but your uncle has; and I hope you will like your visitor."

"Now remember, Clara," resumed my guardian, "it is no wish of mine that you should do so. To me it is a matter of perfect indifference; but your mother and myself agreed that a little society would do you good."

"When is she to come?" I asked, in high displeasure that no one had consulted me.

"He is likely to be here to-morrow."

"Oh," I exclaimed, "the plot is to humanize me through a young gentleman, is it? And how long is he to stay in my house?"

"In your house! I suppose that will depend upon your mother's wishes."

"More likely upon yours," I cried; "but it matters little to me."

He said nothing, but looked displeased; my mother doing the same, I was silent, and the subject dropped. But of course I saw that he wished me to like his new importation, while he dissembled the wish from knowledge of my character.

Two years after my father's birth, his father had married again. Of the second wedlock the only offspring was my guardian, Edgar Vaughan. He was a posthumous son, and his mother in turn contracted a second marriage. Her new husband was one Stephen Daldy, a merchant of some wealth. By him she left one son, named Lawrence, and several daughters. This Lawrence Daldy, my guardian's half-brother, proved a spendthrift, and, while scattering the old merchant's treasure married a fashionable adventuress. As might be expected, no retrenchment ensued, and he died in poverty, leaving an only child.

This boy, Clement Daldy, was of my own age, or thereabout, and, in pursuance of my guardian's plan, was to live henceforth with us.

He arrived under the wing of his mother, and his character consisted in the absence of any. If he had any quality at all by which one could know him from a doll, it was perhaps vanity; and if his vanity was singular enough to have any foundation, it could be only in his good looks. He was, I believe, as pretty a youth as ever talked without mind, or smiled without meaning. Need it be said that I despised him at once unfathomably?

His mother was of a very different order. Long-enduring, astute, and plausible, with truth no more than the pith of a straw, she added thereto an imperious spirit, embodied just now in an odious meekness. Whatever she said or did, in her large contempt of the world, her lady-abbess walk, and the chastened droop of her brilliant eyes, she conveyed through it all the impression of her humble superiority. Though profoundly convinced that all is vanity, she was reluctant to force this conviction on minds of a narrower scope, and dissembled with conscious grace her knowledge of human nature.

To a blunt, outspoken child, what could be more disgusting? But when upon this was assumed an air of deep pity for my ignorance, and interest in my littleness, it became no longer bearable.

This Christian Jezebel nearly succeeded in estranging my mother from me. The latter felt all that kindness towards her which people of true religion, when over-charitable, conceive towards all who hoist and salute the holy flag. Our sweet pirate knew well how to make the most of this.

For myself, though I felt that a hypocrite is below the level of hate, I could not keep my composure when with affectionate blandness our visitor dared to "discharge her sacred duty of impressing on me the guilt of harbouring thoughts of revenge." Of course, she did not attempt it in the presence of my mother; but my guardian was there, and doubtless knew her intention.

It was on a Sunday after the service, and she had stayed for the sacrament.

"My sweet child," she began, "you will excuse what I am about to say, as I only speak for your good, and from a humble sense that it is the path of duty. It has pleased God, in His infinite wisdom, to afflict your dear mother with a melancholy so sensitive, that she cannot bear any allusion to your deeply-lamented father. You have therefore no female guidance upon a subject which justly occupies so much of your thoughts. Your uncle Edgar, in his true affection for you, has thought it right that you should associate more with persons calculated to develop your mind."

Now I hate that word "develop;" and I felt my passion rising, but let her go on:--

"Under these circumstances, it grieves me deeply, my poor dear child, to find you still display a perversity, and a wilful neglect of the blessed means of grace, which must (humanly speaking) draw down a judgment upon you. Now, open your heart to me, the whole of your little unregenerate heart, you mysterious but (I firmly believe) not ill-disposed lambkin. Tell me all your thoughts, your broodings, your dreams--in fact, your entire experiences. Uncle Edgar will leave the room, if you wish it."

"Certainly not," I said.

"Quite right, my dear; have no secrets from one who has been your second father. Now tell me all your little troubles. Make me your mother-confessor. I take the deepest interest in you. True, I am only a weak and sinful woman, but my chastisements have worked together for my edification, and God has been graciously pleased to grant me peace of mind."

"You don't look as if you had much," I cried.

Her large eyes flashed a quick start from their depths, like the stir of a newly-fathomed sea. My guardian's face gleamed with a smile of sly amusement. Recovering at once her calm objective superiority, she proceeded:

"I have been troubled and chastened severely, but now I perceive that it was all for the best. But perhaps it is not very graceful to remind me of that. Yet, since all my trials have worked together for my good, on that account I am, under Providence, better qualified to advise you, in your dark and perilous state. I have seen much of what thoughtless people call 'life.' But in helping you, I wish to proceed on higher principles than those of the world. You possess, beyond question, a strong and resolute will, but in your present benighted course it can lead only to misery. Now, what is the principal aim of your life, my love?"

"The death of my father's murderer."

"Exactly so. My unhappy child, I knew it too well. Though a dark sin is your leading star, I feel too painfully my own shortcomings, and old unregenerate tendencies, to refuse you my carnal sympathy. You know my feelings, Edgar."

"Indeed, Eleanor," replied my guardian, with an impenetrable smile, "how should I? You have always been such a model of every virtue."

She gave him a glance, and again addressed me. "Now suppose, Clara Vaughan, that, after years of brooding and lonely anguish, you obtain your revenge at last, who will be any the better for it?"

"My father and I."

"Your father indeed! How you wrong his sweet and most forgiving nature!"

This was the first thing she had said that touched me; and that because I had often thought of it before. But I would not let her see it.

"Though his nature were an angel's," I cried, "as I believe it was, never could he forgive that being who tore him from me and my mother. I know that he watches me now, and must be cold and a wanderer, until I have done my duty to him and myself."

"You awful child. Why, you'll frighten us all. But you make it the more my duty. Come with me now, and let me inculcate the doctrines of a higher and holier style."

"Thank you, Mrs. Daldy, I want no teaching, except my mother's."

"You are too wilful and headstrong for her. Come to me, my poor stray lamb."

"I would sooner go to a butcher, Mrs. Daldy."

"Is it possible? Are you so lost to all sense of right?"

"Yes, if you are right," I replied; and left the room.

Thenceforth she pursued tactics of another kind. She tried me with flattery and fictitious confidence, likely from a woman of her maturity to win a young girl, by inflating self-esteem: she even feigned a warm interest in my search, and wished to partake in my readings and secret musings. Indeed, I could seldom escape her. I am ready to own that, by her suggestions and quick apprehension, she gained some ascendancy over me, but not a tenth part of what she thought she had won; and I still continued to long for her departure. Of this, however, no symptom appeared: she made herself quite at home, and did her best to become indispensable to my mother.

Clement Daldy had full opportunity to commend himself to my favour. We were constantly thrown together, in the presence of his mother, and the absence of mine. For a long time, I was too young, and too much engrossed by the object for which I lived, to have any inkling of their scheme; but suddenly a suspicion broke upon me. My guardian and his sister-in-law had formed, as I thought, a deliberate plot for marrying me, when old enough, to that tailor's block. The one had been so long accustomed to the lordship of the property, to some county influence, and great command of money, that it was not likely he would forego the whole without a struggle. But he knew quite well that the moment I should be of age I would dispense with his wardship, and even with his residence there, and devote all I had to the pursuit of my "monomania." All his endeavours to make me his thrall had failed, partly from my suspicions, partly from a repugnance which could not be conquered. Of course, I intended to give him an ample return for his stewardship, which had been wise and unwearying. But this was not what he wanted. The motives of his accomplice require no explanation. If once this neat little scheme should succeed, I must remain in their hands, Clement being nobody, until they should happen to quarrel for me.

To show what Clement Daldy was, a brief anecdote is enough. When we were about sixteen years old, we sat in the park one morning, at the corner of the lake; Clement's little curled spaniel, which he loved as much as he could love anything, was gambolling round us. As the boy lounged along, half asleep, on the rustic chair, with his silky face shaded by a broad hat, and his bright curls glistening like daffodils playing, I thought what a pretty peep-show he made, and wondered whether he could anyhow be the owner of a soul.

"Oh, Clara," he lisped, as he chanced to look up--"Couthin Clara, I wish you wouldn't look at me tho."

"And did it look fierce at its dolly?" I said; for I was always good-natured to him. "Dolly knows I wouldn't hurt it, for it's house full of sugar-plums."

"Then do let me go to thleep; you are such a howwid girl."

So I hushed him off with a cradle song. But before the long lashes sunk flat on his cheeks, like the ermine tips on my muff, and while his red lips yet trembled like cherries in the wind, my attention was suddenly drawn to the lake. There was a plashing, and barking, and hissing, and napping of snow-white wings--poor Juan engaged in unequal combat with two fierce swans who had a nest on the island. The poor little dog, though he fought most gallantly, was soon driven into deep water, and the swans kept knocking him under with rapid and powerful strokes. Seeing him almost drowned, I called Clement to save him at once.

"I can't," said the brave youth; "you go if you like. They'll kill me, and I can't bear it; and the water ith tho cold."

In a moment I pushed off the boat which was near, jumped into it, and, seizing an oar, contrived to beat back the swans, and lifted the poor little dog on board, gasping, half-drowned, and woefully beaten. Meanwhile my lord elect had leaped on the seat for safety, and was wringing his white little hands, and dancing and crying, "Oh, Clara'll be throwned, and they'll say it was me. Oh, what thall I do! what thall I do!"

Even when I brought him his little pet safe, he would not touch him, because he was wet; so I laid him full on his lap.

CHAPTER VII.

The spring of the year 1849 was remarkable, throughout the western counties, for long drought. I know not how it may be in the east of England, but I have observed that in the west long droughts occur only in the spring and early summer. In the autumn we have sometimes as much as six weeks without rain, and in the summer a month at most, but all the real droughts (so far as my experience goes) commence in February or March; these are, however, so rare, and April has won such poetic fame for showers, and July for heat and dryness, that what I state is at variance with the popular impression.

Be that as it may, about Valentine's-day, 1849, and after a length of very changeable weather, the wind fixed its home in the east, and the sky for a week was grey and monotonous. Brilliant weather ensued; white frost at night, and strong sun by day. The frost became less biting as the year went on, and the sun more powerful; there were two or three overcast days, and people hoped for rain. But no rain fell, except one poor drizzle, more like dew than rain.

With habits now so ingrained as to become true pleasures, I marked the effects of the drought on all the scene around me. The meadows took the colour of Russian leather, the cornlands that of a knife-board. The young leaves of the wood hung pinched and crisp, unable to shake off their tunics, and more like catkins than leaves. The pools went low and dark and thick with a coppery scum (in autumn it would have been green), and little bubbles came up and popped where the earth cracked round the sides. The tap-rooted plants looked comely and brave in the morning, after their drink of dew, but flagged and flopped in the afternoon, as a clubbed cabbage does. As for those which had only the surface to suck, they dried by the acre, and powdered away like the base of a bonfire.

The ground was hard as horn, and fissured in stars, and angles, and jagged gaping cracks, like a dissecting map or a badly-plastered wall. It amused me sometimes to see a beetle suddenly cut off from his home by that which to him was an earthquake. How he would run to and fro, look doubtfully into the dark abyss, then, rising to the occasion, bridge his road with a straw. The snails shrunk close in their shells, and resigned themselves to a spongy distance of slime. The birds might be seen in the morning, hopping over the hollows of the shrunken ponds, prying for worms, which had shut themselves up like caddises deep in the thirsty ground. Our lake, which was very deep at the lower end, became a refuge for all the widgeons and coots and moorhens of the neighbourhood, and the quick-diving grebe, and even the summer snipe, with his wild and lonely "cheep." The brink of the water was feathered, and dabbled with countless impressions of feet of all sorts--dibbers, and waders, and wagtails, and weasels, and otters, and foxes, and the bores of a thousand bills, and muscles laid high and dry.

For my own pet robins I used to fill pans with water along the edge of the grass, for I knew their dislike of the mineral spring (which never went dry), and to these they would fly down and drink, and perk up their impudent heads, and sluice their poor little dusty wings; and then, as they could not sing now, they would give me a chirp of gratitude.

When the drought had lasted about three months, the east wind, which till then had been cold and creeping, became suddenly parching hot. Arid and heavy, and choking, it panted along the glades, like a dog on a dusty road. It came down the water-meadows, where the crowsfoot grew, and wild celery, and it licked up the dregs of the stream, and powdered the flood-gates, all skeletons now, with grey dust. It came through the copse, and the young leaves shrunk before it, like a child from the hiss of a snake. The blast pushed the doors of our house, and its dry wrinkled hand was laid on the walls and the staircase and woodwork; a hot grime tracked its steps, and a taint fell on all that was fresh. As it folded its baleful wings, and lay down like a desert dragon, vegetation, so long a time sick, gave way at last to despair, and flagged off flabbed and dead. The clammy grey dust, like hot sand thrown from ramparts, ate to the core of everything, choking the shrivelled pores and stifling the languid breath. Old gaffers were talking of murrain in cattle, and famine and plague among men, and farmers were too badly off to grumble.

But the change even now was at hand. The sky which had long presented a hard and cloudless blue, but trailing a light haze round its rim in the morning, was bedimmed more every day with a white scudding vapour across it. The sun grew larger and paler, and leaned more on the heavens, which soon became ribbed with white skeleton-clouds; and these in their turn grew softer and deeper, then furry and ravelled and wisped. One night the hot east wind dropped, and, next morning (though the vane had not changed), the clouds drove heavily from the south-west. But these signs of rain grew for several days before a single drop fell; as is always the case after discontinuance, it was hard to begin again. Indeed, the sky was amassed with black clouds, and the dust went swirling like a mat beaten over the trees, and the air became cold, and the wind moaned three days and three nights, and yet no rain fell. As old Whitehead, the man at the lodge, well observed, it had "forgotten the way to rain." Then it suddenly cleared one morning (the 28th of May), and the west was streaked with red clouds, that came up to crow at the sun, and the wind for the time was lulled, and the hills looked close to my hand. So I went to my father's grave without the little green watering-pot or a trowel to fill the chinks, for I knew it would rain that very day.

In the eastern shrubbery there was a pond, which my father had taken much trouble to make and adorn; it was not fed by the mineral spring, for that was thought likely to injure the fish, but by a larger and purer stream, called the "Witches' brook," which, however, was now quite dry. This pond had been planted around and through with silver-weed, thrumwort and sun-clew, water-lilies, arrow-head, and the rare double frog-bit, and other aquatic plants, some of them brought from a long distance. At one end there was a grotto, cased with fantastic porous stone, and inside it a small fountain played. But now the fountain was silent, and the pond shrunk almost to its centre. The silver eels which once had abounded here, finding their element likely to fail, made a migration, one dewy night, overland to the lake below. The fish, in vain envy of that great enterprise, huddled together in the small wet space which remained, with their back-fins here and there above water. When any one came near, they dashed away, as I have seen grey mullet do in the shallow sea-side pools. Several times I had water poured in for their benefit, but it was gone again directly. The mud round the edge of the remnant puddle was baked and cracked, and foul with an oozy green sludge, the relic of water-weeds.

This little lake, once so clear and pretty, and full of bright dimples and crystal shadows, now looked so forlorn and wasted and old, like a bright eye worn dim with years, and the trees stood round it so faded and wan, the poplar unkempt of its silver and green, the willow without wherewithal to weep, and the sprays of the birch laid dead at its feet; altogether it looked so empty and sad and piteous, that I had been deeply grieved for the sake of him who had loved it.

So, when the sky clouded up again, in the afternoon of that day, I hastened thither to mark the first effects of the rain.

As I reached the white shell-walk, which loosely girt the pond, the lead-coloured sky took a greyer and woollier cast, and overhead became blurred and pulpy; while round the horizon it lifted in frayed festoons. As I took my seat in the grotto, the big drops began to patter among the dry leaves, and the globules rolled in the dust, like parched peas. A long hissing sound ensued, and a cloud of powder went up, and the trees moved their boughs with a heavy dull sway. Then broke from the laurels the song of the long-silent thrush, and reptiles, and insects, and all that could move, darted forth to rejoice in the freshness. The earth sent forth that smell of sweet newness, the breath of young nature awaking, which reminds us of milk, and of clover, of balm, and the smile of a child.

But, most of all, it was in and around the pool that the signs of new life were stirring. As the circles began to jostle, and the bubbles sailed closer together, the water, the slime, and the banks, danced, flickered, and darkened, with a whirl of living creatures. The surface was brushed, as green corn is flawed by the wind, with the quivering dip of swallows' wings; and the ripples that raced to the land splashed over the feet of the wagtails.

Here, as I marked all narrowly, and seemed to rejoice in their gladness, a sudden new wonder befell me. I was watching a monster frog emerge from his penthouse of ooze, and lift with some pride his brown spots and his bright golden throat from the matted green cake of dry weed, when a quick gleam shot through the fibres. With a listless curiosity, wondering whether the frog, like his cousin the toad, were a jeweller, I advanced to the brim of the pool. The poor frog looked timidly at me with his large starting eyes; then, shouldering off the green coil, made one rapid spring, and was safe in the water. But his movement had further disclosed some glittering object below. Determined to know what it was, despite the rain, I placed some large pebbles for steps, ran lightly, and lifted the weed. Before me lay, as bright as if polished that day, with the jewelled hilt towards me, a long narrow dagger. With a haste too rapid for thought to keep up, I snatched it, and rushed to the grotto.

There, in the drought of my long revenge, with eyes on fire, and teeth set hard and dry, and every root of my heart cleaving and crying to heaven for blood, I pored on that weapon, whose last sheath had been--how well I knew what. I did not lift it towards God, nor fall on my knees and make a theatrical vow; for that there was no necessity. But for the moment my life and my soul seemed to pass along that cold blade, just as my father's had done. A treacherous, blue, three-cornered blade, with a point as keen as a viper's fang, sublustrous like ice in the moonlight, sleuth as hate, and tenacious as death. To my curdled and fury-struck vision it seemed to writhe in the gleam of the storm which played along it like a corpse-candle. I fancied how it had quivered and rung to find itself deep in that heart.

My passions at length overpowered me, and I lay, how long I know not, utterly insensible. When I came to myself again, the storm had passed over, the calm pool covered my stepping stones, the shrubs and trees wept joy in the moonlight, the nightingales sang in the elms, healing and beauty were in the air, peace and content walked abroad on the earth. The May moon slept on the water before me, and streamed through the grotto arch; but there it fell cold and ghost-like upon the tool of murder. Over this I hastily flung my scarf; coward, perhaps I was, for I could not handle it then, but fled to the house and dreamed in my lonely bed.

When I examined the dagger next day, I found it to be of foreign fabric. "Ferrati, Bologna," the name and abode of the maker, as I supposed, was damascened on the hilt. A cross, like that on the footprint, but smaller, and made of gold, was inlaid on the blade, just above the handle. The hilt itself was wreathed with a snake of green enamel, having garnet eyes. From the fine temper of the metal, or some annealing process, it showed not a stain of rust, and the blood which remained after writing the letters before described had probably been washed off by the water. I laid it most carefully by, along with my other relics, in a box which I always kept locked.

So God, as I thought, by His sun, and His seasons, and weather, and the mind He had so prepared, was holding the clue for me, and shaking it clear from time to time, along my dark and many-winding path.

CHAPTER VIII.

Soon after this, a ridiculous thing occurred, the consequences of which were grave enough. The summer and autumn after that weary drought were rather wet and stormy. One night towards the end of October, it blew a heavy gale after torrents of rain. Going to the churchyard next day, I found, as I had expected, that the flowers so carefully kept through the summer were shattered and strewn by the tempest; and so I returned to the garden for others to plant in their stead. My cousin Clement (as he was told to call himself) came sauntering towards me among the beds. His usual look of shallow brightness and empty self-esteem had failed him for the moment, and he looked like a fan-tailed pigeon who has tumbled down the horse-rack. He followed me to and fro, with a sort of stuttering walk, as I chose the plants I liked best; but I took little notice of him, for such had been my course since I first discovered their scheme.

At last, as I stooped to dig up a white verbena, he came behind me, and began his errand with more than his usual lisp. This I shall not copy, as it is not worth the trouble.

"Oh, Clara," he said, "I want to tell you something, if you'll only be good-natured!"

"Don't you see I am busy now?" I replied, without turning to look. "Won't it do when you have taken your curl-papers off?"

"Now, Clara, you know that I never use curl-papers. My hair doesn't want it. You know it's much prettier than your long waving black stuff, and it curls of its own accord, if mamma only brushes it. But I want to tell you something particular."

"Well, then, be quick, for I am going away." And with that I stood up and confronted him. He was scarcely so tall as myself, and his light showy dress and pink rose of a face, which seemed made to be worn in the hair, were thrown into brighter relief by my sombre apparel and earnest twilight look. Some lurking sense of this contrast seemed to add to his hesitation. At last he began again:

"You know, Cousin Clara, you must not be angry with me, because it isn't my fault."

"What is not your fault?"

"Why, that I should fall--what do they call it?--fall in love, I suppose."

"You fall in love, you dissolute doll! How dare you fall in love, sir, without my leave?"

"Well, I was afraid to ask you, Clara. I couldn't tell what you would say."

"Oh, that must depend, of course, on who Mrs. Doll is to be! If it's a good little thing with blue satin arms, and a sash and a slip, and pretty blue eyes that go with a string, perhaps I'll forgive you, poor child, and set you up with a house, and a tea-set, and a mother-of-pearl perambulator."

"Now, don't talk nonsense," he answered. "Before long I shall be a man, and then you'll be afraid of me, and put up your hands, and shriek, and want me to kiss you."

I had indulged him too much, and his tongue was taking liberties. I soon stopped him.

"How dare you bark at me, you wretched little white-woolled nursery dog?"

I left him, and went with my basket of flowers along the path to the churchyard. For a while he stood there frightened, till his mother looked forth from the drawing-room window. Between the two fears he chose the less, and followed me to my father's grave. I stood there and angrily waved him back, but he still persisted, though trembling.

"Cousin Clara," he said--and his lisp was quite gone, and he tried to be in a passion--"Cousin Clara, you shall hear what I have got to say. You have lived with me now a long time, and I'm sure we have agreed very well, and I--I--no, I don't see why we should not be married."

"Don't you indeed, sir?"

"Perhaps," he continued, "you are afraid that I don't care about you. Really now, I often think that you would be very good-looking, if you would only laugh now and then, and leave off those nasty black gowns; and then if you would only leave off being so grand, and mysterious, and stately, and getting up so early, I would let you do as you liked, and you might paint me and have a lock of my hair."

"Clement Daldy," I asked, "do you see that lake?"

"Yes," he replied, turning pale, and inclined to fly.

"There's water enough there now. If you ever dare again to say one word like this to me, or even to show by your looks that you think it, I'll take you and drown you there, as sure as my father lies here."

He slunk away quickly without a word, and could eat no lunch that day. In the afternoon, as I sat in my favourite bow-window seat, Mrs. Daldy glided in. She had put on with care her clinging smile, as she would an Indian shawl. I thought how much better her face would have looked with its natural, bold, haughty gaze.

"My dear Clara," began this pious tidewaiter, "what have you done to vex so your poor cousin Clement?"

"Only this, Mrs. Daldy: he was foolish or mad, and I gave him advice in a truly Christian spirit, entirely for his own good."

"I hope, my dear, that some day it may be his duty as well as his privilege to advise you. But, of course, you need not take his advice. My Clara loves her own way as much as any girl I ever knew; and with poor Clement she will be safe to have it."

"No doubt of that," I replied.

"And then, my pet, you will be in a far better position than you could attain as an unmarried girl to pursue the great aim of your life; so far, I mean, as is not inconsistent with the spirit of Christian forgiveness. Your guardian has thought of that, in effecting this arrangement; and I trust that I was not wrong in allowing so fair a prospect, under Providence, of your ultimate peace of mind to influence me considerably when he sought my consent."

"I am sure I am much obliged to you."

"I cannot conceal from you, so clear-sighted as you are--and if I could, I object to concealment of any kind, on principle--that there are also certain worldly advantages, which are not without weight, however the heart be weaned by trials and chastened from transient things. And your guardian has this arrangement so very much at heart. My own dear child, I have felt for you so long that I love you as a daughter. How thankful I ought to be to the Giver of all good things to have you really my own dear child."

"Be thankful, madam, when you have got it. This is a good thing which under Providence you must learn to do without."

It was coarse of me to hint at my riches. But what could I do with her?

"Why, Clara," she asked, in great amazement, "you cannot be so foolish and wilful as to throw away this chance of revenge? If only for your dear mother's sake, as well as your father's, it is the path of duty. Let me tell you, both she and yourself are very much more in your guardian's power than you have any idea. And what would be your poor father's wish, who has left you so entirely to his brother's care and discretion? Will you put off for ever the discovery of his murderer?"

"My father," I said, proudly, "would scorn me for doing a thing below him and myself. The last of the Vaughans to be plotted away to a grocer's doll!"

It had been a trial of temper; and contempt was too much for hypocrisy. Through the rouge of the world, and the pearl-powder of religion, nature flushed forth on her cheek; for she really loved her son. She knew where to wound me the deepest.

"Is it no condescension in us that my beautiful boy should stoop to the maniac-child of a man who was stabbed--stabbed in his midnight bed--to atone, no doubt, for some low act of his own?"

I sprang up, and rang the bell. Thomas Kenwood, who made a point of attending me, came at once. I said to him, calmly and slowly:

"Allow this person one hour to pack her things. Get a fly from the Walnut Tree Inn, and see her beyond the Lodge."

If I had told him to drag her away by the hair, I believe that man would have done it. She shrunk away from me; for the moment her spirit was quelled, and she trembled into a chair.

"I assure you, Clara, I did not mean what I said. You provoked me so."

"Not one word more. Leave the room and the house."

"Miss Vaughan, I will not leave this house until your guardian returns."

"Thomas," I said, without looking towards her, "if Mrs. Daldy is not gone in an hour, you quit my service."

How Thomas Kenwood managed it, I never asked. He was a resolute man, and all the servants obeyed him. She turned round once, as she crossed the threshold, and gave me a look which I shall never forget. Was such the look that had glared on my father before the blow? She lifted the white arm of which she was proud, and threw back her head, like the Fecial hurling his dart.

"Clara Vaughan, you shall bitterly grieve for this. It shall throw you and your mother at the feet of your father's murderer, and you shall crave meat worse than your enemy's blood."

Until she had quitted the house, I could not sit down; but went to my father's bedroom, where I often took refuge when strongly excited and unable to fly to his grave. The thoughts and the memories hovering and sighing around that fatal chamber were enough to calm and allay the sensations of trivial wrong.

But now this was not the case. The outrage offered had been, not to me, but to him who seemed present there. The suggestion, too, of an injury done by my father, though scorned at first, was working and ruffling within me, as children put bearded corn-ears in another's sleeve, which by-and-by work their own way to the breast. Till now, I had always believed that some worldly advantage or gain had impelled my foe to the deed which left me an orphan. But that woman's dark words had started a new train of reasoning, whose very first motion was doubt of the man I worshipped. Among all I had ever met, there existed but one opinion as to what he had been--a true gentleman, who had injured not one of God's creatures, whose life had been guided mainly by the wishes and welfare of others. Moreover, I had my own clear recollections-- his voice, his eyes, and his smile, his manner and whole expression; these, it is true, were but outward things, yet a child's intuition is strong and hard to refute.

Again, during my remembrance, he had never been absent from us, except for a day or two, now and then, among his county neighbours; and any ill will which he might have incurred from them must, from his position, have become notorious.

And yet, in the teeth of this reasoning, and in spite of my own warm feeling, that horrible suspicion clave to my heart and chilled it like the black spot of mildew. And what if the charge were true? In that case, how was I better than he who had always been to my mind a fiend in special commission? His was vengeance, and mine revenge; he had suffered perhaps a wanton wrong, as deep to his honour as mine to my love.

While I was brooding thus miserably, my eyes fell upon the bed. There were the red streaks, grained and fibred like the cross-cut of a fern-stalk; framed and looking down on me, the sampler of my life. Drawing near, I trembled with an unknown awe, to find myself in that lonely presence, not indeed thinking, but inkling such things of my father, my own darling father, whose blood was looking at me. In a storm of self-loathing and sorrow, I knelt there and sobbed my atonement; but never thenceforth could I wholly bar out the idea. Foul ideas when once admitted will ever return on their track, as the cholera walks in the trail of its former pall.

But instead of abating my dogged pursuit, I now had a new incentive--to dispel the aspersions cast on my father's shadow.

CHAPTER IX.

At this particular time of my life, many things began to puzzle me, but nothing was a greater puzzle than the character of my guardian. Morose or moody he was not, though a stranger might have thought him so; nor could I end with the conviction that his heart was cold. It rather seemed to me as if he felt that it ought to be so, and tried his best to settle down as the inmate of an icehouse. But any casual flush of love, any glow of native warmth from the hearts around him, and taken by surprise he wavered for one traitor moment, and in his eyes gleamed some remembrance, like firelight upon frozen windows. But let any one attempt to approach him then with softness, to stir kind interest and feeling into benevolent expression, and Mr. Vaughan would promptly shut himself in again, with a bar of irony, or a bolt of sarcasm. Only to my mother was his behaviour different; towards her his manner was so gentle, and his tone so kind, that but for my conviction that remorse lay under it, I must have come to like him. True, they did not often meet, for dear mother confined herself (in spite of Mrs. Daldy) more and more closely to her own part of the house, and rarely had the spirits now to share in the meals of the family. Therefore, I began at once to take her place, and would not listen to Mrs. Daldy's kind offer to relieve me. This had led quite recently to a little outbreak. One day I had been rather late for dinner, and, entering the room with a proud apology, found to my amazement Mrs. Daldy at the head of the table. For me a seat was placed, as for a good little girl, by the side of Master Clement. At first I had not the presence of mind to speak, but stood by my rival's chair, waiting for her to rise. She affected not to understand me, and began, with her hand on the ladle, and looking me full in the face: "I fear, darling Clara, the soup is cold; but your uncle can give you a very nice slice of salmon. Have you offered thanks for these mercies?"

"Thank you, I will take soup. Allow me to help myself. I am sorry to have troubled you."

And I placed my hand on the back of her chair, presuming that she would get up; but she never stirred one inch, and actually called for a plate to help me. My guardian was looking at both of us, with a dry smile of amusement, and Clement began to simper and play with his fork.--Now for it, or never, thought I. "Mrs. Daldy, you quite mistake me, or pretend to do so. Have the goodness to quit *my* chair."

She had presumed on my dread of an altercation before the servants, but only Thomas Henwood happened to be in the room. Had there been a dozen present, I would still have asserted my right. At last she rose in her stateliest manner, but with an awkward smile, and a still more awkward sneer.

"Your use, my poor child, of the possessive pronoun is far more emphatic than your good breeding is."

"Who cares for your opinion?" Not a hospitable inquiry; but then she was not *my* visitor.

In grand style she marched to the door, but soon thought better of it, and came to her proper place with the sigh of a contrite spirit.

"Poor creature! It is a rebuke to me, for my want of true faith in the efficacy of prayer."

And after all this, she made a most excellent dinner.

About that woman there was something of a slimy pride, no more like to upright prickly self-respect than macerated bird-lime is to the stiff bright holly. Yet no one I ever knew possessed such wiry powers of irritation. Whenever my mother and my guardian met, she took care to be in the way, and watched them both, and appealed to me with all her odious pantomime of sorrow, sympathy, wonder, loving superiority, and spiritual yearnings. And all the time her noisome smile, like the smell of a snake, came over us. She knew, and rejoiced in the knowledge, how hard set I was to endure it, and every quick flash of my eyes only lit up her unctuous glory.

For all I know, it was natural that my antipathy to that woman should, by reaction, thaw sometimes my coldness towards my uncle. Though self-respect had at length compelled him to abandon his overtures to my friendship, now and then I detected him looking at me with a pitying regard. In self-defence, I began to pity him, and ceased to make faces or sneer when the maids--those romantic beings--declared that he must have been crossed in love. At this conclusion, long ago, all the servants' hall had arrived; and even little Tilly Jenkins, not admitted as yet to that high conclave, remarkable only for living in dust-bins, and too dirty to cause uneasiness to the under-shoeboy's mother-- even that Tilly, I say, ran up to me one morning (when I went to see my dear pony) and beat out her dust, and then whispered:

"Oh, please, Miss Clara, to give my very best wishes to Master. What a terrible blight to the heart be unrequited love!" And Tilly sighed a great cloud of brick-dust.

"Terrible, Tilly: I hope you have not fallen in love with the weeding boy!"--a smart young lad, ten stairs at least above her.

"Me, miss? Do you think I would so demean myself?" And Tilly caught up her dust-pan arrogantly.

This little anecdote proves a fact which I never could explain, viz. that none of the servants were ever afraid of me.

To return to the straight line of history. My guardian came home rather late that evening, and some hours after the hasty exit of Mrs. and Master Daldy. While I was waiting in some uneasiness, it struck me that he had kept out of the way on purpose, lest he should seem too anxious about the plot. Mrs. Daldy, as I found afterwards, had written to him from the inn, describing my "frenzied violence, and foaming Satanic fury"--perhaps I turned pale, no more--and announcing her intention to remain at Malvern, until she should be apprised whether uncle or niece were the master. In the latter case she demanded--not that she cared for mammon, but as a humble means for the advancement of the Kingdom--the sum of 300*l.*; that being the lowest salary conscience allowed her to specify for treading the furnace of affliction, to save the lost sheep of the house of Israel. I forgot to say that, before she left the house, she had tried to obtain an interview with my mother, hoping, no doubt, to leave her in the cataleptic state. But this had been sternly prevented by Thomas Kenwood, who performed quite a labour of love in ministering the expulsion. All the servants hated her as a canting sneak and a spy.

That night when I received Mr. Edgar Vaughan's short missive--"Clara, I wish to see you immediately in my study," my heart began to flutter provokingly, and the long speech I had prepared flew away in shreds of rhetoric. Not that I meant for an instant to bate one tittle of what I had done and would do: but I had never asserted my rights as yet in direct opposition to him, nor taken upon my own shoulders the guardianship of myself. But the dreary years of dark preparation and silent welding of character had braced a sensitive, nervous nature with some little self-reliance.

With all the indifference I could muster, I entered the gloomy room, and found him leaning upon the high desk where he kept the accounts of his stewardship. The position was chosen well. It served at once to remind me of his official relation, and to appeal to the feelings as betokening an onerous wardship. Of late his health had been failing him, and after every long absence from home, he returned more jaded and melancholy. Now a few silver hairs--no more than a wife would have quickly pulled out--were glistening among his black locks; but though he was weary and lonesome, he seemed to want none to love him, and his face wore the wonted sarcastic and travelled look.

As our glances met, we both saw that the issue was joined which should settle for life the mastery. He began in a light and jocund manner, as if I were quite a small thing.

"Well done, Miss Clara, you *are* asserting yourself. Why, you have dismissed our visitors with very scant ceremony."

"To be sure I have; and will again, if they dare to come back."

"And don't you think that you might have consulted your mother or me?'

"Most likely I should have done so, in an ordinary case."

"Then your guardian was meant for small matters! But what was the wonder to-day?"

"No wonder at all. Mrs. Daldy insulted my father, and I sent her out of his house."

"What made her insult my brother?"

"My refusal to marry her puppet and puppy."

"Clement Daldy! Did she propose such a thing? She must think very highly of you!'

"Then I think very lowly."

"And you declined, did you, Clara?"

"No. I refused."

"Very good. No one shall force you; there is plenty of time to consider the subject."

"One moment is too much."

"Clara, I have long noticed in you a rude, disrespectful, and I will say (in spite of your birth) a low and vulgar manner towards me, your uncle and guardian. Once for all, I will not permit it, child."

"*Child* you call me, do you? Me, who am just seventeen, and have lived seven such years as I have, and no one else!"

He answered quite calmly, and looking coldly at me:

"I never argue with women. Much less with girls. Mrs. Daldy comes back to-morrow. You will beg her pardon, as becomes a young lady who has forgotten herself. The other question may wait."

"I thought, sir, that you had travelled far, and in many countries."

The abrupt inquiry startled him, and his thoughts seemed to follow the memory.

"What if I have?" he asked, at length, and with a painful effort.

"Have you always found women do just what you chose?"

He seemed not to listen to me; as if he were out of hearing: then laughed because I was looking at him.

"Clara," he said, "you are an odd girl, and a Vaughan all over. I would rather be your friend than your enemy. If you cannot like me, at least forget your dislike of me, and remember that I am your uncle, and have tried to make you love me."

"And what if I do not?"

"Then I must keep you awhile from the management of this property. My dear brother would have wished it, until you recover your senses; and not an acre of it is legally yours."

This he said so slowly, and distinctly, and entirely without menace, that, knowing his manner, I saw it was the truth, at least in his opinion. Strange as it may seem, I began at once to revolve, not the results of dispossession and poverty on myself, or even on my mother, but the influence which the knowledge of this new fact must have on my old suspicions, surmises, and belief.

"Will the property pass to you?" I asked.

"Yes, if I choose: or at any rate the bulk of it."

"What part will be yours? Do you mean to say the house?--"

"Never mind now. I would rather leave things as they are, if you will only be more sensible."

"I will not disguise my opinions for a hundred Vaughan Parks, or a thousand Vaughan Palaces; no, nor even to be near my father's bones."

"Very well," he said, "just as you like. But for your mother's sake, I give you till Christmas to consider."

"If you bring back Mrs. Daldy, I shall leave the door as she enters it."

"I have no wish to hurry you," he replied, "and therefore she shall not return at present. Now take these papers with you. You may lay them before any lawyer you please. They are only copies, but may be compared with the originals, which I have. They will quickly prove how totally you are at my discretion."

"The money and the land may be so, but not I. Before I go, answer me one question. Did you know of these things, whatever they may be, before my father's death?"

He looked at me clearly and calmly, with no withdrawal, or conscious depth in his eyes, and answered:

"No. As a gentleman, I did not."

I felt myself more at a loss than ever, and for the moment could not think.

CHAPTER X.

Thus was I, and, what mattered much more, my mother, reduced quite suddenly from a position of rank and luxury, and a prospective income of £15,000 a-year (so much had the land increased in value) to a revenue of nothing, and no home. Even to me it was a heavy blow, but what could my poor mother do?

We were assured by counsel that a legal struggle could end in expense alone, and advised by the family lawyers to throw ourselves on the good feeling and appeal to the honour of Mr. Edgar Vaughan. Mr. Vaughan he must henceforth be called. I cannot well understand, still less can I explain, small and threadbare technicalities (motes, which too often are the beam of Justice), but the circumstances which robbed me of my father's home were somewhat as follows:--

By the will of my father's grandfather, Hubert Vaughan, who died in the year 1782, the whole of the family property was devised to his son, Vaughan Powis Vaughan, for life, and after his decease, to his sons successively *in tail male*, failing these to his right heirs in general. This will was said to have been prepared in haste: it was, in fact, drawn by a country attorney, when the testator was rapidly sinking. It was very brief, and by no means accurately worded; neither did it contain those powers to meet family exigencies, which I am told a proper practitioner would have inserted.

There was no reason to suppose that the testator had contemplated anything more than a strict settlement of the usual kind, *i.e.* a common estate entail, expectant upon a life-interest; and under which I should have succeeded my father, as his heiress, in the ordinary course. But it is the chief fault of smatterers in the law (and country attorneys at that time were no better) that they will attempt to be too definite. The country lawyer in this case, grossly ignorant of his profession, and caught by the jangle of the words *tail male*, had inserted them at hazard, possibly not without some idea that they would insure a stricter succession than a common entail would do.

When my father became of age, measures were taken for barring the entail created by the will of Hubert Vaughan; and at the time it was believed that these were quite effectual, and therefore that my father was now entitled in fee-simple, and could dispose of the property.

Upon his marriage with my mother, she, with worthy pride, refused most firmly to accept a jointure charged on his estates, alleging that as she brought no fortune into the family, she would not incumber the family property, which had but recently been relieved of incumbrances. More than this--she had even insisted upon expressly abandoning, by her marriage settlement, all claim to dower. This unusual course she had adopted, because of some discontent expressed by relatives of my father at his marriage with a portionless bride, whereby her self-respect had been deeply wounded. So nothing was settled upon her, except her own little estate in Devonshire, which was secured to her separate use.

My father had never permitted this excess of generosity on her part, but that he was by nature careless upon such subjects, and hoped to provide amply for her interests by his will: moreover he was hot to remove all obstacles to their marriage. But it was now discovered that he had no power to charge the real estate for her benefit, in the manner his will imported; that he had never been more than a tenant in tail, and that entail such that I could not inherit. Neither, of course, could I take under his will, as he possessed no power of disposition. One quarter of all that has been written upon the subject I never could understand; and even as to the simplest points, sometimes I seem to apprehend them clearly, and then I feel that I do not. My account of the matter is compressed from what I remember of the legal opinions.

The leading fact, at any rate, and the key to all the mischief, was, that the entail had never been barred at all: the legal process (called a "recovery") which was to have had that effect, being null and void through some absurd informality. They told me something about a tenant to a precipice, but they must have made a mistake, for there was no precipice on the estate, unless some cliffs near the church could be called so, and they were never let.

Be that as it may, my father's will was declared to be waste paper, except as regarded what they called the personalty, or, in good English, the money he had to bequeath. And of this there was very little, for, shortly before his death, he had spent large sums in drainage, farm-buildings, and other improvements. Furthermore, he had always maintained a profuse hospitality, and his charity was most lavish. The lawyers told us that, under the circumstances (a favourite expression of theirs when they mean some big robbery), a court of equity would perhaps consider our application to be "recupped," as they called it, out of the estate, for the money laid out in improvements under a false impression. But we had been cupped enough already. Grossly plundered by legal jargon, robbed by statute, and scourged by scriveners' traditions, we flung away in disgust the lint the bandits offered, and left them "all estate, right, title, interest, and claim, whether at law or in equity, in to or out of" the licking of our blood.

But now my long suspicions, and never-discarded conviction of my guardian's guilt, were, by summary process, not only revived, but redoubled. This arose partly from the discovery of the stake he had on my father's life, and partly, perhaps, from a feeling of hatred towards our supplanter. That he knew not till now the flaw in our title, and his own superior claim, was more than I could believe. I felt sure that he had gained this knowledge while in needy circumstances and sharp legal practice, brought, as he then most probably was, into frequent contact with the London agents who had the custody of the documents.

To be in the same room with him, was now more than I could bear, and it became impossible that we should live any longer in the same house. He, indeed, wished, or feigned to wish, that we should remain there, and even showed some reluctance to urge his unrighteous rights. But neither my mother (who bore the shock with strange resignation) nor myself would hear of any compromise, or take a farthing at his hands, and he was too proud and stern to press upon us his compunctions.

Statements of our case had been prepared and submitted to three most eminent conveyancers, and the three opinions had been found to agree, except upon some trivial points. More than two months had been thus consumed, and it was now once more the anniversary of my father's death. I had spent the time in narrowly watching my ex-guardian's conduct, though keeping aloof, as much as possible, from any intercourse with him.

One night, I stole into the room which he called his study, and where (with a child's simplicity) I believed him to keep his private documents. Through Thomas Kenwood, to whom I now confided almost everything, and whose suspicions were even stronger than mine, I obtained clandestine possession of the keys of the large bureau. As I stood before that massive repository in the dead of night, the struggle within me was intense and long. What letters, what journals, documents, or momentous relics of a thousand kinds, might be lurking here, waiting only for a daughter's hand to turn the lock, and cast the light she bore on the death-warrant of her father! How easy then to snatch away the proof, clutching it, though it should burn the hand or bosom, to wave it, with a triumph wilfully prolonged, before the eyes of justice's dull-visioned ministers; and then to see, without a shudder or a thrill of joy, but with the whole soul gazing, the slow, struggling, ghastly expiation. As this thought came crawling through my heart, lighting up its depth as would a snake of fire, the buhl before me grew streaks of blood, and the heavy crossbars a gallows. I lifted my hand to open the outer lock. Already the old cruciform key was trembling in the silver scutcheon. I raised the lamp in my left hand to show the lunette guard which curved above the hole, when a heavy mass all cold and dark fell across my eyes. I started, and thought for the moment, in my strong excitement, that it was my father's hand. One instant more, and, through the trembling of my senses, I saw that it was only a thick fold of my long black hair, shaken down on the face by my bending and quivering posture. But the check was enough. A Vaughan, and that the last one of so proud and frank a race, to be prowling meanly, with a stolen tool, to violate confidence, and pry through letters! No suspicion, however strong, nothing short of certainty (if even that) could warrant it. Driven away by shame combined with superstition, I glided from the cold silent room, and restored the keys to my faithful friend, whom I had left in the passage, ordering him at once to replace them, and never touch them again.

"Well, miss," he whispered, with a smile, "I knew you couldn't do it, because I seemed, somehow, it wasn't like a Vaughan."

We were already preparing to quit the house, no longer ours, when our dismissal became abrupt, through another act of mine. What drove me to such a wild deed I can scarcely tell. Shame, perhaps, for the furtive nature of my last attempt hurried me into the other extreme; and now I was so shaken by conflicting impulse, that nothing was too mad for me.

On the seventh anniversary of my father's death, and the last which I was likely ever to spend beneath that roof, I passed the whole day in alternate sadness and passion, in the bedroom where he died. All the relics I possessed, both of his love and of his death, I brought thither; and spread them out, and wept upon the one, and prayed upon the other. I also brought my choicest histories of murder and revenge, and pored over them by the waning daylight and the dull lamp, and so on through the night, until my mind became the soul's jetsam.

Then I procured four very large wax candles, and lit them at the head of the bed, two on each side, and spread a long white cloth between, as if my father were lying in state; and hung a row of shorter lights above, to illuminate the letters of blood. Then I took a small alarum clock, given me by dear father, that I might rise for early walks with him, and set it upon a chest by the door, and fixed it so as to ring five minutes before the hour at which the murder befell. A cold presentiment crawled through me that, at the fatal time, I should see the assassin. After all these arrangements I took my volume again, and sat in the shade of the curtain, with a strong light on the page. I was deep in some horrible record, and creeping with terror and hope, when the clear bell rang a long and startling peal. I leaped up, like one shot through the heart, and what I did was without design or purpose. My glance fell on the dagger; I caught it up, and snatched the lamp, and hurried down corridor and staircase, straight to my guardian's private room.

He was sitting at the table, for he never passed that night in bed. At the sound of the lock he leaped up, and pointed a pistol, then hid it. Straight up to him I went, as swiftly and quietly as a spirit, and spoke:

"Seven years ago, at this very moment, my father was killed. Do you know this dagger?" He started back, as if I had stabbed him with it, then covered his eyes with both hands.

"You know it, then?" I said, with a triumph chill all over me. "It was your hand that used it."

Another moment, and I should have struck him with it. I lifted it in my frenzy; when he looked at me by some wonderful effort, calmly, steadily, even coldly. "Yes," he said, "I have seen that weapon before. Alas my poor dear brother!"

Whether it was true feeling that made his voice so low and deep, or only fierce self-control, I knew not then, nor tried to think.

"You know who owned it?" I asked, with my life upon his answer.

"Yes. I know who owned it once; but many years ago. And I know not in the least what is become of him now."

The baffled fury and prostrate hope--for at the moment I fully believed him--were too much for my reeling brain and fasting body. For one minute's command of my faculties, I would have sold them for ever; but I felt them ebbing from me, as the life does from a wound. The hemispheres of my brain were parting one from the other, and a grey void spreading between them. I tried to think, but could not. I strove to say *anything*, but failed. Fainter and fainter grew the room, the lamp, the ceiling, the face at which I tried to look. Things went to and fro with a quicker quiver, like flame in the wind, then, round and round like whirling water; my mouth grew stiff, and the tongue between my teeth felt like a glove; and with a rush of sound in my brain and throat, and a scream pent up, yet bursting, I fell, as I thought, through the earth. I was only on the floor, in a fit.

When I came to myself, I was in my own bed, and my own dear mother bending over me, pale, and haggard, and full of tears. The broad daylight was around us, and the faint sunshine on her face. She had been with me ever since. In my weakness, I looked up at her with a pang of self-reproach, to think how little I had valued her love; and I vowed to myself to make up for it by future care and devotion.

That violent convulsion, and the illness after it, changed me not a little both in mind and body.

CHAPTER XI.

It was indeed high time for me to cherish my mother. Her pain at leaving the place where she had known her little all of happiness--for her childhood had been overcast with trouble--her pain was so acute and overpowering that all my deep impassioned feelings sunk reproved before it.

My guardian now seemed much embittered against me, and anxious for our departure. He came once or twice, in my illness, to ask for and to see me; and he brought back, unperceived by any one, the weapon for which I raved. But ere I was quite recovered, he wrote, requesting to see me on business in his study. I could not speak yet without pain, having bitten my tongue severely.

"Your mother shall have a home here," he said, "as long as ever she wants one; but as for you, malignant or mad, I will try no more to soften you. When first I saw you in your early childhood, you flew at me as a murderer. Soon after you ransacked my cupboards and stole my boots, to compare them with some impressions or casts you kept. Yes, you look astonished. I never told you of it, but I knew it for all that. Of those absurdities I thought little, for I regarded them as the follies of a mad child, and I pitied you deeply, and even liked you for your filial devotion. But now I find that you have grown up in the same belief, and you dare even now to avow it. You know that I have no fear of you."

"Then why had you got that pistol?"

I saw that he was vexed and surprised at my having perceived it.

"In a house like this, where such deeds have been done, I think it right to be armed. Do you think if I had feared you, or your evidence, I would have restored that dagger?"

"Whose was it?"

"I told you the other night that I once saw a weapon like it, for which at first I mistook it, but closer examination convinced me of the difference."

"How does it differ?"

"In this. There was no snake on the handle of the other, though there was the cross on the blade."

"And where did you see the other?"

"Some day I will tell you. It is not right to do so now."

"Not convenient to you, I suppose you mean."

"I have also shown you that the lock of hair found in your poor mother's hand is much finer and more silky than mine; and you know that I cannot draw on my foot a boot so small as the one whose impression you have. But I am ashamed of myself for having stooped to such proofs as these. Dare you to look at me and suppose that I with my own hand could have stabbed my brother, a brother so kind and good to me, and for whose sake alone I have borne so long with you?"

He tried to look me down. I have met but one whose gaze could master mine; and he was not that one.

"So, you doubt me still? Are your things packed?'

"Yes, and my mother's."

"Then if your mother is well enough, and will not let you leave her, you had better go next week."

"No," I replied, "we will go to-morrow."

"Wilful to the last. So be it. Take this; you cannot refuse it in duty to your mother."

He put in my hand an order for a large sum of money. I threw it into the fire.

"There have been criminals," I exclaimed, "who have suffered from a life-long fear, lest the widow and orphans, starved through their crime, should compass their dying bed. Though we starve in a garret, we touch no bread of yours."

"Bravo, Miss Melodrame. You need never starve in the present state of the stage."

"That I don't understand; but this I do. It is perhaps the last time I shall ever see you living. Whether you did that deed or not is known to God, and you, and possibly one other. But whether you did it or not, I know it is on your soul. Your days are wretched, your nights are troubled. You shall die as your brother died, but not so prepared for death."

"Good bye, Clara. My lunch is coming up."

God has much to forgive me, but nothing worse than the dark thought of that speech. In my fury at weakness in such a cause, I had dared sometimes to imagine that my mother knew him to be the murderer, but concealed it for the sake of the family honour!

CHAPTER XII.

No need to recount my bitter farewell to all the scenes and objects I had loved so long, to all which possessed a dark yet tender interest, and most of all to my father's grave. That some attention might still be paid to this, I entrusted it to the care of an old housekeeper of ours, who was living in the village. My last visit was in the moonlight, and dear mother was there. I carried rather than led her away. Slight as my knowledge has been of lightsome and happy love, I am sure that a sombre affection is far the stronger and sweeter.

As we began our journey, a crowd of the villagers met us beyond the lodge, and lined the Gloucester road as far as the old oak-tree. While our hired conveyance passed between them, the men stood mute with their hats in their hands, the women sobbed and curtseyed, and blessed us, and held up their children to look at us.

Our refuge was the small estate or farm in Devonshire, which I have mentioned as my mother's property. This, which produced £45 a-year, was all that now remained to us, except a sum of £1,000 left to me by a godfather, and of which I could not touch the principal. The residue of the personalty, and the balance at the banker's, we had refused to take, being assured that legally we were responsible to Mr. Vaughan, even for the back rents of the Gloucestershire estate. Of course we had plenty of jewellery, some of it rather valuable, but the part most precious was heirloom, and that we had left behind. Most of our own had been my father's gift, and therefore we could not bear to sell it.

As regarded myself, this comparative poverty was not of very great moment, except as impairing my means of search; but for my mother's sake I was cut to the heart, and lost in perplexity. She had so long been accustomed to much attention and many luxuries, which her weak health had made indispensable to her. Thomas Henwood and poor Ann Maples insisted on following our fortunes, at one third of their previous wages. My mother thought it beyond our means to keep them even so; but for her sake I resolved to try. I need not say that I carried all my relics, difficult as it was to hide them from my mother.

When we reached our new home, late in the evening of the second day, a full sense of our privation for the first time broke upon us. It was mid-winter, and in the gloom of a foggy night, and after the weariness of a long journey, our impressions were truly dismal. Jolted endlessly up and down by ruts a foot deep and slaty stones the size of coal-scuttles, entombed alive betwixt grisly hedges which met above us like the wings of night, then obliged to walk up treadmill hills while the rickety fly crawled up behind; then again plunging and lurching down some corkscrew steep to the perpetual wood and rushing stream at the bottom; at length and at last along a lane so narrow that it scraped us on both sides as we passed, a lane which zig-zagged every thirty yards with a tree-bole jutting at every corner, at length and at last we came to the farmyard gate. It was not far from the lonely village of Trentisoe, which lies some six miles to the west of Lynmouth. This part is little known to London tourists, though it possesses scenery of a rarer kind than Lynmouth itself can show.

Passing through an outer court, with a saw-pit on one side and what they call a "linhay" on the other, and where a slop of straw and "muck" quelched under the wheels, we came next to the farmyard proper, and so (as the flyman expressed it) "home to ouze." The "ouze" was a low straggling cottage, jag-thatched, and heavy-eaved, and reminded me strongly of ragged wet horse-cloths on a rack. The farmer was not come home from Ilfracombe market, but his wife, Mrs. Honor Huxtable, soon appeared in the porch, with a bucket in one hand and a candle stuck in a turnip in the other. In the cross-lights, we saw a stout short woman, brisk and comely, with an amazing cap, and cheeks like the apples which they call in Devonshire "hoary mornings."

"A massy on us, Zuke," she called into the house, "if here bain't the genelvolks coom, and us be arl of a muck! Hum, cheel, hum for thee laife to the calves' ouze, and toorn out both the pegs, and take the pick to the strah, and gie un a veed o' wets."

Having thus provided for our horse, she advanced to us.

"So, ye be coom at last! I be crule glad to zee e, zure enough. Baint e starved amost! An unkid place it be for the laikes of you."

So saying, she hurried us into the house, and set us before a wood-fire all glowing upon the ground, beneath an enormous chimney podded with great pots and crocks hung on things like saws. These pots, like Devonshire hospitality, were always boiling and chirping. The kitchen was low, and floored with lime and sand, which was worn into pits such as boys use for marbles; but the great feature was the ceiling. This was divided by deep rafters into four compartments lengthwise. Across some of these, battens of wood were nailed, forming a series of racks, wherein reposed at least a stye-ful of bacon. Herbs and stores of many kinds, and ropes of onions dangled between.

Mrs. Huxtable went to the dresser, and got a large dish, and then turned round to have a good look at us.

"Poor leddy," she said gently, "I sim her's turble weist and low. But look e zee, there be a plenty of bakken yanner, and us'll cut a peg's drort to-morrow, and Varmer Badcock 'll zend we a ship, by rason ourn be all a'lambing." Then she turned to me.

"Whai, Miss, you looks crule unkid tu. Do e love zider?"

"No, Mrs. Huxtable. Not very much. I would rather have water."

"Oh drat that wash, e shan't have none of thiccy. Us has got a brown gearge of beer, and more nor a dizzen pans of mulk and crame."

Her chattering warmth soon put us at our ease; and as soon as the parlour fire burnt up, she showed us with many apologies, and "hopping no offence" the room which was thenceforth to be ours.

After tea, I put my dear mother to bed as soon as possible, and sat by the dying fire to muse upon our prospects. Not the strangeness of the place, the new ideas around me, not even my weariness after railroad, coach, and chaise, could keep my mind from its one subject. In fact, its colour had now become its form.

To others indeed, all hope of ever detecting and bringing to justice the man, for whose death I lived, might seem to grow fainter and fainter. Expelled from that place, and banished from those recollections, where, and by which alone, I could well expect ever to wind up my clue, robbed of all means of moving indifferent persons and retaining strong ones; and, more than this, engrossed (as I must henceforth be) in keeping debt at bay, and shielding my mother from care--what prospect was there, nay what possibility, that I a weak unaided girl, led only by set will and fatalism, should ever overtake and grasp a man of craft, and power, and desperation?

It mattered not: let other things be doubtful, unlikely, or impossible; let the hands of men be clenched against me, and the ears of heaven be stopped; let the earth be spread with thick darkness, as the waters are spread with earth, and the murderer set Sahara between us, or turn hermit on the Andes; happen what would, so God were still above us, and the world beneath our feet--I was as sure that I should send that man from the one to the throne of the other, as he was sure to be dragged away thence, to fire, and chains, and gnashing of teeth.

CHAPTER XIII.

So impulsive, kind-hearted, and honest was Mrs. Huxtable, that we could always tell what was the next thing she was going to say or do. Even at her meals she contrived to be in a bustle, except on Sundays; but she got through a great deal of work. On Sundays she put on, with her best gown, an air of calm dignity which made her unhappy until it was off, which it was directly after the evening service. She seemed a very sensible woman, and whatever the merits of the case she sided always with the weakest. The next morning we asked how it was she appeared not to expect us, as I had written and posted the letter myself on the previous Saturday.

"For sure now," she replied, "and the papper scrawl coom'd on Monday; but us bain't girt scholards, and Varmer said most like 'twas the Queen's taxes, for there was her head upon it; so us put un in the big mortar till Beany Dawe should come over, or us should go to church next Zunday, and passon would discoorse it for us. But"--and off she ran--"But her belongs to you now, Miss Clerer, seeing as how you've coom after un."

So they had only a general idea that we were coming, and knew not when it would be. The following day, Thomas Henwood arrived, bringing our boxes in a vehicle called a "butt," which is a short and rudely made cart, used chiefly for carrying lime.

After unpacking our few embellishments, we set up a clumsy but comfortable sofa for my mother, and tried to divert her sadness a little by many a shift and device to garnish our narrow realm. We removed the horrible print of "Death and the Lady," which was hung above the chimneypiece, and sundry daubs of our Lord and the Apostles, and a woman of Samaria with a French parasol, and Eli falling from a turnpike gate over the Great Western steamer. But these alterations were not made without some wistful glances from poor Mrs. Huxtable. At last, when I began to nail up a simple sketch of the church at Vaughan St. Mary instead of a noble representation of the Prodigal Son, wearing a white hat with a pipe stuck under the riband, and weeping into a handkerchief with some horse upon it, the good dame could no longer repress her feelings.

"Whai, Miss Clerer, Miss, dear art alaive, cheel, what be 'bout? Them's the smartest picters anywhere this saide of Coorn. Varmer gied a pan of hogs' puddens for they, and a Chainey taypot and a Zunday pair of corderahoys. Why them'll shaine with the zun on 'um, laike a vield of poppies and charlock. But thic smarl pokey papper of yourn ha'ant no more colour nor the track of a marly scrarly. A massy on us if I couldn't walk a better picter than thic, with my pattens on in the zider squash."

To argue with such a connoisseur would have been worse than useless; so I pacified her by hanging the rejected gems in her own little summer room by the dairy. Our parlour began before long to look neat and even comfortable. Of course the furniture was rough, but I care not much for upholstery, and am quite rude of French polish. My only fear was lest the damp from the lime-ash floor should strike to my dear mother's feet, through the scanty drugget which covered it. The fire-place was bright and quaint, lined with old Dutch tiles, and the grey-washed walls were less offensive to the eye than would have been a paper chosen by good Mrs. Huxtable. The pretty lattice window, budding even now with woodbine, and impudent to the winds with myrtle, would have made amends for the meanest room in England. Before it lay a simple garden with sparry walks and bright-thatched hives, and down a dingle rich with trees and a crystal stream, it caught a glimpse of the Bristol Channel.

CHAPTER XIV.

When our things were nearly settled, and I was sitting by myself, with dirty hands and covered with dust, there came a little timid tap at the door, followed by a shuffling outside, as if some one contemplated flight, yet feared to fly. Opening the door, I was surprised to find the child whom I expected a massive figure, some six feet and a quarter high, and I know not how many feet in width, but wide enough to fill the entire passage. He made a doubtful step in advance, till his great open-hearted face hung sheepishly above my head.

"Have I the pleasure of seeing Mr. Huxtable?" I asked.

"Ees 'um," he stammered, blushing like a beet-root, "leastways Miss, I ort to zay, no plasure 'um to the laikes of thee, but a honour to ai. Varmer Uxtable they karls me round about these 'ere parts, and some on 'em Varmer Jan, and Beany Dawe, he karl me 'Varmer Brak-plew-harnish, as tosses arl they Garnish,' and a dale he think of his potry as it please God to give 'un: but Maister, may be, is the riglar thing, leastways you knows best, Miss." "Danged if I can coom to discourse with girt folks nohow, no more nor a sto-un." This was an "aside," but audible a long way off, as they always are on the stage.

"But I am a very small folk, Mr. Huxtable, compared at least with you."

"I humbly ax your parding, Miss, but ai didn't goo for to be zuch a beg, nockety, sprarling zort of a chap. I didn't goo for to do it nohow. Reckon 'twar my moother's valt, her were always draining of hayricks." This also was an "aside."

"Come in," I said, "I am very glad to see you, and so will my mother be."

"Noo! Be e now? Be e though undade, my dear?" he asked with the truest and finest smile I ever saw: and I felt ashamed in front of the strong simplicity which took my conventional words for heart's truth.

"Them's the best words," he continued "as ai 've 'eered this many a dai; for ai'll be danged if ever a loi could coom from unner such eyes as yourn."

And thereupon he took my puny weak hand in his rough iron palm, like an almond in the nut-crackers, and examined it with pitying wonder.

"Wull, wull! some hands be made for mulking coos, and some be made of the crame itself. Now there couldn't be such a purty thing as this ere, unless it wor to snow war'rm. But her bain't no kaind of gude for rarstling? and ai be aveared thee'll have to rarstle a rare bout wi the world, my dearie: one down, tother coom on, that be the wai of 'un."

"Oh, I am not afraid, Mr. Huxtable."

He took some time to meditate upon this, and shook his head when he had finished.

"Noo, thee bain't aveard yet I'll warr'ne. Gude art alaive, if e bain't a spurrity maid. But if ere a chap zays the black word on e--and thiccy's the taime when a maid can't help herzell, then ony you karl Jan Uxtable that's arl my dear, and if so be it's in the dead hoor of the naight, and thee beest to tother zaide of Hexymoor, ai'll be by the zaide of thee zooner nor ai could thraw a vorehip."

Before I could thank him for his honest championship my mother entered the room, and all his bashfulness (lost for the moment in the pride of strength) came over him again like an extinguisher. Although he did not tremble--his nerves were too firm for that--he stood fumbling with his hat, and reddening, and looking vaguely about, at a loss where to put his eyes or anything else.

My mother, quite worn out with her morning's walk, surprised at her uncouth visitor, and frightened perhaps at his bulk, sank on our new-fangled sofa, in a stupor of weakness. Then it was strange and fine to see the strong man's sense of her feeble state. All his embarrassment vanished at once; he saw there was something to do; and a look of deep interest quickened his great blue eyes. Poising his heavy frame with the lightness of a bird, he stepped to her side as if the floor had been holy, and, scarcely touching her, contrived to arrange the rude cushions, and to lay her delicate head in an easy position, as a nurse composes a child. All the while, his looks and manner expressed so much feeling and gentleness, that he must have known what it was to lose a daughter or mother.

"Poor dear leddy," he whispered to me, "her be used to zummut more plum nor thiccy, I reckon. Her zimth crule weist and low laike. Hath her been long in that there wai?"

"Yes, she has long been weak and poorly; but I fear that her health has been growing worse for the last few months." I couldn't help crying a little; and I couldn't help his seeing it.

"Dang thee, Jan Uxtable, for a doilish girt zinny. Now doon e tak on so, Miss; doon e, that's a dear. Avore her's been here a wake, her'll be as peart as a gladdy. There bain't in arl they furren parts no place the laike of this ere to make a body ston upraight. The braze cooms off o Hexymoor as frash as a young coolt, and up from the zay as swate as the breath of a coo on the clover, and he'll zit on your chake the zame as a dove on her nestie; and ye'll be so hearty the both on ye, that ye'll karl for taties and heggs and crame and inyons avore e be hout of bed. Ee's fai ye wull." With this homely comfort he departed, after a cheering glance at my mother.

Before I proceed, the Homeric epithet "Break-plough-harness," applied by the poet to Mr. Huxtable, needs some explanation. It appears that the farmer, in some convivial hour (for at other times he detested vaunting), had laid a wager that he and Timothy Badcock, his farm-labourer, would plough half an acre of land, "wiout no beastessy in the falde." Now, it happened that the Parracombe blacksmith had lately been at Barnstaple, and there had seen a man who had heard of ploughing by steam. So when the farmer's undertaking got noised abroad and magnified, all Exmoor assembled to witness the exploit, wondering, trembling, and wrathful. Benches and tables were set in the "higher Barton," a nice piece of mealy land, just at the back of the house, while Suke and Mrs. Huxtable plied the cider-barrel for the yeomen of the neighbourhood. The farmer himself was not visible--no plough or ploughing tackle of any description appeared, and a rumour began to spread that the whole affair was a hoax, and the contriver afraid to show himself. But as people began to talk of "sending for the constable" (who, of course was there all the time), and as cart-whips and knob-sticks began to vibrate ominously, Mrs. Huxtable made a signal to Mr. Dawe, who led off the grumbling throng to the further end of the field, where an old rick-cloth lay along against the hedge. While the tilting was moved aside, the bold sons of Exmoor shrunk back, expecting some horrible monster, whose smoke was already puffing. All they saw was a one-horse plough with the farmer, in full harness, sitting upon it and smoking his pipe, and Timothy Badcock patiently standing at the plough-tail. Amid a loud hurrah from his friends, Mr. Huxtable leaped to the fore, and cast his pipe over the hedge; then settled the breast-band across the wrestling-pads on his chest, and drew tight both the chain-traces. "Gee wugg now, if e wull," cried stout Tim Badcock cheerily, and off sailed the good ship of husbandly, cleaving a deep bright furrow. But when they reached the corner, the farmer turned too sharply, and snapped the off-side trace. That accident impressed the multitude with a deeper sense of his prowess than even the striking success which attended his primitive method of speeding the plough.

To return to my mother. As spring came on, and the beautiful country around us freshened and took green life from the balmy air, I even ventured to hope that the good yeoman's words would be true. He had become, by this time, a great friend of ours, doing his utmost that we might not feel the loss of our faithful Thomas Henwood.

Poor Thomas had been very loth to depart; but I found, as we got settled, that my mother ceased to want him, and it would have been wrong as well as foolish to keep him any longer. He invested his savings in a public-house at Gloucester, which he called the "Vaughan Arms," and soon afterwards married Jane Hiatt, a daughter of our head game-keeper; or I ought to say, Mr. Vaughan's.

Ann Maples remained with us still. We lived, as may be supposed, in the most retired manner. My time was chiefly occupied in attendance upon dear mother, and in attempts to create for her some of those countless comforts, whose value we know not until they are lost. After breakfast, my mother would read for an hour her favourite parts of Scripture, and vainly endeavour to lead me into the paths of peace. Her soul discarded more and more the travel garb and wayfaring troubles of this lower existence, as, day by day, it won a nearer view of the golden gate, and the glories beyond; with which I have seen her eyes suffused, like the lucid heaven with sunrise. It has been said, and I believe, that there is nothing, in all our material world, so lovely as a fair woman looking on high for the angels she knows to be waiting for her.

Even I, though looking in an opposite direction, and for an opposite being, could not but admire that gentle meekness, whose absence formed the main fault of my character. Not that I was hard-hearted, or cross, (unless self-love deceives me), but restless yearning and hatred were ever at work within me; and these repel things of a milder nature, as a bullet cries tush to the zephyr.

CHAPTER XV.

One cold day in March, when winter had come to say "good-bye" with a roar, after wheeling the sofa with my mother upon it towards the parlour fire, I went out to refresh my spirit in the kitchen with Mrs. Huxtable, and to "yat myself" (for the sofa took all the parlour fire) by the fragrant hearth of wood and furze. The farmer's wife was "larning" me some strange words of her native dialect, which I was now desirous to "discoorse," and which she declared to be "the only vitty talk. Arl the lave of thiccy stoof, zame as the Carnishers and the Zummersets and the Lunnoners tulls up, arl thiccy's no more nor a passel of gibbersh, Miss Clerer, and not vitty atarl; noo, nor English nother. Instead of zaying 'ai' laike a Kirsten, zome on em zays 'oi,' and zome on em 'I.'" In the middle of her lecture, and just as I had learned that to "quilty" is the proper English for to "swallow," and that the passage down which we quilty is, correctly speaking, not the throat, but the "ezelpipe," a strange-looking individual darkened the "draxtool" (corruptly called the threshold) and crossed the "planch," or floor, to the fireplace where we sat.

Turning round, I beheld a man about fifty years old, of moderate stature, gauntly bodied, and loosely built, and utterly reckless of his attire. His face was long and thin, the profile keenly aquiline; and the angles made yet sharper, by a continual twitching and tension of the muscles. The skin of his cheeks was drawn, from his solemn brows to his lipless and down-curved mouth, tight and hollow, like the bladder on a jam-pot. His eyes, of a very pale blue, seemed always to stand on tip-toe, and never to know what he was going to say. A long, straight, melancholy chin, grisly with patches of hair, was meant by nature to keep his mouth shut, and came back sullenly when it failed. Over his shoulders was flung a patched potato-sack, fastened in front with a wooden skewer, and his nether clothes were as ragged as poetry. In his air and manner, self-satisfaction strove hard with solemn reserve. Upon the whole he reminded me of an owl who has lost his heart to a bantam hen. I cannot express him justly; but those who have seen may recognise Beany Dawe, the sawyer, acknowledged the bard of the north of Devon.

Mr. Ebenezer Dawe, without any hesitation or salute, took a three-legged stool, and set it between our chairs, then looked from Mrs. Huxtable to me, and introduced himself.

"Wull, here be us three,

And I hopps us shall agree."

"Agray indeed," cried Mrs. Huxtable, "doon 'e zee the quarlity be here, ye aul vule?" Then turning to me. "Doon'e be skeared, Miss Clerer, it be oney that there aul mazed ramscallion, Beany Dawe. Her makth what girt scholards, laike you, karls potry, or zum such stoof. Her casn' oppen the drort of him nohow, but what her must spake potry. Pote[#] indeed! No tino, I'd pote un out of ouze if I was the waife of un. 'Zee zaw, Beany Dawe!' that be arl the name he hath airned vor his rhaiming and rubbish, and too good for 'un too! Rhaime, rhaime, drash, drash, like two girt gawks in a barn! Oh fai, oh fai; and a maight have aimed two zhillings a dai and his zider!"

[#] "Pote." Danmonic for to "kick."

The subject of these elegant strictures regarded her all the time, with that pleased pity which none but a great Poet so placed can feel. Then swinging slowly on his tripod, and addressing the back of the chimney, he responded:

"Poor vule! Her dunno what a saight 'tis haigher

To be a Pout, nor a hunderzawyer!"

Perhaps his lofty couplet charmed her savage ear; at any rate she made a peaceful overture.

"Coom now, Mr. Dawe, wull e have a few broth?"

He assented with an alacrity much below his dignity;

"Taties, and zider, maat, and broth a few,

"Wull, zin you ax ai, ai'll not answer noo."

"E shan't have no cider," replied his hostess, "without e'll spake, for wance, laike a Kirsten, maind that, without no moor of thiccy jingle jangle, the very zame for arl the world as e be used to droon in the zawpit, 'Zee, zaw, Margery Daw,' with the arms of e a gwayn up and doon, up and doon, and your oyes and maouth most chokked with pilm[#] and the vace of e a hurning laike a taypot, and never a drop of out to aise the crickles of your barck. That's the steet you potes be in, and zawyers."

[#] Pilm, Londinicè, "dust."

As she delivered this comment, she swung to and fro on her chair, in weak imitation of the impressive roll, with which he enforced his rhyme. This plagiarism annoyed him much more than her words: but he vindicated his cause, like a true son of song.

"And if zo hap, I be a pout grand,

Thee needn't jah, 'cos thee doon't understand.

A pout, laike a 'ooman, or a bell,

Must have his clack out, and can't help hiszell."

A mighty "ha ha" from the door, like a jocund earthquake, proved that this last hit had found an echo in some ample bosom.

"Thee shall have as much vittels as ever thee can let down," said the farmer, as he entered, "danged if thee bain't a wunnerful foine chap, zure enough. Ai'd as lieve a'most to be a pote, plase God, as I wud to be a ooman: zimth to ai, there bain't much differ atwixt 'em. But they vainds out a saight of things us taks no heed on. I reckon now, Beany, thee cas'n drink beer?"

This was a home thrust, for Mr. Dawe was a notorious drinker. He replied with a heavy sigh and profoundly solemn look:

"Ah noo! a noo! Unless when I be vorced,

By rason, Dactor zaith, my stommirk ba'in exhaust."

"And what was it the doctor said to you, Mr. Dawe?" I asked, perceiving that he courted inquiry. He fixed his eyes upon me, with a searching look; eager, as it seemed, yet fearing to believe that he had found at last a generous sympathy.

"'Twas more nor dree months zince ai titched a drap,

When ai was compelled to consult the Dactor chap;

He zaith, zaith he, "tain't no good now this here,

Oh, Ebenezer Dawe, you must tak beer.'"

These words he repeated with impressive earnestness, shaking his head and sighing, as if in deprecation of so sad a remedy. Yet the subject possessed perhaps a melancholy charm, and his voice relented to a pensive unctuousness, as he concluded.

"'Tak beer!' I zays, 'Lor, I dunnow the way!'

'Then you must larn,' zays he, 'this blessed day:

You'm got,' he zays, 'a daungerous zinking here,

Your constitooshun do requaire beer.'"

"Thee wasn' long avore thee tried it, I'll warr'n," said the farmer, "tache the calf the wai to the coo!"

Scorning this vile insinuation, Mr. Dawe continued thus:

"Wull, after that, mayhap a month or zo,

I was gooin home, the zame as maight be noo:

I had zawed a hellum up for Varmer Yeo,

And a velt my stommick gooin turble low,

Her cried and skooned, like a chield left in the dark,

And a maze laike in my head, and a maundering in my barck.

Zo whun ai coom to the voot of Breakneck hill,

I zeed the public kept by Pewter Will:

The virelight showed the glasses in the bar,

And 'um danced and twinkled like the avening star."

Here he paused, overcome by his own description.

"Wull," said the farmer, brightening with fellow-feeling, for he liked his glass, "Wull, thee toorned in and had a drap, laike a man, and not be shamed of it nother. And how did her tast? A must have been nation good, after so long a drouth!"

"Coom'd down my drort, like the Quane and Princess Royal,

The very sa-am as a drap of oi-al!"

"The very sa-am, the very sa-am," he repeated with an extrametrical smack of his lips, which he wiped with the back of his hand, and cast a meaning glance towards the cellar. The farmer rose, and took from the dresser a heavy quart cup made of pewter. With this he went to the cellar, whence issued presently a trickling and frothing sound, which thrilled to the sensitive heart of Mr. Dawe. The tankard of ale, with a crown of white foam, was presented to the thirsty bard by his host, who did not, however, relinquish his grasp upon the vessel; but imposed (like Pluto to Orpheus) a stern condition. "Now, Beany Dawe, thee shan't have none, unless thee can zay zummut without no poetry in it."

At this barbarous restriction, poor Ebenezer rolled his eyes in a most tragic manner; he thrust his tongue into his cheek, and swung himself, not to and fro as usual, but sideways, and clutched one hand on the tatters of his sack, while he clung with the other to the handle of the cup. Then with a great effort, and very slowly, he spoke--

"If my poor vasses only maks you frown,

I'll try, ees fai I wull, to keep 'em--

A rhyme came over him, the twitching of his face showed the violence of the struggle; he attempted to say "in," but nature triumphed, and he uttered the fatal "down." In a moment the farmer compressed his mighty fingers, and crushed the thick metal like silver paper. The forfeit liquor flew over the poet's knees, and hissed at his feet in the ashes. Foreseeing a storm of verse from him, and of prose from Mrs. Huxtable at the fate of the pride of her dresser, I made a hasty retreat.

Thenceforth I took a kind interest in our conceited but harmless bard. His neighbours seemed not to know, how long it was since he had first yielded to his unfortunate ailment; which probably owed its birth to the sound of the saw. During our first interview, his rhythm and rhyme had been unusually fluent and finished, from pride perhaps at having found a new audience, or from some casual inspiration. Candour compels me to admit that his subsequent works were little, if at all, better than those of his more famous contemporaries; and I am not so proud, as he expects me to be, of his connexion with my sad history.

CHAPTER XVI.

About half a mile from Tossil's Barton (the farmhouse where we lived) there is a valley, or rather a vast ravine, of a very uncommon formation. A narrow winding rocky combe, where slabs, and tors, and boulder stones, seem pasturing on the velvet grass, or looking into the bright trout-stream, which leaps down a flight of steps without a tree to shade its flash and foam; this narrow, but glad dingle, as it nears the sea, bursts suddenly back into a desert gorge, cleaving the heights that front the Bristol Channel. The mountain sides from right and left, straight as if struck by rule, steeply converge, like a high-pitched roof turned upside down; so steep indeed that none can climb them. Along the deep bottom gleams a silver chord, where the cramped stream chafes its way, bedded and banked in stone, without a blade of green. From top to bottom of this huge ravine there is no growth, no rocks, no cliffs, no place to stay the foot, but all a barren, hard, grey stretch of shingle, slates, and gliddery stones: as if the ballast of ten million fleets had been shot in two enormous piles, and were always on the slip. Looking at it we forget that there is such a thing as life: the desolation is not painful, because it is so grand. The brief noon glare of the sun on these Titanic dry walls, where even a lichen dies; the gaunt desert shade stealing back to its lair in the early afternoon; the solemn step of evening stooping to her cloak below--I know not which of these is the most impressive and mournful. No stir of any sort, no voice of man or beast, no flow of tide, ever comes to visit here; the little river, after a course of battles, wins no peaceful union with the sea, but ponds against a shingle bar, and gurgles away in slow whirlpools. Only a fitful moaning wind draws up and down the melancholy chasm. The famous "Valley of Rocks," some four miles to the east, seems to me common-place and tame compared to this grand defile. Yet how many men I know who would smoke their pipes throughout it!

Thinking so much of this place, I long wished my mother to see it; and finding her rather stronger one lovely April morning, I persuaded her forth, embarked on Mrs. Huxtable's donkey. We went, down a small tributary glen, towards the head of the great defile. The little glen was bright, and green, and laughing into bud, and bantering a swift brook, which could hardly stop to answer, but left the ousels as it passed to talk at leisure about their nests, and the trout to make those musical leaps that sound so crisp through the alders. Another stream meets it among the bushes below, and now they are entitled to the dignity of a bridge whereon grows the maidenhair fern, and which, with its rude and pointed arch, looks like an old pack-saddle upon the stream.

From this point we followed a lane, leading obliquely up the ascent, before the impassable steep begins. Having tethered our quiet donkey to a broken gate, I took my mother along a narrow path through the thicket to the view of the great ravine. Standing at the end of this path, she was astonished at the scene before her. We had gained a height of about two hundred feet, the hill-top stretched a thousand feet above us. We stood on the very limit of vegetation, a straight line passing clown the hill where the quarry-like steep begins.

My dear mother was tired, and I had called her to come home, lest the view should make her giddy; when suddenly she stepped forward to gather a harebell straggling among the stones. The shingle beneath her foot gave way, then below her, and around, and above her head, began in a great mass to glide. Buried to the knees and falling sideways, she was sinking slowly at first, then quickly and quicker yet, with a hoarse roar of moving tons of stone, gathering and whelming upon her, down the rugged abyss. Screaming, I leaped into the avalanche after her, never thinking that I could only do harm. Stronger, and swifter, and louder, and surging, and berged with shouldering stone the solid cascade rushed on. I saw dearest mother below me trying to clasp her hands in prayer, and to give me her last word. With a desperate effort dragging my shawl from the gulfing crash, I threw it towards her, but she did not try to grasp it. A heavy stone leaped over me, and struck her on the head; her head dropped back, she lay senseless, and nearly buried. We were dashing more headlong and headlong, in the rush of the mountain side, to the precipice over the river, and my senses had all but failed, and revenge was prone before judgment, when I heard through the din a shout. On the brink of firm ground stood a man, and signed me to throw my shawl. With all my remaining strength I did so, but not as he meant, for I cast it entirely to him, and pointed to my mother below. One instant the avalanche paused, he leaped about twenty feet down, through the heather and gorse, and stayed his descent by clutching a stout ash sapling. To this in a moment he fastened my shawl, (a long and strong plaid), and just as my mother was being swept by, he plunged with the other end into the shingle tide. I saw him leap and struggle towards her, and lift her out of the gliding tomb, gliding himself the while, and sway himself and his burden, by means of the shawl, not back (for that was impossible), but obliquely downwards; I saw the strong sapling bow to the strain like a fishing-rod, while hope and terror fought hard within me; I saw him, by a desperate effort, which bent the ash-tree to the ground, leap from the whirling havoc, and lay my mother on the dead fern and heath. Of the rest, I know nothing, having become quite unconscious, before he saved me, in the same manner.

We must have been taken home in Farmer Huxtable's butt, for I remember well that, amidst the stir and fright of our return, and while my mother was still insensible, Mrs. Huxtable fell savagely upon poor Suke, for having despatched that elegant vehicle without cleaning it from the lime dust; whereby, as she declared, our dresses (so rent and tattered by the jagged stones) were "muxed up to shords." Poor Suke would have been likely to fare much worse, if, at such a time, she had stopped to dust the cart.

When the farmer came home, his countenance, rich in capacity for expressing astonishment, far outdid his words. "Wull, wull, for sure! wuther ye did or no?" was all the vent he could find for his ideas during the rest of the day; though it was plain to all who knew him that he was thinking profoundly upon the subject, and wholly occupied with it. In the course of the following week he advised me very impressively never to do it again; and nothing could ever persuade him but that I jumped in, and my mother came to rescue me.

But his wife very soon had all her wits about her. She sent to "Coom" for the doctor (I begged that it might not be Mr. Dawe's physician), she put dear mother to bed, and dressed her wounds with simples worth ten druggists' shops, and bathed her temples with rosemary, and ran down the glen for "fathery ham" (Valerian), which she declared "would kill nine sorts of infermation;" then she hushed the entire household, permitting no tongue to move except her own, and beat her eldest boy (a fine young Huxtable) for crying, whereupon he roared; she even conquered her strong desire to know much more than all could tell; and showed my mother such true kindness and pity that I loved her for it at once, and ever since.

Breathing slowly and heavily, my poor mother lay in the bed which had long been the pride of Tossil's Barton. The bedstead was made of carved oak, as many of them are in North Devon, and would have been handsome and striking, if some ancestral Huxtable had not adorned it with whitewash. But the quilt was what they were proud of. It was formed of patches of diamond shape and most incongruous colours, with a death's head in the centre and crossbones underneath.

When first I beheld it, I tossed it down the stairs, but my mother would have it brought back and used, because she knew how the family gloried in it, and she could not bear to hurt their feelings.

One taper white hand lay on it now, with the tender skin bruised and discoloured by blows. She had closed the finger which bore her wedding ring, and it still remained curved and rigid. In an agony of tears, I knelt by the side of the bed, watching her placid and deathlike face. Till then I had never known how strongly and deeply I loved her.

I firmly believe that she was revived in some degree by the glare of the patched quilt upon her eyes. The antagonism of nature was roused, and brought home her wandering powers. Feebly glancing away, she came suddenly to herself, and exclaimed:

"Is she safe? is she safe?'

"Yes, mother; here I am, with my own dear mother."

She opened her arms, and held me in a nervous cold embrace, and thanked God, and wept.

CHAPTER XVII.

When the surgeon came, he pronounced that none of her limbs were broken, but that the shock to the brain, and the whole system, had been so severe, that the only chance of recovery consisted in perfect quiet. She herself said that the question was, whether Providence wanted her still to watch over her child.

After some days she came down stairs, not without my support, and was propped once more upon her poor sofa. Calm she appeared, and contented, and happy in such sort as of old; but whenever she turned her glance from me, she observed with starting eyes every little thing that moved. Especially she would lie and gaze through the open window, at a certain large spider, who worked very hard among the woodbine blossoms. One day, in making too bold a cast, he fell; some chord of remembrance was touched, and she swooned away on the couch.

In spite of these symptoms I fondly hoped that she was recovering strength. She even walked out with me twice, in the sunny afternoon. But this only lasted a very short time; it soon became manifest, even to me, that ere long she would be with my father.

Unable to fight any more with this dark perception, I embraced it with a sort of savage despair, an utter sinking of the heart, which defied God as it sank. This she soon discovered, and I fear that it saddened her end.

She was much disappointed, too, that we could not find or thank him who had perilled his life for us. None could tell who he was, or what had become of him; though the farmer, at our entreaty, searched all the villages round. We were told, indeed, by the landlady of the "Red-deer Inn" (a lonely public-house near the scene of the accident) that a stranger had come to her in very great haste, and, having learned who we were, for she had seen us pass half an hour before, had sent her boy to the farm for some kind of conveyance, while he returned at full speed to attend those whom he had rescued. It further appeared that this stranger had helped to place us in the cart, and showed the kindest anxiety to lessen the roughness of its motion, himself even leading old "Smiler," to thwart his propensity to the deepest and hardest ruts. By the time our slow vehicle reached the farm, Mrs. Huxtable was returned from the Lower Cleve orchard, where she had been smoking the fernwebs, in ignorance of our mishap; and our conductor, seeing us safe in her hands, departed without a word, while she was too flurried and frightened to take much notice of him.

Neither could the woman of the inn describe him; she was so "mazed," when she heard of the "vail arl down the girt goyal," as she called our slide of about fifty feet; and for this she quoted the stranger as her authority, "them's the very words as he used;" though, just before this, she had stated that he was a foreigner and could not speak English. Knowing that in Devonshire any stranger is called a foreigner, and English means the brogue of the countryside, I did not attach much weight to this declaration. The only remaining witness, the lad who had come with the butt, was too stupid to describe anything, except three round O's, with his mouth and eyes.

But it mattered little about description; I had seen that stranger under such circumstances, that I could not fail to know him again.

On the morrow, and once in the following week, some kind inquiries were made as to our condition, by means of slips of paper conveyed by country lads. No name was attached to these, and no information given about the inquirer. The bearer of the first missive came from Lynmouth, and of the second from Ilfracombe. Neither lad knew anything (though submitted by Mrs. Huxtable to keen cross-examination), except that he was paid for his errand, but would like some cider, and that the answer was to be written upon the paper he brought.

Whether any motive for concealment existed, beside an excess of delicacy, or whether there even was any intentional secrecy, or merely indifference to our gratitude, was more than we could pretend to say. I am not at all inquisitive--not more so, I mean, than other women--but I need not confess that my curiosity (to say nothing of better feelings) was piqued a little by this uncommon reserve.

So now, beside the engrossing search for my deadly enemy, I had to seek out another, my brave and noble friend.

CHAPTER XVIII.

But for the present, curiosity, gratitude, hate, all feelings indeed and passions, except from the bled vein of love, and the heart-rooted fibres of sorrow, were to be crushed within me. Evening after evening, my dear mother's presence seemed more and more dreamy and shadowy; and night after night she went feebler and feebler to bed. In the morning indeed she had gathered some fragile strength, such strength as so wasted a form could exert, and the breeze and the fresh May sun made believe of health on her cheeks. But no more was I tempted to lay my arm round her waist, and rally her on its delicate girlish span, nor could I now look gaily into her eyes, and tell her how much she excelled her child. Those little liberties, which with less than a matron's dignity, and more than a mother's fondness she had so long allowed me, became as she still expected, and I could not bear to take them, so many great distresses. Even at night, when I twined in its simple mode her soft brown hair, as I thought how few the times my old task would be needed again, it cost me many a shift to prevent her descrying my tears in the glass, or suspecting them in my voice. For herself, she knew well what was coming; she had learned how soon she must be my sweet angel instead of my mother, and her last trouble was that she could not bring me to think the difference small. So calmly she spoke of her end, not looking at me the while for fear we both should weep, so gently and sweetly she talked of the time when I should hearken no more, as if she were going to visit a garden and hand me the flowers outside. Then, if I broke forth in an anguish of sobs, she would beg my forgiveness, as if she could have done wrong, and mourn for my loneliness after her, as though she could help forsaking me.

Looking back, even now, on that time, how I condemn and yet pardon myself, reflecting how little I tried to dissemble my child-like woe.

When all things rejoiced in their young summer strength, and scarcely the breeze turned the leaves for the songs of the birds, and the pure white hawthorn was calm as the death of the good, and the soul of gladness was sad, we talked for the last time together, mother and child, looking forth on the farewell of sunset. The room under the thatch smelled musty in summer, and I had made up a bed on the sofa downstairs. The wasting low fever was past, and the wearisome cough exhausted, and the flush had ebbed from her cheeks (as the world from her heart), and of all human passions, and wishes, and cares, not one left a trace in her bosom, except a mother's love. This and only this retarded her flight to heaven, as the sight of his nest delays the rising of the lark.

"My child," she began, and her voice was low, but very distinct, "my only and darling child, who has minded me so long, and laid her youth, and beauty, and high courageous spirit, at the feet of her weak mother; my child, who fostered in wealth and love, will be to-morrow an orphan, cast upon the wide world"-- here she fairly broke down, in spite of religion, and heaven, and turned her head to the pillow, a true daughter and mother of earth. I would fain have given that fortune, whose loss to me she lamented, for leave to cry freely with her, without adding to her distress.

In a minute or two, she was able to proceed; with her thin hand she parted the hair shaken purposely over my eyes.

"I am sure that my pet will listen, with kindness and patience, while I try to say what has lain so long at my heart. You know how painfully I have always been moved by any allusion to the death of your dear father. It has been a weakness no doubt on my part, but one which I vainly strove against; and for which I trust to be pardoned where all is pardon and peace."

Her voice began to tremble, and her eyes became fixed, and I feared a return of the old disorder; but she shook it off, and spoke again distinctly, though with great labour:

"This is a bitter subject, and I never could bring myself to it, till now, when it seems too late. But, my poor love, I am so anxious about it. For the rest--that Providence which has never forsaken us, repine as I would, I can trust that Providence still to protect my darling child. There is one thing, and only one, by promising which you will make my departure quite happy. Then I shall go to rejoin your father, and carry such tidings of you, as will enable us both to wait, in the fulness of time, your coming."

"Oh, that the fulness of time were come!" I cried in my selfish loneliness; "for me it is empty enough."

"My precious, my own darling Clara, you sob so, you make me most wretched."

"Mother, I will not cry any more;" neither did I, while she could see me.

"I need not tell you," she said, "what is that promise which I crave for your own dear sake."

"No, ma'am," I replied, "I know quite well what it is."

I saw that I had grieved her. How could I call her then anything else than "mother"?

"My mother dear, you wish me to promise this--that I will forego my revenge upon him who slew my father."

She bowed her head, with a look I cannot describe. In the harsh way I had put it, it seemed as if she were injuring both my father and me.

"Had you asked me anything else, although it were sin against God and man (if you could ask such a thing)--I would have pledged myself to it, as gladly as I would die--die, at least, if my task were done. But this, this one thing only-- to abandon what I live for, what I was born to do, to be a traitor to my own father and you--I implore you, mother, by Him whose glory is on you now, do not ask me this."

Her face in its sadness and purity made me bury my eyes and forget things.

"Then I must die, and leave my only child possessed with a murderer's spirit!"

The depth of her last agony, and which I believed would cling to her even in heaven, was more than I could bear. I knelt on the floor and put my hand to her side. Her worn out heart was throbbing again, with the pang of her disappointment.

"Mother," I cried, "I will promise you this. When I have discovered, as I must do, that man who has made you a widow and me an orphan, if I find any plea whatever to lessen his crime, or penitence to atone for it, as I hope to see my father and mother in heaven, I will try to spare and forgive him. Can you wish me to rest in ignorance, and forget that deed?"

"Clara," she answered weakly, and she spoke more slowly and feebly every time, "you have promised me all I can hope for. How you loved your father! Me too you have loved I cannot say how much. For my sake, you have borne poverty, trouble, and illness, without a complaining word. By day, and by night, through my countless wants, and long fretfulness."

I put my finger upon her pale lips. How could she tell such a story then? Her tears came now and then, and would not be stopped, as she laid her weak hand on my head.

"May the God of the fatherless and the poor, who knows and comforts the widow's grief, the God who is taking me now to His bosom, bless with all blessings of earth and heaven, and restore to me this my child."

A sudden happiness fell upon her, as if she had seen her prayer's acceptance. She let her arms fall round me, and laid my cheek by the side of her bright flowing smile. It was the last conscious stir of the mind; all the rest seemed the flush of the soul. In the window the night-scented heath was blooming; outside it, the jessamine crossed in a milky way of white stars, and the lush honeysuckle had flung down her lap in clusters. The fragrance of flowers lay heavy upon us, and we were sore weary with the burden of sorrow and joy. So tranquil and kind was the face of death, that sleep, his half-brother, still held his hand.

The voice of the thrush, from the corner laurel, broke the holy stillness. Like dreams of home that break our slumbers, his melody was its own excuse. My mother awoke, and said faintly, with no gleam in her eyes:

"Raise me upon the pillow, my love, that I may hear him once more. He sings like one your father and I used to listen to every evening, in the days when we watched your cradle."

I lifted her gently. The voice of nature made way for her passing spirit.

"Now kiss me, my child; once more, my own loved child, my heart is with you for ever. Light of my eyes, you are growing dim."

She clasped her hands in prayer, with one of mine between them. My other was round her neck.

Then she spoke slowly, and with a waning voice; but firmly, as if it had been her marriage-response.

"Thou art my guide, and my staff. I have no fear, neither shadow of trembling. Make no long tarrying, oh my God!"

The bird went home to his nest, and she to that refuge where all is home. Though the hands that held mine grew cold as ice, and her lips replied to no kiss, and the smile on her face slept off into stillness, and a grey shade crept on her features;--I could not believe that all this was death.

CLARA VAUGHAN

BOOK II.

CHAPTER I.

"Long-shadowed death," some poet says. How well I know and feel it! the gloom before him deepening as he comes, and the world of darkness stretching many years behind.

I once dared to believe that no earthly blow could ever subdue, or even bend my resolute will. I now found my mistake, and cared not even to think about it.

On the morning after my mother's death I wandered about, and could not tell where to go. The passionate clinging which would not allow me, during that blank and sleepless night, to quit what remained of her presence, and the jealous despair which felt it a wrong that any one else should approach, had now settled down to a languid heaviness, and all that I cared for was to be let alone. All the places where we had been together I visited now, without knowing why, perhaps it was to see if she were there. Then vaguely disappointed, I thought there must be some mistake, and wearily went the dreary round again.

I cannot clearly call to mind, but think it must have been that day, when I was in the corner of the room, looking at the place whence they had taken dear mother. Ann Maples and Mrs. Huxtable came in, followed by the farmer, who had left his shoes at the door. They did not see me, so I suppose it must have been in the evening. They were come to remove the sofa. I have not the heart to follow their brogue.

"Yes to be sure," said Mrs. Huxtable, looking at it with a short sigh. It was odd that it should strike me then, but all she did was short.

"Get it out of her sight, poor dear," said Ann Maples.

"To see her sit and look at it!" exclaimed the farmer's wife.

"With her eyes so dry and stupid like!" returned the other. "Poor child, she must have cried herself out. I have known her sit by the hour, and stare at the bed where her father was killed, but it was a different sort of look to this."

"Ah well, she has lost a good mother," said Dame Huxtable. "God grant my poor little chicks may never be left like her."

"What's your children to talk of along with Miss Clara?" asked my nurse.

Mrs. Huxtable was about to answer sharply, but checked herself, and only said:

"All children is much of a muchness to their mothers."

"Don't tell me," cried Ann Maples, who had never had any.

The farmer came between them, walking on tip-toe.

"For good, now, don't ye fall out at such a time as this here. What's our affairs to speak of now?"

"What's any folks," asked Mrs. Huxtable, "that has the breath of life?"

"And goes forth in the morning, and is cast into the oven, ma'am," continued her antagonist.

"Ah, bless thee, yes!" the farmer replied, "I'll take my gospel oath of it. It's not much good I am at parsoning, and maybe I likes a drop of drink when the weather is fitty; but that young chestnut filly that's just come home from breaking, I'd sell her to a gipsey, and trust him for the money, if so be 'twould make the young lady turn her face to the Lord. Can't ye speak to her now about it, either of you women? Doo'e now, doo'e."

"How could I possible?" his wife exclaimed; "why, farmer, you must be mazed. A high young lady like that, and the tears still hot in her eyes!"

"The very reason, wife, the very time and reason. But likely Mrs. Maples would be the proper person."

"Thank you, sir," my nurse replied, "Mrs. Maples knows good manners a little. Thank you, sir; Mrs. Maples wasn't born in Devonshire."

"I ask your pardon, ma'am," said the farmer, much abashed, "I humbly ask your pardon; I wasn't taught no better. I can only go by what I have seen, and what seems to come inside of me. And I know, in our way of business, when a calf is weaned from the mother, the poor beastess hath a call for some one else to feed it. Maybe it's no harm to let her have the refusal." Therewith he opened my mother's Bible, and placed it reverently on the window-seat. "Waife, do'e mind the time as poor Aunt Betsy died, over there to Rowley Mires?"

"For sure I do, but what have her got to do with it? Us mustn't talk of her, I reckon, any more than of the chillers, though us be so unlucky as to be born in Devonshire. Fie, fie, thee ought to know better than to talk of poor Aunt Betsy along of a lady, and before our betters." Here she curtsied to Ann Maples, with a flash of light in her eyes, and rubbing them hard with her apron.

"Well, well," replied the farmer, sadly, "mayhap so I did. And who be I to gainsay? Mayhap so I did;" he dropped his voice, but added, after some reflection, "It be hard to tell the rights of it; but sure her were a woman."

"Who said her were a man, thee zany?" Mrs. Huxtable was disappointed that the case would not be argued. The farmer discreetly changed the subject.

"Now, if it was me," he continued, "I wouldn't think of taking this here settle-bed away from the poor thing."

"Why not, farmer?" asked Mrs. Huxtable, sharply. "Give me a reason for leaving it, and I'll give you ten for taking it."

"I can't give no reasons. But maybe it comforts her a little."

"Comfort indeed!" said his wife; "breaks her heart with, crying, more likely. Come, lend a hand, old heavy-strap; what can a great dromedary like thee know about young wenches?"

At any rate he knew more than she did. The moment they touched it I burst forth from my corner, and flung myself upon it, rolling as if I would bury myself in the ecstasy of anguish. What they did I cannot tell; they might say what they liked, I had not cried till then.

The next day I was sitting stupified and heavy, trying once more to meet the necessity of thinking about my mother's funeral; but again and again, the weakness of sorrow fell away from the subject. The people of the house kept from me. Mrs. Huxtable had done her best, but they knew I would rather be alone.

The door was opened quietly, and some one entered in a stealthy manner. Regarding it as an intrusion, I would not look that way.

"Miss Clara dear," began the farmer, standing behind me, and whispering, "I humbly ask your pardon, Miss, for calling you that same. But we have had a wonderful fine season, sure enough."

I made him no answer, being angry at his ill-timed common-place.

"If you please, Miss, such a many lambs was never known afore, and turnips fine last winter, and corn, and hay, and every kind of stock, a fetching of such prices. The farmers about here has made their fortune mainly."

"I am glad to hear that you are so prosperous, Mr. Huxtable," I answered, very coldly.

"Yes fie, good times, Miss, wonderful good times, we don't know what to do with our money a'rnost."

"Buy education and good taste," I said, "instead of thrusting your happiness upon such as I."

How little I knew him! Shall I ever forgive myself that speech?

"Ah, I wish I could," he answered, sadly, "I wish with all my heart I could. But we must be born to the like of that, I am afeared, Miss Vaughan."

Poor fellow! he knew nothing of irony, as we do, who are born to good taste, otherwise I might have suspected him of it then.

He suddenly wished me "good evening," although it was middle-day, and then he made off for the door, but came back again with a desperate resolve, and spoke, for him, very quickly, looking all the time at his feet.

"There, I can't make head or tail of it, Miss Clara, but wife said I was to do it so. Take the danged money, that's a dear, and for good now don't be offended, for I cas'n help it."

He opened his great hand, which was actually shaking, and hurriedly placed on the sofa a small packet tied in the leaf of a copy book; then suddenly put in mind of something, he made a dive, and snatching it up, flung it upon a Windsor chair. It fell with a chink, the string slipped off, and out rolled at least forty sovereigns and guineas, and a number of crown-pieces.

Peremptorily I called him back, for he was running out of the door.

"Mr. Huxtable, what is the meaning of this?"

"Meaning, Miss! Lord bless you, Miss Clara, there bain't no meaning of it; only it corned into my head last night, as I was laying awake, humbly asking your pardon, Miss, for that same, that if so be you should desire, that the dear good lady herself might like, if I may make so bold, meaning that it isn't fitly like, that she should lay nowhere else, but alongside of her own husband, till death do them part, Mr. Henry Valentine Vaughan, Esquire, Vaughan Park, in the county of Gloucestershire. There I be as bad as Beany Dawe."

He repeated his rhyme, with some relief, hoping to change the subject. I caught him by both hands, and burst into tears.

"Don't ye now," he said, with a thickness in his voice, "don't ye now, my dearie, leastways unless it does you good."

"It does me good, indeed," I sobbed, "to find still in the world so kind a heart as yours."

Though I longed to look him in the face, I knew that I must not do so. Oh why are men so ashamed of manly tears? Perceiving that I could not speak, he began to talk for both of us, making a hundred blundering apologies, trying to hide his knowledge of my poverty, and to prove that he was only paying a debt which extended over many years of tenancy. He was not at all an imaginative man, but delicacy supplied him with invention. So deep a sense pervades all classes in this English country, that want of money is an indictment, which none but the culprit may sign. Poor or rich, I should not be worth despising, if I had shown the paltry pride of declining such a loan.

The tears came anew to my eyes when I found that what had been brought so freely was the savings of years of honest toil, a truth which the owners had tried to conceal by polishing the old coin. But not being skilled, dear souls, in plate-cleaning, they had left some rotten-stone adhering to the George and Dragons.

CHAPTER II.

Although I find a sad pleasure in lingering over these times, with such a history still impending, I cannot afford the indulgence.

Dear mother's simple funeral took me once more to my native place. Even without Mr. Huxtable's generous and noble assistance, I should have laid her to rest by the side of the husband she loved so well. But difficulties, sore to encounter at such a time, would have met me on every side. Moreover the kind act cheered and led me through despondency, like the hand and face of God.

Caring little what people might say or think, I could not stay at a distance. Nature told me that it was my duty to go, and duty or not, I could not stay away.

And now for the last time I look on the face and form of my mother. That which I have played, and talked, and laughed with, though lately not much of laughter, that which has fed and cared for me, till it needed my care in turn; that which I have toddled beside, or proudly run in front of; whose arms have been round me whenever I wept, and whose bosom the haven of childhood's storms; first to greet me with smiles in the morning, and last to bless me with tears at night; ever loving, and never complaining--in one word for a thousand, my mother. So far away now, so hopelessly far away! There it lies indeed, I can touch it, kiss it, and embrace it; but oh how small a part of mother! and even that part is not mine. So holy and calm it lies, such loving kindness still upon its features, so near me, but in mystery so hopelessly far away! I can see it, but it never will know me again; I may die beside it, and it cannot weep. The last last look of all on earth--they must have carried me away.

I remember tottering down the hill, supported by a stalwart arm. The approach to the house prevented--or something. Two children ran before me, stopping now and then to wonder, and straggling to pick hedge-flowers. One of them brought me a bunch, then stared, and was afraid to offer them. "Nancy, I'll be the death of thee," whispered a woman's voice. The little girl shrunk to me for shelter, with timid tears in her great blue eyes. So I took her hand, and led her on, and somehow it did me good.

At intervals, the funeral hymn, which they sing on the road to the grave, fell solemnly on our ears. Some one from time to time gave out the words of a verse and then it was sung to a simple impressive tune. That ancient hymn, which has drowned so many sobs, I did not hear, but felt it.

We arrived at Vaughan St. Mary late in the afternoon of the second day. The whole of the journey was to me a long and tearful dream. Mr. Huxtable came with us. He had never before been further from home than Exeter; and his single visit to that city had formed the landmark of his life. He never tried to comfort me as the others did. The ignorant man knew better.

Alone I sat by my father's grave, with my mother's ready before my feet. They had cast the mould on the other side, so as not to move my father's coverlet. The poor old pensioner had been true to her promise, and man's last garden was blooming like his first flower-bed.

My mind (if any I had) seemed to have undergone some change. Defiance, and pride, and savage delight in misery, were entirely gone; and depression had taken the place of dejection. Death now seemed to me the usual and proper condition of things, and I felt it an impertinence that I should still be alive. So I waited, with heavy composure, till she should be brought, who so often had walked there with me. At length she was coming for good and all, and a space was left for me. But I must not repose there yet; I had still my task before me.

The bell was tolling faster, and the shadows growing longer, and the children who had been playing at hide-and-seek, where soon themselves shall be sought in vain, had flitted away from sight, perhaps scared at my presence, perhaps gone home to tea, to enjoy the funeral afterwards. The evening wind had ceased from troubling the yews, and the short-lived songs of the birds were done. The place was as sad as I could wish. The smell of new earth inspired, as it always does, some unsearchable everlasting sympathy between the material and the creature.

The sun was setting behind me: suddenly a shadow eclipsed my own upon the red loam across the open grave. Without a start, and dreamily (as I did all things now), I turned to see whence it came. Within a yard of me stood Mr. Edgar Vaughan. In a moment the old feeling was at my heart, and my wits were all awake.

I observed that he was paler than when I had seen him last, and the rigid look was wavering on his face, like steel reflected by water. He lifted his hat to me. I neither rose nor spoke, but turned and watched him.

"Clara," he said in a low, earnest voice, "I see you are still the same. Will no depth of grief, no length of time, no visitation from Him who is over us all, ever bend your adamant and implacable will?"

I heard, with some surprise, his allusion to the Great Being, whom he was not wont to recognise; but I made him no reply.

"Very well," he resumed, with the ancient chill hardening over his features; "so then let it be. I am not come to offer you condolence, which you would despise; nor do I mean to be present when you would account the sight of me an insult. And yet I loved your mother, Clara; I loved her very truly."

This he said with such emotion, that a new thought broke upon me.

Quick as the thought, he asked, "Would you know who killed your father?"

"And my mother, too," I answered, "whose coffin I see coming."

The funeral turned the corner of the lane, and the dust rose from the bearers' feet. He took his hat off, and the perspiration stood upon his forehead. Betwixt suspense and terror, and the wildness of grief, I was obliged to lean on the headstone for support, and a giddiness came over me. When I raised my eyes again, there was no one near me. In vain I wiped them hurriedly and looked again. Mr. Vaughan was gone; but on the grass at my feet lay a folded letter. I seized it quickly, and broke the seal. That moment a white figure appeared between the yew-trees by the porch. It was the aged minister leading my mother the last path of all. The book was in his hand, and his form was tall and stately, and his step so slow, that the white hair fell unruffled, while the grand words on his lips called majesty into his gaze. Thrusting aside the letter, I followed into the Church, and stood behind the old font where I had been baptized; a dark and gloomy nook, fit for such an entrance. She who had carried me there was carried past it now, and the pall waved in the damp cold air, and all the world seemed stone and mould.

But afterwards, on the fair hill-side, while the faint moon gathered power from the deepening sky, and glancing on that hoary brow sealed the immortal promises and smoothed the edges of the grave, around which bent the uncovered heads of many who had mourned before, and after a few bounds of mirth should bend again in mourning, until in earth's fair turn and turn, others should bend and they lie down--beholding this, and feeling something higher than "dust to dust," I grew content to bide my time with the other children of men, and remembered that no wave can break until it reach the shore.

CHAPTER III.

When a long and heavy sleep (my first sleep since dear mother's death) had brought me down to the dull plain of life, I read for the first time the letter so strangely delivered. Even then it seemed unkind to my mother that I should think about it. Mr. Vaughan had placed it in a new envelope, which he had sealed with his own ring, the original cover (if any there were) having been removed. The few words, of which it consisted, were written in a clear round hand, upon a sheet of thin tough paper, such as we use for foreign postage, and folded in a peculiar manner. There was nothing remarkable in the writing, except this, that the words as well as the letters were joined. It was as follows:

"The one who slain your brother is at 19 Grove Street London. You will come in danger of it why you know."

No date, no signature, no stops, except as shown above. In short, it was so dark and vague, that I returned to Devonshire, with a resolution to disregard it wholly. When we reached the foot of the hill, at the corner of the narrow lane which leads to Tossil's Barton, and where the white gate stands of which the neighbourhood is so proud, a sudden scream was heard, and a rush made upon us from behind the furze-bush. The farmer received the full brunt of a most vigorous onset, and the number and courage of the enemy making up for their want of size, his strong bastions were almost carried by storm. To the cry of "Daddy! Daddy's come home!" half a dozen urchins and more, without distinction of sex, jumped and tugged and flung and clung around him, with no respect whatever for his Sunday coat, or brass-buttoned gaiters. Taking advantage of his laughing, they pulled his legs this way and that, as if he were skating for the first time, and little Sally (his favourite) swarming up, made a base foot-rope of the great ancestral silver watch-chain whose mysterious awe sometimes sufficed to keep her eyes half open in church. Betwixt delight and shame, the poor father was so dreadfully taken aback, that he could not tell what to do, till fatherly love suggested the only escape. He lifted them one by one to his lips, and after some hearty smacks sent all (except the baby) sliding down his back.

While all this was going forward, the good dame, with a clean apron on, kept herself in the background, curtseying and trying to look sad at me, but too much carried away to succeed. Her plump cheeks left but little room for tears, yet I thought one tried to find a road from either eye. When the burst was nearly done, she felt (like a true woman) for me so lonely in all this love, though I could not help enjoying it; and so she tried to laugh at it.

For a long time after this, the farmer was admired and consulted by all the neighbouring parishes, as a man who had seen the world. His labourers, also, one man and a boy, for a fortnight called him "Sir," a great discomfort to him; more than this, some letters were brought for him to interpret, and Beany Dawe became unduly jealous. But in this, as in most other matters, things came to their level, and when it was slowly discovered that the farmer was just the same, his neighbours showed much disappointment, and even some contempt.

It was not long before the thought of that letter, which had been laid by so scornfully, began to work within me. Again and again, as time wore on, and the deep barb of sorrow darkly rusted away, it came home to me as a sin, that I was neglecting a special guidance. Moreover, my reason for staying in Devonshire was gone, and as my spirit recovered its tone, it could not put up with inaction.

Three months after our return, one breezy afternoon in August, when the heath had long succeeded the gorse and broom upon the cleve, and the children were searching for "wuts" and half-kerneled nuts, I sat on a fallen tree, where a break in the copse made a frame for one of our favourite views. Of late I had been trying to take some sketches in water-colours of what my mother and I had so often admired together, and this had been kept for the last. Wild as the scheme may appear to all who know the world and its high contempt for woman's skill, I had some hope of earning money in London by the pencil, and was doing my utmost to advance in art. Also, I wished to take away with me some memorials of a time comparatively happy.

Little Sally Huxtable, a dear little child, now my chief companion, had strayed into the wood to string more strawberry beads on her spike of grass, for the wood strawberries here last almost to the equinox; and I had just roughed in my outline, and was correcting the bold strokes, by nature's soft gradations; when suddenly through a cobnut bush, and down the steep bank at my side, came, in a sliding canter, a magnificent red deer. He passed so close before me, with antlers, like a varnished crabstick, russet in the sun, that I could have touched his brown flank with my pencil. Being in no hurry or fright whatever, he regarded me from his large deep eyes with a look of courteous interest, a dignified curiosity too well bred for words; and then, as if with an evening of pleasant business before him, trotted away through the podded wild broom on the left.

Before I had time to call him back, which, with a childish impulse, I was about to do, the nutbush where he had entered moved again, and, laughing at his own predicament on the steep descent, a young man leaped and landed in the bramble at my feet. Before me stood the one whom we had so often longed to thank. But at sight of me, his countenance changed entirely. The face, so playful just before, suddenly grew dark and sad, and, with a distant salutation, he was hurrying away, when I sprang forward and caught him by the hand. Every nerve in my body thrilled, as I felt the grasp that had saved my mother and me.

"Excuse me," he said coldly, "I will lose my prey."

But I would not let him go so curtly. What I said I cannot tell, only that it was very foolish, and clumsy, and cold by the side of what I felt. Whom but God and him had I to thank for my mother's peaceful end, and all her treasured words, each worth a dozen lives of mine? He answered not at all, nor looked at me; but listened with a cold constraint, and, as I thought, contemptuous pity, at which my pride began to take alarm.

"Sir," I exclaimed, when still he answered not, "Sir, I will detain you no longer from murdering that poor stag."

He answered very haughtily, "I am not of the Devonshire hunters, who toil to exterminate this noble race."

As he spoke he pointed down the valley, where the red deer, my late friend, was crossing, for his evening browse, to a gnoll of juicy grass. Then why was he pursuing him, and why did he call him his prey? The latter, probably a pretext to escape me, but the former question I could not answer, and did not choose to ask. He went his way, and I felt discharged of half my obligation.

CHAPTER IV.

The farmer, his wife, and little Sally were now all I had to love. Poor Ann Maples, though thoroughly honest and faithful, was of a nature so dry and precise that I respected rather than loved her. I am born to love and hate with all my heart and soul, although a certain pride prevents me from exhibiting the better passion, except when strongly moved. That other feeling, sown by Satan, he never allows me to disguise.

To leave the only three I loved was a bitter grief, to tell them of my intention, a sore puzzle. But, after searching long for a good way to manage it, the only way I found was to tell them bluntly, and not to cry if it could be helped. So when Mrs. Huxtable came in full glory to try upon me a pair of stockings of the brightest blue ever seen, which she had long been knitting on the sly, for winter wear, I thanked her warmly, and said:

"Dear me, Mrs. Huxtable, how they will admire these in London."

"In Lonnon, cheel!" she always called me her child, since I had lost my mother--"they'll never see the likes of they in Lonnon, without they gits one of them there long glaskies, same as preventive chaps has, and then I reckon there'll be Hexymoor between, and Dartmoor too, for out I know, and ever so many church-towers and milestones."

"Oh yes, they will. I shall be there in a week."

"In Lonnon in a wake! Dear heart alaive, cheel, dont'e tell on so!"

She thought my wits were wandering, as she had often fancied of late, and set off for the larder, which was the usual course of her prescriptions. But I stopped her so calmly that she could not doubt my sanity.

"Yes, dear Mrs. Huxtable, I must leave my quiet home, where all of you have been so good and kind to me; and I have already written to take lodgings in London."

"Oh, Miss Clerer, dear, I can't belave it nohow! Come and discoorse with farmer about it. He knows a power more than I do, though I says it as shouldn't. But if so be he hearkens to the like of that, I'll comb him with the toasting iron."

Giving me no time to answer, she led me to the kitchen. The farmer, who had finished his morning's work, was stamping about outside the threshold, wiping his boots most carefully with a pitchfork and a rope of twisted straw. This process, to his great discomfort, Mrs. Huxtable had at length enforced by many scoldings; but now she snatched the pitchfork from him, and sent it flying into the court.

"Wun't thee never larn, thee girt drummedary, not to ston there an hour, mucking arl the place?"

"Wull, wull," said the farmer, looking at the pitchfork first, and then at me, "Reckon the old mare's dead at last."

"Cas'n thee drame of nothing but bosses and asses, thee girt mule? Here's Miss Clerer, as was like a cheel of my own, and now she'm gooin awai, and us'll niver zee her no more."

"What dost thee mane, 'ooman?" asked the farmer, sternly, "hast thee darr'd to goo a jahing of her, zame as thee did Zuke?"

"Oh, no, farmer!" I answered, quickly, "Mrs. Huxtable never gave me an unkind word in her life. But I must leave you all, and go to live in London."

The farmer looked as if he had lost something, and began feeling for it in all his pockets. Then, without a word, he went to the fire, and unhung the crock which was boiling for the family dinner. This done, he raked out the embers on the hearthstone, and sat down heavily on the settle with his back towards us. Presently we heard him say to himself, "If any cheel of mine ates ever a bit of bakkon to-day, I'll bile him in that there pot. And to zee the copy our Sally wrote this very morning!"

"Wonnerful! wonnerful!" cried Mrs. Huxtable, "and now her'll not know a p from a pothook. And little Jack can spell zider, zame as 'em does in Lonnon town!"

"Dang Lonnon town," said the farmer, savagely, "and arl as lives there, lave out the Duke of Wellington. It's where the devil lives, and 'em catches his braath in lanterns. My faather tould me that, and her niver spak a loi. But it hain't for the larning I be vexed to lose my dearie."

That last word he dwelt upon so tenderly and sadly, that I could stop no longer, but ran up to him bravely with the tears upon my face. As I sat low before him, on little Sally's stool, he laid his great hand on my head, with his face turned toward the settle, and asked if I had any one to see me righted in the world but him.

I told him, "None whatever;" and the answer seemed at once to please and frighten him.

"Then don't e be a-gooin', my dear heart, don't e think no more of gooin. If it be for the bit and drap thee ates and drinks, doesn't thee know by this time, our own flash and blood bain't no more welcome to it! And us has a plenty here, and more nor a plenty. And if us hadn't, Jan Huxtable hisself, and Honor Huxtable his waife, wud live on pegmale (better nor they desarves) and gie it arl to thee, and bless thee for ating of it."

"Ay, that us wud, ees fai," answered Mrs. Huxtable, coming forward.

"And if it be for channge, and plaisure, and zeeing of the warld, I've zeen a dale in my time, axing your pardon, Miss, for convarsing so to you. And what hath it been even at Coom market, with the varmers I've a-knowed from little chillers up? No better nor a harrow dill for a little coolt to zuck. I'd liefer know thee was a-gooin' to Trentisoe churchyard, where little Jane and Winny be, than let thee goo to Lonnon town, zame as this here be. And what wud thy poor moother zay, if so be her could hear tell of it?"

At this moment, when I could say nothing, being thoroughly convicted of ingratitude, and ashamed before natures far better than my own, dear little Sally, who had been rolling on the dairy floor, recovered from the burst of childish grief enough to ask whether it had any cause. Up to me she ran, with great pearl tears on the veining of her cheeks, and peeping through the lashes of her violet-blue eyes, she gave me one long reproachful look, as if she began to understand the world, and to find it disappointment; then she buried her flaxen head in the homespun apron I had lately taken to wear, and sobbed as if she had spoiled a dozen copies. What happened afterwards I cannot tell. Crying I hate, but there are times when nothing else is any good. I only know that, as the farmer left the house to get, as he said, "a little braze," these ominous words came back from the court:

"'Twud be a bad job for Tom Grundy, if her coom'd acrass me now."

CHAPTER V.

That same evening, as I was sitting in my lonely room, yet not quite alone,-- for little Sally, who always did as I bade her, was scratching and blotting her best copy-book, under my auspices,--in burst Mrs. Huxtable, without stopping to knock as usual.

"Oh Miss Clerer, what *have* e been and doed? Varmer's in crule trouble. Us'll arl have to goo to gaol to-morrow, chillers and arl."

She was greatly flurried and out of breath, and yet seemed proud of what she had to tell. She did not require much asking, nor beat about the bush, as many women do; but told me the story shortly, and then asked me to come and hear all particulars from Tim Badcock the farm-labourer, who had seen the whole.

Tim sat by the kitchen fire with a pint of cider by him on the little round table; strong evidence that his tidings, after all, were not so very unwelcome.

"Wull, you zee, Miss," said Tim, after getting up, and pulling his rough forelock, "you zee, Miss, the Maister coom out this arternoon, in a weist zort of a wai, as if her hadn't had no dinner." Here he gave a sly look at "the Missus," who had the credit of stopping the supplies, when the farmer had been too much on the cruise.

"What odds to thee, Tim," she replied, "what odds to thee, what thee betters has for dinner?"

"Noo fai," said Tim, "zo long as ai gits maine, and my missus arlways has un raddy. Zo I zed to Bill, zays I, 'Best maind what thee's at boy, there's a starm a coomin, zure as my name's Timothy Badcock.' Howsomever her didn't tak on atarl wi we, but kitched up a shivel, and worked awai without niver a ward. 'Twur the tap of the clave, 'langside of the beg fuzz, where the braidle road coomth along 'twixt that and the double hadge; and us was arl a stubbing up the bushes as plaisant as could be, to plough thiccy plat for clover, coom some rain, plase God."

"Git on, Tim, wull e," cried his impatient mistress, "us knows arl about that. Cas'n thee tull it no quicker?"

"Wull, Miss," continued Tim, in no hurry whatever, "prasently us zees a girt beg chap on a zort of a brown cob, a coomin in our diraction"--Tim was proud of this word, and afraid that we should fail to appreciate it--"they was a coomin, as you might zay, in our diraction this beg chap, and anither chap langside on him. Wull, when 'um coom'd within spaking room of us, beg chap a' horsebarck hollers out, 'Can 'e tell, my men, where Jan Uxtable live?' Avore I had taime to spake, Maister lifts hissell up, and zaith, 'What doo 'e want to know for, my faine feller?' every bit the zame as ai be a tullin of it to you. 'What's the odds to thee,' zays tother chap, 'thee d'st better kape a zivil tongue in thee head. I be Tom Gundry from Carnwall.' And with that he stood up in his starrups, as beg a feller as iver you zee, Miss. Wull, Maister knowed all about Tom Gundry and what a was a coom for, and zo did I, and the boy, and arl the country round; for Maister have gotten a turble name for rarstling; maybe, Miss, you've a heer'd on him in Lunnon town?"

"I have never been in London, Tim, since I was a child; and I know nothing at all about wrestling."

"Wull, Miss, that be nayther here nor there. But there had been a dale of brag after Maister had thrown arl they Carnishers to Barnstable vair, last year, about vetching this here Tom Gundry, who wor the best man in Cornwall, to throw our Maister. Howsomever, it be time for ai to crack on a bit. 'Ah,' zays the man avoot, who zimth had coom to back un, 'ah, 'twor arl mighty faine for Uxtable to play skittles with our zecond rate men. Chappell or Ellicombe cud have doed as much as that. Rackon Jan Uxtable wud vind a different game with Tom Gundry here.' 'Rackon he wud,' zaith Gundry, 'a had better jine a burial club, if her've got ere a waife and vamily.'"

"Noo. Did a zay that though?" inquired Mrs. Huxtable, much excited.

"'Coom now,' my maister zaith, trying to look smarl behaind the fuzz, 'thee must throw me, my lad, avore thee can throw Jan Uxtable. He be a better man mainly nor ai be this dai. But ai baint in no oomer for playin' much jist now, and rackon ai should hoort any man ai kitched on.' 'Her that be a good un, Zam, baint it now?' zaith Gundry to little chap, the very zame as ai be a tullin it now, 'doth the fule s'pose ai be ratten? Ai've half a maind to kick un over this hadge; jist thee hold the nag!' 'Sober now,' zaith varmer, and ai zeed a was gettin' rad in the chakes, 'God knows ai don't feel no carl to hoort 'e. Ai'll gie thee wan chance more, Tom Gundry, as thee'st a coom arl this wai fram Carnwall. Can 'e trod a path in thiccy country, zame as this here be?' And wi' that, a walked into the beg fuzz, twaice so haigh as this here room, and the stocks begger round nor my body, and harder nor wrought hiern. A jist stratched his two hons, raight and left, and twitched un up, wan by wan, vor ten gude lanyard, as asily as ai wud pull spring inyons. 'Now, wull e let me lone?' zaith he, zo zoon as a coom barck, wi his brath a little quicker by rason of the exarcise, 'wull 'e let me lone?' 'Ee's fai, wull I,' zaith the man avoot. 'Hor,' zaith Tom Gundry, who had been a[#] shopping zumwhere, 'thee cans't do a gude dai's work, my man, tak that vor thee's wages.' And wi' that a lets fly at Maister's vace wi' a light hash stick a carr'd, maning to raide off avore Maister cud coom to's brath again. In a crack Jan Uxtable zet both his hons under the stommick of the nag, one avore the starrup and one behaind, zame as I maight to this here little tabble, and haved un, harse and man, clane over hadge into Muster Yeo's turmot falde. Then with wan heft, a kitched up tother chap, and zent un sprarling after un, zame as if 'twor this here stule after the tabble."

[#] *i.e.* dealing commercially where the staples are liquid.

I thought poor Tim, in the excitement of his story, would have thrown table and stool over the settle to illustrate it; and if he had, Mrs. Huxtable would have forgiven him.

"'Thar,' zaith our Maister, as plaisant as cud be, and ai thought us shud have died of laffing, 'thar now, if zo be the owner of thiccy falde zummons e for traspash, you zay Jan Uxtable zent e on a little arrand, to vaind a Carnisher as can do the laike to he.' And wi' that, a waiped his hons with a slip of vern, and tuk a little drap of zider, and full to's wark again."

"Wull, but Tim," asked the farmer's wife, to lose no part of the effect, "what zort of a hadge wor it now? Twor a little hadge maybe, no haigher nor the zettle barck."

"Wor it though?" said Tim, "thee knows better nor that, Missus. It be the beggest hadge on arl the varm, wi' a double row of saplin hash atap. Her maks the boundary betwixt the two parishes, and ain't been trimmed these vaive year, ai can swear."

"And how be the both on 'em now, Tim? A must have gone haigh enough to channge the mune.

"Wull, Miss," said Tim, addressing me, for he had told his Mistress all the story twice, "Tom Gundry brak his collar boun, and zarve 'un raight, for a brak Phil Dascombe's a puppose whun a got 'un in a trap, that taime down to Bodmin thar; and harse gat a rick of his taial; but the little chap, he vell upon his hat, and that zaved him kindly. But I heer'd down to Pewter Will's, whur I gooed for a drap of zumthin for my waife's stommick, ai heer'd zay there, as how Constable was a coomin to Maister this very naight, if Carnishers cud have perswadded un. But Constable zaith, zaith he, 'Twor all along o you Garnish chaps, fust battery was mad, and fust blow gien, and wi'out you can zhow me Squaire Drake's warrant, I wunt have nout to do wi' it, not ai; and that be law and gospel in Davonsheer and in Cornwall.'"

"Tim," said Mrs. Huxtable, "I'se warrant thee's niver tould so long a spin up in thee's laife avore. And thee's tould it wonnerful well too; hathn't un Miss Clerer? Zuke, here be the kay of zellar, gie Tim a half a paint more zider; and thee mai'st have a drap theesell, gall. Waipe thee mouth fust."

"Ah," said Tim, favouring me with a wink, in the excess of his glory, "rackon they Carnishers 'll know the wai off Tossil's Barton varm next taime, wi'out no saign postesses."[#]

[#] Every word of Tim's story is true, except as regards the names.

CHAPTER VI.

Two or three days after this, I was keeping school in the dairy, the parlour being too small for that purpose, and the kitchen and "wash-up" (as they called the back-kitchen) too open to inroads from Suke and Tim. My class consisted of ten, or rather was eight strong, the two weames (big baby and little baby), only attending for the sake of example, and because they would have roared, if parted from the other children. So those two were allowed to spraddle on the floor, where sometimes they made little rollers of themselves, with much indecorum, and between whiles sat gravely sucking their fat red fingers, and then pointed them in a glistening state at me or my audience, and giggled with a large contempt. The eight, who made believe to learn something, were the six elder Huxtables, and two of Tim Badcock's "young uns." I marshalled them, four on each side, against the low lime-whitened walls, which bore the pans of cream and milk. Little Sally, my head scholar, was very proud of measuring her height, by the horizontal line on the milk-pan where the glazing ended; which Tabitha Badcock, even on tiptoe, could not reach. They were all well "claned," and had white pinnies on, and their ruddy cheeks rubbed up to the highest possible polish, with yellow soap and the jack-towel behind the wash-up door. Hence, I never could relieve them from the idea that Sunday now came every day in the week.

I maintained strict discipline, and allowed no nonsense; but two sad drawbacks constantly perplexed me. In the first place, their ways were so ridiculous, and they laboured so much harder to make me laugh, than they did to learn, that I could not always keep my countenance, and when the spelling-book went up before my face, they knew, as well as possible, what was going on behind it, and peeped round or below, and burst out all together. The second drawback was, that Mrs. Huxtable, in spite of all my protests, would be always rushing in, upon errands purely fictitious; and the farmer himself always found some special business in the yard, close to the wired and unglazed window, whence every now and then his loud haw-haws, and too audible soliloquies, "Dang me! wull done, Zally, that wor a good un; zay un again, cheel! zay un again, wull 'e?" utterly overthrew my most solemn institutions.

"Coom now, smarl chillers"--I addressed them in my unclassical Devonshire dialect, for it kept their attention alive to criticise me when I "spak unvitty"--"coom now, e've a been spulling lang enough: ston round me now, and tull me what I axes you."

Already, I had made one great mistake, by saying "round" instead of "raound," and Billy, the genius of the family, was upon the giggle.

"Now thun, wutt be a quadripade?"

"Ai knoo!" says Sally, with her hand held out.

"Zo do ai," says Jack, thrusting forth his stomach.

"Who wur axing of you?" I inquire in a stately manner. "You bain't the smarl chillers, be 'e? Bill knows," I continue, but wax doubtful from the expression of Bill's face.

"Ees fai," cries Bill, suddenly clearing up, "her be wutt moother zits on vor to mulk the coos. Bain't her now?"

"Thee bee'st ony wan leg out, Bill. Now Tabby Badcock?"

While Tabby is splashing in her memory (for I told them all last week), the farmer much excited, and having no idea what the answer should be, but hoping that one of his own children may discover it first, boldly shows his face at the wired window, but is quite resolved to allow fair play. Not so Mrs. Huxtable, who, in full possession of the case, suddenly appears behind me, and shakes her fist at poor puzzled Tabby. "Thee'dst best pretend to know more than thy betters." She tries to make Tabby hear, without my catching her words. But the farmer hotly shouts, "Lat un alo-un, waife. Tak thee hon from thee mouth, I tull 'e. Spak up now, little wanch."

Thus encouraged, Tabby makes reply, looking cross-wise at Mrs. Huxtable.

"Plase, Miss, it be a beastie wi vour taials."

"Raight," cries the farmer, with admiration conquering his disappointment; "raight this taime, ai'll tak my oath on it. I zeed wan to Barnstaple vair last year, and her wor karled, 'Phanominy Quadripade,' her Kirsten name and her zurname, now ai coom to racollack."

Tabby looks elated, and Mrs. Huxtable chagrined. Before I can redress the situation, a sound of heavy blows, delivered on some leathery substance, causes a new stir. All recognise the arrival of Her Majesty's mail, a boy from Martinhoe, who comes upon a donkey twice a week, if there happen to be any letters for the village below.

Out rush Mrs. Huxtable and Suke (who once received an epistle), and the children long to go, but know better. The boy, however, has only a letter for me, which is from Mrs. Shelfer (a cousin of Ann Maples), to whom I wrote a few days since, asking whether she had any rooms to let. Mrs. Shelfer replies that "she has apartments, and they are splendid, and the rent quite trifling;" so the mail is bribed with a pint of cider, while I write to secure a new home.

My departure being now fixed and inevitable, the women naturally began to remonstrate more than over. It had been settled that Ann Maples should go with me, not to continue as my servant, but to find a place for herself in London.

My few arrangements, which cost me far more pain than trouble, were not long in making; and after saying good-bye to all the dear little children and weanies, and kissing their pretty faces in their little beds, amid an agony of tears from Sally, I was surprised, on entering the kitchen, to find there Mr. Beany Dawe. There was little time for talking, and much less for poetry. We were to start at three in the morning, the farmer having promised to drive us to meet the coach in Barnstaple, whence there would be more than thirty miles of hilly road to Tiverton, the nearest railway station. The journey to London could thus be made in a day, though no one in the parish could be brought to believe it.

The poet had been suborned, no doubt, by Mrs. Huxtable, and now detained me to listen to an elegy upon the metropolis of England. I cannot stop to repeat it, neither does it deserve the trouble; but it began thus:--

"Fayther was wance to Lonnon town,

And a zed, zed he, whan a coom down,

'Don't e niver goo there, Ebenezer my son,

For they mulks a coo, when her ain't gat none.

They kapes up sich a hollerin, naight and day,

And a Devonsheer man dunno the impudence they zay.

Their heads and their hats wags regular, like the

scratchers of a harrow,

And they biles their taties peeled, and ates them

in a barrow.

They raides on a waggon top with their wives squazed

up inside her,

And they drinks black dose and yesty pops in the

place of wholesome zider.

They want take back anything they've zelled,

And the beds can bite, and the cats can speak:

And a well-dress'd man be a most compelled

To channge his shirt in the middle of the week!'"

"Lor," cried Mrs. Huxtable, "however could they do their washing? Thee vayther must a been as big a liar as thee, Beany. Them gifts always runs in the family."

When, with remarkable patience, I had heard out his elegant effusion, the author, who had conceived much good will towards me, because I listened to his lays and called him Mr. Dawe, the author dived with a deep-drawn sigh into a hole in his sack, and produced in a mysterious manner something wrapped in greasy silver paper, and well tied up. He begged me to accept, and carry it about me most carefully and secretly, as long as I should live. To no other person in the world would he have given this, but I had earned it, as a true lover of poetry, and required it as a castaway among the perils of London. In vain I declined the present; refusal only confirmed his resolution. As the matter was of so little importance, I soon yielded upon condition that I should first examine the gift. He gave me leave with much reluctance, and I was surprised at the beauty and novelty of the thing. It was about the size of a Geneva watch, but rather thicker, jet black and shining, and of the exact shape of a human heart. Around the edge ran a moulding line or cord of brilliant red, of the same material as the rest. In the centre was a white spot like a siphuncle. What it was I could not guess, but it looked like some mineral substance. Where the two lobes met, a small hole had been drilled to receive a narrow riband. After putting me through many guesses, Mr. Dawe informed me that it was a pixie's heart, a charm of unequalled power against witchcraft and assassination, and to enthral the affection of a loved one. He only smiled, and rubbed his nose, on hearing that I should never want it in the last capacity. Being greatly pleased with it, I asked him many questions, which he was very loth to answer. Nevertheless I extorted from him nearly all he knew.

As he was sawing into boards a very large oak-tree, something fell from the very heart of it almost into his mouth, for poor Ebenezer was only an undersawyer. As he could not stop the saw without his partners concurrence, and did not wish to share his prize, he kicked some sawdust over it until he could stoop to pick it up unobserved. In all his long experience of the woods, he had seen but two of these rare and beautiful things, and now assured me that any sawyer was considered lucky who found only one in the course of his career. The legend on the subject was rather quaint and graceful, and deserves a better garb than he or I can furnish.

"All in the olden time, there lived

A little Pixie king,

So lovely and so light of foot

That when he danced the ring,

The moonlight always shifted, to gaze upon his face,

And the cowslip-bells uplifted, rang time with every pace.

There came a dozen maidens,

Almost as tall as bluebells;

The cowslips hushed their cadence,

And bowed before the true belles:

The maidens shyly glancing, betwixt the cummer darts,

Espied the monarch dancing, and lost a dozen hearts.

He was fitted up so neatly,

With dewdrops for his crown,

And he footed it so featly

He never shook them down.

The maids began advancing, along a lily stem,

Not to stop the monarch's dancing, but to make him look at them.

The king could not afford them

The proper time to gaze,

But sweetly bowed toward them,

At the turn of every maze:

Till full of pretty faces, and his sandals getting worn,

He was puzzled in his paces, and fell upon a thorn.

The maidens broke the magic ring,

And leaped the cummer dart;

'Alas, our little Pixie king,

The thorn is in his heart!'

They laid him in a molehill, and piteously they cried:

Yet this was not the whole ill, for all the maidens died.

Each took a spindled acorn, found

Below a squirrel's nest,

And set the butt against the ground,

The barb beneath her breast:

So truly she addressed the stroke unto her loving part,

That when the acorn grew an oak, it held her little heart.'

By no means a "little heart," it seemed to me, for a fairy to have owned, but as large as it was loving. I assured Mr. Dawe that he was quite untaught in fairy lore, or he never would have confounded fairies with pixies, a different class of society. But he treated my learning with utter contempt, and reasonably enough declared that he who spent all his time in the woods must know more than any books could tell.

He also informed me, that the proper name for the lignified fairy heart, was a "gordit:" but he did not choose to tell me what had become of the other, which was not so large or handsome as this, yet it had saved him a month's sawing, and earned him "a rare time," which meant, I fear, that the proceeds had been spent in a very long cruise.

After refusing all compensation, Mr. Dawe made his farewell in several couplets of uncouth but hearty blessing, begging me only to shake hands with him once, and venturing as a poet to prophesy that we should meet again. The "gordit" was probably nothing more than a rare accretion, or ganglion, in the centre of an aged oak. However, it was very pretty; and of course I observed the condition upon which I had received it, valuing it moreover as a token of true friends.

But how can I think of such trifles, while sitting for the last time in the room where my mother died? To-morrow all the form and colour of my life shall change; even now I feel once more my step on the dark track of justice, which is to me revenge. How long have I been sauntering on the dreary moor of listlessness and hollow weariness, which spreads, for so many dead leagues, below the precipice of grief? How long have I been sauntering, not caring to ask where, and conscious of existence only through the nerves and fibres of the memory. The things I have been doing, the duties I have discharged, the vague unlinked ideas, startling me by their buffoonery to grief--might not these have all passed through me, every whit as well, if I had been set against a wall, and wound up for three months, and fitted with the mind expressed in the chuckle of a clock? Nay, worse than all--have I not allowed soft thoughts to steal throughout my heart, the love of children, the warmth of kindness, the pleasure of doing good in however small a way? Much more of this, and I shall learn forgiveness of my wrong!

But now I see a clearer road before me. Returning health renews my gall. Death recedes, and lifts his train from the swords that fell before him. Once more my pulse beats high with hatred, with scorn of meanness, treachery, and lies, with admiration of truth and manhood, not after the fashion of fools.

But dare I mount the Judge's throne? Shall the stir of one frail heart, however fresh from its Maker's hand, be taken for His voice pronouncing right and wrong?

These thoughts give me pause, and I dwell again with my mother. But in all the strength of youth and stern will, I tread them down; and am once more that Clara Vaughan whose life shall right her father's death.

CHAPTER VII.

At last we got through our parting with the best of people (far worthier than myself to interest any reader), and after it the dark ride over the moors, and the farmer's vain attempt at talking to relieve both himself and us. The honest eyes were bright with tears, tears of pity for my weakness, which now he scarcely cared to hide, but would not show by wiping away; and how many times he begged for frequent tidings of us, which Sally could now interpret, if written in large round hand. How many times he consulted, commanded, and threatened the coachman, and promised him a goose at Michaelmas, if he took good care of us and our luggage! These great kindnesses, and all the trifling cares which strew the gap of long farewells, were more to think of than to tell. But I ought to mention, that much against the farmer's will, I insisted on paying him half the sum, which he had lent me in a manner never to be forgotten. Moreover, with the same presentiment which he had always felt, he made me promise once more to send for him, if I fell into any dreadful strait.

It was late at night when our cabman, the most polite, and (if his word may be trusted) the most honourable of mankind, rang the bell of Mrs. Shelfer's house. The house was in a by-street near a large unfinished square, in the northern part of London. Mrs. Shelfer came out at once, sharp and quick and short, and wonderfully queer. At first she took no notice at all of either of as, but began pulling with all her strength at the straps of the heaviest boxes, which, by means known to herself alone, she contrived to drag through the narrow passage, and down three low steps into the little kitchen. Then she hurried back, talking all the time to herself, re-opened the door of the fly, jumped in, and felt under both the seats, and round the lining. Finding nothing there, she climbed upon the driver's box, and thoroughly examined both that and the roof. Being satisfied now that none of our chattels were left in the vehicle, she shook her little fist at two or three boys, who stood at the corner near the mews, and setting both hands to the farmer's great hamper or "maun" (as he called it), she dragged it inside the front door, and turned point blanc upon me.

"Pray, my good friend, how many is there?"

"I'm sure I don't know, Mrs. Shelfer, your cousin knows best."

"Ah, they're terrible fellows them cabbies, terrible!" The cabman stood by all the time, beating his hands together. "'Twas only last time I went to Barbican, one of 'em come up to me, 'Mrs. Shelfer,' says he, 'Mrs. Shelfer!' says I, 'pray my good friend, how do you know my name?' 'Ho, I knows Charley well enough,' says he, 'and there ain't a better fellow living.' 'A deal too good for you,' says I, 'and now pray what's your business with me?' 'Why, old lady,' he says, as impudent as the man with the wooden leg, 'you've been and left your second best umbrella under the seat of the Botany Bay Bus.' 'Catch me!' says I. 'It's Bible truth,' says he, 'and my old woman's got it now.' 'If you never get drunk,' says I, 'till that umbrella runs in your shoes, your old woman needn't steal her lights,' and with that I ran between the legs of a sheep, hanging up with my Tuscan bonnet on trimmed with white--nothing like it, my good friend, the same as I've had these two and twenty years."

"What for, Mrs. Shelfer?" I asked in great surprise.

"Why, for the butcher to see me, to be sure, Miss. You see he wanted to get me down the mews, and murder me with my little wash-leather bag, as I was going to pay the interest on Shelfer's double-barrel gun. Ah yes," with a short sigh, "and there'll be four and ninepence again, next Tuesday."

Talking at this rate, and stopping for no reply, she led us into her kitchen, saying that she would not light a fire upstairs, it was so bootiful, the trimmings of the grate, because she wasn't certain that we would come, but she had got supper for us, excuse me, my good friend, in her own snug little room, and bootiful they was sure enough, the wind last week had made them so fat.

She pointed in triumph to a large dish on the table piled up with blue shells.

"Why, Mrs. Shelfer, they are muscles," I exclaimed with some disgust.

"Ah I see you knows 'em, that they are, Miss, and as bootiful as ever you ate. Charley and me sits down to a peck of them. But the man as comes round with the catsmeat's brother the man with the truck and his eyes crossed, he told me there was such a demand for them in Grosvenor Square, and they was so cunning this weather when they gets fat, he hadn't more than half a peck left, but they was the best of the lot. Now I'll have them all bootiful hot, bootiful, boiling my good friend, if you'll just run upstairs, and a teaspoon and a half of salt, and Cousin Ann knows the way, and the apartments is splendid, splendid, Miss Vaughan!"

She drew herself up, at the end of the sentence, with an air of the greatest dignity; then suddenly dropped it again, and began bustling in and out. Now for the first time, I had leisure to examine her, for while she spoke, the short jumps of her ideas unsettled my observation.

She was a little body, rather thin, with a face not strongly peculiar, but odd enough to second the oddities of her mind. No doubt she had once been pretty, and her expression was pleasant now, especially when a glimpse was afforded of her quick grey eyes, which generally avoided the gaze, and dropped beneath a fringe of close-set lashes. But the loss of the front teeth, and the sharpening and wrinkling of the face, with the straggling neglect of the thick black hair fraying out from the black cap, and the habit she had of shutting her mouth with a snap, all these interfered with her credit for pristine good looks. Like Mrs. Huxtable, she was generally in a bustle, but a bustle of words more often than of deeds. She had no deception about her, yet she never knew the difference between the truth and a lie, and could not understand that any one else should do so. Therefore she suspected everything and everybody, till one of her veins of opinion was touched, and then she would swallow anything.

Tired out with the long day's travel, the dazing of railway speed, and the many scenes and faces which had flashed across me, I could not appreciate the beauty of Mrs. Shelfer's furniture; but leaving Ann Maples to eat the muscles, if she could, and to gossip with her cousin, I was not slow to revisit the old farmhouse, and even the home of my childhood, in the winged cradle of sleep.

CHAPTER VIII.

Ann Maples had done her best to persuade me to call on my godmother, Lady Cranberry, but I was quite resolved to do nothing of the sort. In the first place, Lady Cranberry was a person of great wealth, living in a very large house, and keeping up such state as gay widows love, who have forgotten old affections and are looking out for new. In me, therefore, to whose fixed estimate fidelity seemed the very pith of honour, there could be no love towards such a changeling. And even if I had liked her, my circumstances would not admit of our visiting upon equal terms, and it was not likely that I would endure to be patronized by any one. In the second place, the same most amiable lady had written letters of beautiful condolence, and taken a tender interest in our change of fortune, so long as there was any novelty in it; but soon flagged off, and had not even replied to my announcement of dearest mother's death. Finally, I hated her without any compromise, from what I had seen of her, and what she had done to me at Vaughan Park.

So my good Ann set off all alone, for she hoped to obtain some recommendation there, and I was left to receive Mrs. Shelfer's morning visit.

Her queer episodical conversation, and strange biographies of every table, chair, and cushion--her "sticks," as she delighted to call them--I shall not try to repeat, for my history is not a comic one; neither will she appear, unless the connexion requires it. One vein of sympathy between us was opened at once, by her coming into the room with a lame blackbird on her finger; and I was quite surprised at the number of her pets. As for the "splendid apartments," they were two little rooms on the first floor, adjoining one another, and forming, together with the landing outside and a coal-closet, the entirety of that storey. The rooms above were occupied by a young dress-maker. Mr. and Mrs. Shelfer, who had no children kept the ground-floor (consisting of a parlour and kitchen) and the two attics, one of which was always full of onions and carrot seed. Upon the whole, though the "sticks" were very old, and not over clean, until I scoured them, and the drawing-room (as my landlady loved to call it) was low and small, and looked through the rails of a narrow balcony upon a cheese-monger's shop across the road (instead of a wooded dingle), I was very well satisfied with them; and above all the rent was within my means.

In the afternoon, when things were growing tidy, a carriage drove up rapidly, and a violent ringing of the bell ensued. It was Lady Cranberry, who, under the pretext of bringing Ann Maples home, was come to gratify her own sweet curiosity. She ran upstairs in her most charming manner, caught me by both hands, and would have kissed me desperately, if I had shown any tendency that way. Then she stopped to admire me.

"Oh, you lovely creature! How you are grown to be sure! I should never have known you. How delicious all this is!"

Of course I was pleased with her admiration; but only for a moment, because I disliked her.

"I am glad you find it delicious," I replied quite coldly; "perhaps I shall by-and-by."

"What would I give to be entering life under such sweetly romantic circumstances? Dear me! I must introduce you. What a sensation you will cause! With such a face and figure and such a delightful story, we shall all rave about you. And how well you are dressed from that outlandish place! What a piece of luck! It's the greatest marvel on earth that you found me in London now."

"Excuse me," I said, "I neither found, nor meant to find you."

"Oh, of course you are cross with me. I forgot about that. But who made your dress, in the name of all woodland graces?"

"I always make my own dresses."

"Then you shall make mine. Say no more about it. You shall live with me, and make my dresses by day; and by night you shall go with me everywhere, and I won't be jealous. I will introduce you everywhere. 'This is my ward, Miss Vaughan, whose father--ah, I see, you know that romantic occurrence in Gloucestershire.' Do you think it will be a your--and the Great Exhibition season--before you are mistress of a property ten times the size of Vaughan Park? If you doubt it, look in the glass. Ah me! You know nothing of the world, I forget, I am so warm-hearted. But you may take my word for it. Will you cry a bargain?"

She held out her hand, as she had seen the fast men do, whose society she affected. I noticed it not, but led her on; my fury had long been gathering. I almost choked when she spoke in that way of my father, utterly as I despised her. But I made it a trial of self-control, which might be demanded against more worthy objects.

"Are you sure that I shall be useful? Sure that I shall earn my board?"

"Oh, you Vaughans are always so conscientious. I want an eider-down petticoat quilted at once for the winter, and I dare not trust it to Biggs, I know she will pucker it so. That shall be the first little job for my Clara."

Her cup was full. She had used dearest mother's fond appellative, and, as I thought, in mockery. I did not lower myself by any sarcastic language. She would not have understood it. I merely opened the door, and said calmly to my landlady, who was there, of course "promiscuously;" "Mrs. Shelfer, show out the Countess of Cranberry."

Poor godmother, she was so frightened that I was sorry for her. They helped her into the carriage, and she had just strength to draw down the blinds.

Mrs. Shelfer had been in raptures at having so grand a vehicle and two great footmen at her door. Lest the street should lose the effect, she had run in and out a dozen times, and banged the door, and got into talk with the coachman, and sent for beer to the Inn, though she had it in the house. She now came again to my door, in what she called a "terrible quandary." I could not attend to her, but locked myself in, and wrestled with my passionate nature, at one time indulging, then spurning and freezing it. Yet I could not master it, as I fancied I had done.

CHAPTER IX.

Soon afterwards, Ann Maples went to the place which she had obtained in Lady Cranberry's household; and I determined to begin my search.

"Mrs. Shelfer, do you know London well?"

My landlady was feeding her birds, and I had made up for her disappointment about Lady Cranberry, by fitting the lame blackbird with a wooden leg, cut from a skewer, and tipped with a button: it was pretty to see how kindly and cleverly he took to it, and how proudly he contemplated it, when he thought there was no one watching. His mistress now stopped her work, and made ready for a long speech, with the usual snap of her lips.

"Know London, Miss Vaughan! I was born in Red Cross Street, and I've never been further out of town than Chalk Farm fair, or Hampstead Waterworks, and, please God, I never will. Bless me, what an awful place the country is, awful! What with the trees, and the ditches, and the sting-nettles, and the black wainscot with skewers on the top--"

"Too bad of you, Mrs. Shelfer, to be frightened at palings--and your husband a gardener, too! But tell me whereabouts is Grove Street?"

"What Grove Street, my good friend?"

"Grove Street, London, to be sure."

"Why, dear me, Miss, I thought you knew everything; you can doctor Jack, and the Bully, and tell me all about Sandy the squirrel's tail and the hair coming off and when it's going to rain! Don't you know there's a dozen Grove Streets in London, for all I know. Leastways I knows four."

"And where are those four, Mrs. Shelfer?"

"Now please, my good friend, give me just a minute to think. It is dreadful work to be hurried, ever since I fell downstairs, when I were six year old. Let me see now. Charley knows. Can't you wait, Miss, till Charley comes home, and he's coming quite early this evening, and two friends of his to supper."

"No, Mrs. Shelfer, I cannot wait. If you can't tell me, I must go and get a book."

"Oh them books is no good. Why they ain't got Charley in, and he with the lease one time of the garden in Hollyhock Square, and a dahlia named after him at the Royal Heretical Society! And they did say the Queen would have handed him the spade she liked his looks so much, only his nails wasn't clean. Very likely you heard, Miss--And how he was cheated out of it."

"Do you expect me to wait all day?"

"No no, my good friend, to be sure not. You never will wait a minute, partikler when I spill the coals, and when I wants to baste the meat. And how can the gravy run, and a pinch of salt in the dripping-pan--"

"Yesterday, Mrs. Shelfer, you basted my pound and a half of mutton with three pounds of coals. Now don't go off into a treatise. Answer me, where is Grove Street?"

"Bless my heart, Miss Vaughan. You never gives one a chance. And we thought a young lady from the country as had been brought up with tags, and lace, and bobbin, and pigs, and hay--"

"Could be cheated anyhow. No, I don't mean that: I beg your pardon, dear Patty. I often speak very hastily. What I mean is that you thought I should know nothing at all. And I don't know much, but one thing I do know, that you would never cheat me much."

To my surprise she was not at all sensitive on this subject. In fact she had dealt with so many lodgers, that she expected to be suspected. But I believe she never cheated me more than she could help. She answered me quite calmly, after some meditation:

"To be sure, Miss, to be sure, I only does my dooty. A little dripping may be, or a drop of milk for old Tom, and a piece of soap you left in the water, Miss, I kept it for Charley to shave with."

"Now, Mrs. Shelfer, no more of that. Come back to Grove Street; surely, I have given you time enough now."

"Well, Miss, there is one I know close by here. You keep down the Willa Road, and by the fishmonger's shop, and then you turn on the right over against the licensed pursuant to Act of George the Fourth. I knows George the Fourth acted badly, but I never thought it was that way. Sam the Sweep lives with him, and the young man with a hook for his hand that lets out the 'Times' for a penny, and keeps all his brothers and sisters."

"And where are the other three that you know?"

"There's one in Hackney, and one in Bethnal Green, and there's one in Mile-end Road. Bless me, to be sure! I've been there with dear Miss Minto after a cat she lost, a tabby with a silver collar on, and a notch in his left ear. It would make you cry, Miss--"

"Thank you, Mrs. Shelfer; that will do for the present. I'll go up to the 'drawing-room' now."

In a few minutes I went forth with my dark plaid shawl around me, which had saved my mother's life, and was thenceforth sacred. It was the first time I walked all alone in London, and though we lived quite in the suburbs it seemed very odd to me. For a while I felt rather nervous, but no one molested me then or at any other time; although I have heard some plain young ladies declare that they could not walk in London without attracting unpleasant attention. Perhaps because they knew not the way either to walk or to dress.

Without any trouble, I found No. 19, Grove Street, then rang the bell and looked round me. It was a clean unpretentious street, not to be known by its architecture from a thousand others in London. The bell was answered by a neat little girl, and I asked for the Master of the house. Clever tactics truly for commencing a task like mine.

Being told that the Master was from home, I begged to see the Mistress. The little maid hesitated awhile, with the chain of the door in her hand, and then invited me into the parlour, a small room, but neat and pretty.

"Please, Miss, what name shall I say?"

"Miss Vaughan, if you please." Then I said to myself, "What good am I? Is this my detective adroitness?"

Presently a nice old lady, with snow-white hair, came in.

"Miss Vaughan," she asked with a pleasant smile, "do you wish to see me?"

"Yes, if you please. Just to ask a few questions as to the inmates of this house."

Despite her kindness and good breeding, the lady stared a little.

"May I inquire your motives? Do you know me at all? I have not the pleasure of knowing you."

"My motives I must not tell you. But, as a lady, I assure you, that curiosity is not one. Neither are they improper."

She looked at me in great surprise, examined me closely, and then replied:

"Young lady, I believe what you say. It is impossible not to do so. But my answering you must depend on the nature of your inquiries. You have done, excuse my saying it, you have done a very odd thing."

"I will not ask many questions. How many people live here?"

"I will answer you curtly as you ask, unless you ask what I do not choose to answer. Four people live here, namely, my husband, myself, our only daughter--but for whom I might have been ruder to you--and the child who let you in. Also a woman comes every day to work."

"Are there no more? Forgive my impertinence. No strangers to the family?"

"No lodgers whatever. My son is employed in the City, and sleeps there. My only daughter is in very weak health, and though we do not want all the house, we are not obliged to take lodgers. A thing I never would do, because they always expect to be cheated."

"And is your husband an Englishman?"

"Yes, and an English writer, not altogether unknown."

She mentioned a name of good repute in the world of letters, as even I was aware.

"You have quite satisfied me. I thank you most heartily. Very few would have been so polite and kind. I fear you must think me a very singular being. But I have powerful motive, and am quite a stranger in London."

"My dear, I knew that at once. No Londoner would have learned from me the family history I have told you. I should have shown them out at the very first question. Thank you, oh thank you, my child. But I am sure you have hurt yourself. Oh, the shell has run into your forehead."

As she looked so intently at me, on her way to the door of the room, her foot had been caught by the claw of the what-not, and I barely saved her from falling.

"No, Mrs. Elton, I am not hurt at all. How stupid of me, to be sure. And all my fault that you fell. I hope the shell is not broken. Ah, I bring very bad luck to all who treat me kindly."

"The shell is not worth sixpence. The fault was all my own. If you had not been wonderfully quick, I must have fallen heavily. Pray sit down, and recover yourself, Miss Vaughan. Look, you have dropped a letter. Dear me, I know that writing! Excuse me; it is I that am now impertinent."

"If you know that writing, pray tell me how and where."

The letter she had seen was the anonymous one which brought me from Devonshire to London. I had put it into my pocket, thinking that it might be wanted. It fell out as I leaped forward, and it lay on the floor wide open.

"May I look at the writing more closely? Perhaps I am deceived."

For a while I hesitated. But it seemed so great a point to know who the writer was, that I hushed my hesitation. However, I showed the letter so that she could not gather its import.

"Yes," said Mrs. Elton, "I am quite certain now. That is the writing of a Polish lady, whom at one time I knew well. My husband has written a work upon Poland, which brought him into contact with some of the refugees. Among them was a gentleman of some scientific attainments, who had a pretty lively warm-hearted wife, very fond of dancing, and very fond of dogs. She and I have had many a laugh at one another and ourselves; for, though my hair is grey, I am fond of lively people."

"And where is that lady now?"

"My child, I cannot tell you. Her name I will tell you, if you like, when I have consulted my husband. But it will help you very little towards finding her; for they change their names almost every time they move. Even in London they forget that they are not heard every time they sneeze. The furtive habits born of oppression cling about them still."

"And where did they live at the time you knew them?"

Wrung by suspense and anxiety, I had forgotten good manners. But Mrs. Elton had good feeling which knows when to dispense with them. Nevertheless I blushed with shame at my own effrontery.

"Not very far from here, in a part that is called 'Agar Town.' But they have now left London, and England too, I believe. I must tell you no more, because they had reasons for wishing to be unknown."

"Only tell me one thing. Were they cruel or violent people?"

"The very opposite. Most humane and warm-hearted They would injure no one, and hated all kinds of cruelty. How pale you are, my child! You must have a glass of wine. It is useless to say no."

As this clue, which seemed so promising, led to nothing at all, I may as well wind it up at once, and not tangle my story with it. Mr. Elton permitted his wife to tell me all she knew about the Polish exiles, for they were gone to America, and nothing done here could harm them. But at the same time he made me promise not to mention to the police, if my case should ever come before them, the particulars which he gave me; and I am sure he would not wish me to make free with the gentleman's name. A gentleman he was, as both my kind friends assured me, and not likely to conceal any atrocious secret, unless he had learned it in a way which laid it upon his honour. Mr. Elton had never been intimate with him, and knew not who his friends were, but Mrs. Elton had liked the lady who was very kind and passionate. Also she was very apt to make mistakes in English names, and to become confused at moments of excitement. Therefore Mrs. Elton thought that she had confounded the Eltons' address with that of some other person; for it seemed a most unlikely thing that she should know the residents at two Nos. 19 Grove Street. However so it proved--but of that in its place. It was now six months since they had quitted London, perhaps on account of the climate, for the gentleman had been ill some time, and quite confined to the house. It would be altogether vain to think of tracing them in America. While living in London they owned a most magnificent dog, a truly noble fellow but afflicted with a tumour. This dog suddenly disappeared, and they would not tell what had become of him, but the lady cried most violently one day when he was spoken of. Directly after this they left the country, with a very brief farewell.

All this I learned from Mr. and Mrs. Elton during my second visit, for Mrs. Elton was too good a wife to dispense with her husband's judgment. Also I saw their daughter, a pleasing delicate girl; they learned of course some parts of my story, and were most kind and affectionate to me; and I am proud to have preserved their friendship to the present time. But as they take no prominent share in the drama of my life, henceforth they will not be presented upon its stage.

As I returned up the Villa Road, thinking of all I had heard, and feeling down at heart, something cold was gently placed in my ungloved hand. Turning in surprise and fright I saw an enormous dog, wagging his tail, and looking at me with magnificent brown eyes. Those great brown eyes were begging clearly for the honour of my acquaintance, and that huge muzzle was deposited as a gage of love. As I stooped to ascertain his sentiments, he gravely raised one mighty paw and offered it to me delicately, with a little sigh of self-approval. Upon my accepting it frankly and begging to congratulate him upon his noble appearance and evident moral excellence, he put out his tongue, a brilliant red one, and gave me a serious kiss. Then he shrugged his shoulders and looked with patient contempt at a nicely-dressed young lady, who was exerting her lungs at a silver whistle some fifty yards down the road. "Go, good dog," I said with a smile, "run, that's a good dog, your Mistress wants you immediately." "Let her wait," he said with his eyes, "I am not in a hurry this morning, and she doesn't know what to do with her time. However, if you think it would be rude of me--" And with that he resumed a long bone, laid aside while he chatted to me, tucked it lengthwise in his mouth, like a tobacco-pipe, and after shaking hands again, and saying "Now don't forget me," the great dog trotted away sedately, flourishing his tail on high, like a plume of Pampas grass. At the corner of the railings he overtook his young Mistress, whose features I could not descry; though from her air and walk I knew that she must be a pretty girl. A good-tempered one too she seemed to be, for she only shook her little whip lightly at the dog, who made an excursion across the road and sniffed at a heap of dust.

CHAPTER X.

Although Ann Maples was not so very talkative, it would be romantic to suppose that Mrs. Shelfer had failed to learn my entire history, so far at least as her cousin knew it.

Having now disposed of one Grove Street, I was about to try the same rude tactics with another, viz. that in Hackney; when my landlady gave a little nervous knock, and hurried into the room. "Oh, Miss Vaughan, is it about them willains you are wandering about and taking on so, and frightening all of us nearly to death?"

"Mrs. Shelfer, I shall feel obliged by your leaving me to manage my own affairs."

"Bless you, Miss, so I will. I wouldn't have them on my mind for the Bank of England, and Guildhall, paved with Lombard Street, and so I told Charley last night. Right, my good friend, quite right, you may depend upon it." Here she tapped her forehead, and looked mysterious.

"That being so, Mrs. Shelfer, I need say nothing more;" and with that I was going away.

"No, no, to be sure not. Only listen to me, Miss, one minute; and I knows more about willains, a deal more than you do of course, Miss. Why, ever since that rogue who come to Miss Minto's with brandyballs and rabbitskins on a stick."

"Once more, Mrs. Shelfer, I have no time to spare for gossip--"

"Gossip! No, no, Miss Vaughan; if you ever heard any one say Patty Shelfer was a 'gossip,' I'll thank you for their name. Gossip! A mercy on me with all I has to do, and the days drawing in so, and how they does charge for the gas, and the directors holds a meeting first Tuesday in every month, and fills up the pipes with spittle, that's the reason it sputters so, Charley told me."

"Good bye, Mrs. Shelfer."

"No, no. One minute, Miss Vaughan; you are always in such a hurry. What Charley and me was talking about last night was this. My Uncle John, a very high class man, first-rate, first-rate, Miss Vaughan, has been for ever so long in the detective police. There's nothing he don't know of what goes on in London, from the rats as comes up the drain pipes to the Queen getting up on her throne. A wonderful man he is. I said t'other day--"

"Is he like you, Mrs. Shelfer?"

"Like me, my good friend! No, no. And I wouldn't be like him for something. With all them state secrets upon him. Why he daren't sneeze out of his hat. But if you'll only put off going again till to-morrow, he'll be here this very night about the plate they stole in the Square. And I'm sure you can't do better than hear what he thinks about you. He'll be sure to know all that was done at the time. Bless you, he has got to make all the returns; what that is, I don't know. It's a kind of tobacco Charley says, that they smokes in the Queen's pipe. But I think it's the convicts as returns from Botany Bay."

"Well, Mrs. Shelfer, I'll think of what you say, and I am much obliged to you for the suggestion; but I can't bear the idea of coming before the Police again, with a matter in which they failed so signally."

"But you know, my good friend, it need not be put on the books at all. He'll tell us what he thinks of it, private like, and for the love of the thing."

"If I see him at all, I must beg to see him alone."

"To be sure, my good friend. Quite right, Miss Vaughan, quite right. I'm sure I would rather have the plumber's ladle put to my ear, than one of them horrible secrets."

"Mrs. Shelfer, have I told you any? Now remember, if you ever again allude to this subject before me, I leave your house that day. You ought to know better, Mrs. Shelfer."

"You are quite right, Miss Vaughan; I ask your pardon, you are quite right. The very words as Charley said to me the other night. 'You ought to have knowed better, Patty, that you did.'"

Away she went, smoothing her apron, patting the fray of her hair--for she never wore side-combs--and mumbling down the stairs. "Quite right, my good friend, quite right, I ought to have knowed better, poor thing."

She brought up my dinner and tea, without a single word, but with many sly glances at me from her quick grey eyes. Once or twice she was at the point of speaking, and the dry smile she always spoke with fluttered upon her face; but she closed her lips firmly and even bit them to keep herself in. I could scarcely help laughing, for I liked the odd little thing; but she was so free with her tongue, that the lesson was sadly wanted.

Late in the evening, she came to say that Inspector Cutting was there, and would come up if I wished it. Upon my request he came, and one look was enough to show that his niece had not misdescribed him. An elderly man, but active looking and wiry, with nothing remarkable in his features, except the clear cast of his forehead and the firm set of his mouth. But the quick intelligence that shot from his eyes made it seem waste of time to finish telling him anything. For this reason, polite though he was, it became unpleasant to talk to him. It was something like shooting at divers--as my father used to describe it--for whom the flash of the gun is enough.

Yet he never once stopped or hurried me, until my tale was done, and all my thoughts laid bare. Then he asked to see all my relics and vestiges of the deed; even my gordit did not escape him.

"L.D.O." he said shortly, "do you speak Italian?"

"I can read it, but not speak it."

"Is it commoner for Italian surnames to begin with an O, or with a C?"

"There are plenty beginning with both; but more I should think with a C."

When all my particulars had been told, and all my evidence shown, I asked with breathless interest--for my confidence in him grew fast--what his opinion was.

"Allow me, young lady, to put a few questions to you, on matters you have not mentioned. Forgive me, if they pain you. I believe you feel that they will not be impertinent."

I promised to answer without reserve.

"What was your mother's personal appearance?"

"Most winning and delicate."

"How old was she at the time of her marriage?"

"Twenty-one, I believe."

"How old was your father then?"

"Twenty-five."

"How many years were they married?"

"Sixteen, exactly."

"When did your guardian first leave England?"

"In the course of a year or two after the marriage."

"Had there been any misunderstanding between him and your father?"

"None, that I ever heard of."

"Did your father, at any time, travel on the continent?"

"Only in Switzerland, and part of Italy, during his wedding tour."

"Your guardian returned, I believe, at intervals to England?" I had never told him this.

"Yes. At least I suppose so, or he would not have been in London."

"Did he visit then at Vaughan Park?"

"Not once within my memory."

"Thank you. I will ask no more. It is a strange story; but I have known several much more strange. Of one thing be assured. I shall catch the criminal. I need not tell you that I heard much of this case at the time."

"Were you sent down to Gloucestershire?"

"No. If I had been--well, I will not say. But I was not then in my present position. Had I been so, it would have become my special department."

"Pray keep me no more in suspense. Tell me what you think."

"That I must not do, or you should know it at once, for my opinion is formed. It would be a breach of duty for me to tell you now."

"Oh," I cried in my disappointment, "I wish I had never seen you."

"Young lady, you have done your duty in placing the matter before me, and some day you will rejoice that you did so. One piece of advice I will give you: change your name immediately, before even the tradesmen about here know it."

"Change my name, Inspector Cutting! Do you think I am ashamed of my name?"

"Certainly not. You have shown great intelligence when a mere child; exert but a little now, and you will see the good sense, or rather the necessity, of my recommendation. When you have gained your object, you may resume your name with pride. You have given your information, Miss Vaughan, as clearly as ever I knew a female give it."

If I detest anything, in the way of small things, it is to be called a "female." So I said coldly; "Inspector Cutting, I thank you for the compliment. It would be strange indeed if I could not tell with precision, what I have thought of all my life."

"Excuse me, Miss, it would not be strange at all, in a female. And now I will wish you 'good night.' You shall hear from me when needful. Meanwhile, I will take charge of these articles."

He began, in the coolest manner, to pack up my sacred relics, dagger, casts, and all.

"Indeed you won't," I cried, "you shall not have one of them. What are you thinking of?"

He went on with his packing. I saw he was resolute; so was I. I sprang to the door, locked it, and put the key in my pocket. He said nothing, but smiled.

"Now," I exclaimed in triumph, "you cannot take those away, unless you dare to outrage a young lady."

I was wholly mistaken. He passed by, without touching me, drew some instrument from his waistcoat pocket, and the door stood open before him. All my treasures were in his left hand. I flew at, and snatched them, and then let go with a scream. A gush of blood poured from my hand. He had taken the dagger folded in paper only, and I was cut to the bone. I sank on a chair and fainted.

When I came to myself, Mrs. Shelfer was kneeling before me, with her feet in a basin of water, while two other basins, and numberless towels, were round. Mrs. Shelfer was rubbing my other hand, and crying and talking desperately about her bad luck that day, and a man with eyes crossed whom she had met in the morning. In the background stood Mr. Shelfer himself, whom I had hitherto failed to see, though I believe he had seen me often. He had a pipe in his mouth about a yard long, and seemed wholly undisturbed. "All right, old 'ooman," he said deliberately through his nose, as he saw that I perceived him, "she'll do now, if you don't make too much rumpus." And with that he disappeared, and I had time to pity myself. The hand the poor farmer used so to admire, and which I was proud of no doubt, in my way, lay in a dishcloth covered and oozing with blood. But my relics were on the table, all safe. A quick step was heard on the stairs, and Inspector Cutting came in, carrying a small phial.

"Out of the way, Patty," he cried, "you are doing more harm than good."

He took up a basin of cold water, and poured half the contents of the little phial into it.

"Now hold her arm up, Patty, as high as you can. I never knew arnica fail."

My hand was put into the water, and the bleeding was stanched in a minute or two. However he kept it there for a quarter of an hour, till it was quite benumbed.

"Now you may look at your hand, Miss Vaughan; it will not be disfigured at all. There will be no inflammation. Patty, fetch me some cambric and the best lard; put the young lady to bed at once, and prop her arm up a little."

I looked at my hand, and found three parallel gashes across it, for every edge of the weapon was keen. But only one wound was deep, viz. that across the palm, which was very deep under the thumb. I have the mark of it still. All the wounds were edged with a narrow yellow line.

"Inspector Cutting," I cried, "no power will move me from here, until you promise not to steal my property. Stealing it is, and nothing else. You have no warrant, and my information to you was wholly unofficial."

The last word seemed to move him. They all like big words, however clear-headed they are.

"Miss Vaughan, under these special circumstances, I will promise what you require; upon condition that you give me accurate drawings, for I see that you can make them."

"Certainly, when my hand is well enough."

"Believe me, I am deeply concerned at what has occurred. But the fault was all your own. How dare you obstruct the Police? But I wish some of my fellows had only half your spirit. A little more experience, and nothing will escape you. Come, Miss Vaughan, though you are a lady, or rather because you are one, give me your left hand, in token that you forgive me."

I did so with all my heart. I liked him much better since I had defeated him; and I saw that it was well worth the pain, for he would do his utmost to make amends. He wished me good night with a most respectful bow. "I will come and inquire how you are to-morrow, Miss Vaughan. Patty, quiet, and coolness, and change the lard frequently. No doctor, if you please; and above all hold your queer little tongue."

"Never fear me, Uncle John; you are right, my good friend, it is a little tongue, but no queerer than my neighbours."

Inspector Cutting would have formed a far lower opinion of my spirit, if he had seen how I cried that night; not from the pain of the wounds, I am sure, but to think of the fuss dear mother would have made about them.

CHAPTER XI.

In spite of the arnica, my cuts were not healed for a month; not enough, I mean, for me to handle a pencil. Mr. Cutting, when he came, according to promise, told me something to quiet me, because I was so feverish. Whether he believed it, or only acted medically, was more than I could decide. The opinion he gave me, or the substance of it, was this.

That the deed was done, not for money, or worldly advantage in any way, but for revenge. Here I thought of Mrs. Daldy. What wrong the revenge was wreaked for, he could not even guess, or at any rate would not hint to me.

That the straightest clue to the mystery was to be sought in Italy, where my guardian's track should be followed carefully. The idea of forcing, or worming, the truth from him was rejected at once through my description of his character; although the Inspector quite agreed with me, that, even if guiltless of the crime, Mr. Edgar Vaughan knew all about it now.

That no importance should be attached to the anonymous letter from London; in accordance with my promise to Mrs. Elton, I did not mention the Polish lady's name; and Mr. Cutting did not press me to do so, for he firmly believed from what I said that she had made a mistake in the address she gave, and would not help us now, even if we could find her. That nevertheless a strict watch should be kept in London, whither flock nine-tenths of the foreigners who ever set foot in this country. London moreover was likely, ere long, to draw nearly all the migratory strangers to the business or pleasure of next year's "Great Exhibition," provided only that it should prove successful, as the Inspector thought it would.

As for my enemy being attracted by works of industry, it seemed to me quite against nature that a base assassin should care for art or science, or any national progress. But the remembrance of several cases, among the dark annals I used to delight in, soon proved to me my error; while the long experience of a man, versed from his youth in criminal ways, convicted me of presumption.

To put myself more on a level with fraud, and stealth, and mystery, I did a thing for which I felt guilty to myself and my mother. I changed my name. But, in spite of Inspector Cutting, I did not travel out of the family. My father's second name was "Valentine," taken from his mother. This name I assumed in a shorter form, becoming "Clara Valence;" it saved change of initials and a world of trouble, and I felt warmer in it, because it seemed to have been my father's. In the neighbourhood I knew no one except Mrs. Elton, to whom (as I grew intimate with her) I partly explained my reasons. As for Mrs. Shelfer, she was delighted at the change. She said that her Uncle John had christened me, that it sounded much prettier, and would always remind her of Valentines. Nevertheless I longed for the day when I might call myself "Clara Vaughan" once more.

By the time I was able to go about freely again and use my hand as of old, it was the middle of November. The first use I made of my pencil was to copy most carefully all that Inspector Cutting required. He promised to keep these drawings, and indeed the whole matter, most jealously to himself; by which term he meant, as I afterwards found, Inspector Cutting and those to whom he was bound to report.

What I now wanted was money, to send an adroit inquirer throughout the North of Italy, and other parts where my guardian's shifting abode had been. I knew that he dwelt awhile at Pisa, Genoa, and Milan, also at an obscure little village named "Calva," which I could not find in the maps. All I had learned of his rovings was from the lessons my father would give me sometimes, when he used to say, "Now, Tooty, put your finger on Uncle Edgar." To every one, but myself, it seemed a strange thing that after so many wanderings, Mr. Edgar Vaughan had brought no valet, major domo, or courier, no dependant or retainer of any kind, and not even a foreign friend to England, or at any rate to Vaughan Park.

But now for the needful resources--the only chance of procuring them lay in my young and partly self-tutored art. I braced myself with the remembrance, that while none of my family ever laid claim to genius, the limner's faculty had never been wanting among them. Inferior gifts are often as heirlooms in the blood, though high original power follows no vein except its own. The latter none of us ever possessed; but taste and the knack of adaptation had seldom been alienated. Observation too, in a small way, and the love of nature seemed inborn in us all. My father's drawings were perfect, but for the one thing wanted; and in sketches from outdoor nature that want was less perceived. My grandfather had been known among the few amateurs of the day as a skilful colourist. As to habits of observation, a little tale handed down in our family will show that they had existed in one of its members seven generations ago.

In the autumn of 1651, when King Charles was stealing along from Colonel Wyndham's house to the coast of Hampshire and Sussex, the little band was overtaken by nightfall, somewhere near the New Forest. It was shortly after the narrow escape of the King from that observant blacksmith, who saw that his horse was shod with North-country iron. Though he was taking it easily, his three trusty friends knew well that a Roundhead Squadron was near, and that his last chance depended on speed and night travel. What could they do now in the tempestuous darkness? They were in a tract thinly inhabited, half woodland, half heather, and the road was hopelessly lost. No rain fell as yet it was true, and the wind was waiting for rain, but the lightning came fitfully from the horizon all round. The King alone was on horseback, his three companions afoot. They stood still in doubt and terror, for they could not tell north from south. Suddenly Major Cecil Vaughan espied a faint gleam familiar to him of old in the waste land round Vaughan Park. To an accurate eye there could be little doubt as to the source of the lambent light--flame it could not be called. It played in a pale yet constant stream on a certain kind of moss, known to botanists, not to me, for the waste lands have been reclaimed. This light is to be seen at no time, except when the air is surcharged with electricity.

"Follow me all; I know the way!" cried Major Vaughan, right cheerily.

"And if you do, man," said the King, "your eyes are made of dashers."

[What this meant, I used as a child to wonder; but now I know.]

For six dark miles the Major led them without default, until they came to a lonely heathman's house, where they slept in safety. He never told them how he did it; being apt, I suppose, as men of the second order are, to hug superior knowledge. But it was a most simple thing. That strangely sensitive moss follows the course of the sun, and therefore the lambent light can only be seen from the west. So all the time he could see it--the others never saw it at all--he knew that they were wending from west to east, which was their proper course.

To return to myself. I put the finishing touch to a view of rock and woodland scenery, north-west of Tossil's Barton, and set off to try my fortune with it. Some young ladies, born to my position, would have thought this errand one of much degradation, but it did not appear so to me. So I walked briskly--for I hate an omnibus, and could ill afford a cab--to the shop of a well-known dealer in pictures, not far from the Haymarket. It was my first venture into the heart of London, but I found the way very easily, having jotted it down from a map. The day was dark and drizzly; the pavement grimy and slimy, and hillocked with mud at the joints of the flags. It was like walking on a peeled kneading-trough with dollops of paste left in it. Along the far reach of the streets, and the gardens in the squares, wisps of fog were crawling, and almost every one was coughing.

The dealer received me politely. Too politely in fact: for it seemed to savour of kindness, which I did not want from him. What I wanted was business, and nothing else. He took my poor drawing, done only in water-colours, and set it up in a square place made perhaps for the purpose, where the brown flaw fell upon it from a skylight formed like a Devonshire chimney. Then he drew back and clasped his hands, then shaded his eyes with them, as if the light were too strong, whereas the whole place was like a well turned upside down. He seemed uneasy because I did not care to follow him throughout all this little performance.

"And now," I said, for my foolish pride was up, and I spoke as I would have done to the porter at our lodge, not with the least contempt--I was never so low as that--but with a long perspective, "Now, Mr. Oxgall, it will soon be dark. What will you give me for it?"

"Allow me, Miss; allow me one moment. The light is a leetle too strong. Ah, the mark of the brush comes out. Strong touch, but indiscreet. A year of study required. Shade too broad and massive. A want of tone in the background. Great feeling of nature, but inexperienced rendering. More mellowness desiderated. Full however of promise. All the faults on the right side. Most energetic handling; no weak stippling here. But water-colours are down just now; a deal depends on the weather and time of year."

"How so, Mr. Oxgall?"

"Hot sun, and off they go. Fog and murk and frost, and the cry is all for oil. Excuse me, Miss--a thousand pardons, your name escaped me, you did not pronounce it strongly."

"Miss Valence!" I said, with an emphasis that startled him out of his mincing.

"Miss Valence, you think me very long. All young ladies do. But my object is to do them justice, and if they show any power, to encourage them."

"Thank you, I want no encouragement. I know I can draw a little; and there it is. The fog is thickening. I have far to go. Your price, if you please?"

I went up many steps in his opinion, by reason of my curtness and independence.

"Miss Valence, I will give you three guineas, although no doubt I shall be a loser."

"Then don't give it," said I in pure simplicity.

I went up several steps more. How utterly men of the world are puzzled by plain truth!

"Miss Valence, if you will forgive the observation, I would beg to remark that your conversation as well as your painting is crisp. I will take this little piece at all hazards, because it is full of character. Will you forgive me for one word of advice?"

"There is nothing to forgive. I shall thank you heartily for it."

"It is simply this:--The worst part of your work is the perspective. And figure-drawing will be of service to you. Study at a school of design, if you have one near you; and be not above drawing stiff and unsightly objects. Houses are the true guides to perspective. I cannot paint or even draw; but I am so much with great artists, that I know well how to advise."

"Thank you. Can you kindly suggest anything more?"

"Yes. Your touch is here and there too harsh. Keep your hand light though bold, and your brush just a leetle wetter. But you have the grand things quite unattainable, when not in the grain. I mean, of course, freedom of handling and an artist's eye."

"Do you think I could do any good in oils?"

"I have no doubt you could, but not for a long time. If fame is your object, take to oils. If speedy returns, stick to water-colours. Leave me your address, if you have no objection; and bring me your next work. If I do well with this, I will try to give you more."

He took from a desk three new sovereigns and three new shillings, wrapped them neatly in silver paper, and handed them to me. I never imagined I could be so proud of money.

Light of heart I left the shop, not that I had made my fortune yet, but what was greater happiness, I thought myself likely to make it.

Soon I perceived, with some alarm, how thick and murky the air had grown. The fog was stooping heavily down, and was now become like a wash of gamboge and lamp-black. All the street-lamps were lit, though they could not see one another, and every shop-keeper had his little jet. The pavement was no longer slippery, but sticky and dry; and a cold, that pierced to the bones, was stealing along. Already it had begun to freeze; and I, so familiar both with white and black frost, observed with no small interest the grey or fog-frost, which was new to me. How different from the pure whiteness when the stars are sparkling, and the earth is gleaming, and the spirit of man so buoyant! This grey fog-frost is rather depressing to most natures, and a chilly damp creeps to the core of all things. Thick encrusting rime comes with it, and sometimes a freezing rain.

Before I reached the New Road, the fog had grown so dense and dark, that I was much inclined to take a cab, for fear of losing my way. But I could not see one, and finding myself at last in a main thoroughfare called the Hampstead Road, I walked on briskly and bravely till I reached Camden Town, when I knew what course to pursue.

Slowly wending up College Street, for I was getting tired and the fog thicker than ever, indeed every step seemed a thrust into an ochred wall, I heard a plaintive, and rather musical, voice chanting, much as follows:--

"Christian friends, and sisters in the Lord, all who own a heart that feels for undeserved distress, aid, I implore you, a bereaved wife and mother, who has this very moment seven small lovely children, starving in a garret, three of them upon a bed of sickness, and the inhuman landlord, for the sake of a few shillings about to turn them this bitter night into the flinty streets. Christian friends, may you never know what it is to be famished as I and my seven darlings are this very night, in the midst of plenty. From Plymouth in Devonshire, I walked two hundred and fifty miles afoot all the way to join my beloved husband in London. When I came to this Christian city--Georgiana, pick up that halfpenny--he had been ordered off in the transport ship Hippopotamus, to shed his blood for his Queen and country; and I who have known the smiles of plenty in my happy rustic home, I am compelled for the sake of my children to the degradation of publicly soliciting alms. The smallest trifle, even an old pair of shoes or a left off garment will be received with the heartfelt gratitude of the widow and orphan. My eldest child, ma'am, the oldest of seven, bad in the whooping cough. Georgiana, curtsey to the pretty lady, and show her your broken chilblains."

"No thank you," I said: I could just see her through the fog. She looked like one who had seen better days, and the thought of my own vicissitudes opened my heart towards her. How could I show my gratitude better for the money I had just earned, than by bestowing a share in charity upon worthy objects? So I took out my purse, an elegant little French one given me by dear mother, and placed my three new shillings in the poor creature's hand, as she stood in the gutter. She was overpowered with gratitude, and could not speak for a moment. Then she came nearer, to bless me.

"Sweet lady, in the name of seven famishing innocents, whom you have saved from death this night, may He who guards the fatherless and the widow from His mercy-seat above, may He shower his richest blessings--"

Snap--she had got my purse and was out of sight in the fog. Georgiana's red heels were the last thing I saw. For an instant I could not believe it; but thought that the fog had affected my sight. Then I darted across the road, almost under the feet of a horse, and down a place called "Pratt Street." It was hopeless, utterly hopeless; and not only my three pounds were gone, but half besides of all I had in the world. I had taken that money with me, because I meant, if fortunate with my landscape, to buy a large box of colours in Rathbone-place; but the fog had deterred me. She had snatched my purse while I tried to clasp it, for my glove had first got in the way. All was gone, dear mother's gift, my first earnings, and all. More than all I felt sore at heart from the baseness of the robbery. Nothing is so bitterly grievous to youth as a blow to faith in one's species.

I am not ashamed to confess that feeling all alone in the fog, I leaned against some iron railings and cried away like a child. Child I was still at heart, despite all my trials and spirit; and more so perhaps than girls who have played out their childhood. In the full flow of my passion, for I was actually sobbing aloud, ashamed of myself all the while, I felt an arm steal round my waist, and starting in fear of another thief, confronted the loveliest face that human eyes ever looked on. With soft caresses, and sweetest smiles, it drew close to my own stormy and bitter countenance.

"Are you better now, dear? Oh don't cry so. You'll break your poor little heart. Do tell me what it is, that's a dear. I'll do anything to help you."

"You can't help me:" I exclaimed through my sobs: "Nobody can help me! I was born to ill luck, and shall have nothing else till I die."

"Don't say so dear. You mustn't think of it. My father, who never is wrong, says there's no such thing as luck."

"I know that well enough. People always say that who have it on their side."

"Ah, I never thought of that. But I hope you are wrong. But tell me, dear, what is the matter with you. I'm sure you have done no harm, and dear papa says no one can be unhappy who has not injured any one."

"Can't they though? Your papa is a moralist. Now I'll just tell you facts." And to prove my point, I told her of this new trouble, hinted at previous ones and my many great losses, of which money was the least. Even without the controversial spirit, I must have told her all. There was no denying anything to such a winning loving face.

"Dear me!" she cried very thoughtfully, with her mites of hands out of her muff--she had the prettiest set of fur I ever beheld, and how it became her!--"Dear me! she couldn't have meant it, I feel quite sure she couldn't. You'll come to my opinion when you have time to consider, dear"--this was said so sagely that I could have kissed her all over like a duck of a baby. "To steal from you who had just given her more than you could afford! Now come with me, dear, you shall have all the money I have got; though I don't think it's anything like the nine pounds you have lost, and I'm sure it is not new money. Only I haven't got it with me. I never carry money. Do you know why, dear?"

"No. How should I?"

"Well, I don't mind telling you. Because then I can't spend it, or give it away. I don't care a bit about money. What good is it to me? Why, I can never keep it, somehow or other. But papa says if I can show five pounds on Christmas-day, he will put five more on the top of it, and then do you know what I'll do? I'll give away five, and spend the rest for Pappy and Conrad." And the lively little thing clapped her hands at the prospect, quite forgetting that she had just offered me all her store. Presently this occurred to her.

"No. Now I come to think of it, I won't have the five pounds on Christmas-day. As the girls at the College say, I'll just sell the old Pappy. That will be better fun still. He will find a good reason for it. He always does for everything. You shall have every bit of it. Come home with me now, that's a dear. You are better now, you know. Come, that's a love. I am sure I shall love you with all my heart, and you are so terribly unlucky."

I yielded at once. She was so loving and natural, I could not resist her. She broke upon me like soft sunshine through the fog, laughing, smiling, dancing, her face all light and warmth, yet not a shallow light, but one that played up from the fount of tears. Her deep rich violet eyes seldom used their dark lashes, except when she was asleep. She was life itself, quick, playful, loving life, feeling for and with all life around; pitying, trusting, admiring all things; yet true as the hearth to household ties. I never found another such nature: it was the perfection of maiden womanhood, even in its unreason. And therefore nobody could resist her. With me, of ten times her strength of will, and power of mind--small though it be--she could do in a moment exactly as she liked; I mean of course in trivial matters. It was impossible to be offended with her.

When she had led me a few steps towards her home--for I went with her (not, of course, to take her money, but to see her safe), she turned round suddenly:--

"Oh I forgot, dear; I must not take you to our house. We have had new orders. But where do you live? I will bring you my little bag to-morrow. They won't let me out again to-night. Now I know you will oblige me. I am so sorry that I mustn't see you safe home, dear." This she said with the finest air of protection imaginable.

I gave her my name and address, and asked for hers.

"My name is Isola Ross, I am seventeen and a half, and my papa is Professor at the College. I ran away from old Cora. It seemed such fun to be all alone in the fog. What trouble I shall get into! But they can't be angry with me long. Kiss me, darling. Mind, to-morrow!"

Off she danced through the fog; and I went sadly home, yet thinking more of her, than of my serious and vexatious loss.

CHAPTER XII.

Inspector Cutting, upon the first tidings of the robbery, came at once, and assured me that he knew the "party" well, and wanted her for several other plants, and crafty as she was ("leary" was the elegant word he used) he was sure to be down upon her in the course of a very short time.

Isola Ross, to my great surprise, did not come the next day, nor even the day after; so I set out to look for her, at the same time wondering at myself for doing so. Knowing that College Street must take its name from some academic building in or near it, I concluded of course that there I should find Professor Ross and my lovely new friend. So without consulting Mrs. Shelfer, who would have chattered for an hour, away I went one tine frosty morning to ask about the College.

I found that a low unsightly building, which I had often passed, near the bottom of the street, was the only College there; so I entered a small quadrangle, to make further inquiries.

The first person I saw was a young man dressed like one of my father's grooms, and cracking a long whip and whistling. He had a brilliant scarlet neckcloth, green sporting coat, and black boots up to his knees. I studied him for a moment because it struck me that he would look well in a foreground, when toned down a little, as water colours would render him. He appreciated my attention, and seemed proud of it.

"Now, Polly, what can I do for you, dear?"

He must have been three parts drunk, or he would never have dared to address me so. Of course I made no answer, but walked on. He cracked his whip like a pistol, to startle me.

"Splendid filly," I heard him mutter, "but cussed high action." What he meant I do not know or care.

The next I met was a fussy little man, dressed all in brown, who smelt of musty hay.

"Will you kindly tell me," I asked, "where to find Professor Ross?'

"Ross, Ross! Don't know the name. No Ross about here. What's he Professor of?"

"That I was not told. But it is something the young ladies study."

"No young ladies about here. But I see you have brought your dear mamma's lapdog. Take it out of the bag. Let me look at it."

"Is not this the College?"

"Yes to be sure. The best College in London. Quick, let me see the dog."

"I have no dog, sir. I have made some mistake."

"Then you have got a pony. Pet over-fed. Shetland breed."

"No indeed. Nothing except myself; and I am looking for Miss Ross."

"Young lady, you have made a very great mistake. You have kept me five minutes from a lecture on the navicular disease. And my practice is controverted by an upstart youth from the country. I am in search of authorities." And off he darted, I suppose to the library.

It was clear that I had made some mistake, so I found my way back to the street, and asked in the nearest shop what building it was that I had just left.

"Oh, them's the weterans," said the woman, "and a precious set they be!"

"Why, they did not look like soldiers."

"No, no, Miss. Weterans, where they takes in all the sick horses and dogs. And very clever they are, I have heard say."

"And where is the College where the young ladies are?"

"I don't know of no other College nearer than High Street, where the boys wear flat caps. But there's a girls' school down the road."

"I don't want a school. I want a College where young ladies go."

"Then I cant help you, Miss." And back I went to consult Mrs. Shelfer.

"Bless my soul, Miss Valence," cried the little woman, out of breath with amazement, "have you been among them niggers? It's a mercy they didn't skin and stuff you. What do you think now they did to my old Tom?"

"How can I guess, Mrs. Shelfer?"

"No, no, to be sure not. I forgot, my good friend. Why, they knowed him well it seems, because he had been there in dear Miss Minto's time, for a salmon bone that had got crossways in his oesop, so they said at least, but they are the biggest liars--so only a year ago come next Boxing-day, here comes to the door half a dozen of them, bus-cad and coachman all in one, all looking as grave as judges. When I went to the door they all pulled their hats off, as if I had been the Queen at the very least. 'What can I do for you, my good friends?' says I; for Shelfer was out of the way, and catch me letting them in for all their politeness. No, no, thank you. 'Mrs. Shelfer,' says the biggest of them, a lantern-jawed young fellow with covers over his pockets, 'Mrs. Shelfer, you are possessed of a most remarkable cat. An animal, ma'am, of unparalleled cemetery and organic dewelopment. Our Professor, ma'am, is delivering a course of lectures on the Canonical Heapatightness of the Hirumbillycuss."

"Well done, Mrs. Shelfer! What a memory you must have!"

"Pretty well, Miss, pretty well. Particular for long words, when I likes the sound of them. 'Well sir,' I says, feeling rather taken aback, 'thank God I haven't got it.' 'No, ma'am,' says he, 'your blooming countenance entirely negatives any such dyingnoses. But the Professor, in passing the other morning, observed some symptoms of it in your magnificent cat, for whom he entertains the most sincere attachment, and whom he will cure for our advancement and edification upon the lecture table. And now, ma'am, Professor Sallenders desires his most respectful compliments, and will you allow us to take that dear good cat to be cured. The Professor was instrumental once in preserving his honoured existence, therefore he feels assured that you will not now refuse him.' Well you see, Miss, I didn't half like to let him go, but I was afraid to offend the Professor, because of all my animals, for I knew that he could put a blight upon them, birds and all, if he chose. Old Tom was lying roasting his back again the fender, the same as you see him now, poor soul; so I catched him up and put him in a double covered basket, with a bit of flannel over him, because the weather was cold; and he was so clever, would you believe it, he put up his old paws to fight me, he knew he was going to mischief, and that turned me rather. 'Now will you promise to bring him back safe?' I says. 'Ma'am,' says the lantern-jawed young man, bowing over his heart, and as serious as a pulpit, 'Ma'am, in less than an hour. Rely upon the honour of Weteran Arian Gent."

"Well, Mrs. Shelfer, I am astonished. Even I should never have been so silly. Poor old Tom among the Philistines!"

"Well, Miss, I began to feel very uneasy directly they was gone. I thought they looked back so queerly, and old Tom was mewing so dreadful in the basket. Presently I began to hear a mewing out of the cupboard, and a mewing out of the clock, and even out of the dripping-pan. So I put on my bonnet as quick as I could, and ran right away to the College, and somehow or other by the time I got there, I was in a fright all over. As good luck would have it, the man was at the gate; a nice respectable married man, and a friend of Charley's. 'Curbs,' I says, 'where is Professor Sallenders?' 'Down in the country,' says he, 'since last Friday. He never stops here at Christmas, Mrs. Shelfer, he's a deal too knowing for that.' My heart went pop, Miss, like an oyster shell in the fire. I held on by the door, and I thought it was all up with me. 'Don't take on so, Missus,' says Curbs, 'if any of your museum is ill, there's half a dozen clever young coves in the operating room over there, only they're busy just now, cutting up a big black cat. My eyes, how he did squeal!' I screamed out and ran--Curbs thought I was mad, and he was not far out--bang went the door before me, and there on the table, with the lantern-jawed young man flourishing a big knife over him, there lay my precious old Tom strapped down on his back, with his mouth tied up in white tape, and leather gloves over his feet, and sticks trussed across him the same as a roasting rabbit, and a streak of white all along his blessed stomach--you know, Miss, he hadn't got one white hair by rights--where the niggers had shaved and floured him, to see what they were about. He turned up his dear old eyes when he saw me; it would have made you cry, and he tried to speak. Oh you precious old soul, didn't I scatter them right and left? I scratched that lantern-jawed hypocrite's face till I gave him the hirumbillycuss and hirumtommycuss too, I expect. I called a policeman in, and there wasn't one of them finished his Christmas in London. But the poor old soul has never been the same cat since. The anxiety he was in, turned his hair white on both sides of his heart and all round the backs of his ears. He wouldn't come to the door, he shook so, at the call of the cat's-meat man for better than a month, and he won't look at it now, while there's a skewer in it."

The poor little woman was crying with pity and rage. Old Tom looked up all the time as if he knew all she said, and then jumped on her lap, and showed his paws, and purred.

Meanwhile, a change had come over my intentions. Perhaps all the rudeness I had met with that day had called my pride into arms. At any rate, much as I liked pretty Isola, and much as I longed for her fresh warm kindness, I now resolved to wait until she should choose to seek me. So I did not even ask Mrs. Shelfer whether she knew the College where the Professor lectured. What were love and warm young hearts to me? I deserved such a rebuff for swerving so from my duty. Now I would give all my thoughts to the art, whence only could spring any hope of attaining my end, and the very next day I would follow the picture-dealer's advice.

CHAPTER XIII.

There was a school of design not very far from my lodgings, and thither I went the next morning. My landlady offered to come with me and see me safe in the room; and of course her Charley, who seemed to know everybody, knew some one even there, to whom she kindly promised to recommend me. So I gladly accepted her offer.

In some respects, Mr. Shelfer was more remarkable than even his wife. He was so shy, that on the rare occasions when we met, I never could get him to look at me, except once when he was drunk; yet by some mysterious process he seemed to know everything about me--the colour of my eyes, the arrangement of my hair, the dresses I put on, the spirits I was in--a great deal more, in fact, than I ever cared to know. So that sometimes my self-knowledge was largely increased, through his observations repeated by his wife. But I was not allowed to flatter myself that this resulted from any especial interest; for he seemed to possess an equal acquaintance with the affairs of all his neighbours. Mention any one anywhere around, and he, without seeming to mean it, would describe him or her unmistakably in half a dozen words. He never praised or blamed, he simply identified. He must have seen more with a blink of his eye, than most people see in five minutes of gazing. He seldom brought any one home with him, though he often promised to do so; he never seemed to indulge in gossip, at any rate not with his wife. "Cut it short, old 'ooman," was all the encouragement he ever gave her in that way. When he was at home--a thing of rare occurrence--he sat with his head down and a long pipe in his mouth; he walked in the street with his head down, and never accosted any one. Where did he get all his knowledge? I doubt if there were a public-house in London, but what Shelfer knew at the furthest a cousin of the landlord, and a brother of one of the potboys. "Charley Shelfer" everybody called him, and everybody spoke of him, not with distinguished respect, but with a kindly feeling. His luck was proverbial; he had a room full of things which he had won at raffles, and he was in constant requisition to throw for less fortunate people. As for his occupation--he called himself a nurseryman, but he had no nursery that I could discover. He received a pound a week for looking after the garden in the great square; but when any one came for him, he was never to be found there. I think he spent most of his time in jobbing about, and "swopping" (as Mrs. Shelfer called it) among his brother gardeners. Sometimes, he brought home beautiful plants, perfectly lovely flowers, unknown to me even by name, and many of these he presented to me by Mrs. Shelfer's hands. Every Sunday morning he was up before the daylight, and away for an excursion, or rather an incursion, through the Hampstead, Highgate, and Holloway district. From these raids he used to return as I came home from the morning service. By the way, if I had wanted to puzzle him and find a blank in his universal acquaintance, the best chance would have been to ask him about the clergyman. He never gave the pew-openers any trouble, neither indeed did Mrs. Shelfer, who called herself a Catholic; but the lively little woman's chiefest terror was death, and a parson to her was always an undertaker. If Mr. Shelfer had not spent the Sunday morning quite so well as I had, at any rate he had not wasted his time. I think he must have robbed hen-roosts and allotment grounds; and yet he was too respectable for that. But whence and how could he ever have come by the gipsey collection he always produced from his hat, from his countless pockets, from his red cotton handkerchief, every Sunday at 1 P.M.? Eggs, chickens, mushrooms, sticks of horseradish and celery, misletoe-thrushes, cucumbers, cabbages red and white, rabbits, watercress, Aylesbury ducks--I cannot remember one quarter of his manifold forage. All I can say is, that if these things are to be found by the side of the road near London, Middlesex is a far better field for the student of natural history than Gloucestershire, or even beloved Devon. Mrs. Shelfer said it was all his luck; but I hardly think it could have rained Aylesbury ducks, even for Mr. Shelfer.

All the time he was extracting from his recesses this multifarious store, he never once smiled, or showed any symptoms of triumph, but gravely went through the whole, as if a simple duty.

How was it such a man had not made his fortune? Because he had an incurable habit of "backing bills" for any one who asked him; and hence he was always in trouble.

Mrs. Shelfer and I were admitted readily into the school of design. It was a long low room, very badly lighted, and fitted up for the time until a better could be provided. It looked very cold and comfortless; forms instead of chairs, and desks like a parish school. The whitewashed walls were hung with diagrams, sections, tracings, reductions, most of them stiff and ugly, but no doubt instructive. At one end was a raised platform, reserved for lecturers and the higher powers. Shelves round the wall were filled with casts and models, and books of instruction were to be had out of cupboards. Of course we were expected to bring our own materials, and a code of rules was exhibited. The more advanced students were permitted to tender any work of their own which might be of service to the neophytes. From no one there did I ever receive any insolence. At first, the young artists used to look at me rather hard, but my reserved and distant air was quite enough to discourage them.

After the introduction, which Mrs. Shelfer accomplished in very great style, I dismissed her, and set to in earnest to pore once more over the rudiments of perspective. One simple truth as to the vanishing point struck me at once. I was amazed that I had never perceived it before. It was not set forth in the book I was studying; but it was the sole key to all my errors of distance. At once I closed the book; upon that one subject I wanted no more instruction, I had caught the focus of truth. Books, like bad glass, would only refract my perception. All I wanted now was practice and adaptation of the eye.

Strange as it seemed to me then, I could draw no more that day. I was so overcome at first sight by the simple beauty of truth, mathematical yet poetical truth, that error and obscurity (for there is a balance in all things) had their revenge for a while on my brain. But the truth, once seen, could never be lost again. Thenceforth there were few higher penances for me, in a small way, than to look at one of my early drawings.

When my brain was clear, I returned to do a real day's work. For the cups, and vases, and plates, and things of "æsthetic art" (as they chose to call it), I did not care at all; but the copies and models and figures were most useful to me. Unless I am much mistaken, I made more advance in a fortnight there, than I had in any year of my life before.

With my usual perseverance--if I have no other virtue, I have that--I worked away to correct my many shortcomings; not even indulging (much as I wanted the money) in any attempts at a finished drawing, until I felt sure that all my foundations were thoroughly laid and set. "And now," I cried towards Christmas, "now for Mr. Oxgall; if I don't astonish him this time, my name is not Clara Vaughan!" It did me good when I was alone, to call myself by my own name, and my right to be my father's daughter.

CHAPTER XIV.

Meanwhile old Christmas was come, and all I was worth in the world was change for half a sovereign. True, my lodgings were paid for, a fortnight in advance, because good Mrs. Shelfer wanted to treat all her pets to a Christmas dinner; but as for my own Christmas dinner--though I can't say I cared much for it--if I got one at all, it must be upon credit, since my drawing would not be finished for another week. Credit, of course, I would not think of. Any day in the week or year, I would rather starve than owe money. However, I was not going to cry about plum-pudding, though once or twice it made me hungry to think of the dinner in the great hall at Vaughan Park on the Christmas eve; a much more elaborate matter in the old time, than the meal served in the dining-room next day.

Now I sat in my little room this dreary Christmas eve; and do what I would, I could not help thinking a little. It was a gusty evening, cold and damp, with scuds of sleet and snow, as yet it had not made up its mind whether to freeze or thaw. Nevertheless, the streets were full of merry laughing parties, proud of their bargains for the Christmas cheer; and as they went by, the misletoe and the holly glistened in the flickering gaslight.

For old recollection's sake, I had made believe to dress my little room with some few sprigs of laurel and unberried holly; the sceptre branch, all cobbed with coral beads, was too expensive for me. Misletoe I wanted not. Who was there now to kiss me?

From the sheer craving of human nature for a word of kindness, I had called, that afternoon, upon Mrs. Elton. But good as she was and sweet to me, she had near relatives coming; and I saw or fancied, that I should be in the way. Yet I thought that her mother heart yearned toward me as she said "Good bye," and showed me out by the Christmas tree, all trembling to be lighted.

Now I sat alone and lonely by the flickering of three pennyworth of wood which I had bought recklessly for the sake of the big ash-tree that used to glow with the lichen peeling round it on the old Christmas hearth, where I was believed the heiress. The little spark and sputter of my sallow billet (chopped by the poor old people at St. Pancras workhouse) led me back through eight sad years to the last merry time when my father was keeping his latest Christmas, and I his pride and hope was prouder than all, at being just ten years old.

How he carved and ladled the gravy; how he flourished his knife and fork with a joke all hot for every one; how he smiled when the thrice-helped farmers sent for another slice, and laughed when the crow-boy was nearly choked with plum-pudding; how he patted me on the head and caught me for a kiss, when I, dressed up as head-waitress, with my long hair all tied back, pulled his right arm and pointed to widow Hiatt's plate--the speech he made after dinner, when I was amazed at his eloquence and clapped my little hands, and the way he made me stand up on a chair and drink the Queen's health first--then the hurrahs of the tenants and servants, and how they kissed me outside--all this goes through my memory as the smoke of the billet goes up the chimney, and the tears steal under my eyelids.

Then I see the long hall afterwards, with the tables cleared away and the lights hung round the tapestry, and the yule log roaring afresh; my father (a type of the true English gentleman, not of the past but the present century), holding the hand of his wife (a lady of no condescending airs, but true womanly warmth and love)--both dressed for the tenants' ball as if for the lord-lieutenant's; both eager to lead off the country dance, and beating their feet to the music. Next them, a laughing child in a little white frock and pink slip (scarce to be known for myself), hand-in-hand with my brave chevalier, Master Roderick Blount, accounted by Cooky and both lady's-maids, and most of all by himself, my duly affianced lord.

Then the housekeeper, starched beyond measure, yet not too stiff to smile, and open for the nonce even to jokes about courtship, yielding her gracious hand for the dance to the senior tenant, a man with great calves, red face, and snow-white hair. After them come--

Hark! a loud knock and a ring. It is just in time before I begin the palinode. Who can want me to-night? I want no one but those I cannot have, whom the fire has now restored me, though the earth has hidden them.

Mrs. Shelfer is hard at work in the kitchen, preparing a wonderful supper for Charley, who has promised to come home. She has canvassed the chance of his keeping this promise fifty times in the day. Hope cries "yes;" experience whispers "no." At any rate the knock is not his, for he always carries a latch-key.

She calls up the stairs "Miss Valence!" before she goes to the door, for who knows but she might be murdered in the midst of her Christmas pudding? I come out to prove my existence and stand in the dark on the landing. She draws back the bolt; I hear a gruff voice as if it came through a hat.

"Young 'ooman by the name of Clara Waun live here?"

"Yes to be sure; Miss Valence you mean, my good friend."

"The name on this here ticket ain't Walence, but Waun."

"All right, my good friend. All right. It's just the same."

"Hor, I don't know that though. Jim, the name of the party here ain't Waun after all. It be Walence. And three blessed days us has been all over London!"

Jim, from the top of the van, suggests that, after all, Walence and Waun be much of a muchness. For his part, he'll be blessed if he'll go any further with it. Let him and Ben look at the young lady, and see if she be like the card. Meanwhile, of course, I come forward and claim the parcel, whatever it is. Mrs. Shelfer redoubles her assurances, and calls the man a great oaf, which has more effect than anything.

"Why, Jim, this must be Charley's missus; Charley Shelfer's missus! Him as beat you so at skittles last week, you know."

"Ah, he did so. And I'd like to back him again you, Ben, for a quart all round."

This fact is decisive. Who can doubt any more? But for all that, the book must be signed in the name of "Waun," with which of course I comply. When the two strong men have, with much difficulty (of which they made much more), lowered the enormous package from the van, Ben stands wiping his forehead. "Lor, how hot it be to-night to be sure! And the job us has had with this big lump sure*ly*! Both the handles come off long ago. I wish my missus had got a featherbed half the weight of that. Five-and-twenty year I've been along of this company, man and boy, but I never see such a direction as that there in all my born days. Did ever you, Jim?"

"Well," replies Jim, "I've seed a many queer ones, but none as could come up to that. And who'd a thought after all their trouble--for I'm blessed if they wrote that there under a week--who'd a' thought they'd a put 'Waun' on it when they meant 'Walence.' But the young lady is awaiting for us to drink her health, Ben, and a merry Christmas to her."

"How much is the carriage?" I ask, trembling for my change of the half-sovereign.

"Nothing, miss. Only eightpence for delivery. It be paid to Paddington, and if ever our Company airned eightpence, I'm blessed if they haven't airned it now. Thank you, Miss, and werry handsome on you, and us hopes the contents will prove to your liking, Miss, and make you a merry Christmas."

Away they go with the smoking horses, after carrying into the little kitchen the mighty maun, which Mrs. Shelfer, with my assistance, could not stir.

"Bless me, Miss Valence, what a direction!" cries Mrs. Shelfer, when the full light falls upon it.

The direction was written in round hand upon a strip of parchment, about four inches wide and at least eight feet in length. It came from the bottom all up over the cover and down upon the other side, so that no one could open the basket without breaking it asunder. It was as follows:--

"Miss Clara Vaughan lodges at number seven in Prince Albert Street in London town near Windsor Castle in Gloucestershire the daughter of Mr. Henry Valentine Vaughan Esquire a nice tall young lady her always wears black things and walks very peart pale with a little red on her cheeks when they lets her alone can't be no mistake without it be done a purpose If so be this here little maun hain't brought to her safe and sweet and wholesome will be prosecuted with the *utmost rigour of the law* signed John Huxtable his mark x witness Timothy Badcock his'n X."

I wondered much whether Mr. Beany Dawe had been called in to achieve this masterpiece of manuscript, which was all in large round hand, but without any stops. It seemed beyond poor Sally's art, yet were some loops and downstrokes that must be dear little Sally's. I took it off with much trouble--the parchment was joined in four places--and I have it now.

Meanwhile Mrs. Shelfer was dancing around it, neglecting her supper in the wonder of this gigantic hamper. "Let me get a chopper, Miss, you'll never get it open. Why it's sewed as tight as an oyster."

However, I did get it open at last, and never shall I forget the contents. There was a month's food for a family of twelve. First came hay, such as I never smelt out of Devonshire; then eighteen rolls of butter, each with a snowy cloth around it; the butter so golden even at that time of year, that Mrs. Shelfer compared it to the yolk of an egg looking out of the white. Then a storey of clotted cream and beautiful lard and laver, which they knew I loved. Then a floor of hay. Below it a pair of guinea fowls, two large turkeys, and most carefully wrapped from the rest a fine hare filled with dried sweet herbs. Below these a flitch of bacon, two wood-smoked hams, a pair of tongues, a leg of Exmoor mutton, and three bottles of best elder wine. Then a brown paper parcel containing Sally's last copy-book (I had set her copies for half a year to come) and a long letter, the first I had ever received from Tossil's Barton.

When all was out at last, after the greatest delight and laughter as each thing appeared, I fell back in utter dismay at the spectacle before me. Mrs. Shelfer sat on the floor unable to find her way out, she was so flounced and tippeted with good things. When I came to her relief, she did nothing but go round and round what was left of the little room, humming a Catholic hymn, and pressing both hands to her side.

But something must be done at once. Waste is wickedness; how could we stave it off? Everything would depend upon the weather. At present all was beautifully fresh, thanks to the skilful packing and the frost, albeit the mighty package had made the round of all the Albert Streets in London. Mrs. Shelfer would have looked at it for a month, and at intervals exclaimed, "Bless me, my good friend, that beats Charley's pockets. How they must eat in Devonshire!"

"Come, Mrs. Shelfer, what good are you at housekeeping? You don't help me at all. Let us put most of it out of doors at once. You have no cellar, and I suppose they have none in London. At least we can give it the chance of the open air, and it is not snowing now."

"Oh, but the cats, Miss!"

"Well, I must find some plan for them before we go to bed. Now come and help, that's a good little creature, and I'll give you some elder wine when we have done."

So we got all that was taintable into the little yard, while Tom, who never stole, except when quite sure of impunity, looked on very sagely. There we fixed it all up to the wall secure, except from cats, of whom a roving band serenaded me every night. I presented Mrs. Shelfer at once with a turkey--a specimen of natural history not found by the roadside, even on Mr. Shelfer's Sabbath journey--also a ham, and three rolls of butter. As to the rest, I would think what to do with it afterwards.

Mrs. Shelfer kept off the cats until midnight, after which I held them at bay by the following means. With one of my mineral paints mingled with some phosphorus, I drew upon a black board a ferocious terrier, the size of life, with fangs unsheathed, bristles erect, and eyes starting out of his head. We tried the effect in the dark on poor Tom, who arched his back, and sputtered with the strongest execration, then turned and fled ignobly, amid roars of laughter from Mr. Shelfer, who by this time was come home. This one-headed Cerberus being hung so as to oscillate in the wind, right across the cat-leap, I felt quite safe, so long as my chemical mixture should continue luminous.

CHAPTER XV.

Dear little Sally's letter gave me the greatest delight. It was all in round hand, and had taken at least a week to write, and she must have washed her hands almost every time. There were no stops in it, but I have put some. The spelling was wonderfully good for her, but here and there I have shaped it to the present fashion.

"Please Miss Clara dear, father and mother and I begs their most respectable duty and love and they hopes no offence and will you be so kind as to have this here little hamper and wishes it was ten times as much but hopes you will excuse it and please to eat it all yourself Miss. All the pegmate be our own doctrine, and very wholesome, and we have took all the hair off, please Miss, because you said one time you didn't like it. Likely you'll remember, Miss, the young black sow as twisted her tail to the left, her as Tim was ringing the day as I wrote first copy, and the other chillers ran out, well most of it be she, Miss. Father say as he don't think they ever see butter in London town, but Beany Dawe says yes for they makes a plenty out of red herrings and train oil.

Please Miss, Tabby Badcock would go on the ice in the old saw-pit last Sunday, by the upper linhay when I told her it would not bear, and so her fell through and would have been drownded at last, only our little Jack crawled over the postesses and give her his heel to hold on by, and please Miss it would have done your heart good, mother says, to see how Tim Badcock dressed her when he come home from church for getting her best frock all of a muck.

Please Miss, Beany Dawe come when you was gone, and made a poem about you, and father like it so much he give him free of the cider and as he was going home he fell into a bit of a ditch down Breakneck hill, and when he come to himself the road had taken to run the wrong way Beany don't know how for the life of him, so he come back here 'nolus wolus' he saith and that be the way to spell it and no mistake, and here he have been ever since a-making of poems and sawing up hellums out of the lower cleeve, and he sleepth in the onion loft and Suke can't have no rest of nights for the noise he makes making verses. Mother tell Suke to pote him down stairs and too good for him, but father say no, he be a fine chap for sure and airneth his meat and drink, let alone all the poetry.

Please Miss he wanted to larn me to write, but father say no I had got better learning than hisn, and I say he may learn Tabby Badcock if he will, but he shan't learn me. No tino."

How she tossed her pretty curls when she wrote this I'll be bound. I wished that I could see her.

"Please Miss I be forced to write this when he be away, or he'd a made it all in poetry; and Tim Badcock tell me to be sure to tell you as how at the wrastling to Barnstaple fair, week after you was gone, father was so crule unkid that in playing off the ties he heaved a Cornisher up through the chandelier, and a come down with a candle stuck so fast down his throat doctor was forced to set it a-fire and blow with a pair of bellises afore he could put him to rights. Cornisher be all right again now, Tim saith, but he have a made up his mind not to wrastle no more in Devonshire.

Please Miss, father saith before this here goes he'll shoot the old hare as sits in the top of the cleeve if Queen Victoria transports him for it with hard labour. Tim have made four pops at her, but he say the powder were crooked.

Please Miss Clara, all the eggs as my little black hen have laid, since the last of the barley was housed, is to be sewed up inside the Turkey with the black comb; he be strutting about in the court and looking at me now as peart as a gladdy; but her have not laid more than a dozen to now, though I have been up and whistled to her in the tall at every morning and evening same as we used to do when you was in good spirits. But the other hens has not laid none at all.

Please Miss, father say as how he have sold such a many beasties, he be afeared to keep all the money in the house, and he have told mother to sew up the rent for next Ladyday in the turkey with the white comb when he be killed and he humbly hope no offence.

Please Miss Clara, us has had three letters from you, and I reads them all to father and mother every Sunday evening, and Joe the Queen's boy don't know but what he lost another one in leathering the jackass across the brook after the rain. Joe tells as he can't say for certain, because why he baint no scholar the same as us be, and Joe only knows the letters by the pins they sticks in his sleeve afore he leaves Martinhoe. Whoever 'twas for he thinks there was crockery in it by reason it sunk so quick. Anyhow mother give him a little tap with a mop on the side of his head, to make him mind the Queen's business, and didn't he holler a bit, and he flung down the parson's letters all in the muck, but us washed them in a bucket and let parson have them on Sunday. Joe Queen's boy haven't been nigh us since, and they did say to Martinhoe us shouldn't have no more letters, but father say if he don't he will show the man there what a forehip mean pretty smart.

Please Miss Clara, us would have written afore, but mother say no, not till I finish twelve copybooks one every week, that the folks to London town might see the way as they ought to write and spell. Father say London be in Gloucestershire, but I am most sure it baint, and Beany Dawe shake his head and won't tell, and mother believe he don't know.

Please Miss, there be a new babby come a month agone and better, and mother find out as how it be a girl, and please if you have no objection Miss, and if you don't think as it would be a liberty, us has all made up our minds upon having it christened Clara, and please to say Miss if it be too high, or any way unfitty. Father be 'most afeared that it sound too grand for the like of us, but mother says as the Huxtables was thought brave things on, to Coom and Parracombe a hundred years agone.

Please Miss, father heard to Coom market last week, as there's going to be a French invasion, and they be sure to go to London first, and he beg you to let him know as soon as ever there be one, and he come up at once with the big ash-stick and the ivy on it as growed in Challacombe wood, and see as they doesn't hurt you, Miss.

Please Miss, the young chap as saved you from the great goyal come here to ask for you, day after you was gone, and mother believes he baint after no good, by token he would not come in nor drink a drop of cider.

Please Miss, father say it make his heart ache every night, to think of you all to yourself in the wicked London town, and he go down the lane to the white gate every evening in the hope to see you acoming, and mother say if you be a selling red and blue picturs her hope you will send for they as father gave the hog's puddens for, and us wont miss them at all.

And Miss Clara dear, I expect you'll be mazed to see how I writes and spells, father say it must be in the family, and I won't write no more till I have finished another dozen of copy books; and oh dear how I do wish that you were come back again, but father say to me to say no more about it for fear to make you cry, Miss. All the little childers except the new babby who have not seen you yet, sends their hearts' loves and duty and a hundred kisses, and father and mother the same, and Timothy Badcock, and Tabby, and Suke, and Beany Dawe, now he knows it.

I remain, Miss Clara dear, your thankful and loving scholar to command,

SARAH HUXTABLE.

Signed all this here papper scrawl in the settle by the fire.

JOHN   HUXTABLE   his   mark   X
HONOR HUXTABLE hern X."

CHAPTER XVI.

I was much grieved at the loss of my last letter to Tossil's Barton, because it contained my little Christmas presents for all the family. It was registered for security, but I suppose they "took no count" of that where the delivery of letters depended so much upon luck. Of their Christmas present to me I resolved to give the surplus to those who would be the better for it, and not (according to the usual law of such things) to those who did not want it, and would make return with interest. So on the Christmas morning Mrs. Shelfer and myself, each carrying a large basket, went to the mews round the corner, and distributed among the poor lodgers there, more Christmas dinners than had ever entered those doors before; and how grateful the poor things were, only they all wanted the best.

Now the school of design was closed for a while, and I worked hard for several days at the landscape for Mr. Oxgall, though the store of provisions sent me and the rent enclosed in the turkey had saved me from present necessity.

On the day of all days in the year the saddest and darkest to me, I could not keep to my task, but went for a change of thoughts to the school, now open again.

It was the 30th of December, 1850, and, though I crouch not to the mumming of prigs scolloped out at the throat, who block out with a patchwork screen the simple hearth of religion, and kneel at an ashbin to warm themselves; though I don't care a herring for small anniversaries dotted all over the calendar, and made by some Murphy of old; yet I reverence deeply the true feasts of Church and Chapel, the refreshings of faith and charity, whereupon we forgive and are sorry for those who work hard to mar them. Neither does it seem to me--so far as my timid and wavering judgment extends--to be superstition or vanity, if we dare to set mark by those dates in our own little span which God has scarred on our memory.

In the long dark room so bare and comfortless, and, to-day, so lonely and cold, I got my usual books and studies, and tried, all in vain, to fix my attention on them. Finding the effort so fruitless, I packed up my things in the little black bag and rose to depart. Turning round, I saw on the table, where students' works were exhibited, a small object newly placed there. It was a statuette in white marble of a magnificent red deer, such as I had seen once or twice in the north of Devon. The listening attitude, the turn of the neck, the light poise of the massive head, even the mild, yet spirited eye, and the quivering sensitive lip, I could answer for them all, they were done to the very life. Truth, power, and elegance triumphed in every vein of it. For a minute I stood overcome with wonder. If this were the work of a youthful sculptor, England might hope at last for something beyond the grotesque.

Before me rose at once all the woodland scenery, the hill-side garbed with every shade of green, the brambled quarry standing forth, the trees, the winding vales embosoming the light, the haze that hovers above the watersmeet, bold crests of amaranth heath behind, and far away the russet wold of Exmoor. The stag in the foreground of my landscape, I feel so grateful to him for this expanse of vision that I stoop down and kiss him, while no one can see me. As I bend, the gordit drops from its warm home in my breast. By some impulse undefined I lift the ribbon from my neck, and hang the little fairy's heart on the antlers of the Devonshire deer. Out springs from behind a chest full of casts and models--what model can compare with her?--the loveliest of all lovely beings, my little Isola Ross.

I hide the tears in my eyes, and try to look cold and reserved. What use is it? One smile of hers would have disarmed Belial.

"It isn't my fault, dear. It isn't indeed. Oh, please give me that cordetto. No don't. That is why I loved you so at first sight. And here is all my money dear. I have carried it about ever since, though I sewed up the purse not to spend it, and only once cut it open. They made me promise, and I would not eat for three days, and I tried to be sulky with Pappy because he did not care; they made me promise with all my honour not to go and see you, and Cora came about with me so that I had no chance of breaking it. And I would not tell them where you lived, dear; but I led old Cora a dance through your street on the side you live, till she began to suspect. But I could never see you, though I looked in at all the windows till I was quite ashamed, and the people kissed their hands to me."

Poor little dear! I lived upstairs, and could not have seen her without standing out on the balcony, which was about the size of a chess-board. If she had not been so simple as to walk on my side of the street, she must have seen me ere long, for I sat all day near the window to draw, when I was not away at my school.

I forgave her most graciously for having done me no wrong, and kissed her with all my heart. Her breath was as sweet as violets in Spring clover, and her lips warm and soft as a wren's nest. On receiving my forgiveness, away she went dancing down the long room, with her cloak thrown off, and her hair tossing all out of braid, and her exquisite buoyant figure floating as if on a cloud. Of course there was no one there, or even impulsive Isola would hardly have taken her frolic; and yet I am not sure. She never thought harm of any one, and never imagined that any one could think harm of her.

After a dozen flits of some rapid elegant dance quite unknown to me (who have never had much of dancing), but which I supposed to be Scotch, back she came out of breath, and kissed me ever so many times, and kissed my gordit too, and told me never to part with it. One thing she was sure of, that her Papa could not resist me now, and when he was told of it I should come to their house the next day. And she knew I was dreadfully proud, but would I, for her sake, forgive her Pappy? Of course, he knew nothing about me, and she had never told him my name, though she could not help telling my story, at least all she knew of it; but he was so dreadfully jealous of her, he did not want any one to have a touch of her glove but himself.

Looking at her pure sweet face, I could well believe it; but how could he bear to see that dear little thing go three days without food? Most likely she had exaggerated. Although she was truthful as light, sometimes her quick fancy and warmth, like the sunshine itself, would bring out some points too strongly. However, I was prepared, without that, to dislike the Professor, for, as a general rule, I don't like men who moralise; at least if their philosophy is frigid. Nevertheless, I promised very readily to forgive her Papa, for I did so love that Isola. Her nature was so different to mine, so light and airy, elastic and soft; in short (if I must forsake my language), the complement of my own. We chatted, or rather she did, for at least half an hour; and then she told me old Cora was coming to fetch her at three o'clock. Once more I rose to depart, for I feared she might get into trouble, if the old nurse should find her so intimate with a stranger.

But Isola told me that she did not care for her a bit, and she had quite set her heart on my meeting her brother Conrad, the sculptor of that magnificent stag. Perhaps he would come with Cora, but he was so altered now, she could never tell what he would do. Since the time she first saw me, Conrad had come of age, and she could not guess what it was all about, but there had been a dreadful disturbance between him and his father, and he had actually gone to live away from the family. She thought it must be about money, or some such nasty thing; but even Cora did not know, or if she did, the old thing would not tell. It had made poor Isola cry till her eyes were sore, but now she supposed she must make up her mind to it all. But she would tell the truth, she did hate being treated like a baby when she was a full-grown woman; how much taller did they expect her to be? And what was much worse, she did want so to comfort them both, and how could she do it without knowing what was the matter? It was too bad, and she wished she was a boy, with all her heart she did.

She went on talking like this till her gentle breast fluttered, and her coral lips quivered, and the tears stole down her long lashes, and she crept to me closer for comfort.

I was clasping her round little waist, and kissing the bright drops away, when in burst a dark, scraggy woman, who must, of course, be old Cora. She tore the poor child from my arms, and scowled at me fiercely enough to frighten a girl unacquainted with real terrors.

I met her dark gaze with a calm contempt, beneath which it quailed and fell. She mumbled some words in a language or patois, which I supposed to be Gaelic, and led off her charge towards the door.

She had mistaken her adversary. Was I to be pushed aside, like a gingerbread woman tempting a weak-stomached child? I passed them; then turned and confronted the hag.

"Have the goodness, old woman, to walk behind this young lady and me. When we want your society, we will ask for it. Isola Ross, come with me, unless you prefer a rude menial's tyranny to a lady's affection."

Isola was too frightened to speak. I know not what would have been the result, if the old hag, who was glaring about, rather taken aback, but still clutching that delicate arm, had not suddenly spied my fairy's heart, as yet unrestored to its sanctuary.

She stared, for a moment, in wide amazement; then her whole demeanour was altered. She cringed, and fawned, and curtseyed, as if I had worn a tiara. She dropped my dear Isola's arm, and fell behind like a negress. My poor little pet was trembling and cold with fright, for (as she told me afterwards) she had never seen old Cora in such a passion before, and the superstitious darling dreaded the evil eye.

As we went towards Isola's home, I could not help thinking how fine the interview would be between Mrs. Shelfer and Cora, if I only chose to carry that vanquished beldame thither; but sage discretion (was I not now eighteen?), and the thought of that solemn day prevented me. So I took them straight home, leading Isola while she guided me, and turning sometimes, with complacency, to encourage old Cora behind us.

The house they lived in was a high but narrow one, dull-looking and dark, with area rails in front. Some little maiden came to the door, and I took my leave on the steps. Dear Isola, now in high spirits again, kissed me, like a peach quite warm in the sun, and promised to come the next day, about which there could now be no difficulty.

Old Cora bent low as she wished me good evening and begged leave to kiss my cordetto. This I granted, but took good care not to let it pass out of my hands; she admired it so much, especially when allowed to examine it, and there was such a greedy light in her eyes, that I was quite sure she would steal it upon the first chance; and therefore I went straightway and bought a guard of thick silk cord, as a substitute for the black riband, which was getting worn.

And so I came home before dark, full of wonder, but feeling rather triumphant, and greatly delighted at having recovered dear Isola.

END OF VOL. I.

BOOK II. (*continued*).

CHAPTER XVII.

Late in the evening of that same day, I sat in my room by the firelight only (for I could not work) and tried to look into myself, and find out the cause of my strange attraction or rather impulsion towards Isola. Somehow or other I did not wonder so much that she should be drawn quite as strongly towards me, although an impartial observer would perhaps have wondered far more. Alter puzzling myself in vain with this inquiry, my thoughts began to move, in their usual gloomy train.

Eight years had now elapsed, and what had I discovered? Nothing; but at long dark intervals some impress of the deed itself, more than of the doer. Had I halted in pursuit, or had my vengeance cooled? To the former question my conscience answered "yes," to the latter "no." Gentle influences had been shed around me, sorrow had bedewed the track of hate, intercourse with happy harmless people, and gratitude for unmerited kindness; it was not in human nature, however finely constitute for evil, entirely to repulse these powers.

I could not deny, that the religion of my heart, during the last twelvemonth, had been somewhat neglected. For my devotion to dear mother, no plea was required. But the time since that, what business had I with laughing children, and snug firesides, with dickybirds, and Sandy the squirrel? Even sweet Isola caused me a pang of remorse; but no, I could not quite abandon her. But now, thank God, I was in the right road again, and plodding resolutely as my father could expect. To his spirit, ever present with me, I knelt down and poured out my remorse; and swore to make amends, whatever it might cost me. Yet even then, a gentle shadow seemed to come as well, and whisper the words that calmed the face of death.

My musings, if so mild a word may suit them, were roughly interrupted by a loud step on the stairs. Inspector Cutting, who could walk when needful like a cat, loved to redress this injury to the Goddess Echo, by making double noise when not on business. Farmer Huxtable, a man of twice the weight, would have come up those stairs at half the expense in sound.

When he entered the room, he found himself in a semi-official state again, and I saw that he was not come for nothing. In a few brief words, he told me what he had done, which was not very much; or perhaps my suspicion was right, that he only told me a part of it. Then he said abruptly,

"Miss Valence, I know pluck when I see it."

"What do you mean, Mr. Cutting?"

"Excuse me, I forgot that you have been reared in the country. What I mean is, that I believe you possess an unusual share of courage."

"As to that, I cannot say, having never been severely tried; but in such a cause as mine, I could go through a good deal."

"And not lose your presence of mind, even in real danger?"

"That again I cannot say, and for the same reason. But I am quite ready to make the trial."

I felt the colour mounting in my cheeks. How glad I should be to prove to myself that I was not ignoble. He observed me closely, and appeared quite satisfied.

"What I have to propose to you, is attended with no little danger."

"I will do my utmost not to be afraid. I am more impulsive perhaps than brave, but what is life worth to me? I will try to think of that all the time. No doubt you have a good reason for exposing me to danger."

"Certainly I have, Miss Valence. For your own purpose it is most important that you should be able to identify certain persons, whom I shall show you to-night; that is, unless I am misinformed."

"To-night! so late as this?" And I began to tremble already.

"Yes, we must go to-night, or wait for another fortnight; and then it would be no earlier, even if we got such a chance again. And for your sake it is better than to be in a fright for a fortnight."

"Inspector Cutting, I am in no fright whatever. At least I mean no more so than any other girl would be, who felt a vague danger impending. I hope and trust that my father's memory and the justice of God will be with me."

"Young lady, I see that I may safely venture it. If you had boasted, I should have hesitated, though I have had some proof already of your determination. The chief, and indeed the only danger, is lest you lose your presence of mind, and that most females would do, if placed as you will be. Now I wish you to make deliberate choice, and not to be carried away by impulse vindictiveness, or the love of adventure; which, when the spirit is high like yours, too often leads young females into trouble, from which it is not always possible even for the most capable members of the force to extricate them."

"Of course I know all that. How much longer are we to talk? Must I disguise myself? When am I to be ready? And where are we going?"

"Now you are growing impatient. That is not a good sign. Remember, I can easily procure another witness; but for your own sake I wish to give you the chance. Probably you will see to-night the man who killed your father."

As he spoke my flesh was creeping, and my blood ran cold, then suddenly flushed through my system like electric fluid. He began again as coolly as if he were reporting a case of some one discovered "drunk and incapable." From force of habit, he touched his forehead, and stood at attention, as he spoke. "In consequence of information which I have received, I have been induced to make certain inquiries, which have resulted in the conviction that the criminal I am in search of will be present at a certain place this night, at a certain hour. It is therefore my intention to embrace the opportunity of--"

"Catching him!" cried I in a breathless hurry.

"To embrace the opportunity," continued the Inspector, like a talking oak, "of conducting my investigations personally, and in the presence of a witness. The effect thereby produced upon my mind shall be entered duly, the moral effect I should have said, and the cause of justice will be promoted as rapidly as is consistent with the principles of our glorious constitution."

"Do you mean to say that you will let him go?"

"No, I shall not let him go, Miss Valence, for the simple reason that I shall not apprehend him. I see that you are inclined to take the law into your own hands. That will never do for me."

"Oh no, I am not. A year ago I would have done so. But I am older and wiser now."

I was thinking of dear mother; and began to feel already that my character was changing.

CHAPTER XVIII.

Inspector Cutting gave me some minute instructions, and in less than half an hour we set forth upon our enterprise. I was wrapped in a loose grey cloak having a hooded cape; and carefully hidden I carried for self-defence a very keen stiletto. I had procured it indirectly from the best cutler in London, but neither workmanship nor material could be compared to that of Italy.

The night was dark and cold, the streets were almost deserted, and all the shops except the chemists' and the public-houses closed. We walked straightway to the nearest cabstand, where Mr. Cutting ordered a vehicle, and put me inside, himself riding with the driver. So little did I know as yet of London, that after the first turn or two, I could not even guess what direction we were taking. I had such confidence in my guide, a staid respectable man with a grown up family, that I never thought there could be harm in my journeying with him at night. And even had I thought so, most likely I should have done it all the same. Ever since the time he wounded me, or allowed me to wound myself, his manner towards me had been most kind, considerate, and respectful; though he found it his duty now and then to repress my impetuosity.

With all my perception alert, I kept a sharp look-out from the window, but vainly strove to find anything that might serve for a landmark. Once we stopped for about five minutes, at a police-station somewhere in Clerkenwell, where, by the light of a lamp, I read, without leaving the cab, the ghastly descriptions of all the dead bodies recently found in London and waiting identification. Hereupon my courage began to ooze, and the weather seemed much colder. The type was hard to read at that distance, and the imagination had fair play, as it does when words come slowly.

Anon the inspector reappeared, so altered in dress and countenance, that I did not know him until he made me a bow. With a glance of encouragement, and a little grin of dry humour, he mounted the box again. After another long drive, in the course of which we ran silently over a wooden road,--probably High Holborn,--we stopped in a broad but deserted thoroughfare, very badly lighted. Here Mr. Cutting opened the door, helped me out, and discharged the cab, but whispered something to the driver before he let him go.

"Now take my arm, Miss Valence, if you please. I have escorted many a lady of higher birth than yours."

"Of higher title perhaps, Mr. Cutting; and their grandfathers money-lenders, or perhaps far worse."

"I am sure I don't know; we must take things as we find them. I thought you despised such nonsense. But the cabbage that runs to seed is the tallest in the field. No Englishman sees the nonsense of it, unless he happens to be a detective or a grave-digger."

"Do you mean to say that those of lofty birth are worse than those of low birth?"

"No, I mean nothing of the sort. But I do mean that they ought to be better, and on the whole are not so. Nature holds the balance, and temptation and education chuck into the opposite scales, and I think the first chucks fastest. At any rate I would rather have a good drunken navvy than a lord to take to the station. I mean of course when my own rank was not what it is."

This little dissertation was meant to divert my thoughts. I made no reply, being ignorant of such matters; neither did I care to talk about them then. Nevertheless, I believe Inspector Cutting was wrong. As we entered a narrow street he suddenly turned and looked at me.

"Poor child! how you tremble! Draw your cape more forward; the bitter cold requires it. Are you trembling from fear?"

"No; only from cold." But I tried in vain to think so.

"A steady hand and steadfast nerve are wanted for your task. If you cannot rely on them, say so at once. In five minutes you will have no retreat."

"I shall be better directly. But I am so cold. Inspector Cutting, it must be freezing hard--ten degrees, I should think."

"It does not freeze at all. I see we must warm you a little. But no more 'Inspector Cutting,' if you please, until to-morrow."

Hereupon he led me into a little room, fenced off from the bar of some refreshment-house. A glorious fire was burning, by which he set and left me. Presently he returned, with a small glass in his hand.

"Drink this, young lady. It will warm you, and brace your nerves."

I saw by the firelight that it was brandy, or some dark-coloured spirit.

"No, I thank you. Do you suppose that I require Dutch courage?"

I threw such emphasis on the personal pronoun, and looked at him so indignantly, that he laughed outright.

"I thank you in turn. You suppose that I do. I will justify your discernment." And with that he tipped it off, and then returned to business, all the graver for the interlude.

"Now, if you are really warm, we will start again. Stop one moment. I have heard you cough two or three times. Can you keep it under?"

I assured him that I could very easily do so, and that it was nothing but the sudden effect of the cold. Forth we went again into the winter night, after I had learned from him that we were now in Whitechapel, not far from Goodman's Fields.

After another short walk, we came to the end of a narrow by-street, where there was an archway. Passing through this archway, we descended some steep and broken steps. Then the Inspector produced a small lamp brightly burning, which he must have lit at the public-house. It was not what is called a bull's-eye, but a reflector-lamp. By its light I saw that the chief entrance to the house must be round the corner, and perhaps in another street. With a small key which he took from his pocket, Mr. Cutting unlocked a little iron gate, and we entered a narrow passage. At the end of it was a massive door studded with great nails. Here my guide gave a gentle knock, and hid the lamp as before.

Presently we heard a shrill sound from the keyhole, like a dryad's voice. The Inspector stooped thereto, and pronounced the password. Not without some difficulty the lock was turned and the bolts withdrawn, and we stood inside. A child, under-sized and unnaturally sharp, stared at us for a moment, then dodged away from the lamp, as if more accustomed to darkness. Mr. Cutting closed the door and refastened it, then led me through some basement rooms unpaved and unfurnished, until we came to an iron step-ladder. This he ascended, and helped me up, and we found ourselves in a small dark lobby, containing no furniture, except a high three-legged stool. When he closed his lamp all around was dark, but on the rafters overhead a faint patch of light appeared--ceiling there was none.

"Do you see that light?" he whispered to me, pointing, as I could just perceive, to a narrow glazed opening high in the wall, whence the faint gleam proceeded.

"Then jump upon this stool, and do your best to see through."

He cast the light of his lamp upon the stool for a moment, while I did as he bade me. Standing there, I found that I was tall enough to look through; but the narrow pane which formed the window was thickly covered with size, or some opaque integument. All I could tell was, that the space beyond was lighted.

"I know you can't see now," he said, as I came down despairing, "but you shall see by and by. The fools who were here before sized the glass on the wrong side, and this lot, though much sharper, have not corrected the error. They keep that window for escape in the last resort. Now take this bottle and this camel's-hair brush; it will make the glass transparent without the smallest noise. The men are not there yet. We could easily rub it clear now, but they will examine it. When the time comes, use the liquid most carefully and lightly, and don't spread it higher than an inch from the bottom of the frame. The lights are at this end; the shadow of the sill will allow you just an inch."

"And how far may I go horizontally?"

"The whole length of the glass, to command as much view as possible. The effect will pass in three or four minutes, but you must not do it again. If you do, the glass will fly, and you will be in their hands. Desperate men they are, and though I shall be near, I might be too late to save you. See all you can, to be able to swear to them all."

"How shall I know the one?"

"I cannot tell you. I must leave it to your instinct, or your intuition. I only know myself that he is one of the four. My information, such as it is, was obtained very oddly, and I trust to this night's work to make it more precise. One thing more: No noise, if you value your life. Keep the bottle stopped. Don't let the stuff drop on you; don't put your eyes to it, or it will blind you for ever. There is very little of it, because it is so deadly."

"When shall I do it?"

"In one hour from this time. Take this repeater. I have shown you how to use it. Look well at it now, while you have the light."

I looked at the watch; it was nearly midnight.

"Am I to be left in the dark--all in the dark here, by myself?"

"Yes. I must be seen elsewhere, or the whole thing fails. They know me even in this dress, and they watch me as I do them. But for to-night I believe I have misled them. When it is over, wait here till I come for you, or the little girl you saw."

"Oh! I wish I had never come; and all so vague and indecisive!"

"You can go back now, if you please; though ever that would be dangerous."

"I will not go back. No doubt I shall know him. When will you secure him?"

"When my evidence is completed. Now, remember, you have to deal with men keen as hawks, and stealthy as tigers. But there is no real danger, if you keep your self-command. Observe all four as narrowly as you can, both for your own sake and for mine. Be careful to stand on the centre of the stool. But you had better not get upon it until they have searched the room. Now, good-bye. I trust to your courage. If any harm comes, I will avenge you."

"A comfort that! What good will it be to me?"

"If vengeance is no good, what are you doing here?"

"Thank you. That is no business of yours. Don't let me detain you."

He told me afterwards that he had vexed me on purpose to arouse my mettle. And I am sure I needed it.

"Ah! now you are all right. If your caution fails you, the man who slew your father will be sure to escape us."

"If it fails me, 'twill be from anger, not from terror."

"I know it. Let me look at you."

He threw the full light on my face. The burnished concave was not brighter or firmer than my eyes.

"Pale as death, and quite as resolute. Rely only upon yourself."

"God and myself," I whispered, as he glided out of sight along the vaults below. I could see no other entrance to the place in which I sat; but how could I tell?

For a minute excitement kept me hot; but as the last gleam of the light died upon the wall below, my heart began to throb heavily, and a chill came over me. The pulse thumped in my ears, like a knocking in the cellar. "Was it fear?" I asked myself, in scorn that I should ask. No, it was not fear, but horrible suspense. The balance of life and death, of triumph and disgrace, swung there before me in the dark, as if my breath would turn it. No dream of a child, no vagary of the brain--the clear perception of strong will and soul poised upon this moment.

The moment was too long; the powers began to fail, the senses grew more faint and confused at every heavy throb. Little images and little questions took the place of large ones. In vain I looked for even a cobweb, or the skeleton of a fly, where the dull light flickered through the pane of glass. In vain I listened for a mouse. Even a rat (much as I hate him) would have been welcome then. The repeater was purposely made so low of tick, that I got no comfort thence. All was deep, unfathomable silence, except the sound of my rebel heart.

As a forlorn hope, I began to reckon sixty slowly, as a child keeps with a ticking clock.

It would not do. My heart was beating louder than ever, and my hands were trembling; even my teeth rattled like dice in a box as the time approached.

The nerves will not be hoodwinked; the mind cannot swindle the body. I once slapped the cheeks of my governess. I cannot treat nature so. Try the sweet influence, and the honest coin of reason. It will not do. All trembling, I strike the repeater. Five minutes more, and the trial must come. My heart is fluttering like a pigeon's throat. The long suspense has been too much. Oh! why was I submitted to this cruel ordeal? The walls are thick. I can hear no movement in the secret room.

There comes a creeping, fingering, sound, as of one whose candle is out, groping for the door. It passes along the pane of glass, and a shadow is thrown on the rafter. Who can it be? What stealthy hand but that of my father's murderer?

The word--the thought is enough. What resolution, reason, justice, all in turn, have failed to do, passion has done at once--passion at myself, as well as at my enemy. Is it Clara Vaughan, who, for eight long years of demon's reign, has breathed but for this moment--is Clara Vaughan to shake like the wooden-legged blackbird now her chance is come?

A rush of triumph burned, like vitriol, through my veins. Every nerve was braced, every sense alert and eager. Against the light of that window, dull as it was, I could have threaded the finest needle that ever was made.

I struck my repeater again. It was the hour, the minute, when my father died. With the mere spring of my instep I leaped upon the stool. I could see it clearly now. I dipped the broad camel's-hair brush in the flat phial, holding it carefully at arm's length, and then drew it lightly along the pane, quite at the bottom, from corner to corner. One more dip, one more stripe above, a steam hovered on the glass, and there was a gazing-place, clear as crystal, and wide enough to show most of the narrow room. Of the room itself I took no heed; the occupants were my study.

Only four in all. One man at a high desk writing rapidly; three men sitting round a small table, talking earnestly, and with much gesticulation, but the tone too low for me even to guess their language. From the appearance, manner, and action of the speakers, I felt sure that it was not English, and I thought that it was not French. Why, I cannot say; but my attention fixed itself upon the man who was writing at the top of the room. Perhaps it was because I could see him best, for he stood with his face full towards me.

He was a man of middle age and stature, strongly framed, closely knit, and light of limb, with a handsome, keenly oval face, broad forehead, black eyes, glancing quickly and scornfully at his three comrades, long hair of an iron grey, falling on his shoulders, and tossed back often with a jerk of the head. His hands were white and restless, quick as light in their motion. On the left thumb flashed a large red jewel. Though I could not see the paper, I knew by the course of the quill that the writing was very small. But one minute I watched him, for the film was returning upon the glass, and I must scan the others; yet in that time he had written several lines, half of them without looking at the paper, but with his eyes upon the other three.

I knew him now he was in clear light, I could swear to him anywhere again. The last glance I could spare him sent a shudder through me, for in his impatience he shifted one foot from the shade of the desk. It was small, pointed, and elegant.

The film was thickening, like frost upon the pane, when I began to observe the others. But I saw enough to print their faces on my memory, or those at least of two. The third I could not see so well. He seemed older than the rest. All the men wore loose grey tunics, with a red sash over the left shoulder. I judged that the three were debating hotly, as to some measure, upon which the fourth had resolved. Every now and then, they glanced at him uneasily.

At him I gazed again, with deadly hatred, cold as ice, upon my heart. I felt my dagger handle. Oh for one moment with him! In my fury I forgot the Inspector's warning. The film was closing over. I touched the glass with my lashes. A flash of agony shot through my eyes. With a jerk I drew back, the stool rocked under me, one foot of it struck the wall. I clutched the window sill, and threw my weight inwards. Down came the foot of the stool, loud as the bang of a door.

I thought it was all over. How I stifled a scream I know not; had it escaped me, I should never have told this story. I had the presence of mind to stand still, and watch, though my eyes were maddening me, what the cut-throats would do. Through the agony, and the dimness, I could just see them all start, and rush to the door at the side of the room. The writer stood first, with his papers thrust anyhow into his bosom, a pistol in one hand, a poniard in the other. Did I know the shape of it? The other three were armed, but I could not see with what. They crouched behind a heavy screen, presenting (I supposed) their pistol muzzles at the door. Finding no attack ensue, they began to search. Now was the real danger to me. If they searched that window before the size returned, my life ended there. Fear was past. Desperation seized me. If I was doomed to blindness, just as well to death. But I clutched my dagger.

My left ear was against the wall. I heard a hand graze the partition inside, then a chair placed under the embrasure, and a step upon it. I was still upon the stool, stooping close beneath the window frame. Suddenly the light streak vanished, the size flew over it, as the breath flies over glass in the hardest frost. The hand felt along the window frame, the dull shadow of a head flitted upon the beam. It was within a foot of mine. The searcher passed on, without suspicion.

Strange it was, but now the deadliest peril was over, triple fear fell upon me. The heat flew back to my heart, just now so stanch and rigid; my hair seemed to creep with terror. Dear life, like true love scorned, would have its way within me. Quietly I slid down from the stool, and cowered upon it, in a storm of trembling. My eyelids dropped in agony, I could not lift them again, but blue and red lights seemed to dance within them. I had made up my mind to blindness; but not, oh not just yet, to death.

How long I remained in this abject state, scorning myself, yet none the braver, is more than I can tell, or even cared to ask. May it never be the lot of any, not even the basest murderer! Worn out at last, in a lull of pain and terror, I fell into deep sleep, from which I was awakened by a hand upon my shoulder.

I tried to look up, but could not. Sight was fled, and as I thought for ever. But I felt that it was a friend.

"Ah, I see how it is"--the voice was Inspector Cutting's--"my poor child, there is now no danger. Give me your hand:" he tried to lift me, but I fell against the wall.

"Take a sip of this, we must restore circulation. It is the cold as much as anything; another sip, Miss Vaughan." He used my true name on purpose; it helped to restore me. He was most humane and kind; he did not even remind me of Dutch courage.

CLARA VAUGHAN

BOOK III.

CHAPTER I.

In the morning I dreamed of Isola. Across a broad black river, I saw her lovely smile. Thick fog rose from the water, in which two swans were beating a dog, and by snatches only could I see my darling. She waved her little hand to me, and begged me, with that coaxing smile which bent cast iron and even gold, to come across to Isola. In vain I looked for a boat, even in my dream I knew that I could not swim, and if I could, the lead upon my eyelids would have sunk me. So I called to her to come to me, and with that cry awoke.

It was striking ten--my own little clock which my father gave me. I counted every stroke. What was Mrs. Shelfer doing, that she had not called me yet? What was I doing, that I lay there so late; for I always get up early? And what was the sun about, that no light came into the room? I knew it was ten in the morning.

I felt all round. I was in my little bed, the splinter at the side of the head-board ran into my finger as usual. There I was, and nowhere else. Was it a tremendous fog? If it was, they should have told me, for they knew that I liked fogs. At least they thought so, from the interest I felt.

I groped for the little bell-pull, a sleezy worsted cord, which meant to break every time, but was not strong enough to do it. I jerked with all my strength, which seemed very little somehow. What a pleasure! The bell rang like a fire-peal. I fell back on the pillow, exhausted, but determined to have it out with Mrs. Shelfer. I put my hands up to arrange my hair, to look a little more like Clara Vaughan, when the light should enter, and to frighten Mrs. Shelfer.

There was something on my head. I never wear a night-cap; my long black hair would scorn it. Am I in a madhouse, is this put to keep me cool? Cold it is, and my brain so hot. All Wenham lake on Dives, and he will only hiss. While I am pulling at it, and find it streaming wet, in comes--I know her step--Mrs. Shelfer. But there is no light from the passage!

"Mrs. Shelfer, what do you mean by this?"

"By what, my dear good soul? I have done all the blessed things I was told to do for you. You might have put a ostrich feather or a marabout to my mouth, Miss Valence, and tucked me up, and a headstone, and none the wiser, when Uncle John brought you home last night."

"I suppose I am dreaming. But I am sure I rang the bell."

"Miss Valence, you did so, and no mistake. Bless me! I started in my shoes. A good job, Shelfer wasn't home, he's so nervous. He'd have gone for gin straightways. Now get up, that's a dear good soul, and when you have had some breakfast, we'll talk over it, Miss Valence. Let me see how your eyes are. Uncle John said they was bad, and I was to keep them covered. I expects him here every minute. Now turn them up to the light. What large eyes you have, to be sure. Bless me! Where are your long black lashes?"

"Mrs. Shelfer, there is some strange mistake. Let the light into the room."

I had risen in the bed, and her breath was on my forehead.

"Light, dear child, I can't let more. The sun is on your face."

I fell back upon my pillow, and could rise no more. The truth had been tingling through me, all the time she talked. I was stone-blind. I flung the bandage from me, and wished my heart would break. Mrs. Shelfer tried some comfort. She seemed to grieve for my eyelashes, more than for my eyes; and addressed her comfort more to my looks than sight. Of course, I did not listen. When would the creature be gone, and let me try to think?

Poor little thing! I was very sorry; what fault was it of hers? Who and what am I, blind I, to find fault with any one who means me well? I drop my eyelids, I can feel them fall; I lift them, I can feel them rise; a full gaze, a side gaze, a half gaze; with both eyes, with one; it is all the same; gaze there may be, but no sight. Henceforth I want no eyelids.

The sun is on my face. I can feel his winter rays, though my cheeks are wet. What use is he to me?

I have the dagger somewhere by which my father died. Let me find it, if I can.

I could have sworn that the box was in that corner carefully concealed. I strike against a washing-stand. Ah, now I have it; the box is locked, my keys are in the top-drawer. I bear the box to the bed, and go groping for the chest of drawers. Already I can tell by the sun-warmth on my face, which way I am going. Surely, if I wait, I shall have the instinct of the blind.

What care I for that? The coward love of life suggested that poor solace. Now I have the keys. Quick unlock the box.

At length I throw the cover back. The weapon handle is to the right. I stoop to seize it. I grasp a square of colour. Pretty instinct this! I have got my largest drawing box.

Oh paints, my paints, so loved but yesterday, that ape the colours I shall never see, my hot tears make you water-colours indeed! If God has robbed my eyes of sight, He has not dried my tears.

The gushing flood relieves me. What right have I to die? Even without asking if my case be hopeless! Who knows but what these lovely tints may glow for me again? May I not once more intone the carmine damask of the rose, the gauzy green of April's scarf? Softening scenes before me rise. I lay my box of colours by, and creep into my bed for warmth.

Presently the doctor comes. Inspector Cutting has chosen him, and chosen well. From his voice I know that he is a gentleman, from his words and touch instinctively I feel that he understands the case.

When he has finished the examination he sees me trembling for the answer which I dare not seek.

"Young lady, I have hopes, strong hopes. It is quite impossible to say what course the inflammation may pursue. All depends on that. At present there is a film over the membrane, but the cornea is uninjured. Perfect quiet, composure, so far as in such a case is possible, cold applications, and the exclusion of light, are the simple remedies. All the rest must be left to nature. Avoid excitement of any kind. Diet as low as possible. Do not admit your dearest friends, unless they will keep perfect silence. Even so, they are better away, unless you pine at loneliness."

"Oh no. I am quite accustomed to that."

"That is well. I shall make a point of calling daily, but shall not examine your eyes every time. The excitement and the effort would strain the optic nerve. Our object is to keep the inflammation from striking inwards. I should not tell you all this, but I see that you have much self-command. On that and your constitution, under Providence, the cure depends. One question. I am not a professed ophthalmist, would you prefer to have one?"

"Oblige me with your opinion."

"It is a delicate point for me. There is no operation to perform. It is a medical, not a surgical case. I have dealt with such before. Were you my own child I would call in no ophthalmist, but as you are a stranger to me, I wish you to decide for yourself."

"Then, I will have none. I have perfect confidence in you."

He seemed gratified, and took his leave. "Please God, Miss Valence, you shall look me in the face ere long."

CHAPTER II.

"Composure is my only chance." What chance have I of composure until I know the meaning of what I saw last night? Blind though I am, one face is ever before me. No thickening of the membrane can exclude that face. Inspector Cutting is still below; I will send for him at once.

Mrs. Shelfer remonstrates. "It will excite you so, my good friend. The doctor said perfect quiet."

"Just so. I can have none, until I have spoken to your Uncle John. Let him stay in my sitting-room, open the folding-door a little, and then, Mrs. Shelfer, please to go down stairs."

I hear the Inspector's step, not so heavy this time. He asks how I am, and expresses his sorrow. I feel obliged to him for not reminding me that the fault was all my own. Then I implore him, if he wishes me ever to see again, to tell me all he knows about the men I saw last night.

Thus entreated, he cannot refuse me, but first looks up and down the stairs, as I know by the sound of his steps; then he shuts the door of the sitting-room. All he knows is not very much. They are refugees, Italian refugees; two political and two criminal exiles, leaders now of a conspiracy to revolutionize their country.

"But why does he not arrest them?'

"Simply because he has no right. As for the political refugees, of course, we never meddle with them; as for the two criminals, they have not been demanded by their Government. Wonderful now, isn't it? The two fellows who have committed murder their Government would not give sixpence for them; but the two men who have only spouted a little, it would give a thousand pounds for either of them. He can't understand such a system."

And Inspector Cutting sucks his lips--I know it by the sound--he always does it when he is in a puzzle. Being a true Englishman, he knows no more of serfdom, than of the dark half of the moon. I mean, of course, political serfdom. Of social slavery we have enough to last ten generations more.

"Would he be afraid to arrest them? He said they were desperate men."

"He should rather hope he wouldn't. They had got their knives, and pistols, and all that humbug. But it was more show than fight. They were desperate men in a private quarrel, particular when they could come round a corner, and when women were concerned; but as for showing honest fight, he would sooner come across three of them, than one good Irish murderer."

"What was his proof against my enemy? I need not ask him which it was."

The excitement of this question sent needles through my eyes. And I could not see him, to probe his pupils.

"Well, his proof was very little. In fact it was no proof at all as yet. But he was not like a juryman. He was quite convinced; and his eyes should never be off that man, until he had him under warrant, and the whole case clear. Would that satisfy me?"

He spoke with such hearty professional pride, that I could not help believing him. But as for being satisfied--why should his evidence be a mystery to me? "Catch him at once," was my idea; but a hot and foolish one. "Get up the evidence first," was Inspector Cutting's, "I can catch him at any time." That was the whole gist of it. Could he always catch him?

He scorned the idea of there being any difficulty about it. The man could leave for no part of the Continent; he was a political refugee. America was his only bourne beyond the Inspector's jurisdiction. And thither he could not try to go without the Police being down upon him at once.

By this time I was worn out, though my reasons were not exhausted. In a word, I was only half satisfied, but I could not help myself. If, in my helpless blindness, I offended Inspector Cutting, the whole chance disappeared. Only one question remained. "Why did he take me thither?"

"For excellent reasons. As to the one, it was most important that I should always know him again. Moreover, it saved my energies from waste. As to the other three, he had his own reasons for requiring an intelligent witness about their proceedings."

I thought of the thousand pounds, and said no more. Inspector Cutting was an Englishman, and proud, in his way, of English freedom. But, like nine-tenths of us, he thought that we alone understand what freedom is. What good was it to such fellows as those? They would only be free of one another's throats. And like all of us, with most rare exception, next to freedom, he valued money. For our love of this, many foreigners jeer us. All we can say is, that with us it is second, with them it is first. But we are of such staple, our second is stronger than their first.

When the Inspector was gone, I formed a very sensible resolve. Since there was nothing more to be done or learned at present, my only care should be the recovery of my sight. If I were to be blind till death, the purpose of my life was lost, and I might as well die at once. But now the first blind agony, the sudden shock, was over; and I had too much of what the Inspector denominated "pluck," to knock under so.

In the afternoon, when all was quiet, lovely Isola came. Strict orders had been given that no one should be admitted. But Mrs. Shelfer was not proof against the wiles of Isola.

"She smiled so bootiful, when I opened the door, Miss, it fetched out all my hair pins; and when I told her you was ill in bed, and struck stone blind along of some chemical stuff, two big tears came out of her long blue eyes, same as the wet out of a pennorth of violets, Miss; and as for stopping her, she threw her muff at me, and told me to stop that if I liked, and to run and tell you that she was coming, quick, quick!

"To be sure, and here I am!" cried the cheery voice I loved so well. "Oh, Clara dear, dear Clara!" The little darling flung her soft warm arms around me, utterly forgetful of her dress, forgetful of all the world, but that little bit of it she held. Her delicious breath came over my fevered cheek, her cool satin flesh was on my burning eyelids. What lotion could be compared to this? How long she stayed, I cannot tell; I only know that while I heard her voice, and felt her touch, blindness seemed no loss to me. She pronounced herself head nurse; and as for doctors, what were they, compared to her own father? If she could coax him, he should come next day, and deliver his opinion, and then the doctor might betake himself to things he understood, if indeed he understood anything, which she did not believe he did, because he had said she was not to come. My drawings too she admired, much more than they deserved, and her brother Conrad must come and see them, he was so fond of drawing, and there was nothing he could not do. She was so sorry she must go now, but old Cora must be tired of patroling, and she herself had a lecture to attend upon the chemical affinity of bodies. What it meant she had no idea, but that would not matter the least; some of the clever girls said they did, but she would not believe them; it took a man, she was sure, to understand such subjects. She would bring her work the next day, such as it was, and the nicest bit of sponge that was ever seen, it could not be bought in London; and she would answer for it I should be able to paint her likeness in a week; and she would not go till it was dark; and then the Professor should come for her when his lectures were over, and examine me; he knew all about optics, and retinas, and pencils of light, and refraction and aberration, and she could not remember any more names; but she felt quite certain this was a case of optical delusion, and nothing else.

How I wished I could have seen her, when she pronounced this opinion, with no little solemnity. She must have looked such a sage! The thought of that made me laugh, as well as the absurdity of the idea. But I only asked how the Professor was to examine my eyes, if he did not come till dark.

To be sure! She never thought of that. What a little goose she was! But she would make him come in the morning, before his work began; and then old Cora would fetch her home to tea. And she had very great hopes, that if she could only persuade her papa to deliver a lecture in my room, it would have such an effect on my optic nerves, that they would come all right directly, at any rate I should know how to treat them.

Delighted with this idea, she kissed me, and hugged me, and off she ran, after telling me to be sure to keep my spirits up, and the bandage not too tight.

The latter injunction was much easier to obey than the former. She had enlivened me wonderfully, as well as nursed me most delicately; but now that she was gone, the usual reaction commenced. Moreover, although as the saying is, the sight of her would have been good for sore eyes, the effort at seeing her, which I could not control, when she was present, was, I already felt, anything but good for them. And the loss, when she was gone, was like a second loss of light.

Light! What million thoughts flash through me at that little word! Swiftest thing the mind has met, too like itself to understand. Is it steed or wing of mind? Nay, not swift enough for that. Is it then the food of life, prepared betimes ere life appeared, the food the blind receive but cannot taste? If so, far better to be blind from birth. Well I know the taste from memory; shall I never taste it else? Has beauty lost its way to me? The many golden folds of air, the lustrous dance of sunny morn, the soft reclining of the moon, the grand perspective of the stars (long avenue to God's own home), are these all blank to me, and night made one with day?

Oh God, whose first approach was light, replenisher of sun and stars, whence dart anew thy gushing floods (solid or liquid we know not), whose subtle volume has no bourne or track; light, the dayside half of life, leaping, flashing, beaming; glistening, twinkling, stealing; light! Oh God, if live I must, grudge me not a ray!

CHAPTER III.

Low fever followed the long prostration to which the fear of outer darkness had reduced my jaded nerves. This fever probably redeemed my sight, by generalizing the local inflammation, to which object the doctor's efforts had been directed. Tossing on my weary bed, without a glimpse of anything, how I longed for the soft caresses and cool lips of Isola! But since that one visit, she had been sternly excluded. The Professor had no chance of delivering his therapeutic lecture. In fact he did not come. "Once for all," said Dr. Franks, when he heard of that proposal, "choose, Miss Valence, between my services, and the maundering of some pansophist. If you prefer the former, I will do my utmost, and can almost promise you success; but I must and will be obeyed. None shall enter your room, except Mrs. Shelfer and myself. As to your lovely friend, of whom Mrs. Shelfer is so full, if she truly loves you, she will keep away. She has done you already more harm than I can undo in a week. I am deeply interested in this case, and feel for you sincerely; but unless you promise me to see--I mean to receive--no one without my permission, I will come no more."

It sounded very hard, but I felt that he was right.

"No crying, my dear child, no crying! Dear me, I have heard so much of your courage. Too much inflammation already. Whatever you do, you must not cry. That is one reason why I will not have your friend here. When two young ladies get together in trouble, I know by my own daughters what they do. You may laugh as much as you like, in a quiet way; and I am sure Mrs. Shelfer can make any one laugh, under almost any circumstances. Can't you now?"

"To be sure, my good friend, I have seen such a many rogues. That is, when I know Charley's a-coming home."

"Now good bye, Miss Valence. But I would recommend you not to play with your paints so. There is an effluvium from them."

"Oh, what can I do, what am I to do to pass the endless night? I was only trying to build a house in the dark."

"Sleep as much as you can. I am giving you gentle opiates. When you can sleep no longer, let Mrs. Shelfer talk or read to you, and have a little music. I will lend you my musical box, which plays twenty-four tunes: have it in the next room, not to be too loud. And then play on the musical glasses, not too long at a time: you will soon find out how to do that in the dark."

He most kindly sent us both the boxes that very day; and many a weary hour they lightened of its load. Poor Isola came every day to inquire, and several times she had her brother with her. She made an entire conquest of Mrs. Shelfer, who even gave her a choice canary bird. I was never tired of hearing the little woman's description of her beauty, and her visit to the kitchen formed the chief event of the day. Mrs. Shelfer (who had Irish blood in her veins) used to declare that the ground was not good enough for them to walk on.

"Such a pair, Miss! To see her so light, and soft, and loving, tripping along, and such eyes and such fur; and him walking so straight, and brave, and noble. I am sure you'd go a mile, Miss, to see him walk."

"You forget, Mrs. Shelfer, I may never enjoy that pleasure."

"No, no. Quite true, my good friend. But then we may, all the same."

Exactly so. There lay all the difference to me, but none to any other. This set me moralising in my shallow way, a thing by no means natural to me, who was so concentrated and subjective. But loss of sight had done me good, had turned the mind's eye inward into the darkness of myself. I think the blind, as a general rule, are less narrow-minded than those endowed with sight. Less inclined, I mean, to judge their neighbours harshly, less arrogant in exacting that every pulse keep time with their own. If eyes are but the chinks through which we focus on our brain censoriousness and bigotry, if rays of light are shafts and lances of ill will; then better is it to have no crystalline lens. Far better to be blind, than print the world-distorted puppets of myself. I, that smallest speck of dust, blown upon the shore of time, blown off when my puff shall come; a speck ignored by moon and stars; too small (however my ambition leap) for earth to itch, whate'er I suck; and yet a speck that is a mountain in the telescope of God; shall I never learn that His is my only magnitude; shall I wriggle to be all in all to my own corpuscle?

CHAPTER IV.

Is there any Mocha stone, fortification agate, or Scotch pebble, with half the veins and mottlings, angles, flux and reflux, that chequer one minute of the human mind? Was ever machine invented to throw so many shuttles?

At present I am gauged for little threads of thought--two minutes since, the smallest thing I could think of was myself. Now it is the largest. Must I grope from room to room, shall I never be sure where the table is, where my teacup stands; never read, or write, or draw; never tell when my hands are clean, except by smelling soap; never know (though small the difference) how my dress becomes me, or when my hair is right; never see my own sad face, in which I have been fool enough to glory, never--and this is worst of all--never catch another's smile?

Here am I, a full-grown girl, full of maiden's thoughts and wonderings, knowing well that I am shaped so but to be a link in life; must I never think of loving or of being loved, except with love like Isola's; sweet affection, very sweet; but white sugar only?

When my work is over, and my object gained, when my father's spirit knows the wrong redeemed, as a child I used to think I would lay me down and die. But since I came to woman's fulness, since I ceased to look at men and they began to look at me, some soft change, I know not what, has come across my dream.

Is my purpose altered? Is my tenor broken? Not a whit of either. Rather are they stronger set and better led, as my heart and brain enlarge. Yet I see beyond it all, a thing I never used to see, a glow above the peaks of hate, a possibility of home. "Saw" I should have said, for now what have I to do with seeing?

On the fourteenth morning, I had given up all hope. They told me it was bright and sunny; for I always asked about the weather, and felt most cruelly depressed upon a sunny day. By this time I had learned to dress without Mrs. Shelfer's aid. Still, from force of habit I went to the glass to do my hair, and still drew back, as far as was allowed, the window curtain.

Off with my wet bandage, I am sick of it; let me try no longer to delude myself.

Suddenly a gleam of light, I am sure of it; faint indeed, and like a Will of the Wisp; but I am quite sure it was a gleam of light. I go nearer the window and try again. No, there is no more for the present, it was the sudden change produced it. Never mind; I know what I have seen, a thing that came and cheated me in dreams; this time it has not cheated me; it was a genuine twinkle of the sun.

I can do nothing more. I cannot put another stitch upon me. I am thrilling with the sun, like Memnon. I fall upon my knees, and thank the Father of light.

When the Doctor came that day, and looked into my eyes, he saw a decided change.

"Miss Valence, the crisis is over. With all my heart I congratulate you. Another fortnight, and you will see better than ever."

I laughed, and wept, and, blind as I was, could hardly keep from dancing. Then I wanted to kiss the Doctor, but hearing Mrs. Shelfer's step, made a reckless jump and had it out upon her.

"Bless me, why bless me, my good soul, if I was a young gentleman now--"

"Why, Miss Valence, I am perfectly astonished," said Doctor Franks, but I knew he was laughing; "if I had been requested, only two minutes ago, to pick out the most self-possessed, equable, and courageous young lady in London, I should have said, 'I don't want any looking, I know where to find her,' but now, upon my word--"

"If you are asked to point out the most delighted, grateful, and happy girl in London, you know where to come for her. Let me kiss you, Dr. Franks, only once. I won't rob your daughters. It is to you I owe it all."

"No, to Providence, and yourself, and an uncommonly good conjunctiva. Now be prudent, my dear child; a little ecstasy must be forgiven; but don't imperil your cure by over-excitement. It is, as I hoped it would be, a case of epiphytic sloughing" (I think that was what he said), "and it may become chronic if precipitated. The longer and more thorough the process, the less chance of recurrence."

"Oh I am satisfied with one eye, or half an eye. Can you promise me that?"

"If you will only follow my directions, I can promise you both eyes, more brilliant than ever; and Mrs. Shelfer says they were wonderfully bright. But what I order must be done. Slow and sure."

He gave me short directions, all upon the same principle, that of graduation.

"And now, Miss Valence, good-bye. Henceforth I visit you only as a friend; in which I know you will indulge me, from the interest I feel in the case, and in yourself. Mrs. Shelfer's wonderful young lady may be admitted on Thursday; but don't let her look at your eyes. Girls are always inquisitive. If there is any young gentleman, lucky enough to explain your strange anxiety to see, you will make short work of him, when your sight returns. Your eyes will be the most brilliant in London; which is saying a great deal. But I fear he will hardly know you, till your lashes grow; and all your face and expression are altered for the time."

"One thing will never alter, though it can find no expression, my gratitude to you."

"That is very pretty of you, my dear child. You kissed me just now. Now let me kiss you."

He touched my forehead and was gone. He was the first true gentleman I had met with, since the loss of Farmer Huxtable.

CHAPTER V.

When Isola came on the Thursday, and I obtained some little glimpse of her, she expressed her joy in a thousand natural ways, well worth feeling and seeing, not at all worth telling. I loved her for them more and more. I never met a girl so warm of heart. Many women can sulk for days; most women can sulk for an hour; I believe that no provocation could have made Isola sulky for two minutes. She tried sometimes (at least she said so), but it was no good.

And yet she felt as keenly as any of the very sulkiest women can do; but she had too much warmth of heart and imagination to live in the folds of that cold-blooded snake. Neither had she the strong selfishness, on which that serpent feeds.

In the afternoon, as we still sat together, in rushed Mrs. Shelfer with her bonnet on, quite out of breath, and without her usual ceremony of knocking at the door. I could not think where she had been all the day; and she had made the greatest mystery of it in the morning, and wanted to have it noticed. Up she ran to me now, and pushed Isola out of the way.

"Got 'em at last, Miss. Got 'em at last, and no mistake. No more Dr. Franks, nor bandages, nor curtains down, nor nothing. Save a deal of trouble and do it in no time. But what a job I had to get them to be sure; if the cook's mate hadn't knowed Charley, they would not have let me had 'em, after going all the way to Wapping." She holds up something in triumph.

"What is it, Mrs. Shelfer? I am sorry to say I cannot see."

"And right down glad of it, I am, my good friend. Yes, yes. Or I should have had all my journey for nothing. But Miss Idols knows, I'll be bound she does, or it's no good going to College."

"Let me look at it first," says Isola, "we learn almost everything at college, Mrs. Shelfer; but even we senior sophists don't know every thing without seeing it yet."

"Then put your pretty eyes on them, Miss Idols; I'll be bound it will make them caper. I never see such fine ones, nor the cook's mate either. Why they're as big as young whelks."

"Mollusca, or Crustacea, or something!" exclaims Isola, with more pride than accuracy, "what queer little things. I must take them to my papa."

"Now, young ladies," cried Mrs. Shelfer in her grandest style, "I see I must explain them to you after all. Them's the blessed shells the poor sailors put in their eyes to scour them out, and keep them bright, and make them see in the dark against the wind. Only see how they crawls. There now, Miss Valence, I'll pick you out two big lively fellows, and pop one for you in the corner of each eye; the cook's mate showed me how to lift your eyelids."

"How kind of him, to be sure!'

"And it will crawl about under the lid, you must not mind its hurting a bit; and it won't come out till to-morrow when the clock strikes twelve, and then it will have eaten up every bit, and your eyes will be brighter than diamonds. Charley has seen them do it ever so many times, and he says it's bootiful, and they don't mind giving five shillings a piece for them, when they are scarce."

"Did Mr. Shelfer ever try them? His eyes are so sharp: perhaps that is the reason."

"No. I never heard that he did, Miss. But bless you he never tells me half he does; no, nor a quarter of half." At this recollection, she fetches a little short sigh, her nearest approach to melancholy, for she is not sentimental. "Care killed the cat," is her favourite aphorism.

"Then when he comes home, Mrs. Shelfer, pop one of these shells, a good big one, into each of his eyes; and let us know the effect to-morrow morning, and I'll give you a kiss, if you do it well."

This is the bribe Isola finds most potent with everybody.

"Lor, Miss Idols, bless your innocent heart, do you suppose he would let me? Why he thinks it a great thing to let me tie his shoe, and he won't only when he has had a good dinner."

"Well," cries Isola, "I am astonished! Catch me tying my husband's shoes! I shall expect him to tie mine, I know; and he shall only do that when he is very good."

With a regal air, she puts out the prettiest foot ever seen. Mrs. Shelfer laughs.

"Lor, Miss, it's all very well for girls to talk; and they all does it, till they knows better. Though for the likes of you, any one would do anything a most. Pray, Miss Idols, if I may make so bold, how many offers of marriage have you received?"

"Let me think! Oh I know! it's one more than I am years old. Eighteen altogether, Mrs. Shelfer; if you count the apothecary's boy, and the nephew of the library; but then they were all of them boys, papa's pupils and that, a deal too young for me. They were all going to die, when I refused them; but they are all alive so far, at any rate. Isn't it too bad of them?"

"Well, Miss Idols, if you get as good a husband as you deserve, and that is saying a deal, he'll tie your shoe may be for a month, and then he'll look for you to tie his."

"And long he may look, even if he has shellfish in his eyes. Why look, Mrs. Shelfer, they're all crawling about!"

"Bootiful, isn't it? Bootiful! I wish Miss Valence could see them. And look at the horns they goes routing about with! How they must tickle your eyelids. And what coorious eyes they has! Ah, I often think, Miss Idols, I likes this sort of thing so much, what a pity it is as I wasn't born in the country. I should never be tired of watching the snails, and the earywigs, and the tadpoles. Why, I likes nothing better than to see them stump-legged things come to table in the cabbage. I have not seen one now for ever so long. Oh that Charley, what dreadful lies he do tell!"

"What about, Mrs. Shelfer?"

"Why, my good friend, he says them green things with stripes on, and ever so many legs, turns to live butterflies, after they be dead. But I was too many for him there. Yes, yes. The last one as I boiled, I did not say a word about it to him, but I put it by in a chiney-teacup, with the saucer over, in case it should fly away. Bless your heart, young ladies, there it is now, as quiet as anything, and no signs of a butterfly. And when he tells me any lies, about where he was last night, I just goes to the cupboard, and shows him that; and never another word can he say. And so, Miss Valence, you won't try these little snails, after my journey and all!"

"Of course I won't, Mrs. Shelfer. But I am sincerely obliged to you for your trouble, as well as for all your kind nursing, which I can never forget. Now let me buy those shellfish from you, and Miss Isola will take them as a present to her papa."

"No, no, unless he will put them in his eyes, Miss. I won't have them wasted. Charley will sell them again in no time. He knows lots of sailors. Most likely he'll get up a raffle for them, and win them himself."

Away she hurries to take off the bonnet she has been so proud of, for the last two and twenty years. Though I declined the services of the ophthalmist snails, my sight returned very rapidly. How delicious it was to see more and more every day! Plenty of cold water was the present regimen. Vision is less a vision, every time I use it. In a week more, I can see quite well, though obliged to wear a shade.

One morning, dear Isola runs upstairs, out of breath as usual; but, what is most unusual, actually frowning. Has Cora tyrannised, or what? Through the very shade of her frown, comes her sunny smile, as she kisses me.

"Oh, I am so vexed. I have brought him to the door; and now he won't come in!"

"Who, my darling?"

"Why, Conny, to be sure. My brother Conrad. I had set my heart on showing him to you, directly you could see."

"Why won't he come in?"

"Because he thinks that you ought not to see strangers, until you are quite well. He has not got to the corner yet. I can run like a deer. Send word by me, that you are dying to see him."

"Not quite that. But say how glad I shall be."

"I'll say that you won't get well till you do."

"Say what you like. He will know it's only your nonsense."

Off she darts; she is quick as light in her movements, and soon returns with her brother.

I lift my weak eyes to his bright ones, and recognise at once the preserver of my mother and myself. But I see, in a moment, that he has not the faintest remembrance of me. My whole face is altered by my accident, and even my voice affected by the long confinement. When he met me in the wood, he seemed very anxious not to look at me; when he saved my life from the rushing mountain, he had little opportunity. Very likely he would not have known me, under another name; even without this illness. So let it be. I will not reveal myself. I thanked him once, and he repulsed me; no doubt he had a reason, for I see that he is a gentleman. Let that reason hold good: I will not trespass on it.

He took my hand with a smile, the counterpart of Isola's. He had heard of me so constantly, that I must excuse the liberty. A dear friend of his sister's could be no stranger to him. A thrill shot through me at the touch of his hand, and my eyes were weak. He saw it, and placed a chair for me further from the light. On his own face, not the sun, for the "drawing-room" windows look north, but the strong reflection of the noon-day light was falling.

How like he is to Isola, and yet how different! So much stronger, and bolder, and more decided, so tall and firm of step. His countenance open as the noon, incapable of concealment; yet if he be the same (and, how can I doubt it?), then at least there seemed to be some mystery about him.

Isola, with the quickness of a girl, saw how intently I observed him, and could not hide her delight.

"There now, Clara dear, I knew you would like him. But you must not look at him so much, or your poor eyes will be sore."

Little stupid! As I felt my pale cheeks colouring, I could almost have been angry, even with my Isola. But she meant no harm. In spite of lectures and "college," she was gentle nature personified; and no Professors could make anything else of her. All these things run in the grain. If there is anything I hate, I am sure I hate affectation. But there is a difference between us.

Probably it is this: I am of pure English blood, and she is not. That I know by instinct. What blood she is of, I am sure I cannot tell. Gentle blood at any rate, or I could not have loved her so. How horribly narrow-minded, after all my objectivity! Well, what I mean is, that I can like and love many people who are not of gentle, but (I suppose) of ferocious blood; still, as a general rule, culture and elegance are better matches for nature, after some generations of training. My father used to say so about his pointers and setters. The marvel is that I, who belong to this old streak, seem to have got some twist in it. My grandmother would have swooned at the names of some people I love more than I could have loved her. My mother would not. But then she was a Christian. Probably that is the secret of my twist.

All this has passed through my mind, before I can frown at Isola. And now I cannot frown at all. Dear little thing, she is not eighteen, and she knows no better. I have attained that Englishwoman's majority three weeks ago; and I am sorry for Isola.

To break the awkwardness, her brother starts off into subjects of art. He has heard of my drawings, may he see them some day? I ask him about the magnificent stag. Yes, that is his, and I have no idea how long it took him to do. He speaks of it with no conceit whatever; neither with any depreciation, for the purpose of tempting praise. As he speaks, I observe some peculiarity in his accent. Isola's accent is as pure as mine, or purer. Her brother speaks very good English, and never hesitates for a word; but the form of his sentences often is not English; especially when he warms to his subject; and (what struck me first, for I am no purist as to collocation of words) his accent, his emphasis is not native. The difference is very slight, and quite indescribable; but a difference there is. Perhaps it is rather a difference of the order of thought than of language, as regards the cast of the sentence; but that will not account for the accent; and if it would, it still shows another nationality.

There is a loud knock at the door. I am just preparing (with Isola's help) my little hospitalities. If London visits mean much talk and no food, I hold by Gloucestershire and Devon. I have a famous North Devon ham, and am proud of its fame. Surely no more visitors for me.

No; but one for Mrs. Shelfer. The Professor has heard of the eyeshells; and what politeness, humanity, love of his daughter failed to do, science has effected. He is come to see and secure them. His children hear his voice. Of course, we must ask him to come up. Mr. Conrad rises. Isola runs to fetch her father. Isola loves everybody. I do believe she loves old Cora. Conrad is of sterner stuff: but surely he loves his father. As for me--we were just getting on so well--I wanted no Professor. Isola's brother will not tell a lie. He does not remember, all at once, any pressing engagement. He holds out his hand, saying simply,

"Miss Valence, I heartily beg your pardon for leaving so suddenly; and just when we were giving you so much trouble. It would be impertinence for me to tell you the reason. It is a domestic matter. I trust you will believe me, that no light reason would make me rude. May I come again with Isola, to see your drawings soon?"

He meets the Professor on the stairs. The latter enters the room, under evil auspices for my good opinion.

CHAPTER VI.

If Professor Ross entered my room under evil auspices, it was not long before he sent the birds the other way. For the first time, since my childhood, I met a man of large and various knowledge; a man who had spent his life in amassing information, and learning how to make the most of it. A little too much perhaps there was of the second, and more fruitful branch, of the sour-sweet tree. Once I had been fool enough to fancy that some of my own little bopeeps at nature were original and peculiar. To Thomas Kenwood, Farmer Huxtable, and even Mr. Shelfer, a gardener, I had been quite an oracle as to the weather, the sky, and the insects about. Moreover, in most of the books I had read, there were such blunders, even in matters that lie on nature's doorsteps, that, looking back at them, I thought I had crossed her threshold.

As the proverb has it, nature always avenges herself; and here was I, a mere "gappermouth" (I use a Devonshire word), to be taught that I had not yet cropped even a cud to chew. True, I did not expect (like Mr. and Mrs. Shelfer) that a boiled caterpillar would become a live butterfly; neither did I believe, with Farmer Huxtable, that hips and haws foretell a hard winter, because God means them for the thrushes; but I knew no more than they did the laws and principles of things. My little knowledge was all shreds and patches. It did not cover even the smallest subject. Odd things here and there I knew; but a person of sound information knows the odd and the even as well. My observations might truly be called my own; but instead of being peculiar to me, nearly all of them had been anticipated centuries ago. I was but a gipsey straying where an army had been.

All this I suspected in less than ten minutes from the Professor's entrance; he did not leave me long in doubt about it. It is just to myself to say that the discovery did not mortify me much. My little observations had been made, partly from pure love of nature's doings, partly through habits drawn from a darker spring. At first I had felt no pleasure in them, but it could not long be so. Now they were mine as much as ever, though a thousand shared them with me.

As the Professor laid bare my ignorance and my errors, and proved that the little I did know was at second hand--which it certainly was not--I attempted no reply; I was too young for argument, and too much interested to be impatient. So he demolished my ham and myself, with equal relish and equal elegance of handling. He seemed to have no intention of doing either, but managed both incidentally, and almost accidentally, while he opened his mental encyclopædia.

At length, Isola, who was tired of lectures, such as she got and forgot every day, felt that it was high time to assert her prerogative, and come to my rescue.

"Come, Pappy, you fancy you know everything, don't you?"

He was just beginning to treat of mosses; and I knew that he was wrong upon several points, but did not dare to say so.

"My dear child, of the million things I never shall discover, one is the way to keep you at all in order."

"I should hope not, indeed. Come now, here is another thing you don't know. How long did it take to boil this delicious ham? Clara knows, and so do I."

"Upon that matter, I confess my total ignorance."

"Hear, hear! Pappy, you can lecture by the hour upon isothermic laws, and fluids, and fibrine, and adipose deposits, and you can't tell how long it took to set this delicate fat. I'll tell you what it is, Pappy, if you ever snub me in lecture again before the junior sophists, as you dared to do yesterday, I'll sing out, 'Ham, Pappy, ham!' and you'll see how the girls will laugh."

"No novelty, my dear, for them to laugh at you. I fear you never will learn anything but impertinence."

His words were light, and he strove to keep his manner the same; but his eyes belied him.

Isola ran round, and administered her never-failing remedy. There was that sweetness about her nobody could resist it. Returning to her seat, she gave me a nod of triumph, and began again.

"Now, Papples, when you are good again, you shall have a real treat. Clara will show you her cordetto, won't you, dear? It is twice as big as yours, and more than twice as pretty."

I took it from my neck, where it had been throughout my illness. Isola told me continually that it had saved my sight; and so old Cora devoutly believed, crossing herself, and invoking fifty saints. Long afterwards I found that Cora knew it to be the heart of the Blessed Virgin, perpetuated in the material which her husband used. If so, it had been multiplied as well.

Dr. Ross took my pretty gordit, and examined it narrowly, carrying it to the window to get a stronger light.

"Beyond a doubt," he said at last, "it is the finest in Europe. I have only seen one to compare with it, and that had a flaw in the centre. Will you part with it, Miss Valence?"

"No; I have promised never to do that."

"Then I must say no more; but I should have been proud to add it to my collection."

"To carry it about with you, you mean, Pappy. You know you are a superstitious old Pappy, in spite of all your learning."

Weak as my eyes were, I could see the scowl of deep displeasure in his. Isola was frightened: she knew she had gone too far. She did not even dare to offer the kiss of peace. No more was said about it, and I turned the conversation to some other subject. But when he rose to depart, I found a pretext for keeping Isola with me.

"Good-bye for the present, Miss Valence," Dr. Ross said gracefully--he did everything but scowl with an inborn grace--"I hope that your very first journey in quest of natural history will terminate at my house. I cannot show you much, but shall truly enjoy going over my little collection with you whenever you find that your sight is strong enough. Meanwhile, let me earnestly warn you to abstain from chemical experiments"--this was the cause of my injury assigned by Mrs. Shelfer--"until you have a competent director. Isola, good-bye. I will send Cora for you in good time for tea. Your attendance at lecture will be excused."

All my interest in the subjects he had discussed, and in his mode of treating them, all my admiration of his shrewd intellectual face, did not prevent my feeling it a relief when he was gone. He was not at all like his children. About them there was something so winning and unpretentious, few could help liking them at first sight. They did all they could to please, but without any visible effort. But with the Professor, in spite of all his elegance and politeness, I could not help perceiving that he was not doing his best, that he scorned to put forth his powers when there was neither antagonist nor (in his opinion) duly qualified listener. Nevertheless I could have told him some things he did not know concerning lichens and mosses.

When I was left with my favourite Isola, that gentle senior sophist seemed by no means disconsolate at her Papa's departure. She loved him and was proud of him, but there were times, as she told me, when she was quite afraid of him.

"Would you believe it, dear, that I could be afraid of old Pappy?"--his age was about four and forty--"It is very wicked I know, but how am I to help it? Were you like that with your Papa, when he was alive?"

"No, I should think not. But I am not at all sure that he wasn't afraid of me."

"Oh, how nice that must be! But it is my fault, isn't it?"

I could not well have told her, even if I had known it, that the fault in such cases is almost always on the parent's side.

· CHAPTER VII.

That same evening, when dear "Idols" was gone, and I felt trebly alone, Mrs. Shelfer came to say that her uncle John was there, and would be glad to see me. Though he had been several times to ask how I was, he had not seen me since the first day of my blindness.

After expressing his joy and surprise at my recovery, he assured me that I must thank neither myself nor the doctor, but my luck in not having touched the liquid until its strength was nearly expended.

"Have you any news for me?" I asked abruptly. As my strength returned, the sense of my wrong grew hotter.

"Yes; and I fear you will think it bad news. You will lose my help for awhile in your pursuit."

"How so? You talk of my luck; I am always unlucky."

"Because I am ordered abroad on a matter too nice and difficult for any of my colleagues. To-morrow I leave England."

"How long shall you be away?"

"I cannot tell. Perhaps one year; perhaps two. Perhaps I may never return. Over and above the danger, I am not so young as I was."

I felt dismayed, and stricken down. Was I never to have a chance? All powers of earth and heaven and hell seemed to combine against me. Then came a gleam of hope, obscured immediately by the remembrance of his words.

"Are you going to Italy?"

"No. To Australia."

Thereupon all hope vanished, and for a time I could not say a word. At last I said--

"Inspector Cutting, the least thing you can do before you go, and your absolute duty now, is to tell me every single thing you found out, in the course of your recent search. Something you must have learned, or you would not have done what you did. All along I have felt that you were hiding something from me. Now you can have no motive. Now I am your successor in the secret; I, and no one else. To no other will I commit the case. How much I have suffered from your secresy, none but myself can know. Henceforth I will have no help. Three months you have been on the track, and I almost believe that you have discovered nothing."

I spoke so, partly through passion, partly in hope to taunt him into disclosure. His chief weakness, as I knew well, was pride in his own sagacity.

"You shall suffer no more. I had good reasons for hiding it, one of them your own hastiness. Now I will tell you all I know. In fact, as you well said, it has become my duty to do so, unless you will authorise me to appoint a successor before I go."

"Certainly not. My confidence in you cannot be transferred to a stranger."

"One chance more. Let me report the matter officially. It is possible that my superiors may think it more important than my new mission, which is to recover a large amount of property."

"No. I will not allow it. I have devoted myself to one object. I alone can effect it. It shall not pass to others. I feel once more that it is my destiny to unravel this black mystery; myself, by my own courage. In asking your aid I was thwarting my destiny. Since then I have had nothing but accidents. There is a proverb in some language, 'Who crosses destiny shall have accident.'"

"Miss Valence, I could never have dreamed that you were so superstitious."

"Now tell me all you have done, all you have discovered, and your own conclusion from it."

He told me all in a very few words, and his conclusion was mine. To any other except myself, the grounds on which he had based it, would have seemed insufficient. I took good care to secure every possible means of following up the frail clue. Ere he wished me good-bye, he offered one last suggestion. "If, during my absence, Miss Valence, you press your evidence far enough to require the strong hand, or if before you have done so you require a man's assistance, apply at once to my son--you can always find him through Patty Shelfer. He is only a serjeant as yet, and not in the detective force; but he has qualities, that young man has, he has got all my abilities, and more! Ah, he will be at the top of the tree when I am in my grave, please God."

His shrewd eyes softened as he spoke, and I liked him ten times as well for this little flaw in his sheathing. Of course he knew that I could not entrust myself to a young man, as I could to him. When he was gone, with many good wishes on both sides, and a little keepsake from me, I felt that I had lost an intelligent, honest, and true friend.

CHAPTER VIII.

Vigorous and elastic as I am, I cannot deny that the air and weather have great dominion over me. It was always so with my own dear father. Two days spent indoors, without any real exercise, would make him feel as uneasy as a plant in a cellaret. Crusty and crabbed, nothing could ever make him--not even gout I believe, if he had lived long enough for it--but when he had lost his fishing, or shooting, or bit of gardening, too long, he was quite unlike himself. It was a bad time then to coax for anything--no song, no whistling, no after-dinner nap.

I too am not of a sedentary nature, though upon due occasion I can sit writing or drawing for some hours together. But how fine a thing all the while to see any motion outside--a leaf that can skip, or a cloud that can run! How we envy a sparrow his little hop, even across the gutter. It is now a long month since I have been out of doors, except just to sniff the air, without any bonnet on. I have never been boxed and pannelled so long since first I crawled out of my cradle. It is a sharp bright frost--it seems to freeze harder in London than in the west of Gloucestershire, but not half so cleanly.

Isola comes, like a tea-china rose bedded in poplin and ermine. Her close-drawn bonnet of velvet, mazarin blue, is freaked with snowdrops, nod, nod, nodding, not too many of them. I hail the omen of spring, and my spirits rise already. Idols is up for a lark (as the junior sophists express it) and she has set her heart upon leading me such a dance. Shall she ever set that sweet heart upon anything, and not obtain it at once? Who knows? Never, I am quite sure, when another heart is the object.

"Come, you grave old Grandmother. You are younger than me, I believe, in spite of all your stories; and you are old enough in your ways, for old mother Hubbard that lived in a cupboard. Oh my tippets and furbelows, if I wore as tall as you, and half as long in the waist, what a dress I would have. Fifteen guineas at least. Come along, you bed-ridden dump of a Clara; it's freezing like bricks and silica, and I am in such spirits, and Giudice is frightening Tom out of his life in the kitchen."

She danced round my little room, like a leaf when the wind is rising. The Pixie-king of my gordit could not have been lighter of foot, nor half so lovely of form. How she managed to spin so between the "sticks," none but herself can tell. What would poor Mrs. Shelfer have said? In spite of her fears for the furniture, she would have laughed, I believe, and blessed the pretty feet.

"Come along, Clara child. Do you think I am going to stand still here all day?"

"If you call that standing still, pray give me the senior sophist's definition of motion."

"Oh I want to skate, so dreadfully. And Pappy and Conrad won't let me. They say it isn't becoming. But what on earth can be more so? Wouldn't I skim on one foot? I'll skate, in spite of them, Clara, if you'll only keep me in countenance."

"Can you imagine me skating?"

"No. I know you won't do it, you are so fearfully grave. But there's more fun in you, when you like, or when you can't help yourself, as I've seen you once or twice, than there is in a hundred such Merry-Andrews as me. At any rate we'll go and see them. On with your bonnet now, I cannot wait a minute. Have something to cover your eyes. Conny '11 be there I know."

On went my bonnet, nothing loth to have an airing again. It was fading in the box.

"Now lots of warm things, darling. You have no idea how cold it is, and scarcely sun enough to thaw the long frost in your eyes. Let me look at them, Donna. Oh if mine were half as bright. You can't have got them in England."

"Now, Idols, don't talk nonsense. Every inch of me is English, and not an inch of you; although your eyes are so blue. You are Scotch all over, or else you are all Swiss."

For answer she began singing "the Merry Swiss Boy," and was going to dance to her song, when I danced her off down stairs. Giudice was in the kitchen, with Tom, from the top of the coffee-mill, sputtering anathemas at him. A magnificent dog he was, of the race of Maltese bloodhounds, now so scarce, fawn-coloured, long in the flank, deep in the jowl, pouch-eared, and grave of eye. He regarded Tom no more than if he had been an old hat brushed the wrong way; and the birds, who were all in a flutter, he took for British butterflies. He came leisurely to me, walking one side at a time, and solemnly deposited his great moist nose in my hand. I knew him then as the friend who addressed me, long since, in the Villa Road.

"Why, you graven images"--a popular person always has fifty nicknames; Isola had a hundred at least, and she liked them all--"what depth of secresy and statecraft is this! You know how I love dogs, and you never even told me of this splendid fellow's existence!"

"Well, Donna dear, don't look so indignant. He doesn't belong to me, and he won't come with me unless he is told, and then he makes such a favour of it. See his long supple stride. He walks just like a leopard--don't you, you pious panther? I wonder he took to you so. He is not fierce at all, except when he ought to be; but he hardly ever makes friends."

"Whose dog is he?'

"Conrad's to be sure. And I do believe Conny thinks more of him than he does of me. Get along, you yellow mammoth! Why he would keep his head there all day?"

"All dogs love me, Idols. It was so when I was a child. They know how honest I am."

"Well, I believe you are, Donna; and too honest sometimes. But I am honest enough, and Giudice does not appreciate it. Come along, Judy. Are you going to stick there all day?"

Away we went, and the great dog walked behind, keeping his head most fairly adjusted between us, never shifting its place an inch, whether we walked or ran--as we did where the street was empty, and when we got into the Park.

Oh the cold air of heaven, fresh from the clear North Pole, where the Great Bear stalks round the Little Bear with the vigilance of a mother, how it tightens the clip of the joints, puts a sting into every step, flushes the cheeks with Aurora, and sparkles in young eyes! For the nonce we forget who we are, never think how our clothes blow about, our spirits are on the north wind, what are we more than snow flakes, let us glisten and lift on the air.

Crossing the Park (lightly furrowed with snow at the drains, like our hair when we part it) we came to a broad sheet of ice. We had heard a long way off a crisp musical hollow sound, like tapping a box with a hole in it. The ice was not like the old ice at Vaughan Park, but seamed and channeled, and up and down, and powdered light grey with scrapings from skates and shoes. Thousands of people were on it, some skating, some sliding, some rushing about and playing hot game with crooked sticks, some sweeping away with short brooms, some crying things for sale and offering skates for hire, many standing still and wistfully eyeing the land; but all in the height of good humour, laughing, chaffing, holloaing, drinking, and ordering more. Every now and then some great performer (in his own eyes) would sail by the women grandly (like a ship heeling over), with his arms folded and foot over foot, and a long cigar in his mouth. For these one devoutly desired a fall. The skaters of real eminence scorned this common show-off, and each had his special admirers forming a ring around him, where he had cut his own circus of smoother and greener ice.

Along the brink of firm land, stood nurses and children innumerable; the maids on the giggle at every challenge borne to them from the glazed waters, the little ones tugging, and kicking, and frantic to get on. The background of all the cold scene, whiter as it receded, and broken by gliding figures, was formed by some low fringed islets, with open water around them, and crane-necked wild fowl wheeling about, and warning boards, and icemen pushing flat-bottomed boats along. In the far distance, to the right, were two or three canvas tents, where they kept the range of the mercury, and the list of the accidents. The long vista was closed now and then, as high as hats and bonnets, by scuds of the drifting ice and snow.

Here as we stood on the bank, Giudice forsook us shamefully, and bounded over the ice, with a levity quite scandalous for a serious-minded dog, towards one of the charmed circles, where eminent skaters whirled, like peg-tops full of steam-engines. Was it likely that we, two girls of spirit, would halt ignobly there? First on the ice went I, holding Isola's hand, and tempting her nothing loth. In spite of her boast about skating, Idols was frightened at first, and held very tightly by me, and wanted to run back. But the little feet grew braver at every step, and she ventured even to clap her hands and dance. To me the thing was no novelty, except from the number of people, and the puckering of the ice. I had even the courage to slide with one foot, but never with both at a time. As for the cracking and bending when some heavy man scoured by, on purpose, I dare say, to frighten us, I laughed with my heart in my mouth. Isola was amazed. She never could have conceived that I had so much effrontery. What cared I, if a hundred people stared at me? I was doing nothing unseemly, and dozens of ladies were there. The scene, and the air, and the spirits of youth set my blood all on the bound, and oh, blessing of blessings, my blessed sight was come back. How manly, and stirring, to feel, that a slip--and a limb may be broken; a crack--and one may be drowned.

But, as usual, I suffered for my temerity. First we followed Giudice, and found him in the centre of the ring, where the greatest throng was gathered, the dog skating with his master, who was one of the very best skaters in the world. Giudice was graver than ever, but wistfully glanced as he whirled round, at every point of escape. With his heavy fore feet on his master's shoulders, and his tongue lolling out, and his eyes rolling sadly at each reluctant caper, and his poor tail between his jerked legs, it was impossible not to see that his dignity and self-respect were suffering. So when Conrad came to speak to us, I earnestly begged that Giudice might be set free, which was done in a moment, to the great disappointment of the bystanders, and the boundless delight of the dog, who came and gratefully kissed my hand.

"Why, Donna," cried Isola in a small pet, "Giudice takes you for his mistress: he would never do that to me, if I coaxed him a hundred years."

Through, the colour the north wind had spread on my cheeks, I felt the warm blood rushing, and bent over the dog to hide it; then much as I longed to see Isola's brother skate, I dragged her off rather rudely towards the rougher part of the ice. Conrad looked rather surprised and hurt, but resumed his figuring with much apparent philosophy.

Idols and I, with the flush in our cheeks, and the flash in our eyes, and our forms all buoyant with innocent fun, came suddenly round a corner on a party of low-looking men, who were casting flat stones, bowling, or curling, or playing at drake, with a great tin can for their mark. We turned and were off in a moment; but we had been observed by the sharpest and slyest eyes in London. A man gave chase in half-skating fashion, having bones tied under his boots, in lieu of skates. We could easily have escaped, in spite of his bones; but was I going to run away, like a skittish servant-maid? I drew up Miss Isola sharply, whether she would or no, and confronted the enemy. It was Mr. Shelfer himself, the man so modest and bashful, who could never bear to look at me. Though a dozen more came after him, I felt no alarm at all, knowing his wonderful shyness and diffidence. But his first address amazed me.

"Now's your time, lads. At 'em, I say. Here's the two prettiest gals in London."

The low scoundrel! I saw that he was quite tipsy. But frightened as I was, for none but they were near, I could hardly help laughing at him. He had his usual slouch, and the long sly nose, and the pent-house gleam of the eye, and his gaunt cheeks drawn as if he was always sucking them, and the chimneypot hat, that had once belonged to some steady going Churchman, with the crown flapping in, like the gills of a fish. All this was balanced by the skill and comical courage of Bacchus, upon a pair of grating marrow-bones. Behind him his countless pockets yawned and looked brown on the wind. And this was the being bowed down to by Mrs. Shelfer!

"Clara dear, stop, Clara!" the impudent sot cried out.

I had stopped without that, and was already facing him. For a moment he was abashed, for my eyes were full upon his; but the others were coming up.

"Now this is what I calls harmony, dashed if it isn't. Why look at the trees and the bushes. There's harmony in them trees, ay in every one on 'em. Fine trees and pretty gals, them's the jockeys for me. That's what I calls natur' and something like. Houses! Lor, there's no harmony in houses and pantiles. Fine trees is all harmony, and so is lovely woman. Don't tell the old gal at home. She never would understand. Why Idols there is a pretty duck as ever swam on the ice. But Clara's a ---- fine swan, and no mistake. Ducks is all very well, but a swan is the jockey for me. There's something to lay hold on there. Give me a swan I say, and the harmony of them trees. Bob Ridley, I'll lay you a tanner I kisses that there swan. Ever see such eyes, Bob, and look at the way she stands. Wonder there's a bit of ice left here."

The low rogue had a long pipe "in his head,"--as Farmer Huxtable expressed it,--and at every leering sentence blew out a puff of smoke.

"Bet you a tanner, Charley, you don't kiss that stunnin' gal," cried his friend, as drunk as himself.

"Here goes, neck or nothing;" and the niddering made a dash at me. I drew my clenched hand from my muff, where it had been tingling in my glove, and in his tipsy rush, his face came full against it. It was a very odd thing, and I know not how it happened. He reeled on his bones from the collision, and staggered in staring amazement. Before he had time to recover, Conrad dashed up like a hawk at an owl; by some wonderful back-stroke he stopped in an instant, wrung Shelfer's crooked stick from his hand, hooked him under the collar, struck out again, and towed the poor wretch away backward, at the speed of a mile in a minute. The fire flew from his skates as he dashed towards the open water. Giudice, at full gallop behind, tried in vain to keep up. Every man and woman there turned to watch the issue. Shelfer threw out his hands wildly, and screamed: he was utterly helpless, his teeth rattled more than the bones on his boots. At the edge of the open water, three hundred yards away, Conrad stopped suddenly, like an engine in collision, unhooked Mr. Shelfer, and let him go with full impetus. Sprawling and yelling in vain, he flung up his arms, and fell backward into the water headlong. The icemen came running with boats, and ropes, and grapnels. But before the first splash was over, another was seen; Giudice, at a sign from his master, plunged in, drew the poor man of harmony out, and laid him high and wet on the ice. He was taken at once to the tent; where, as I afterwards heard, he made a fine afternoon of it with the society's men; most of whom, it is needless to say, he knew. Be that as it may, the lesson did him good. He never insulted a lady again, or (what is still worse) a poor honest girl, with no education, and no one to defend her. As for me, I really believe he never durst blink his sly eyes in my direction again.

I love good justice, in or out of the pod. The bean is as sweet to me from the rough air of heaven as from a juryman's pocket. But I thought Master Conrad had overdone it this time. He had no right to risk the poor man's life. And so I told him when he came back, as calm as if he had cut a spread eagle. He assured me that he had not risked the man's life at all. He knew the depth of the water there by the island. It was five feet and no more. Then I felt all of a glow and longed to give him the kiss which had cost Mr. Shelfer so much. The next minute I felt humiliated, and burst into a passion of tears, to think what my father would say at his pet of grace and luxury being insulted like that. Idols and Conrad, not knowing my story, could not understand it at all.

They came home with me at once. Conrad, "under the circumstances," ventured to offer his arm, which I, under the circumstances, ventured to accept. At the door he left me; but Idols came in with Giudice, commissioned to see her safe home. She came in partly lest I should feel lonely, partly to arraign Mrs. Shelfer (already condemned by both of us girls) for daring to have such a reprobate drunken husband.

CHAPTER IX.

When Isola had told Mrs. Shelfer everything, and a little more than everything (for her imagination was lively), the dominant feeling in the little woman's bosom was not indignation, as we had expected, but terror. Terror of two evils; the first and chief evil, the possibility of Charley catching cold; the other, the probability that he would crush Conrad, and tread him into the earth, at the earliest opportunity. I assured her warmly that Mr. Conrad could well defend himself, even if Shelfer should dare to meddle with him.

"Oh, my good friend, you have no idea what a terrible fellow Charley is. Why he broke the head of the skittleman at the "Load of Hay." So he told me himself. Ah, he's a terrible fellow, when he's put out."

"But you forget, Mrs. Shelfer, he hasn't been put out this time; he was put in." That Isola always loved small jokes.

"Put in, Miss Idols?" Mrs. Shelfer never understood any joke but her own--"oh yes, put into the water you mean. True, true, and serve him right (so long as he don't take cold) for calling me, his lawful wife who keeps him together, 'the old gal at home!' But Charley's a terrible fellow, terrible."

"Terrible coward more likely," I cried, "or he would never have dared his low insolence to me. I am sorry for it, Mrs. Shelfer, utterly as I scorn him, because it compels me to leave your house; and you have been truly good and kind to me." I thought of Mrs. Huxtable; but how different was the fibre of her kindness!

"Leave my house, Miss Valence! No, no, my good friend, that will never do, not to be thought of, and us so used to you and all, and Tom, and the blackbird, and the new squirrel! A likely story, my good friend, and with your eyelashes coming! And do you know who would come instead of you?"

"Of course not, Mrs. Shelfer."

"Why a nasty stinking hussy, that would steal the feathers out of my best bed again, the same as they did before. My very best bed, Miss Idols, as dear Miss Minto left me by her will, not a better bed in London, unless it's the Queen's, and so I used to tell her when I helped to shake it up. My mouth watered over it so, that she said one day, and the knife-boy heard her on the stairs, 'Patty, you've been a good girl to me, and you deserves it, and you shall have it, when I am tucked up for good and all.' And so I did, very honourable, and all above board. Yes, yes; I had a commercial gent one time, a wonderful heavy man to be sure, and he stayed with me three year for the sake of that same bed. And he knew what beds was, and no mistake. It was bootiful to see when he was a getting up. It began to rise up, up, the same as Tom's back, when he see your dog, Miss Idols."

"Come, Mrs. Shelfer, I fear we can hardly wait."

"'Twas like dough put afore the fire, Miss. There's no such Dantzic now. You couldn't put your fist into one side of it, but out it would come the other. Oh Lor, I could cry; that nasty sly minx, she was softer than parsnips, you'd say, and one leg more than the other. I couldn't think why it was she would always make her own bed. 'Thank you, Mrs. Shelfer'--with her lips sucked in like a button-hole--'thank you, you are too kind. It doesn't at all fatigue me, and my doctor pronounces the exercise good for my chest and arms.' Thank God, she got some exercise good for her legs as well. Six months on the treadmill. Charley got me an order, and it did my heart good to see her. But my twenty pounds of best feathers never came back again, and that wasn't the worst of it neither."

"Oh dear no," says Idols, "the worst of it was the sin, Mrs. Shelfer."

"The worst of it was that she stuffed it with sawdust, and oakum, and jovanna, I do believe, by the smell of it."

"What do you mean, Mrs. Shelfer?"

"Lor, Miss Valence, don't you know jovanna that the kingfishers lays on the top of the sea, and the gardeners make water with it?"

"And what did she do with your feathers?"

"Sneaked them out of the house in the crown of her bonnet, and sold them at eightpence a pound, and they worth three and sixpence, every flue of them. But the rag and bottleman got two months, thank God for it. Ah, it will never be a bed again under 5*l.* at least."

"Is it the one I sleep on, Mrs. Shelfer?"

"Yes, my good friend, the very same."

"And you have put me to sleep on guano! Well, I thought it smelt very odd."

"No, no, my good friend, wait a bit. We got most of that out again, and gave it to our geraniums. She stole it out of a sack as Charley kept in the washhouse. There was feathers in it. That put it into her head, I suppose. But as for your going, Miss Valence, that will never do. Never, never. Will it now, Miss Idols? And to see her dress, to be sure, that baggage! Why, my best tarlatan, as dear Miss Minto give me to be married in, wasn't good enough for her to sweep the stairs in. Sweep the stairs--yes, yes, she did sweep the stairs when I see her last; and she had afore, I know; she was so clever at it; and that was why one leg was so much more than the other."

"Mrs. Shelfer, do you expect us to listen to you all night?"

"True, my good friend, quite true. But when I thinks of my feathers, something comes over me, I must out with my troubles, or burst. But you musn't go, Miss Valence. That will never do, never; ask Miss Idols now." And she turned to Isola, who was quite ready to be turned to.

"Of course it won't, Mrs. Shelfer. You are quite right, my good friend. I won't hear of it for a moment. Why Mr. Shelfer was drunk. I know it by the way he held his pipe. Quite 'drunk and incapable,' you know. And he will be so sorry, and he'll never do it again. And he did not mean to be drunk at all, but the frost was very hard, and the cold got into his head. I am sure it would into mine, if I had stayed much longer; and he didn't understand brandy-balls, as we do at College--you could not expect it, you know."

The pure good faith of this last was too much for me. I laughed outright, having no husband concerned in it. As for the dry little woman, she actually cried. I had never seen a tear in her quick, shy eyes before, though the feather-bed nearly brought them, and so did the death of the elder Sandy, the squirrel. She turned away. She was always ashamed of emotion.

"Bless your innocent heart, Miss Idols, if you don't marry a king! Not one of us is good enough to tie your shoes as you talked of, you are that simple and good of heart."

Is there any goodness more touching to a veteran than a soft young nature's disbelief in evil? But for bitter experience, I might have been sweet as Isola. Thank God, that in spite of all vinegar, the ailment is still infectious. Isola could not make it all out.

"To-morrow morning, Miss Valence," began Mrs. Shelfer again, "to-morrow morning, after I have wigged him well all night, and then given him a good breakfast, he'll come and beg your pardon like a child, and be ashamed to look any higher than your flounces; and I know you'll forgive him."

"Mrs. Shelfer, I have forgiven him long ago. I cannot bear enmity against such people"--these last three words had better been away--"for such little wrongs. And I owe you a great deal for all your kindness to me. The only question is, whether self-respect and prudence allow me to stay here. I will leave the decision to Miss Isola. Young as she is, and innocent and confiding, she cannot be wrong on a question of delicacy. As for prudence, she knows more of London than I do."

Hereon I sat down with a womanly air. But I could hardly help laughing when the senior sophist jumped up, proud to deliver judgment. To look taller, she shook her flounces down, threw back her plump white shoulders--her bonnet and cloak were off--drew her rich flowing hair down the pearly curve of her ears and, scarcely satisfied yet, thought of mounting a stool, then took her foot off the too convictive bema. After all these anabolisms, she began with much solemnity. She was thinking of the College, and her father in the rostrum.

"Miss Valence and Mrs. Shelfer, since you have honoured my weak judgment by appointing me umpire, and as I am led to believe without any right of appeal, I will do my utmost to be discreet and impartial. In the first place I award that Miss Valence remain in this house, forget and forgive her wrongs. In the second place I recommend (in such a matter I will not presume to command) that till Mr. Shelfer has made a humble apology and promised faithfully never to be intoxicated again, however cold the weather is, Mrs. Shelfer shall not permit him to have a single kiss, nor a single bit of hot dinner. Now I have delivered my decree."

"Lor, Miss Idols, you are too soft for the Old Bailey. He never kiss me, unless it is when he knows I have got some money. But he do like a good hot dinner. Right enough there, my good friend."

So this knotty point was settled; and Giudice, who was very loth to leave me, escorted Miss Idols home, Before going, he made another solemn deposit of his great jowl in my hand, and looked at me with an air so tutelary and encouraging, that I could not help laughing; at which he felt hurt, but condoned it. Isola told me that when he was put in charge of her, he felt the responsibility so strongly that he would not stir from her side, not even to speak to the most colloquially gifted dog; though at other times he would stay gossiping near a lamp-post for five minutes together. One evening when he was thus commissioned, a rude fellow pushed between them, and said something to Isola. Giudice had him down in an instant, and stood over him, like a tawny thundercloud, with growlings so fearful and such flashing eyes, that two policemen felt it wiser not to act as conductors. Idols herself was obliged, at the entreaty of her prostrate foe, to coax the great dog off; but when the ungrateful man got up, he insisted on giving Giudice into charge, and having him dragged to the Station. "Very good, Sir," said the policeman, "we'll enter the charge when you bring him there; let him go, Miss, for the Gent to collar him." The "Gent" was away in no time, and Giudice and his mistress walked off amid loud hurrahs from all the boys of the neighbourhood.

Conrad called with his sister the day after Mr. Shelfer's ducking, to reassure himself as to my nerves, which were never better. He looked over some of my drawings, and without seeming to give, but rather to seek information, afforded me many a hint, which I afterwards found most useful. I now learned what his profession was; and it gave me pleasure to find that he was not, as I had feared, a mere lounger upon town. Instead of that, he was working very hard, being (as he told me) nothing more or less than a journeyman sculptor. Though, as himself admitted, by no means a novice, he was going through the regular course of study and hand-labour under an eminent artist. But Isola told me, and no doubt it was true, that he could beat his master out and out, and that for any choice design, where original power and taste were needed, they always came to him. Of late the frosts had lightened his tasks; for warm the room as they would, the weather always affected the material; and they feared to attempt the more delicate parts of the work during the rigours of winter. So when the thaw came, he must lose the pleasure of seeing me for a while, unless dear Isola wished to be escorted home on a Sunday; if, indeed, I allowed her to come on that day. Why, that was the very day when I could best indulge in a walk with my gentle friend, after going to church; and I was sure her society did me more good than the sermons. On her part, Isola found that the services always made her so nervous (her nerves were as good as mine), and that she did not much like walking about with a big dog on Sundays, and Cora was always cross all the day after mass, so Conrad must promise upon his honour always to come for her, rain, hail, or shine, on a Sunday. This he promised so readily, that, for a moment, I fancied it had all been preconcerted. Then I despised myself for the suspicion. The trick would have been not out of the compass of Isola, but very unworthy of Conrad.

CHAPTER X.

Soon as ever my sight was fully restored, and I had Dr. Frank's permission, I took to my drawing again, and worked at it till my eyes ached. This was the symptom upon which I had promised immediately to leave off. Then out I would rush, towards dusk, and away into the great square, full of the pure air of heaven, round by the church at the top, and six times round it till my breath was short. The senior sophist reminds me that round a square is impossible. After squaring the circle, extract the square root, dear Idols, by the binomial theorem. You do learn so much at college: but I write simple and often foolish English. Never mind; I would rather write bad English, than the best French ever written. One is the tongue of power and multitude: the other the language of nicety and demarcation. Which of the two is the more expansive, even a woman may guess.

High time it was for me to recruit my exchequer. Dr. Franks had charged me far less than I even dared to hope. How I trembled when I opened the envelope! What quick terror is half so bad as the slow fear of gathering debt? I was accustomed to medical charges of the time when I was an heiress: but his appeared to me now to be even below reason. The sum could hardly have paid him for his numerous walks to and fro. Then a wretched idea shot through me: had he charged me so little, because he knew I was poor? I took Mrs. Shelfer into my confidence; she was likely to know what the London scale should be. The little thing soon reassured me: it was quite enough, she declared; if she were in my place, she would demand a discount for ready money!

"Oh you dreadfully mean little woman! I should lose my sight, and deserve it, if I did."

However, in spite of all this, money was scarce and scarcer every day, and none of my grand revenues would fall due for ever so long. So another visit must be paid to Mr. Oxgall. Isola insisted on coming with me; to my surprise I found that, with all her soft simplicity she had much more idea of making a market than I had. The reason probably was that she had much less pride. No pocket would hold mine, when a tradesman attempted any familiarity. And whoso stands on a pedestal to sell, is like to find the buyer's arm too short.

Whether it were that, or the golden charm of her manner, or of something else, let Mr. Oxgall say; certain it is that the man of crackly canvas (for whom, by-the-bye, I have a sincere respect, because he cheated me so little and so neatly)--this man, I say, regarded her with a wide-mouthed, brooch-eyed, admiration, which he hardly ever expended on anything out of oils. For the king of painters himself she was a vision sweeter than dreams of heaven. Such a tint in her lustrous eyes, such tone in her dainty cheeks, such perfection of line in her features, and every curve of her exquisite shape. And bounding and sparkling through all, from the rippled wealth of her hair to the light-curved arch of her foot, the full play of her innocent, joyous, loving life.

No wonder the picture-dealer shaded his eyes and gazed, and rubbed them and gazed again. I have frequently seen respectable elderly gentlemen, whose rakishness has never been more than found vent in the cock of a hat, magisterial men I mean, who would no more think of insulting a girl in London or anywhere else, than of giving their daughters as prizes for competitive skill in poaching, such good men and true, also simple-hearted clergymen (for some there still are from the country) these and the like, I Clara Vaughan have seen, when they met my Isola, stop short, wink frequently, and without much presence of mind, until she was gone by; then shumble hotly across the street, with hands in their tail-coat pockets (for these gentlemen always expect most to be robbed when there is least chance of it) pretend to look at a shop, then march at top speed, fumbling all the while for their spectacles, until they got well a-head of us. Then I have seen them cross again, some thirty yards in front, with spectacles nicely adjusted, and become again wholly absorbed by the beauty of metropolitan goods. But when the light foot sounded, from a fair gazing distance, these same gentlemen have (by some strange coincidence) alway turned full upon us, in an absent and yet nervous manner, and focussed their green or pale blue eyes upon the rich violet orbs of Isola. I have even known them to look at me (when they could see her no more), to find some sympathy for their vague emotions. Idols knew it: of course she did. And she rather gloried in it. She had much respect for a fine old gentleman; and I know not how it was, but nobody ever thought of insulting her when she could be clearly seen.

A "pretty girl" you would never call her--though Mr. Shelfer did--the term would be quite unworthy; even a "beautiful girl," sweetly beautiful though she was, would hardly be your expression, at least for a while. But a "lovely girl," and the loveliest one ever seen, that is what she would be called at once, if you could take your eyes off, to analyse your ideas.

Isola knew it of course, as I said before, she knew all her wondrous gifts; but as for being conceited, a trull with a splay foot and a crop of short-horn carrots has often thrice her conceit. A certain pretty graceful pride she had, which threw a rosy playful halo round her, but never made other women look plain in her eyes. She will not value her beauty much, until she falls in love; and blessed is he who shall be the object, if she is allowed to abide with him.

Meanwhile Mr. Oxgall wished for nothing but to hear and see her talk; and this she did to some purpose. I like a man who at the age of sixty is still impressible to the gay vein of youth. I know at once by his eyes whether his admiration is abstract and admissible. If it be, I reciprocate it. What clearer proof can we find, that his heart has not withered with his body; that he is not a man of mammon, tinsel, or phylactery,--in a word, no mummy?

Shall I ever finish this bargain? I have never been so reflective before; and all the time no less a sum than five pounds hangs upon it. Five guineas (which sounds better) was the amount at which dear Idols let off Mr. Oxgall. I believe she might have got ten, but she had an excellent conscience. It worked like a patent chronometer, with compensation balance. Mine was still more sensitive. I could hardly think my landscape, perspective mare's nest and all, worth that amount of money, and I wished to throw off a guinea, but Idols would not hear of it.

"Miss Valence, I am your factor for this beautiful landscape, which has cost you so much labour. Either accept my terms, inadequate as they are, or take the agency from me, and recommence with Mr. Oxgall 'de novo,' as we say at College."

Betwixt her beauty and my stately integrity, poor Mr. Oxgall knew not where he stood. I heard him mutter that he would rather go through fifty auctions, even if it was George Robins. But if she had come to sell him a picture the very next day, he would have gone through it all again with the same infatuation. So I took the money; and now my evil demon, who had chafed beneath all this trampling, had his turn again. We had foolishly brought the great dog Giudice, for our delight and the expansion of his mind. In Mr. Oxgall's shop he behaved to admiration. With the air of a connoisseur he walked from picture to picture, closed one eye, and faintly wagged his tail. Then he found a Scotch terrier scarcely worth a sniff, and a mastiff whom he saluted with a contemptuous growl. The only work of high art he could discover was an interior, with a flitch of bacon in the foreground uncommonly well drawn. Before this he sat down, and receiving no invitation, bedewed the boards with a stalactite from either side of his mouth. The dog was so well behaved, he never took anything without leave and saying t a long grace.

Unluckily Mr. Oxgall, mainly I believe to prolong his interview with Idols, insisted upon taking us to the shop of a carver and gilder close by; where my first drawing (which had been sold) was to be seen in its frame. He declared that we could not tell what a painting was like, until we had seen it framed. Observing several large mirrors in this shop, I begged that Giudice might be left outside. And so he was, but he did not stay there. Scarcely had we begun to discuss the effect of the frame on my drawing, when Giudice pushed his way in, and looked about with a truly judicial air. The shop was long, and the owner was with us at the further end. I saw what would follow, and dashed off to stop him, but it was too late. Giudice had seen the very finest dog he ever beheld in his life--a dog really worth fighting. Up went his crest and his tail, one savage growl, and he sprang at him. Crash,--and the largest mirror there was a wreck, and Giudice the rock beneath it. For a time he lay quite stunned; then to my great delight he staggered to me, not Isola, laid his cut paws in my hands and his bleeding nose in my lap, and explained it all to me with much entreaty for sympathy. This I gave him readily, even to tears and kisses. Isola wanted to scold and even to beat him, but I would not hear of it. He had seen another great dog between himself and us, how could he help attacking him? I ordered a sponge and some water at once, and bathed his fore paws, which were terribly cut; then remembering the Inspector, I sent Idols for some arnica. But the blood was not stanched by it as I expected; perhaps the drug was not pure, or the hair obstructed its action. So I held his paws in the basin, and he whinged, and licked me, and made my face all bloody.

Meanwhile the poor carver and gilder thought much more of his looking-glass than of noble flesh and blood. The picture-dealer as well was in a great predicament.

"Mr. Oxgall," I cried, still sponging the wounded dog's nose, "let us hear no more about it. Tell me the full value of the mirror, and I will pay for it. What are glass and quicksilver, or even gold, compared to a noble dog like this? Not worth a wag of your tail, are they, my duck of diamonds? Give me another kiss, you delicious pet of a dog."

The delicious dog was entirely of my opinion. His beautiful eyes were unhurt. His nose tasted wholesomely salt. But Isola was not half so romantic. Little she cared about money for herself; yet she had no idea of seeing a friend disburse. Empowered by nature to wind all men round her finger, she now called art to her aid, and Mr. Oxgall, who was half-way round already, had no chance of escape.

She settled it thus: the carver and gilder, in consideration of his dealings with Mr. Oxgall and his own "careless exposure" of the mirror, should accept cost price for the article. That amount should be paid in equal shares by all three of us: by Mr. Oxgall because he would drag us thither, by herself as the mistress of the dog, and by me as the cause of the expedition. She had attended a course of lectures upon jurisprudence, and her decision was better than that of a judge, because she had seen the whole of it, and because the dog was hers-- at least her brother's, which was all the same. As for the owner of the mirror, he must think himself wonderfully lucky in having met with such honest people, and in having sold his glass, and hadn't he got all the pieces, and she must have the largest one for Judy to dress his hair by. And so indeed she did.

After our dear Portia had finished, and the whole thing was settled, it struck me that no lectures upon jurisprudence could turn wrong into right. Mr. Oxgall was quite blameless, so was I, so was Idols, except in bringing unlucky Giudice with her, which, from the outset, I had discouraged. She, as the temporary owner of the dog, should have borne all the loss; and so she would have done gladly, only she did not see it in that light. As it was, she tried afterwards to force upon me her last three guineas (that being the sum which I had paid, as my third of the whole), but of course I would not accept them. She had no money with her, so I paid her contribution, but allowed her to repay me. Mr. Oxgall's third I made good to him (without consulting her) when he paid me for my next drawing. So I had earned five guineas, and lost six. Is it always to be so when I labour to make a little money?

At my earnest entreaty--Idols could refuse me nothing, when I was in earnest-- darling Giudice was brought home in a cab to my lodgings. I knew that he would not be cared for at the stables where he was boarded; and his wounds were very serious. As for home, Professor Ross, who detested dogs in general, would not admit him into the house. He even thought it a great stretch of grace to allow old Cora to watch the dog back to the stables, after he had been patrolling all the afternoon with his mistress. How I hate such low ingratitude! An animal is to serve us, body and soul, to crouch and fawn for our notice--not that Giudice ever fawned to him, but growled awfully--and we are to think it well off with a curse or a kick, which we durst not give it but for its loyalty to us.

What pleasure I had in nursing that poor Giudice, and how grateful he was! When we got home, I washed his wounds again, with warm water this time, as the bleeding was stanched; and then I "exhibited" (as the doctors absurdly say) a little friar's balsam. "Oh, it does smart so!" Giudice exclaimed with his eyes, "but I know it's for the best, and you won't see me give one wince." Neither did I. Then a nice soft bandage over his lovely paws, and a plaister across his nose, and he lies snugly, at the proper distance from the fire, as proud as possible of being nursed, and with an interesting air of pallid refinement on his features. He will hardly notice Idols, but exclaims, at length, with the petulance of an invalid, "Isola, can't you let me alone? Clara understands a dog, and I like her much the best." So he followed me all round the room with his eyes, and begged me to come and talk to him, which I would not do, because he needed quiet and composure.

CHAPTER XI.

Beloved Giudice remained many days under my care, until he became convinced that he was my dog absolutely, and had no claim on any other human being. He more than paid for his board and medical attendance, by sitting repeatedly for his portrait; in which at last I succeeded to his and my own satisfaction. Though by no means a conceited dog, there was nothing he loved better than having his likeness taken; and directly after breakfast he always assumed the most becoming attitude, and watched intently for the appearance of the pencil with his massive head a little on one side, and his dark brown eyes full of dignified interest, and his great ears curving down through russet tufts, like tawny cascades in autumn, he seemed fit study for a real artist, who should quicken as well as copy him. However, he was too much of a gentleman to sneer at my weak efforts, for he saw that I did my best. Oftentimes he would gaze steadfastly at the portrait and then at me, and hobble up, and nudge me, and whine, a little, and then sigh in self-abasement at his want of speech. Whenever he did this, I knew that he wished to have something altered; but it was long before I could discover what that something was. I tried every change of line or colour that I could think of--all to no purpose. At length it struck me that as he criticised more with nose than eyes, the defect must be in the smell. Happy idea! I satisfied my Giudice at last, and did it thus. After shading around the nose and mouth, before laying on the colour, I took a clean dry brush, and passed it lightly round the hollows of his own sweet saltish nostrils, carefully avoiding the cut; then one turn of the brush, not on the palette, but on a dry square of colour, and with that I expressed the dear dog's nose so well, that he would have spoiled it in a sniffing ecstasy, if I had not pulled it away. His portrait now possessed the life which he required.

Meanwhile I received almost daily visits from Isola and her brother; the latter was, of course, very anxious about his poor dog, and could only relieve that anxiety by long interviews with him. It happened strangely enough, yet more and more often as time went on, that Isola during these interviews felt an especial desire for Mrs. Shelfer's society, which she could only enjoy by betaking herself to the kitchen. There, with all the pets, except old Tom, who was constancy itself, and the lame blackbird who was all gratitude, her influence began to supersede mine, and even Mrs. Shelfer's; for this I cared but little, so long as Giudice kept to me.

Over that great dog, as he turned upon his side, and lifted one hind leg (the canine mode of showing submission to the will of God), over him we bent, Conrad and I, in most interesting diagnosis, until it seemed the proper thing that our hair should flow together, and our breath make one soft breeze. From this position we would rise with a conscious colour in our cheeks, and a flutter at the heart, and a certain awe of one another. Then it would be ever so long before either of us dared to seek the other's eyes. Haply when those eyes were met--unwitting yet inevitably--they would drop, or turn away, or find some new attraction in the dog or clouds.

Then some weak remark would follow, for which the hearer cared no whit, yet feigned deep interest therein.

Why labour thus to cheat ourselves--each other we cannot cheat--why feel we so confused and guilty, why long so heartily to be a hundred leagues away, yet knowing thoroughly that, if it were so, all the space between were void and heartache? The reason neither we nor other mortal knows; the cause is this, that we love one another.

I have felt that it must be so, at least on my part, ever since the day he came with Isola, and knew me not, though I knew him so well. Does he know me now as the Clara Vaughan whom he once avoided? These eyelashes are as long and dark as ever; the large eyes, shaded by them, are as deep a gray as twilight in a grove of willows. My cheeks have regained their curve, my hair was never injured; let me hie to the glass now he is gone, and see if I be like myself, and whether I have face and form likely to win Conrad's love.

No, I am not like myself. No wonder he does not know me. The gloom habitual to my face is gone. It is the difference betwixt a cavern well and a sunny fountain. I see a laughing graceful girl, with high birth marked in every vein, and self-respect in every motion; her clear cheeks glowing with soft wonder, her red lips parted with delight, her arching neck and shoulder curve gleaming through a night of tresses, her forehead calm and thoughtful still, half-belying the bright eyes where love and pleasure sparkle. For a moment self-approval heightens the expression. At my silly self my foolish self is smiling; but the smile has warmer source than maiden's light conceit. I smile because I see that, as regards exterior, he who slights me must be hard to please; and some one, whom I think of, is not hard to please. Straight upon the thought of him--Ah well.

My father used to quote from the "Hero and Leander" a beautiful verse, which neither he nor any other could in English render duly,

[Greek: *Aidoûs   hyròn   éreuphos   apostazousa   prosôpou.*]--v.   173. "Showering from her cheek the flowing carmine of her shame."

CHAPTER XII.

But when Conrad should have learned who it was that nursed his dog, would he feel the tender gratitude and delight which he now displayed so freely? Would he say, as in his fervour he now said every day, "Miss Valence, I do believe there is no one like you in the world!" Would he not rather say, "Miss Vaughan, how basely you have deceived me! Giudice, come away!" A whistle and the last sound of the foot, for which I listened now by the hour.

This thought was continually with me. It poisoned half the flavour and ruined all the digestion of my happy moments. But what could I do? How unmaidenly, how presumptuous of me to imagine that he was likely to break his heart for me! And if he did--why then he should break my own as well. I am not one of the drawing-room young ladies, who receive a modified proposal every Sunday afternoon, and think much more about the sermon afterwards. I cannot play with the daffodils upon the brink of love, sleepily thrusting my admirers in, and lounging with half-open breast, which neither love-knots may secure, nor fluttering sighs unzone. No, here I am, such as I am, such as God has made me. No usury, no auction for my heart: once for all I give it, and my life goes with it.

So it must always be with a girl of any feeling, who has trained her own existence. But for my wild ignorance, I would dare to say--so it must be always with a girl of feeling, twist and warp her as you will. Yet I am told, by those who know the world, that it is not so with nine girls out of ten among the lady caste. If, beneath the roc of fashion, they prefer the diamond to the meat, let them have it, and starve thereon. The choice is of their own young crops. No parent bird can force the bauble down. But what have I to do with this? All I know is that neither I, nor any child of mine, will or shall be gulleted thus for life.

After every little burst of thought, every feeble sally of imagination, came (as always is the case with me) came the slow pusillanimous reaction. All that I had any right to do was to paint, earn money, and be off for Italy.

Little as I knew about the expense of travelling, I felt sure that it would be vain to start with less than a hundred pounds. Enormous sum! How could I ever hope to win it, though I painted day and night, and lived on bread and water. To this diet, or what in London is quite synonymous, bread and milk, I had already reduced myself, in my stern resolve to lay by two pounds every week. Farewell to meat, so soon as my Devonshire "pegmate" was gone, and farewell to what I cared much more about, a glass of good London stout. I suppose there is something horribly "vulgar" in my tastes, for I will confess that the liquid called "black draught" by Mr. Dawe had much charm for me. However, I abjured it with all other luxuries, and throve no whit the worse. The kindly little woman, whose summum bonum (next to her "sticks") was plenty of good fare, took it much to heart that I should live so plainly.

"Why, Miss Valence, you are the queerest young lady as ever I set eyes on. All as ever I see, and I've see'd a many, they picks a little bit so dainty, like a canary cracking a hemp seed when the gentlemen is by: then off they goes when there's nobody looking, and munches like so many pigs in a potato bury. Miss Violante you know. But as for you, why bless me and keep me, you feeds that great horse of a dog with all the fat of the land, and you lives on a crust yourself. Now do come down, that's a good soul; there's a clod of beef a-biling with suet dumplings, and such lovely parsnips, you can smell it all up the stairs, galloping, galloping, my good friend, and that rogue of a Charley won't come home I know, he's got along with that thief Bob Ridley; and I expects the boy every minute with a little drop of stout, and the best pewter pot for you. Now if you won't come down, Miss Valence, my dinner will all stick in my throat, and I am so hungry."

"So am I, Mrs. Shelfer, you have made me so."

In her excitement, she slipped from the edge of the chair, whereon she always balanced herself when I made her sit down. She thought it disrespectful to occupy too much room, and cuddled herself in the smallest compass possible.

Let no ill be thought of Giudice. Who thinks ill of me I care not, for I can defend myself, if it be worth while. So can Giudice with his teeth--the finest set in London--but he has no tongue, no merop tongue, I mean. It was true that Giudice had good fare, and thoroughly he enjoyed it. That dog knew a juicy bit of meat, short of staple, crisp, yet melting, quite as well as I did. True, he had a love of bones, transparent gristle, and white fibres, which I, from inferior structure, cannot quite appreciate. Yet all this was no part of his mind, much less did it affect the greatness of his soul. He kept, as all of us do who are good for anything, a certain alter ego, a higher voice, a purer sense, a vein which fashion cannot leech, or false shame tourniquet. So the good dog used to come to me, before he touched his breakfast, lunch, or dinner, and entreat me to devour all I could, there would be lots still left for him.

In my hurry to get start of time, to spin a little faster the revolving moons, I did a thing which I could ill-approve to myself, even at the moment. I wrote to Sally Huxtable to obtain Mr. Dawe's permission for me to sell my gordit. Professor Ross had offered me no less than ten guineas for it. As a gentleman he should not have made the offer, after what I had told him. But the love of science--falsely so called by collectors--drives men to discern propriety "by the wire-drawn line of their longings."[#] However, I was not quite so blind upon right and wrong, as to mean to keep all the money. I offered Mr. Dawe half, if the plaything should be sold.

[#] "Exiguo fine libidinum."

I knew not why, but I could not bear the idea of a bargain and sale with Conrad's father, wide apart as the two always were in my mind. I rather hoped that Beany Dawe, though sorely tempted, would refuse.

And now the time was almost come for news from Tossil's Barton. Dear Sally must have filled the twelve copybooks, at the rate of one a week. Ere I quite expected it, the letter came; but before its tidings are imparted, I must in few words describe the visit of Inspector Cutting's son. George Cutting came one evening to see his good Aunt Patty, for so he called Mrs. Shelfer, who was in truth his cousin. Though I had been so assured that my enemy could not escape, I was not equally convinced, and at times a deep anxiety and despair possessed me.

Therefore I went to the kitchen to see the Inspector's son, and requested Mrs. Shelfer to allow me five minutes of conversation with him. He stood all the while, and seemed rather shy and confused. He had not heard from his father, since the ship sailed; but he had seen in the papers that she had been spoken somewhere. "The party as I knew of" was still safe in London--my blood ran like lava at the thought--or I should have heard of it. He, George Cutting, had his eye upon him, and so had two of the detective force; but what were they in comparison with his father? This he asked, despite his shyness, with so large a contempt, that I began to think the Cutting family admired the Cuttings only.

Upon me, who am no Cutting, he left the simple impression that the qualities, so lauded by his father, lay as yet beneath a bushel. However, his Aunt Patty declared that he could eat three times as much as Charley. Not unlikely, if he only drank one-third of Charley's allowance.

Mrs. Shelfer, who knew that I was laying by a fixed sum every week, began to look upon me as a fine young miser. Of course she quite fell in with what she supposed to be my ideas, for she never contradicted any one, unless it was a cabman.

"Oh, I do love money, my good friend; gold, gold, it is so bootiful. Did you ever hear tell of the marrow bone I had? Oh dear!"

"What marrow bone, Mrs. Shelfer?"

"Why a big beef marrow bone, that long, full of sovereigns and guineas after dear Miss Minto. I stopped it with a bung and a piece of bladder, and for better than a twelvemonth, while they was executing her will, I slept with that beneath my pillow for fear the priest should get it. Lord, how they did fight over the poor old lady's rags and bones, that leathery priest and three yellow kites of cousins, they said they was, as come from Portugal. At last they got a ministration[#] with the testament and text, and they robbed me shameful, shameful, my good friend. Never catch me going to mass again, or you may tell me of it."

[#] ? Letters of Administration cum testamento annexo.

"And what became of the marrow bone, Mrs. Shelfer?"

At this inquiry, she winked both eyes rapidly, and screwed up her little mouth.

"Oh what a thief that Father Banger was, to be sure! You see, Miss, I had strict orders to shut him out, when Miss Minto was near her end, because he had kicked her dear cat Filippina from the top of the stairs to the bottom, after he had gived her unction. What a pretty sight it was to see them seven dear cats, all sitting round the fire, each one on his proper stool with his name done on it in different coloured worsted. I had so much a year left me on the Bank of England, honourable to the day, for each one of those cats, and change of diet every week, and now there's only one of them left, and that is my dear old Tom."

"But, Mrs. Shelfer, about the marrow bone--"

"Well, my good friend, I was going to tell you. The way that Father Banger got into the house again to steal the poor old lady's money, for building a school or some such villany. He knowed how fond the poor soul was of cats, so he borrowed a cat somewhere, and he got two boys to let it down the area with a whipcord round its stomach, and to jerk, jerk, jerk away at it, and the poor thing did squeal sure enough. 'Pain, Patty,' says my poor mistress, and she could hardly speak--'Oh, Patty, there's some cruel Englishman torturing a cat again.' So out I runs into the area, and in pops Father Banger, who had his back to the wall, with a great sheet of paper; and he begins to make a list of all the things in the house. I took the cat to dear Miss Minto, and how pleased she was! 'Please God,' says she, 'to let me live a few days more till I make a Catholic of this poor heretic'--she always converted her cats the first thing--'and then it shall have a stool and a good annuity.' But next day the poor thing went."

Little Mrs. Shelfer had so great a fear of death, that like some ancient nations she shunned all mention of his name, by euphemistic periphrase. She had never known real illness, and even a stitch or a spasm would frighten her for days. When I spoke calmly, as I sometimes did, of our great inevitable friend, whom we so labour to estrange, up would jump Mrs. Shelfer with a shudder and a little scream.

"Oh don't, my good soul, oh don't! How can you? Let us live, Miss Valence, let us live while we can, and not think of such dreadful things. You make my blood run cold."

"But, Mrs. Shelfer, surely you know that we all must die."

"Of course, my good friend, of course. But then you needn't remind one of it. I met Doctor Franks to-day, and he said, 'Why, Mrs. Shelfer, I do declare, you look younger than ever,' and a very clever man he is, yes, yes; and not a gray hair in my head, and my father lived to eighty-eight."

"And how old are you, Mrs. Shelfer, now?"

"Oh I am sure I don't know, Miss Valence, I don't keep no account. Let us talk of something else. Did you hear what Tom did to your Judy to-day?"

Ah, poor little thing! But I am not going to moralise. Shall I ever know the history of that marrow bone?[#]

[#] I have now ascertained that a roving dog popped in and away with the marrow bone, sovereigns, guineas, and all.--C.V. 1864.

CHAPTER XIII.

Tossil's Barton, estimating the British Post by the standard of Joe Queen's boy, placed but little confidence in that institution. Moreover, Tossil's Barton held that a "papper scrawl," as it termed a letter, was certain to be lost for want of size, unless it were secured in something large, "something as a man can zee and hold on to," as the farmer himself expressed it.

Therefore I was not surprised at receiving, instead of a letter by post, a packet delivered by the parcels van. This packet was bound round like the handle of a whip. and stuck at either end with a mass of cobbler's wax. bearing the vivid impress of a mighty thumb. Within the wrappings first appeared an ominous crumpled scroll. Ye stars, where angels so buffooned by eminent painters dwell! Once more I behold Eli on the turnpike gate, the Great Western steamer, Job with a potsherd of willow-pattern plate, the Prodigal Son, and worse than all, that hideous Death and the Lady. Recklessly I tumble out all the rest of the packet. Three great bolts with silver clasps, three apostle spoons, two old silver salt-cellars marked W.H.J.H., a child's christening cup, a horn tobacco-stopper with a silver tip, an agate from the beach, a tortoise-shell knife with a silver blade, half a dozen coins and a bronze fibula found upon the farm, an infant's coral, a neck-pin garnished with a Bristol diamond, a number of mother-of-pearl buttons and blue beads, and a mass of mock jewelry bought by the farmer from the Cheapjacks at Barum fair with the produce of his wrestling triumphs. Separate from the rest, and packed most carefully, were all but two of the trinkets I had sent as Christmas gifts for the family.

Touched to the heart by all this loving kindness, I felt so ashamed of my paltry petulance at Eli, Jonah, and the rest, that I would not indulge in a peep at Sally's letter, which came last of all, until I had starved myself for a day. That literary effort showed so much improvement, both in writing and in spelling, that any critic would have endorsed Mr. Huxtable's conclusion that the gift must be in the family. A few words still there were of rather doubtful texture, but who can bind or bound the caprice and luxury of the English language? Moreover, Sally's stops were left once more to the discretion of the reader. But if Lord Byron could not grasp the mysteries of punctuation, how could Sally Huxtable? Yet that eager little maid would have learned in half an hour the art which might have mellowed the self-tormentor's howling. Sally's was a healthy, sweet, and wholesome nature.

Tossil's   Barton   Farm,   Trentisoe.
The tenth day of March A.D. 1851.

"DEAR MISS CLARA DEAR,--If you please, father and mother and me and our little Jack hope this letter will find you in good health as it leaves all of us at this present, or when it will be finished, thank God for the same, and hoping no offence. The baby as was born on the 20th day of October last is a very fine and lusty wench at this time of writing, and have got two teeth, and her hair coming again, and answers to the name of Clara, as you know Miss you was so kind to give her leave and liberty, and father call Clara to her now, and so do I and Jack, but mother will call her Babby still, and so the chillers does.

Father often say, "Babby! Why there be a hundred babbies in the world, and a thousand either, for ought I knows again it, but I reckon there isn't half a dozen Claras." But mother say she can't help it: she always did call them babbies till they was put into short-clothes, and longer too, if so be there wasn't another, and she feels a call on her to do it, and no offence Miss Clara for that same. If you please Miss, when the parson say "Name this child," and Aunt Muxworthy, from over to Rowley Mires, say, quite peart, "Clara, sir"--father had been learning her, you see Miss, all the morning--parson look, so mother say, the same as a skinned sheep all skivered out to dry; and Tim Badcock go haw haw, till father was forced to slip behind the godmothers and fetch him a little clout on the side of his head. Then parson say at last, "Clara maam! There be no child of that name to this side of Coom, and it seem to me to go again the rub rick." Father say the parson must be a high farmer, for none of us ever hear tell of that rick in this country. "Now take my advice and think better of it Mrs. Muxworthy," the parson say again. So she looks to father, for you see Miss she were not edified about it being right, because she could not find it in the Bible nowhere. And she say, "Think better of it farmer now; if you wants a handsome name, there's Tryphena and Tryphosa, and has been in the family afore." "Mother," says my father, and he looked the way he do when he don't intend to talk about a thing, "Mother, go home with the child, and I'll take her to Parracombe Church next Sunday: and tell Suke not to put the goose down."

You see, Miss, we was going to have a supper after church, and the best goose on the farm, and the parson was coming too. "Sober now," say the parson, "if so be now, farmer John, you have put your mind upon naming this here infant Clara, why I will christen her so, only an under Protestant, and with difference to the chapter." Father only say "Amen, so be it;" and then parson do it, and do it uncommon well too, father say. and she only laugh when they give her the splash. Father told us afterwards as he believed parson was feared he couldn't spell Clara fitty; but mother say he be wrong there, and all along of his pride, for parson be a college chap and so he can spell anything amost, in one way or another.

Miss Clara, all them beautiful things as you sent for us to Christmas time, with the forepart of all our names upon them, except Sally, was sunk in the bottom of the brook in the hole below the stickle by the hollow ash, where the big trout hath his hover, all along of Joe the Queen's boy; and we never knew ought about it till your after letter come. Then our little Jack, who be quite a big boy now, and button his own corduroys, go down to the brook at once, and pull off all his things, and there he rake and feel among the stones for the biggest part of a day, though the ice was on the edge but the water were quite clear; and Tabby Badcock want to pull off her things and go in too, but Jack would not let her, and be ashamed of herself, and I sat on the bank and Tabby, and Jack pull out nine beautiful things, as were meant for father, and mother, and him, and Billy, and little Honor, and Bobby, and Peggy, and the two weanies, but he couldn't find nothing as were meant for me Sally, unless Tabby stole it, and she be quite equal to it I am afeared: and we all returns you many many kind thanks and love, especially the ones as had it, and me. Our Jack say, No her wouldn't do it, he'll go bail for that, no fie! But I shake my head; though perhaps she never had the chance, if so be there wasn't none marked Sally, and thank you every bit the same, Miss, so long as there wasn't none for Tabby."

Poor little Sally! She must have cried bitterly to think of her being forgotten. But the best of all, next to the farmer's, was for her, and there was one for Tabby too.

"Miss Clara dear, the things was not hurt at all by being under water for a week, and father say they must be made of the very same gold as Queen Victoria's crown and sceptre is, as never can rust with the briny waves; and Beany Dawe feel cock sure as it was the fairy of the brook stole them from Joe's breeches pocket, and keep mine still he say because it be the prettiest. But there, he never know much, any more than Tabby does.

If you please Miss, asking your pardon, when Aunt Muxworthy were here, to the christening time, she said she never see such writing in her life as mine, and it wasn't my best copy neither, and she said it was a sin to make a scholar of a honest wench like that, and I should want to be the parson next, and read the forty-two generations and play the fort piano; and I didn't know, Miss, whether to laugh or cry, so I began to eat an apple; but father say quite slowly, "Sister Muxworthy, you was never gifted with no eddication no more nor I Jan Uxtable, and how be us to know if it be good or bad? Once I had a horse, say father, as afore ever he went into the field, turned up his nose at the grass like, and with turning up so much he died at last of the glanders. But I never see that there horse persuade the others to starve." Aunt Muxworthy toss her head, and we thought she wouldn't eat no goose, but the smell of the stuffing and the weather was too many for her; and she eat a wing, and a leg, and one side of the breast, and it do her good. And afore she had had much brandy, "John," she say, "you was right and I was wrong. Let the little wench crack on, and some day they'll hear of her to tother side of Hexmoor." So father laugh and kiss her, and the chillers was put to bed, and we drink your health Miss, and Clara's nine times nine, and father say he'll learn himself some day, when he give up wrestling, only he fear it would make his hand shake terrible, and then some laugh and some of us cry, and they has more hot water, and Beany Dawe set to, and make so many poems he turn the stairs somehow inside out, and Suke and Tim was forced to heave him into the tallat, and keep him from going abroad by a rope of onions round him and two truss of hay on the top. Next day, he make no poems at all till he drink more than a gallon of cider.

Oh Miss Clara dear, what ever is the matter with you? Father be in such a taking I never see. To-day your letter come about selling that knob-thing of Beany Dawe's, and we knows it must be all along of the crown jewels you bought for us, as we meant to keep in the family to the end of all our time. Mother double up, and cry into the churn, and spoil all the butter; and father were that upset he stamp out of the house a trying hard to whistle, and he couldn't see no one there to let it off on but Timothy Badcock, and he were a little saucy, so he toss Tim up on the linhay roof and his legs come through the thatch, and father was forced to ease him out with the pitchfork. Tim was stiff a bit in the evening, and serve him right say mother, for laughing so at the Cornishers; but father give him some neatsfoot oil and cider, and we knew us couldn't hurt him because he be double-jointed.

And if you please Miss Clara dear, we would not stoop to ask Beany Dawe and he nothing but a sawing poet; so father go to the old oak chest with the whitewash on it, and pull it open without the key, and take out some old rubbish he saith, and order mother to pack it without a word, and mother want to put in a pair of linen sheets and the best table-cloth, but father say quite crusty like, "Do e take our Miss Clara for a common packman?" And when I say, "Please father what shall I say about it all?" he answer me quite low, "How ever can I tell child? Ask your mother there. Only give my best respects and most humble duty, and tell Miss Clara I wishes I could find a man to throw me all four pins, for being such a drunken hosebird not to have more to send her. But I know her won't take money from the likes of us. Stop," father say, "ask her to please to lift our horn up as the horn of an unicorn. I knows where to go for lots of money and all to be had for asking. I'll go to Bodmin town next week," say father, "and show them Cornishers a trick of Abraham Cann. Since honest Abraham took the sprain, he left it all to me, though God knows, and thank him for the same, I never want it yet. I should like to see the Cornisher as could stand my grip." And then father pull both his hands out of his pockets. Mother say he wear them out he do spraddle both his thumbs so.

It seems a curious thing, Miss Clara dear, father never get vexed or weist like, but what he want to wrestle, and other times he never think of it, unless it be to fair or revel time.

When I asked mother and said as father tell me to, the tears was in her eyes, and she try to look angry with me, and then she broke out crying as loud as Suke when the cow Molly kick her. So between the both of them, Miss, I can't know what to say, so please to make it yourself Miss, for I am sure I can't find any thing only the best love of our hearts and a side of bacon us would like to send, and the butter from my own little cow, all sweet hay and no turmots; I be to sit in Coom market, all by myself, on Saturday, and mother not come nigh me, and I know you'll let me send you the money, and I expects elevenpence a pound, because you never was proud with your loving scholar ever to command and obey. SALLY HUXTABLE.

All this here underneath and over the leaf is going to be written after the rest of this here paper.

If you please Miss Clara dear, there come now just a very fine spoken gentleman with a long coat the colour of udder, and blue flaps, and blue at the hands, and ever so many great silver buttons with a print like pats of best butter, and gold ribbon round his hat. We seemed at first he be an officer of dragoons, till we see'd the flour in his hair, and then us knowed he was the Queen's miller. Father was a great mind to show him a forehip and send his buttons to you Miss, because he see they be worth ever so much more than these little things all put together, only mother stop him.

Then the gentleman say he know Mr. Henwood well, and respect him much, and he be sent here by expression to discover where you be Miss Clara, and it be most particular, and if we wished you well, us would tell him to once. Father and mother and me puts him in the parlour and gives him a jug of the very best cider, and then we goes and lays our heads together about him in the cheese-room, and mother and me was for telling him, only father say no. You never give us leave, and us wants to do what is right and upright, unless you order us contrary, and us has no right to tell without ask you, and you so full of enemies.

So father say, very grand for him: "Honoured sir, us hopes the honour of a papper scrawl from Miss Clara in ten days time, or may be a fortnight, according to the weather please God, and us be satisfied too. My eldest daughter here be writing to Miss Clara for a week or more, and if so be she have got room left on the papper scrawl she ask Miss Clara's leave, and us shall have time enough to hear what her say in a fortnight, or mebbe three weeks."

"Oh then, she be gone to Hitaly at the least." The gentleman say. Father never hear tell of Hitaly whether it be in London town or no, but he look to mother and me to hold our noise. The gentleman say something sound very much like "Dang," and father hoped he would be saucy, because then he send his buttons in spite of mother and me; but when he look at father he think better of it, and go off very civil in the carriage he come by, only say he would find out in spite of us.

And please Miss Clara dear, mother say she be ashamed to send you a parcel all rubbage, except the pictures, but she do hope they wont cheat you about them there, for they be the finest ever come to these parts, and warranted real London made. All the farmers hereaway want to buy them of us. And father say, "Dang the pictures, tell Miss Clara to come to us, and her shan't want Beany Dawe's things, nor the Queen's miller either." Oh do come, Miss Clara dear, the banks be yellow with primroses, and white and blue with violets, and I know three blackbirds nests already and an ousel's down by the river. Oh do come. I have got such a lot to tell you, things as I can't make head or tail of when I try to spell them, and you shall milk my own cow Sally, and have all my black hen's eggs, and the ducks too if they hatch,--and sling all the small potatoes from the plough field to the hazel hedge. Your best scholar as ever was and loving pupil.

SALLY HUXTABLE."

CHAPTER XIV.

From Sally's eager description of the coat and buttons, I concluded easily that a servant from Vaughan St. Mary had been sent in quest of me. My father hated showy liveries and loathed hair-powder, but Mr. Edgar Vaughan returned to the family usages, or rather allowed them to re-establish themselves; for on such questions he was wholly indifferent. Now what could be his motive for sending so expressly to discover me? I knew not, neither cared very greatly, but wrote at once to Tossil's Barton, first to return their loving contribution, which consisted mainly of ancestral relics prized for generations, secondly, to set free the secret of my address.

Into my own self I returned once more. Somehow I seem to expand whenever I come in contact with the yeoman's family, and their lowly greatness. I am like a worm when it rains, after the drought of summer. Surely the God, who leaves us to stifle ourselves with the dust of fashion and convention, has His own gracious times to breathe upon and scatter it. At intervals we may see through the reek of our own exuding, and inhale a more bracing air than sleeps in mausoleums. But instead of being exalted and fed by the open breeze, we shudder at the draught and replace our respirators.

I returned into myself, and found little comfort there. I do not live inside myself, as most people live in theirs. True, I am apt to resent any slight to it offered from the outside. True, I seek its keep and comfort in a mechanical sort of way. But as for crusting in its bottle, ripening in its husk, rusting in its watch-case, I have been too long the toy of wind and weather not to be turned inside out. Never can I moulder into the fungoid nucleus the British taste admires. And yet there is about me, if I must not say within me, a stanch cleaving, a cohesion, a concrete will, which is of genuine Anglo-Saxon fibre. So I thrust aside all dreams of Tossil's Barton and Vaughan Park, and certain wilder sweeter dreams which have begun to flutter and thrill through me, and in earnest I return to my task of money-making.

Giudice still is faithful, and comforts much my solitude. He has never asked his master's leave or mine, he has never received any formal invitation, yet here he looks all at home, sleek and unblushing, though long since quite convalescent and equal to livery stable diet. Once indeed, as we passed the entrance, he pretended to me that his conscience pricked him. To ease it, he sniffed about, and halted just for a moment, then turned his nose up, recocked his tail, and trotted jauntily on. Since then he has always avoided that left side of the street. He is affable still to Isola, but clearly regards her as no more than a pleasant acquaintance. Whenever she enters the room, he walks from his corner with a stretch and a yawn, sniffs all round her dress, to learn where she has been, and what dogs she has spoken to; then, in the absence of any striking discovery, he looks into her face with a grave complacence, and brings me his conclusion. Tom, and the birds, the squirrel, and the little marmoset (Mrs. Shelfer's newest and dearest pet), he gazes upon from a lofty standing as so many specimens of natural history, interesting so far, but otherwise contemptible. He is now allowed free run of the house, understands all the locks, and presents himself in every room at the proper meal-time. Even the little dress-maker is then honoured with his attentions. Everybody loves him, he is so gentle and clever and true. Back he comes to me, with his mouth rather greasy I must admit, gives me one kiss (as a form, I am afraid), and exclaiming, "Dear me! What a life this is!' sits down on his rug to think.

No one can tempt him further than the corner of our street, except his master or myself. Miss Flounce, with my permission, granted not without jealousy, once aspired to the escort of Giudice. Although she carried a bag of his favourite biscuits (made perhaps of bone-dust), and kept one of them in her hand, Judy flattered her only to the corner; then he turned abruptly, and trotted firmly (rudely she called it) home, with his eyes upon my balcony. I gave him more of his biscuits than he would have got from her.

All this was very delightful. But there were two sad drawbacks. In the first place, Giudice expected me to forego every other line of art, and devote all my time to portraiture of himself. This was unreasonable, and I could not do it. Apart from other considerations, Mr. Oxgall, after buying three studies of him, declined to take any more until those three should be sold. To Giudice himself I had based my refusal upon more delicate grounds. I had quoted to him,

"Although, lest I profane your hallowed part,

Queen Nature chills the blood around my heart;

Sweet dog, permit me to indulge my dream

Of country valleys, and the mazy stream."

But he took no heed, and never would permit me so to do, without the keenest jealousy.

The other drawback was still more serious. Either by maintaining the dog, I placed his owner under an obligation; or by engrossing the dog's society, I laid myself under obligation to his owner. Either view of the case was unpleasant; the latter, which I adopted, soon became intolerable. So I spoke about it to Isola, for I could not well explain myself to her brother, who ought indeed to have perceived my dilemma.

"Oh Donna," she cried, "what nonsense you do talk! Obliged to us indeed! I am sure we are all greatly obliged to you; and many a stir it saves us at home, for the dog detests papa so; and when Conrad comes to see us, he can't bear to have Judy shut out like a thief, and he the most honourable dog that ever wagged a tail."

"To be sure he is. You know you are, don't you, oh combination of Bayard and Aristides?"

That union of justice and chivalry wagged his tail to me, and nodded gravely to Isola.

"But I have said all along that Conny should pay for his board, and he feels it too: but we could not tell how to propose it to you, dear Donna, you are so very outrageous."

"I should hope so indeed."

"And then I am sure it would break poor Judy's heart to go. Wouldn't it now, Judy?"

Giudice did not answer her, but came and laid his great head on my lap, and looked up at me as only a dog can look. In that wistful look he said as plainly as possible--

"You know I am only a dog. But you, Clara, happen to be a human being; and so you know all we dogs know, and ever so much besides. Only you can't smell. You can talk, as fast as you like, both to each other and to us, but we can talk to none except our fellow dogs. Now don't take a mean advantage of me. I know that I was made only to be your servant, and I love you with all my heart, that I do. I can't tell at all where I shall go when I die, or if I shall go anywhere; and I am sure I shall die, if you cast me away like this."

So I kissed his dotty whiskers, and promised not to desert him, though I should go all the way to the stables twice a day to see him.

"And another thing, Clara dear," resumed his master's sister, "I consider him now more my dog than Conny's. You know he was given between us"--this was the first time I heard of it--"and I only lent Conrad my half as long as he liked to pay for him."

Lovely Isola, like most other lovely girls, was keen about money-matters. Not that she was ungenerous. That impulsive little mortal would give away all her substance, the moment her heart was touched, and it was not hard to touch, despite all the quick suspicions which her London life and native shrewdness had now begun to produce. But as regards small dealings, she was thoroughly qualified to keep a meat-pie shop, or go upon board wages, or even to take furnished lodging: by which climax I mean no disrespect to Mrs. Shelfer, who (considering her temptations) is the very pink of honesty, especially since Giudice can.

As to these small matters, and as to many large ones, I was dear Isola's cardinal opposite. She would make, for most men, a far better wife than I should; although she will never love with a tenth part of the intensity. She can't even hate like me. When I hate, I loathe and abhor. I never hate any one lightly, and hardly ever am reconciled, or suppress it. Isola talks about hating, but has never learned what it means. Spite she can carry, and nurse like a doll, and count it a minor virtue, albeit she cannot be sulky; hate is too heavy a burden. Scorn, which is with women the hate of things beneath them, Isola hardly knows. Perhaps she will learn it when her knowledge of the world narrows and condenses, as with most women it does.

Another great difference there is between Isola and me. Although she never would think of deceiving any one seriously, and would on no account tell a downright malicious lie, yet she is not so particular about telling little fibs, or at any rate colouring matters so highly that others are misled. This she can justify to herself in a charming warm-hearted way. And yet she rarely makes mischief. Her departures are half unconscious, and always arise from good will.

"And so now, Clara dear," concluded the senior sophist, "as Conrad has owned all the dog so long, it is my turn to own every bit of him for an equal period, and I must pay you half a crown a week for his keep, and half a guinea for doctoring him so well."

I was much inclined to take her at her word, it would have been such a surprise. But what a disgrace to Giudice and to me!

"Oh Donna," she continued, "you have no idea how fond dear Conny is of you. I am getting so jealous. He thinks much more of you than he does of me."

I bent over my drawing with more carmine on my cheeks than was on the palette. What folly to be sure! And Isola would come round in front.

"Why don't you answer me, Clara? Did you ever know such a shame? Well, I do believe you like being admired every bit as much as I do, in spite of all your sublimity. Why there comes Conny himself;" and to my great relief she stepped into the balcony. "I thought so. I knew the ring of his heel. He will wear such clumsy boots, though his foot is as pretty as mine. I always know his step, and so does Judy."

Alas! and so do I. How weak and paltry of me, with a life like mine before me!

"I will go and open the door," cries his sister; "how rude he is to come when you are so busy, Clara."

Away she runs, then ushers him grandly in, and away again to nurse the marmoset. I know that I look slightly discomposed. There is a glow upon me as if I had stepped into sunlight. Conrad fails to notice it, or conceals the perception. He stands before my easel. How I long for his approbation! That of course is only from his knowledge of art and his native taste. Yet I fear to look at his face, but wait for him to speak. With a stretch like a windlass, and a cavernous yawn, up comes Giudice, and pokes himself right in front of my work. Could I have foreseen that effrontery and execrable taste, less bread and milk would he have had for breakfast. Conrad perceives my vexation, and despite his good breeding is too natural not to smile. The smile is infectious, and I obtain no more than a look of commendation. But that is enough for me. I resolve to keep the drawing: Mr. Oxgall may bid what he likes.

As our eyes meet, Conrad's and mine, I see that he is not in his usual spirits. Something has happened to vex him. Oh that I dared to ask what it is. I also am heavy at heart, and ill at ease with myself. Is it any wonder? My nature is true and straight-forward as well as proud and passionate. But here have I been, for weeks and weeks, stooping below its level. I have even been deceitful. Perhaps there was no dishonour in my change of name, with such an object in view. Perhaps there was good excuse for maintaining disguise with Conrad, when first we met in London. But was it right and honourable to persist in my alias, when I could not help suspecting his growing attachment to me? Peradventure my conscience alone would not account for all the misery I felt about this. Had I no selfish misgivings as well? Now as I stood before him, my breast began to flutter with fear, not so acute, but deeper than my alarm in the dark, when I crouched from the conspirators.

"Miss Valence," at last he began, "I am grieved in my heart by hearing that you were not treated at all politely last night." He was greatly moved, and began to lose his command of colloquial English. I had spent an evening at the Professor's house in Lucas Street, the second time only of my being there. Now I came to recollect it, Dr. Ross had certainly been a little overbearing, but I did not feel hurt thereby, because I cared not for him, and knew it to be his manner. Isola had told her brother, but without meaning any harm. Her father no doubt had been vexed, because I could not sell him my gordit.

"Oh, Mr. Ross," I replied, "I think nothing at all of that. A learned man like your father cannot be expected to bear with every ignorant girl's curiosity."

"To a lady's love of knowledge every gentleman should administer and be gratified. All men of lofty science enjoy to meet with a gentle mind inquiring."

It was not the first time Master Conrad had disparaged, by implication, his father's great acquirements. To me it seemed scarcely graceful, and very far from dutiful, but many of my sentiments are dreadfully old-fashioned. An awkward pause ensued; how could I answer without condemning one or the other? Though I could not quite acquit Conrad, my heart was entirely with him, for I had long been aware that he was not happy at home. There he stood, with an angry countenance, having declined the chair I had offered him. Suddenly he took both my hands and looked me full in the face, though his eyes were glistening. I gazed full at him, with vague apprehensions rising. How or why, I know not, but at that very moment my hair, which is always a trouble to me, fell in a mass down my cheeks and neck. He started back, but still held my hands.

"I am made certain that I have seen you long ago. I will think, I will think."

I saw at once how it was, the fear on my face reminded him. I meant to tell him some day, but I never meant him to find out. Scorning myself for a hypocrite, I looked stedfastly at him and smiled.

"You will forgive me, Miss Valence, you know that I would not use a freedom."

He saw in my eyes that I knew it, and dropped my hands, and went on.

"You will think me the weakest in mind and most wicked, but I am most unhappy."

I started in turn, and how I longed to console him. What use is pride if it cannot even command one's eyes?

"It is to me a disgrace to come to you with my troubles. But I do it from no unmanly temper. I do it alone for the sake of my precious sister Isola. I have no longer any one whom I dare to love but her, and now I am compelled to abandon her at the last."

"Do you mean to be long away?" This I managed to ask pretty well, though it was sore work.

"I shall not be away from London, but I shall be departed from Isola. The house where she lives I am no more to visit. A long time I have gone there only a little, and alone to see her. She is ordered now to come no more to me. This day I spoke very violently. But I will not detain you with that. I will confess I did wrong; but I was richly provoked. My object in burdening you is double:--First to implore you, if I may without using liberty, to endure well with the Professor, lest she should be interdicted from coming to visit you, and then she would have no one remaining to love her. Second to ask, a thing that I hesitate because I cannot narrate to you all things, whether you would indulge me, if there is no wrong, to come now and then to see my own and my only sister."

"Of course you do not mean without her father's knowledge."

"I would never insult you, Miss Valence, by asking a thing like that. I desire nothing of what you call clandestine. You are so free and open, you would never have to do with any sort of concealment. Neither am I in the habit to do anything like that. It has only been commanded that I may not go there, or invite her to come to my house. The Professor has great power in the present, but he does not pretend to interdict me from my sister."

His eyes flashed, as he spoke, with an expression quite unfilial. Remembering how differently I had loved my own dear father, I felt disappointed and grieved, but had no right to show it.

"Only one more thing I will entreat of you, Miss Valence; poor Isola has never learned what means any grief. If she is vexed by this, I pray you to sustain and comfort her; for I shall never make a wrong advantage of your most kind permission, so as to see her very often."

He raised my hand to his lips in gratitude for what he called a kindness beyond all value to him, and his voice was trembling as he turned away. But I had done no kindness, I had given no permission; for I was not calm enough to distinguish right from wrong. Strange indeed it seemed to me that I, for the most part so decided, could not now determine, but was all perplexity. My great iceberg self-reliance, built in bleak and lonesome years, was now adrift and melting in the bright sun of friendship and the warm sea-depths of love.

CHAPTER XV.

Isola happened that day to leave me before the usual time, being afraid that her father, who was not in his sweetest mood, would be angry with her. She was grieved of course at the new dissension, and thought me (her ideas were of loose texture) somewhat to blame somehow. Nevertheless she soon forgave me the crime I had not committed.

That day I could paint no more, but sat me down to meditate. Suddenly a loud ring and a louder knock echoed through the house. Quickly Mrs. Shelfer's little feet came pattering up the stairs, and her grey eyes actually seemed to come in first at the door. On the crown of her head her black cap hung, like the top of a chaise doubled back.

"Oh my good friend, look here! I was never so frightened in all my life."

She held as far from her as she could reach a closed envelope, addressed "Miss Clara Vaughan." I tore it open and read--"Mr. Vaughan is dying, come instantly. Sent by Mrs. Fletcher."

"Telegraph, my good soul," cried Mrs. Shelfer, "Electric Telegraph Company, all screams the wires red hot, and you must sign the message he says. And is there any answer? And they give him eighteen pence. Oh dear, I shall never get over it. Never had such a turn since my brother John went, and they tucked him up so bootiful, and I said to the clerk at Barbican--"

"Out of my way if you please. Let me sign the form, and leave me alone a minute. There is no answer."

Should I go or not? Bitterly as I disliked him, could I let him die among hirelings and strangers--I, his brother's daughter! A year ago I would have done so and thought it the judgment of God. Now I remembered my dear mother's death, and doubted about going only because I knew not how he would take it. My hesitation was very brief. A cab was ordered, Giudice entrusted to Mrs. Shelfer's care, a short note left for Isola, a few things put together anyhow, and I was ready to start.

Even in this hurry a selfish terror smote me, and I cautioned Mrs. Shelfer strictly to conceal both name and destination. She had only to say that some relative was suddenly taken ill, somewhere down in the country; the country being to her mind a desert marked with milestones, my description did not seem unreasonably vague.

As I stood in the passage waiting for the cab, the poor dog, who had been quite flurried, and scented indefinite evil, commenced, prolonged, and would not conclude a howl of passing sadness.

"Oh, my good friend," cried Mrs. Shelfer, "let me stop the cab. All waste of money to go. The good gentleman, whoever he is, is as dead as a crabshell now. There was a terrier with a split ear, next door but one, when my poor brother John was ill; his name was Jack, I think, no, Tom; bless me, no, what am I thinking of, Bob--Charley knows, I dare say--"

"Well, send me his name by telegraph. Here's the cab, Mrs. Shelfer."

Heavy thumps of weary wambling feet, grating of wheels, a needless "whoa," and we open the door.

Giudice bolts first into the cab, and sitting upright with his tongue out and a sprightly pant, occupies the whole. It takes the united strength, address, and authority of cabman, landlady, and myself to get him out again. Then he coils his tail to his stomach, droops his ears and eyes, and receiving two hot tears and a kiss is sidled and deluded into the narrow passage. The last thing I hear is a howl that winds far round the corner and beyond the square.

In an hour and a half from the delivery of the message, I was in a second-class carriage, and we shrieked away from Paddington. The hurry and rush overcame me for a while. Soon the April evening was spread with shadowy gray, and we were rushing past the wooded waves of Pangbourne, and casting silver rings of steam on the many-fingered spruce, before I could collect and feel my thoughts again. As we glided through plantations and between the winding hills, with the partridge beginning his twilight call, the pheasants come out of the coppice to feed, and the late rook plying his dusky wings, at length the dust and city turmoil lagged round the corner miles away, and we sparkled in the dewy freshness of the silent moon. Though all alone in the carriage, I vainly tried for prudence' sake to creep into the cloak of sleep. Every vein and every pore was full of gushing thrilling electric life. The country, the country! the heavenly country's glory! how had I breathed and groped in the city grave so long? For every thought that dribbled there and guttered in my brain, a hundred thousand now flow through me, not of brain, but soul. Thoughts I cannot call them, for there is no volition, neither have they sequence, impress, or seen image: only a broad stream gliding, whence and whither I know not. How can I describe to others what I cannot tell myself?

"Glost'! Glost'! change here for Chelt'm!" &c. broke my dreaming suddenly. It was eleven at night. I had come unwrapped; the heavenly country and nature's tide forgot to keep me warm. Out I came upon the platform, and dreamily began to seek my carpet-bag, for I had no heavy luggage. The moon was struggling with the gas-lights, as nature in me fought with modern life.

"Fly, Miss, fly?" the lonely porter asked.

"Yes, please," said I.

"Where for, Miss?"

"Vaughan St. Mary."--At this part of my life, I dropped the grand "Vaughan Park;" it seemed too fine for me, and I was well content to be of Conrad's class in the world.

"Oh, there's a carriage waiting at every train, if you please, Miss."

And with tenfold politeness the porter showed me across the square to one of the family hearses, which my father and I so detested. It so happened that the driver and footman were taking some light refreshment at the bar of a neighbouring edifice, while the horses champed their bits and whinnied. The men came out against their will, and stared at me in the broad moonshine. I was very simply, plainly, and cheaply dressed, in deep mourning still for my darling mother; but no servant of even slight experience could take me, I think, for anything but a lady; little as it matters. The men were half-drunk, very surly at being disturbed, and inclined to form a low estimate of my dress and carpet-bag.

"You mean to say you be Miss Vaughan, young 'ooman?" stuttered the reeling coachman, with his hands beneath his flaps and a short pipe in his mouth, "Now I tell you plainly, there's no mistake about me mind, I can't noway credit it. It don't seem likely, do it, Bob?"

"Likely, Jacob? Yes, like enough to a fool; but nohow creditable to the like of us. Think I don't know now? Perhaps the young 'ooman will answer a few questions, Jacob."

"Ah, let you alone; let you alone, Bob! Specially for young women!"

"Porter, a cab at once, if you please; or a fly I think you call it here." Oh my London impudence!

"To be sure, Miss; the best in Gloucester directly. And, Miss"--confidentially, "if I was in your shoes, I'd walk them chaps about their business to-morrow. How they have been carrying on here, to be sure, ever since the six o'clock train come in. Why, in the time of the old Squire Vaughan--"

"Thank you, the fly, if you please."

In two minutes I was off for my father's home with mighty rattle of glass, and many jerking noises. About three miles from Gloucester we were passed by Jacob and Robert, who were sitting side by side and driving furiously. Convinced at last by the porter of my genuine Vaughanship, they had set off full speed to secure first audience.

At length we passed the lodge, where the gates creaked as of yore, and dear old Whitehead trembled at my voice, and so along the great avenue where I had studied the manners and ways of every tree, and where Tulip (Nestor among deer) came to stare at us with his grey face silver in the moonlight. Poor old friend, he knew me as well as Giudice did, but I could not stop to talk to him. Soon as the bell was rung the broad bolt of the great lock, which I was once so proud to draw, flew back with suspicious promptitude.

Albeit he had changed the cloth too ochrously described by Sally, for a suit of gentle gray, and had drawn out his face to a most unjovial length, and assumed an attitude of very profound respect, there he was, quite unmistakeable to observant eyes, the Bacchanalian Bob.

"And please, Miss"--after he had fussed awhile--"what train did you please to come by? I understand that the carriage has been waiting there all day; indeed, I saw it come back from the pantry window myself, and they said in the yard the last train was in afore they come away."

"I came by the train that ought to be there at half-past ten o'clock."

"Well to be sure! That must be the very train as Samuel and Humphry said they waited for; but they never has much judgment, them two men. And to let you come in a common fly, Miss!"

"I saw my father's carriage at the station, and two low-looking servants quite tipsy. Their names, however, were not Samuel and Humphry, but Jacob and Robert."

Strange servants now came thronging round, with an obsequiousness so long unknown that it quite disgusted me. No familiar face among them, none whom I could bring myself to ask how my guardian was. But from their servility to me I concluded that his time was short.

"Will you step into the small drawing-room, if you be so kind, Miss? There is a good fire there, Miss, and a lady waiting for you."

"Thank you. Take my things to my own little room, if you please; that is, if you know which room was called mine."

"Tilly knows, Miss. I'll run and fetch Tilly," cried the officious Bob.

"If Matilda Jenkins is still here, let her answer my bell as long as I remain."

And therewith I was shown into the room where the lady was expecting me. She sat with her back to the door, and I could only see that she was richly attired in full evening dress. There was a powerful smell of vinegar in the room, and two pastiles were burning. As I walked round the table she rose with some reluctance, and I confronted Mrs. Daldy.

CHAPTER XVI.

We stood for a moment, examining each other. She was fattening nicely on what she called "holy converse and spiritual outpourings at Cheltenham." She rushed forward with great enthusiasm.

"Why, Clara, darling, is it possible? Can this be you--so grown, and improved in every way? I never should have known you, I do declare! Why, you have quite a brilliant colour, and your eyes, and your hair--oh dear, how proud your sweet mother would have been! You lovely creature, I must have a kiss! What, not even your pretty hand?"

"No, Mrs. Daldy; never more my hand to a person who dared to insult my father. Me you might have insulted a thousand times, and I would have forgiven you."

"Come now, let bygones be bygones, that's a dear. Oh for a little more of the essence of Christianity! Let us stoop to the hem of the garment of the meek and lowly"--I will not write the sacred name she used--"let us poor grovelling fellow-sinners--"

"Don't couple me with yourself, I beg." I was losing my temper, and she saw her advantage.

"Not even as a sinner, dear? I thought in my humility that we all were sinners."

"So we are; but not all hypocrites."

She kept her temper wonderfully, in all except her eyes.

"Ah, you impetuous young people cannot understand the chastened lowly heart, which nothing but heavy trials and the grace of God produce. You know, Clara, you never could."

This last truth was put in the form of an exclamation, and in such a different tone from the rest, moreover it was so true, that I could hardly help smiling.

"Since last I saw you, I have been tried severely and chastised most heavily. I bow to the rod. All works together for our spiritual good. Until that blessed day, when all the sheaves--"

"Mrs. Daldy, I as well have seen and suffered much since last we met. If I could not be hoodwinked then by this sham religion, is it likely that I can be now? I wonder that you waste your time so."

The truth was that she talked in this strain less from hope than habit.

"Then if I must treat you, Miss Vaughan, but as a sister worldling, let us at least combine, for Providence has seen fit to make our interests the same."

"How so?" I was doing my utmost to bear with her awhile.

"First, before I tell you anything, have you as keen an eye for the perception of your own sweet interest as for the discovery of what you kindly call 'hypocrisy?' Ah well, it is all for my good."

Her rolling compendious eyes glistened at the thought that she was about to catch me here. I pretended to be caught already.

"What of it, if I have?"

"Then I will tell you something. Sit down by me, Clara."

"Thank you, I will stand."

"Now first, before I tell you anything, we must make some little arrangement for our mutual benefit, and then resolve upon united action. You must give me one little pledge. That being done I will tell you everything, and it is of the last importance to you."

"Is it about my father?'

"No. It has nothing to do with him; it is about your uncle, who now lies at the door of death. All, it is all for the best. There is, I fear, no chance of his recovery, and the disposal of this splendid property is in our hands, if we know how to play our cards, and if we act together. But there is no time to be lost. Only think, 15,000*l.* a year, for it is now worth every farthing of that, besides this beautiful place. Why, Clara, all the pleasures of life will be at our feet!"

In her greedy excitement, she forgot all her piety; but I liked her better so. In a moment she saw that she had laid her wicked heart too open. In my eyes there was no co-partner flash of avarice.

"What is the matter with my poor uncle?"

"First a paralytic stroke; since that low gastric fever, and entire prostration. Do you remember when you came to your dear mother's funeral?"

"Of course, I do."

"And could you help observing how altered he was even then? The hour he heard of her death, he was seized with violent illness, yet he would go out of doors alone, on the very day of the funeral. Something then excited him; he came home worse, and in the night was visited with a slight paralytic stroke. However, he quite recovered the use of his limbs for a time, though never his former spirits--if we can call them spirits. For several months he went about as usual, except that instead of a horse he rode a quiet pony. He saw to the property, received the Michaelmas rents, and invested large sums of money both in land and the funds; he even commenced some great improvements, for he has always been, as you know, a most skilful and liberal steward and manager."

"That I never denied. There could not be a better one."

"But suddenly, after no Christmas festivities (for he would hear of none, for the sake of your dear mother), he was found on the morning of the last day in the year bolt upright in his study chair, and fully dressed, with two pistols, loaded and cocked, on the table, no sign of life in his face or pulse, his body stiff yet limp, like a sand-bag tightly stuffed. The man who found him described it better than I can. 'Poor master, whichever way I put him, there he stop, like a French dog doing tricks."

"How terrible!"

"Yes, but it was true. At first they thought it was catalepsy only; but when that passed off, paralysis remained. I wanted to send for you at once."

Here she met, for she could not help it, but did not answer, my gaze; and I knew it was a lie.

"However, I was over-ruled; and your poor uncle lay bed-ridden, but in no actual danger, until this horrid low fever came. He must have a frame of iron to have borne up as he has. The doctor says this fever is partly from the prostration of the nerves."

"Who is the doctor?" I felt almost as if I could love my uncle.

"A very eminent man. His name is Churchyard."

"That is not our old medical man. Where does this gentleman come from?"

"Cheltenham, I believe."

"Surely, you must know that, if he is an eminent man; living there yourself!"

I saw that she had brought him.

"Well," she answered sharply, "it matters little where he comes from, and I have not verified his residence. I fear all the doctors in Europe could not save your poor dear uncle." And here (from habit when death was thought of) she fell into the hypocritical vein once more--"Ah, how true it is! The thing that will most avail him now, when his poor sinful frame is perishing, and the old man with all its works--"

"Thank you. I know all that. Which room does my uncle occupy?"

"Surely, you never would think of disturbing him at midnight!"

"Does death look what o'clock it is? If he is really dying, I must see him at once."

She seemed resolved to prevent me. I was determined to do it. It is needless to tell all her stratagems, and needless to say (unless I have failed to depict myself) that they proved utterly vain. I was only surprised that she did not come with me.

CHAPTER XVII.

How vast the rooms appeared to me, how endless the main passages, after the dimensions long familiar at Tossil's Barton, and Mrs. Shelfer's. I even feared to lose the way, where my childish feet had measured every step. First I hurried to my own snug room, or rooms--for I had parlour and bedroom adjoining--in the western wing, where mother used to live. Everything there was in beautiful order, a lamp and a good fire lighted; and Matilda Jenkins met me at the door.

Directly after our departure for Devonshire, Mr. Vaughan had thought fit to discharge all the old servants, except the housekeeper and Matilda. They were all in league against him, for they could not bear that the "rightful owners," whom they had known so long, should be ejected. Moreover, his discipline was far more stern than ours; for my father and mother had always ruled by love. The housekeeper, a great friend of mine, was retained from respect and policy, and poor Tilly (who entered life through a dust-bin) from contempt of her insignificance. By that time she had risen to the rank of scullery-maid and deputy dishwasher; now she had climbed in the social scale to the position of under-housemaid.

"Why, Matilda, how well you look, and how smart! I declare you are getting quite tall. I suppose the new times agree with you better than the old."

"Oh don't say that, Miss Clara, please don't! I'd tear the gownd off my back"-- looking savagely at the neat print--"if I thought it make you think that. No, I gets a little more wages, but a deal more work, and I never gets a kind word. Oh it does my heart good to see you here again, in your own house, Miss Clara dear, and evil to them as drove you out"--and she lifted the corner of her new white muslin apron;--"and I have tended your rooms all myself, though it wasn't in my part, and never let no one else touch them, ever since I was took from the kitchen, and always a jug full of flowers, Miss, because you was so fond of them."

"Thank you, Matilda. How kind of you, to be sure!"

"Many's the time I've cried over them, Miss, and the new shilling you give me, when we was little girls together. But please to call me 'Tilly,' Miss, the same as you always used."

"I can't stop to talk to you now, Tilly; how is Mrs. Fletcher?"

"Quite hearty, Miss, all but the rheumatics. Ah, she do suffer terrible from them. Us both waited up, Miss, and I to and fro the door, till the carriage come home; and then she went off to bed, and I was up with her, and never knowed when you come. But she's getting up now, Miss, to come here to see you."

"Go and stop her, at once. I will see her to-morrow. Stop, show me first your master's room; knock gently and bring out the nurse. The doctor is gone I believe."

"Yes, Miss, he left here at eight o'clock, for he had a long way to drive, and he couldn't do nothing more. But you must not go, Miss, oh pray, Miss, don't go there!"

We went along the passage, until we came to the door. I was surprised to see a new door across the lobby, very closely fitted. There was an inner door also, and the nurse did not seem very wakeful. Instead of knocking again, Matilda retreated hastily. At last the nurse appeared, and I found her to be a very respectable woman, who had been with my mother, through several attacks of illness. A dark suspicion, which I had scarcely confessed to myself, was partly allayed hereby. After whispering for a few moments, she led me into the dimly lighted room, and to my uncle's bed.

I started back in terror. Prepared as I was for a very great change, what I saw astounded me. The face so drawn and warped aside, withered and yet pulpy, with an undercast of blue; the lines of the mouth so trenched and livid, that the screwed lips were like a bull's-eye in a blue diamond pane; and the hair, so dark and curly when last I saw him, now shredded in patches of waxy gray. The only sign of life I saw, was a feeble twitching of the bed-clothes, every now and then. The poor eyes were closed, hard, and wrinkled round; one wasted arm lay on the quilt, the hand bent up at the wrist, the fingers clutched yet flabby, and as cold as death. It was a sight for human pride to cower at, and be quelled.

"Is he like this always?"

"No," she replied, "but he has been so now for ten hours and more: generally he is taken with pain and thirst, every six hours; and it makes my heart ache to hear him moan and cry."

"Does he say anything particular then?"

God knows I was not pursuing my own fell purpose in asking this. Thank Him, I was not such a fiend as that. All I wished was to relieve him whom I pitied so.

"Yes, he opens his eyes and stares, and then he always says, and he tries to shake his head only he isn't strong enough, 'My fault, ah me, my fault, and to rob them too! If I could but see her, if I could but see her, and die!' He always says that first, and then that exhausts him so, he can hardly say 'water' after, and then he moans so melancholy, and then he goes off again."

The tears stood in her eyes, for she had a tender heart. I burst into my usual violent flood, for I never have any half-crying.

"Have you any medicine to give him?"

"No, Miss, no more; he has taken a shopful already, though he can only swallow at the time he wakes up. The doctor said to-night he could do no more; this awful black fever must end in mortification; no medicine moves it at all."

"Did the doctor call it black fever?"

"Yes, the very worst form of typhus of the real Irish type, such as they have had once or twice in Manchester. It has settled most on the stomach, but all the blood is poisoned."

And she sprinkled herself, and the bed again, with disinfecting fluid, and threw some over me.

"Excuse me, Miss, you wouldn't allow me, so I am bound not to ask you. You know you came in dead against my will, and dead against all orders"--this was what the whispering had been about--"and if anything happens to you, Miss Vaughan, who is to have all the property, but that bad Mrs. Daldy?"

Oh! In a moment I saw the whole; though it was too black for belief, blacker than any fever that festers the human heart. This was the purpose with which that woman had sent for me. She had lied to me as to the character of the disease. She had opposed me, because she knew it the surest way to urge me. She had brought me too at night, when fevers are doubly infectious.

"You see, Miss, we are forced to keep the three windows open, and the passage doors all closed. It's a wonder I had any of the fluid left, for they never sent it up this afternoon; but I had a drop put by, no thanks to them for the same. Mrs. Daldy brought the first nurse, but she ran clean away when the fever took the turn; and they were forced to send for me, for nobody else would come near him. But my poor old man has no work, and I've minded as bad a case as this, and they say I be fever-proof. But you, Miss, you; I should never forgive myself, if anything happened to you, and in your youth and bloom. Though I could not stop you, you know I did my best. And they say you catch things most when you come off a journey."

"Jane, whatever happens, you are not to blame. I have no fear whatever; and now I am here, I will stay. It is safer so, both for myself and others."

"Well, Miss, so I have heard say. Once in for it, keep to the air. But come into this little room, if you want to talk to me, Miss. We can hear the poor gentleman move, or even sigh; and the air is a little fresher there. But we must keep the window open."

She led me into the dressing room; but even there the same crawling creeping smell pervaded, as if a grave had been opened, when the ground was full of gas. Instead of talking to the nurse, I began to think. It broke upon me vaguely, that I had heard of some very simple remedy for a fever of this nature, and that my dear mother, who in her prosperous times was the village doctoress, had been acquainted with the case. But in the whirl of my brain, I could not bring to mind what it was. Oh what would I give, only to think of it now! Though not, I am sorry to say, at all of a pious turn (at least if Mrs. Daldy is so), in the strong feeling of the moment, I fell upon my knees, and prayed for help. So had my mother taught me, and Mother Nature taught me now. I will not be so daring as to say that my prayer was answered. Perhaps it was only that it calmed my mind.

"Jane, have they been brewing lately?" Alas the bathos! But I can't help it.

"Yes, Miss; last Thursday and Friday. They won't let me go near the kitchen part: but I know it all the same."

"Go and get me a nice jug of fresh yeast. I will watch your master."

She stared, and hesitated; but saw that I was in earnest.

"I don't know where to find it, Miss; and none of them will come near me; and they'll stop me too if they can. Why they won't bring my food to the door, but put it half-way down the passage. They wanted to lock me in, only I wouldn't stand that; and they break all the plates and dishes, and to-day they sent word that my dinner must come in at the window to-morrow."

"Low cowards and zanies! Now find the yeast, Jane, if you have to search for an hour. They must all be gone to bed now, except Matilda Jenkins; and she dare not stop you if you say you have my orders."

"Bless you, Miss; she'll run away as if I was a ghost."

"Then call to her, that I say she must go to bed directly."

After a few more words, Jane went her way stealthily, like a thorough-bred thief; and I was left alone with my poor dying uncle. Wonderful as it seemed to me, I felt now a tender affection for him, I the resolute, the consistent, the bitter Clara Vaughan. Even if he had told me that moment, that he had plotted my father's death, I would have perilled my life for his; because I should have known that he was sorry. Yet I was full of cold fear, lest he should awake to consciousness, and utter that awful cry, while I alone was with him, in the dead hour of night.

Sooner than I expected, the nurse came back with a jug of beautiful yeast, smelling as fresh as daybreak. We put it outside the window on the stone sill, to keep it cool and airy. She had seen no one except Matilda, who was waiting for me, and crying dreadfully, predicting my certain death, and her own too; if she should have to attend me. She kept at a most respectful distance from Jane; and, with all her affection, was glad to be clear of me for the night.

For nearly two hours, the nurse and I sat watching, with hardly a spoken word, except that I asked one question.

"How often has Mrs. Daldy been to see my uncle?"

"She would hardly leave his bedside, until the fever declared itself. Since then she has not been once."

Broad awake at that strange hour, and in that strange way, I began to pass through the stereoscope of my brain the many strange slides of my life. Of all of these, the last for the moment seemed the strangest. Suddenly we heard a low feeble moan. Running into the bedroom, there we saw the poor sick one with his eyes wide open, vainly attempting to rise. I put my arms around him, and raised him on the pillow. He tried to say 'thank you,' for he was always a gentleman in his manners; then he gazed at me with hazily wondering eyes. Then he opened his mouth in a spasmodic way, and began that bitter cry.

Ere he closed his mouth again, I poured well into his throat a table-spoonful of yeast, handed to me by Jane. To my great pleasure, it glided beyond the black tongue; and I gave him two more spoonfuls, while he was staring at me with a weak and rigid amazement.

"No water, Jane, not a drop of water! It will work far better alone. He doesn't know what it is, and he thinks he has had his water. Keep him thirsty that he may take more."

As he lay thus in my arms, I felt that one side was icily cold, and the other fiery hot. His face looked most ghastly and livid, but there was not that mystical gray upon it, like the earth-shine on the moon, which shows when the face of man is death's mirror, and the knee of death on man's heart. In a minute he slid from my grasp, down on the pillow again, and, with a long-drawn sigh, became once more stiff and insensible. My hope was faint indeed, but still it was hope: if he had hope's vitality, he might yet be saved.

The rest of that night was passed by the nurse and myself in heavy yet broken sleep. Jane assured me that there was no chance of my poor uncle becoming conscious again, for at least six hours. I was loth to forego my watch, and argued that the dose we had given might cut short this interval; but lo--while I kept repeating at weary and weary periods, that I could do no harm, since the physician gave up, and I might do good--sleep, the lover of repetition, laid his hand alike on my formula and myself. Dear Judy's howl was in my dream, and Mrs. Shelfer's never ceasing prattle.

CHAPTER XVIII.

Cold and fresh was the morning air, and the open window invited the sounds of country life. Who could think of fever with the bright dew sparkling on the lawn, the lilac buds growing fat enough to claim their right of shadow, the pleasant ring of the sharpening scythe, and the swishing sweep of the swathe? From the stable-yard, round the corner, came the soothing hiss of the grooms, the short stamp of the lively steed (I fancied I knew my own favourite "Lilla"), and the gruff "Stand still, mare, wull'e?" Far down the avenue whistled the cowboy, waddle-footed, on his way to the clover leys, or the milkmaid sung with the pail on her hip, and the deer came trooping and stooping their horns along. Was it not one of my own pet robins, who hopped on the window-sill, peered bravely at himself in the jug, and tried to remember the last of his winter notes?

But it is cold, Jane, very cold indeed; and we have never been to bed; and now the mowers have descried us, why do they stop their work, and shake their heads together so, and keep outside the ranunculus bed, and agree that the grass beneath our windows does not require cutting? Why, if they were Papists, they would cross themselves, and that saves many an oath. But the grass does want cutting, Jane. It cannot have been cut for a week. I will call to them. No, it might disturb my uncle.

There is no sound from the bed-room yet: all deep and deadly silence. I will go and see.

There my patient lies, just as when I saw him first, except that I have arranged the wreck of his hoary locks, and applied a lotion to his temple on the burning side. And yet, now I look closer, the face is not quite so livid; or is it the difference between the candle-light and the morning ray?

Even while I looked, he started up, as if my eyes revived him. He did not moan or cry; but opened wide his filmy eyes, and gazed feebly and placidly at me. For a time he did not know me: then a great change gradually crept through his long faltering gaze. Fearing the effects of excitement upon him, I tried to divert his attention by another good dose of yeast. Three times he took it with resignation like a well-trained child, but his eyes all the time intent on me. Presently they began to swim and swerve; the effort of the faint blood-tissued brain and the exertion of swallowing had been too much for his shattered powers. He fell off again into the comatose state, but with a palpable difference. The pulse, which had throbbed on the hot side only, could now be felt most feebly moving in the other wrist, and the tension of the muscles was relaxed: circulation was being restored and balanced, and the breathing could now be traced, short as it was and irregular.

I have not time to describe all the symptoms of gradual improvement, and I have not the medical knowledge needful to do so clearly. Enough that the six-hour interval was shortened that day by half, that the breathing became more regular, and a soft perspiration broke through the clogged and clammy pores. Jane wanted to second this by an additional blanket, but I feared to allow it in a case of so utter prostration. When the perspiration was over, then I prescribed the blanket for fear of a chill reaction.

At every return of consciousness, our patient made an effort to speak, but I hushed him with my hand on his lips, and he even managed to smile, when he found that I would be obeyed. In the evening he tried to open his arms to me, and then tried to push me away, in some faint recollection of the nature of his disorder. To me the interest was so intense, and the delight so deep, that if I had lost him now, it would surely have broken my heart.

At sunset of that day, as nurse and I sat near the dressing-room window, watching the slant rays flickering on the sward, and the rooks alighting and swinging over their noisy nests, a black cloud hung for a moment just above the sun, a black cloud with a vivid edge of gold. It tempered the light in a peculiar manner, and seemed to throw it downwards. Peering through my fingers at it, for it was very beautiful, I saw a whitish mist or vapour steaming and hovering above the disk of the setting sun, between my eyes and that golden marge. I wondered what this could be; there was no heat to cause strong evaporation, nor any mist or dewy haze about, nor was the sun "drawing water." But what I saw was like that trembling twinkle of the air, which we often observe on a meadow footpath in the hot forenoon of July. I drew Jane's attention to it, not expecting any solution, but just for something to say.

"Dear me, Miss, don't you know what that is? I see it every evening; it will be twice as plain when the sun goes down, and then it will be quite white."

"Well, what is it? Why can't you tell me? Is everything here a secret?"

I was rather irritable, but vexed with myself for being so. Too much excitement and too little sleep were the causes.

"No, Miss, there's no secret at all about that. Every one knows what that is. It's only the scum that rises through the grass from the arched pool that takes all the drains of the house. Some of the arch fell in they say, and the ground shakes when they mow it; they are afraid to roll there."

"Is it possible? And you knew it, a practised nurse like you! Did my uncle know it?"

"I am sure, Miss, I can't tell: most likely not, or he would have had it mended, he hates things out of repair. But it can't do any harm, with the mould and the grass above it."

"Can't it indeed? And you can see it rise. Shut all the bedroom windows in a moment, Jane. I'll shut this."

She thought my wits were wandering, from what I had gone through; nevertheless she obeyed me.

It happened that I had attended, at Isola's urgent request, one lecture of the many delivered by Dr. Ross. She forgot what the subject was to be. It proved to be an unsavoury and "unlady-like" one--Mephitis. Isola wanted to run away, but I have none of that nonsense about me, when human life is concerned, and listened with great attention, and even admiration; for he handled the matter eloquently and well.

"Now, Jane, throw all the doors open, and the lobby window that looks in the other direction. When do you think it will be possible to move our poor patient from these rooms? The air here is deadly poison."

"Well I'm sure, Miss! And he couldn't have a nicer nor a more airy room; and all my things in order too, and so handy, and so many cupboards!"

"Out of this poison he must go. When can he be moved?"

"Well, Miss, he might be moved to-morrow, if we could only get plenty of hands, and do it cleverly."

"Surely we can have plenty of hands. There used to be twenty-five servants here; and I have not heard that my uncle has lessened the number."

"No, Miss; but save and keep us, we shan't get one of them here."

"Nonsense! I will have them, or they leave the house. Of course I won't peril their lives. We shall only want two or three; and they may take a bath of disinfecting stuff, with all their clothes on, before they come; and they may smoke all the while."

The nurse laughed grimly, and shook her gray head.

"And we will fumigate, Jane, fumigate tremendously. Surely Englishmen have more self-respect than to be such babies, and you a woman, and I a girl, shaming them out of face."

"It doesn't matter, Miss; they won't come. I know them well, the lot I mean that are in the house now."

"Very well, Jane, we'll have Gamekeeper Hiatt, and his eldest son; they are men I know. And if that is not enough, we'll send to Gloucester for Thomas Henwood. But why don't you open the lobby door, as I told you?"

"If you please, Miss, I can't. They have fastened it outside."

"Do you mean to say that they have dared to lock us in?"

"Indeed I do, Miss; we have been fastened in since the morning."

"And pray, why did you not tell me?'

"Because I feared to excite you, Miss. I know your temper when you are wronged, ever since you was that high; and in this fever air, excitement is sure to kill you. Brutes! But I suppose they don't know it."

"They know it well; at least the master-spirit does. And for that very reason I will crush my indignation. Since I was that high, Jane, I have passed through much tribulation, and have dropped my lady-heiress tone. I can now command myself."

"Then, Miss, I will show you what they sent this morning, round the handle of the coffee-jug. I was afraid to let you see it before." She gave me a twist of paper, on which was written as follows:--

"For the safety of the household, Mrs. Fletcher orders that the persons in the fever-room be allowed no communication with the other servants. The intercepting door is fastened, because a most sinful un-Christian act was perpetrated last night. Due supplies will be delivered once a-day, at 10 A.M. No empty vessels and no correspondence received. Any attempt to break these rules will be punished by suspension of supplies. Servants are forbidden to come beneath the sick-room windows. May the Lord have you in His keeping, in His tender mercy, according to His holy will. You are requested to read Philippians i. 8-11 inclusive. There are three holy bibles on the drawers and dressing-tables."

When I had read this, and perceived, by the blasphemy at the end, that it could proceed from no other than that awful woman, I confess that my spirit was cowed within me. Not from selfish fear, nor yet from the taming of passion, but from the lowering thought that I belonged to the same race of being as the author of such Satanity. Presently, I became too indignant to speak, or even think. It added, if that were possible, to my indignation, that I had seen her leave the house, about nine o'clock that morning, in our best close carriage. She kept the windows up until she was past the lawn and the light iron gates, beyond the arcade of roses; then, at the first turn in the avenue, she let down the glass and gracefully kissed her hand to me. I did not believe, however, that she was gone back to Cheltenham. With so much at stake in our house, and depending on her direction, she would surely stop in the neighbourhood, if only to watch the course of events.

Sooner than I dared to expect, I regained the command of myself; horror within me was stronger than wrath, and stronger than either became the resolve to survive and win. "There can be no God," I exclaimed, in my presumptuous ignorance, "if this scheme of the devil is permitted to triumph."

First I tried the door, which severed us from the rest of the house. My uncle's rooms were in the western wing, very near those which my dear mother had occupied, and not very far from my own. They formed one floor of the western gable; the three bedroom windows and that of the dressing-room looked to the west, while the great lobby window, from which I had seen Mrs. Daldy's departure, looked southward along the avenue, the curve of which could be seen also from the bedroom windows. An oaken door, at the end of the main passage, cut off the rooms in this storey of the gable from all the rest of the house. This door Jane had left locked from the inside, fearing lest others should lock her in, as they had threatened to do. But now we found that a strong iron bolt had been fixed upon the outside, while we were asleep in the morning, and that we had no chance of forcing it.

Next I asked Jane, whether she thought that the house, now Mrs. Daldy was gone, would be still in the hands of our enemies. Would not Mrs. Fletcher at once re-assert her authority? Might not Matilda Jenkins be expected to fly to the rescue? The nurse, knowing all the politics of the servants' hall, assured me that there was no hope of either of these events. Robert, a drunken Wesleyan, turned out of the sect in Cheltenham, was Mrs. Daldy's lieutenant, and would take all care of Matilda, to whose good graces he had been making overture. As for Mrs. Fletcher, she was probably in the same plight as ourselves. From what I heard about Robert, I began to believe that he had private orders to disown me at the station, for the double purpose of yielding a tit-bit of insolence, and warning of my arrival.

However, that mattered very little; but out of those rooms I must get, either by door or by window; and that, too, without delay. Do they expect to triumph so easily over Clara Vaughan? And in her father's house? The windows were about twenty feet from the ground, as nearly as I could guess, and the rooms beneath were empty. At once I resolved to attempt an escape that way, and to do so before the moon, which was southing now, should shine on the western aspect. Good Jane was terrified at the thought; and then, upon my persisting, implored me to let her make the attempt, if it must be made at all.

"Now, Jane, no more, if you please. We can't waste time about that. You have a husband partly dependent upon you, and several children to think of. For me nobody cares." But I hoped somebody did. "And you know I am far more active and much lighter than you are. Help me out with the feather bed."

The little bed in the dressing-room, which she had to sleep on, was speedily brought to the window, and dropped just underneath it. It fell upon the grass with a pleasing and quiet flop. Then the two strong bell-ropes, already cut down and plaited together, were tied round the bars of the double window sashes, the lower sash being thrown up to the full extent, the glass pressed quietly out with a pair of wet towels, and the splinters removed, so as not to cut the rope. The latter still failed to reach more than half-way to the ground, but I would venture the drop if I could only descend so far. After winding a linen sheet around my body and dress, with the end tied round one ankle, so as to leave me free use of my limbs, I sat upon the window-sill in the broad shadow, and calculated my chances. Should I begin the descent with face, or with back, to the wall? Face to the wall I resolved on, for though I should have to drop backward so, yet what I feared most of all was having the back of my head crushed against the house. Next to this I dreaded a sprain of the ankle, but all our family are well-knit and straight in the joint.

So I launched myself off, beginning as gently as could be, Jane having firm hold of one hand, until I was well on the voyage. Though not well versed in calisthenic arts, I got on famously almost as far as the end of the rope, keeping away from the wall by the over-saling of the window-sill, and the rapid use of my feet. Then I rested a moment on a projecting ledge--called, I believe, a "stringing-course"--and away hand below hand again. But I struck my knuckles terribly against that stringing-course, and very nearly lost hold from the pain of the blow; then bending my body forward I gave one good push at the wall, and shutting both eyes, I believe, let go the rope altogether. Backward I fell, and rolled over upon the feather bed. I was not even stunned, but feared for a moment to try if my limbs were sound.

There I sat and stripped off the winding sheet. Presently, up I got, and, in my triumph, alas! could not help crying "All right, Hurrah!" like a foolish little child. In a moment I saw that my cry had been heard, where it should not have been. A rapid flitting of lights along the lower windows and in the stableyard, and I knew that chase would be given.

But after leaving my father's house in such a dignified manner, was it likely that I would give in and be caught? Now, Clara, you could beat all your nurses in running, off and away like the wind! Away I went full speed towards the shade of the avenue, while Jane had the wit to scream out of the window, "Help! Help! Here's the house on fire!" This made some little diversion; I had a capital start, and it was but half a mile to the lodge where old Whitehead lived. Once there, I should care for nobody. I must have escaped very easily, for my feet seemed as swift as a deer's; but, as my luck would have it, the light iron gates between the lawn and the park were fastened. What on earth should I do? I saw men running across the lawn, and, what was worse, they saw me. In vain I pulled at the gates; they rattled, but would not yield. Had I owned true presence of mind, I should have walked boldly up to the men, and dared them to touch me fresh from the fever-room. In the flurry of the moment I never thought of that, but darted into the shrubbery, and crouched among thick laurels. Presently I heard them rush down the main drive and begin the search, with some heavy swearing. Two of them came to the very clump I was hiding in, and pushed a pitchfork almost into my side, but the stupid fellows had lanterns, which blinded them to the moonlight. On they went with grumblings and growlings, which told me exactly where to shun them. Judging at length, from the silence, that the search had passed to the right, I slipped from my tangled lair, and glided away to the left, beyond the shrubbery spring, where a little gate, as I knew, led to a glade in the park. The deep ha-ha which I had feared to jump in the dark, because of the loose stones at the bottom, was here succeeded by a high oak paling, and probably through that gate had come the murderer of my father.

With a cold shudder at the remembrance, I stole along through the shadowy places, and had almost reached the little gate, when I saw two of the searchers coming straight towards me. To the right of me was the park-paling, on the left a breastwork of sod, which I could not climb without being clearly seen; to fly was to meet the enemy; should I yield, and be baffled after all; insulted too, most likely, for I knew that the men were tipsy?

In my hand was the tightly-wound sheet, used as a rope to confine my dress. I had folded it short and carried it, on the chance of its proving useful. In a moment I was under the palings in deep shadow, with the white sheet thrown around me, falling from my forehead, and draped artistically over the right arm. Stock still I stood against the black boards, and two great coils of long black hair flowed down the winding sheet. The men came up, tired of the chase, and grumbling; and by their voices I knew them for my good friends Jacob and Bob. Suddenly, they espied a tall, white figure, of tremendous aspect. They stopped short, both tongue and foot, and I distinctly heard their teeth chatter. With a slow and spectral motion, I raised my draped white arm, and fetched a low, sepulchral moan. Down fell the lantern, and, with a loud yell, away went the men, as hard as their legs could carry them.

Laughing heartily, I refolded my sheet, and taking the short cut across the park to the lodge where old Whitehead lived, arrived, without having met even my old friend "Tulip."

The old man, in hot indignation, drew forth his battered musket--for he had once been in the militia--and swore that he would march upon the ---- rogues at once. Instead of that I sent him for the two Hiatts, and the village constable; and soon, without invitation, half the village attended. With my torn dress tucked up by good Mrs. Whitehead, and a hat on my head, newly bought for her clean little grandchild, I set forth again in the moonlight, at the head of a faithful army, to recover my native home.

Hiatt easily opened the gate, which had defied my flurried efforts, and we presented ourselves at the main entrance, a force that would frighten a castle. It is needless to say that we carried all before us. The state of siege was rescinded, Mrs. Fletcher and Tilly set free, all the ringleaders turned away neck and crop, and what was far more important, my poor uncle removed, without being conscious of it, to a sweet and wholesome room. The sturdy Gloucestershire yeomen scorned all idea of danger.

Tired with all my adventures, before I slept that night--still near my uncle's bed--two reflections came dreamily over my mind.

The first was a piece of vanity. "Ah, Mrs. Daldy, you little know Clara Vaughan!"

The second was, "Dear me, how Conrad would be astonished at this! And how strange that his father should thus have saved my uncle's life! For he must have died, if left in that noisome room."

CLARA VAUGHAN

BOOK IV.

CHAPTER I.

Before that week was over, my uncle could sit up in bed for a short time every day, being duly propped in a downy nest of pillows. One arm, however, remained quite impotent, and part of one side rigid and numb. His recovery was slow and tedious, as might well be expected with one who had been dragged not from the jaws but the very throat of death. For a long time also his mind was feeble and dim, a mirror overcast by the vapours of the body.

To me, who am fond of observing, in my own little childish way, it was interesting as well as delightful to note how, day by day, the mind and body, hand in hand, rose stronger. More than all was I taught, and humbled in my own conceit, by taking heed how tardily came back the power to guide and control the imagination. That object-glass of the mind--not achromatic even in first-rate intellects--had long been out of the focal distance from the lens of reason's eye. Upon it had been glancing loose distorted images, rendered home imperfectly, if at all, to the retina of the brain. Herein its state was the very opposite to that of my own phrenoscope. I have no large imagination; but the images it presents are vivid, and I see well round them. Every one of them is not cast, but cut, on my sensorium. Whether I can strike them off in words-- whether my telegraph can print its message--is quite another question, and beside its purpose. Having rendered home to me the idols (oftentimes inverted, though distinct) it leaves expression and judgment to do their best with the copyright.

Now, both in fabric and in mould, my uncle's mind was different. Naturally his powers were far superior, but he seemed to take no pride in them. No dark and settled purpose had ever thrown its shadow, and even its weight, upon them; nor had they felt, so far as I knew, the rough grasp of adversity. Therefore they were longer in recovering from the blow, than I think my own would have been.

There were few things, among the many desired by Mrs. Daldy, which she failed to reconcile with her strong sense of religion. "There is not one"--I have heard her say--"not one of the things we believe to be for our good, which we should scruple to lay before the Throne of Grace. Even the throbbings of that little unregenerate heart"--Clara Vaughan's to wit, who had kicked her that morning, quite by accident of course--"even they are known and sifted there"-- slight confusion of metaphor caused by strong conviction of sin--"Infinite mercy knows the things that be for our edification, and confirmation in the faith. Yes, backsliding sinner, the want of real heart-felt spiritual life can be supplied by prayer alone. Is it not so in your experience, Elder?" "Prayer, my dear Madam, and searching of the heart. Oh the depth of the wickedness of the unconverted heart!" And he took another glass of sherry. That night I remember she worked very hard, for her; and the next day she presented me with markers the size of a gallows, progged with many holes; on one was done in cross-stitch, "Pray without ceasing," and upon the other "Wrestle thou in prayer. Gen. xxxii. 24." Both of these I threw into the fire there before her eyes.

From this it will be clear, that in her devotions she still remembered me, and doubtless prayed in good Scriptural phraseology for my release from this wicked world. Dr. Churchyard's last report had raised her terror to the highest pitch, and instead of wrestling in prayer, she had run away in high panic, upon hearing that the fever-nurse was seen at large the night before. "We must use the means of grace," she said to Mrs. Fletcher, before she locked her in, "and accept the mercies vouchsafed to us. And it would be sinful, dear Mrs. Fletcher, in me to neglect such a warning as this."

It was wise, as well as righteous, in her to keep aloof for a time, while her devices worked their consummation. For the present it appeared to me that they were failing signally. My uncle was regaining strength of mind and body; while native air, a sense of triumph, and daily exercise, kept me in blooming health. My patient, who otherwise could hardly bear me to leave him for an hour, insisted upon my taking a long ride every day. Lilla was charmed, and so was I, with the sweet spring air, and the rich familiar scenery. And how it did make me eat! Thankful indeed I ought to be, and am, that it pleased God to spare me that awful and deadly pestilence. But the worst injury done by canting hypocrites is, that the repulsion they create drives away others from good. Truly I may say, that for days after being in contact with that slimy sanctity, I could not say my own prayers, as a little child should do.

Of that fever there had been three fatal cases in the village, before it entered our house; and I found that it was spreading rapidly. With my uncle's authority, I had the drainage surveyed and amended at once; and so the pest was stayed. Of course we did not neglect our own weak point; and the crawling noisome smell was no longer perceived in the room, nor the white vapour on the grass.

And so three weeks went by; no news from London or Devonshire, no explanation between my uncle and myself, no arrangements as to my expectations in life. As yet my uncle was too weak to bear any sort of excitement, and seemed desirous only to be passive in my hands. His eyes always followed me to every part of the room, and he would even be propped on the sofa to see me ride down the avenue; and there I always found him watching for my return. Meanwhile I yearned to be once more in a certain little room with a north aspect, opposite a cheesemonger's shop in an obscure street of London. Nightly I dreamed of Giudice, and daily I dreamed of dear Isola and Conrad. The dog in the stableyard, who had hitherto owned no especial attractions for me, suddenly found himself petted, and coaxed, and fed (which he thought much more of) to the scandal of Mrs. Fletcher, and the great alarm of the grooms, who would rather not have me there. Moreover, the dog himself, though I strove to invest him with every chivalrous attribute, was of a low and ungenial order, adorned with no graces of mind, and little taste, except for bones and gravy. But perhaps my standard was too high: peradventure I even commenced with more prejudice than a bulldog's. Be that as it may--and if I can see round things, I ought to see round myself--every day fell heavier and heavier from the fair balance of time; and every night the stars--for there was now no moon--looked wearier in the heavens, and less inclined for business. How long, how long shall you go round the pole in your steady pacing way, as if the sky were for auction, and you were pacing the lots; while I, with more fire in me than you can strike or steal, am ditched like a glow-worm kicked under a dock-leaf, and see no polestar at all?

Here is May, the height of May: I am full of life and spirit: the garb of death, like an April cloud, blows over. Let me see. Last birthday I was eighteen: I have known more troubles than years, and enjoyed no youth as yet. Last year I spent in growing, and pining, and starving. Now the Power, that balances earth and heaven, has filled me with joy and light.

Neither am I renegade to my life, in opening wide my heart to this flood of love and happiness. Still am I set upon one strong purpose. Still am I sworn, and will not repent, that if filial duty demand it, I will trample love under my feet, and cut the throat of happiness.

During most of this time, I had no idea where the queen of hypocrites was; though doubtless she knew all that was happening to us. As soon as he heard of my uncle's surprising rally, Dr. Churchyard came over, and claimed all the merit for his own last prescription. Brought face to face with the awkward fact that the medicine had not been procured, he was not in the least disconcerted, but found that we had misunderstood him, the prescription to which he referred was the one before the last. At any rate, he enhanced his own fame immensely, and became "instrumental under Providence" in killing more people than ever. In reply to Mrs. Fletcher, for I would not deign to ask him, he stated that the excellent and devoted Mrs. Daldy had not been seen lately in Cheltenham. Her son, however, was there, and foremost in the ranks of Pump-room Lady-killers. Just what he was fit for.

The doctor entertained a belief, and spread the report in Cheltenham, that Dorcas was lodged in a humble cot among the haunts of pestilence, imperilling her life and lavishing her substance to relieve the fever-stricken. This being more than I could stand, I asked the worthy doctor--who, after all, was a man of the world--what three wealthy persons Dorcas had carried with her. At first he feigned not to understand me, then looked sly, and changed the subject cleverly. Of course I referred to the well-known fact, that she supported her grandeur and her son's extravagance by playing an admirable rubber. She was playing a better one now.

Dr. Churchyard finished by writing another prescription, which, after his departure, I handed to the husband of Venus, legitimate disposer of mineral medicines.

CHAPTER II.

London! London! was still the cry of my heart; and was I not summoned thither by duty long ago? What might become, during all this time, of the man whom I was bound to watch at every turn, and whom I was now in a better condition to deal with? My first visit, every morning, was to my parents' graves, and neither of them would be there but for his ruthless hand. As I sat there how lonely I felt! how sadly forlorn in the world, be my lot wealth or poverty, victory or defeat!

One morning as I sat there my spirit was moved by dreams of the night before, and I vowed, in that bodily but invisible presence, that none, except one whose name I whispered, should ever kneel on that turf hand in hand with me.

Borne out of my usual vein by the deed myself had done, I entered the ancient church, always left open for me, and, kneeling at the altar-rails, with many a Vaughan supine in prayer, pennons, helms, and trophies round me, stately dames in marble white, and old crusaders clutching still the cross--there I made my vow upon the knee-cupped stones, that if he claimed me not, the race should end with me.

It was a presumptuous and unholy act, with all around me quelled by time, with ages laid aside in dust, with many a stouter heart and larger mind than mine, helpless even to superintend the wasting of his tenement, with all his bygone bliss and woe, stanchest love and deadliest hate, less eloquent now than the fly whom the spider has caught in his skull.

Returning across the park, after a warm interview with "Tulip," who insisted mainly upon having his ears well scratched, I found my uncle in his snug wheel-chair, waiting near the side-door for me to help and accompany him forth. This was our best way to take him out, because of the steps at the front-door. He had not yet been in the open air since his terrible illness, but, judging by my own experience, I thought that he pined for the breeze, and, after long council, it was resolved to trust him forth this day. With all his heart he was longing to be out; but, instead of expressing impatience, smiled gratefully at me. I now observed that he had a sweet and winning smile--a gift bestowed not rarely on faces of a sombre cast.

In return for it I kissed him, and we sailed smoothly out. How he revelled, to be sure, in the first clear breath from the lips of heaven! Stretching one poor arm forth--the other he could not move--he tried to spread himself like a flower to the sun. Then he drew long draughts of liquid freedom, and was for a time as one intoxicated. In the glorious crystal bath he seemed to float away from earth. Coming to himself at length, he looked at me, and said, "Now John may go, if he pleases." A year ago he would have said, "Go, John," and no more. But illness is a great refiner. When John was out of sight he allowed free vent to the tears of joy and gratitude, whereof, in my opinion, he had no call to be ashamed. I kissed him many times. My warm impassioned nature always felt for and delighted in any touch like this. Then he placed his better hand on the cold and rigid one, lifting this with that, and poured forth silent thanks to the Giver of all things.

"Clara, darling," at length he said, "how can I ever show you a thousandth part of my gratitude for all the lovingkindness you have heaped on me? Coals of fire, indeed! and they have warmed my selfish heart. With loathsome death before your face, in all the pride and bloom of early youth and richest--"

I will not repeat his words, because it would not become me; but I am forced by all that has happened to show what his feelings were.

"And all this for me--me who have been your bitterest enemy, who have turned you out of your father's house, and caused your mother's death!" Here I stopped him, lest he should be overcome.

"Dear uncle, talk no more of this--never even think of it. The fault was all my own. You know I would not stop, often as you asked me. There always was a bar between us, and it was my obstinacy."

"No, it was my pride. Clara, in my better mind I loved you all along. How could I help admiring your truth and courage and devotion to your father? Although I own that you were very bitter against me, yet, if I had only used the proper means, I might have got the better of it. If I had told you all my story, you would have pitied more even than condemned me. But my pride forbade, and I made the common mistake of regarding you as a child, because you were that in years. I forgot to allow for the forcing powers of grief. Even now, pulled down as I am, and humbled by the wisdom of Heaven, I cannot tell you my strange history without the acutest pain."

"Then I am sure, uncle, I will never let you do it."

"Yes, it is my duty, and the sooner done the better. Rescued though I am, for the present, by your wonderful courage and skill, I feel that one more blow, even a slight one now, and time for me is ended. But if it were God's will to cut me off to-morrow, I should die in happiness, having made my peace, and won your kind forgiveness."

"You shall not tell me now at any rate. And I won't have you talk so, uncle. Mind, I am head-nurse still. Now come and see how lovely the ranunculus are getting."

I began to wheel him over the grass and gather flowers (which "he played with like a child), to change, if possible, the current of his thoughts. Stupid thing! I took the wrong way to do it.

"Oh, uncle dear! you will laugh at me, and say I am as bad as ever; but as soon as you get better I want to be off again, kind and good as you are to me."

He trembled so violently, that I feared the chair would be upset.

"What, Clara, can't you live with me even now? Everything shall be yours, as it ought to be. I will never meddle with you in any way, but keep to some lonely corner, and not see you very often. Oh, Clara! dear Clara! don't go away! You know I am quite helpless, and I can't live long, and you are all in all to me, and I am so proud of you, darling! But it is not for myself I care. I cannot tell, much less can you, what mischief may be done if you leave this house again. That low, crafty woman will be back again directly--she who made cowards of all the household, and acted the coward herself, who left me to die in my lonely bed, while she took all my keys. If her treachery succeeds, I shall rise from my grave. And I know she will poison me yet, if she gets the chance, and can make anything by it."

It was the first time he had spoken to me of Mrs. Daldy, and I was amazed at his bitterness, for I had heard of no quarrel between them. What on earth did it mean?

"Don't go, Clara!" he implored me, with the cold sweat on his forehead, and every line in his poor thin face a-quivering. "Don't go, my darling, blessed Clara! I have had none to love for years and years, and to love you is so sweet! If you go I must die at once, and, worse than that, die wretched in the knowledge that you will be robbed."

He fell back in the chair, from which, in his excitement, he had striven to rise, and for some minutes there he lay insensible. When I had succeeded in bringing him to himself, he looked at me so piteously, with so much death in his eyes, that I promised, with a sinking heart, never to leave him more, except upon absolute necessity, until he should be well, or need my care no longer.

He even tried to persuade me not to go to London for the things I had left there, but to send a trusty person to pack and bring them home. To this, however, I could not yield, feeling, as I did, that, after all my love for Isola, and all her kindness to me, I was bound to see her and say farewell; and what harm could there possibly be in so short an absence? My uncle wished me to bring her down for a good long visit, but this at such a time could not be thought of. Moreover, lively, impulsive Idols would have grown very long-faced in a dull sick house, which ours must be for the present. It was settled at last that I should go to London the following Monday, stay there one entire day, and come back the day after with all my trifling chattels. One thing more my uncle proposed which I would not hear of. It was, that he should transfer to me, by deed of gift, all the estate, both real and personal, reserving only a small annuity for himself, and a sum of 10,000*l.* for some special purpose, which he would disclose to me at leisure. Thus, he said, he should feel as if justice had been done, and there would be some security against Mrs. Daldy's schemes. Of the latter I felt no fear whatever, and thought it the effect of a shaken mind that he attached so much importance to them. Under no circumstances would I think, for a moment, of allowing him so to divest himself. Money, to any amount, I could have, though I wanted very little, seeing that now, once more, a solemn duty would withdraw me from my long pursuit, and from all the frivolities which many girls delight in. I begged my uncle to appoint an honest steward for the estate, and to assign me a moderate yearly allowance, which would save much trouble. To this he at last consented, and proposed for me so large a revenue, that, after removing the last cipher, I had more than I knew how to spend. The first thing I did was to send the kind farmer the residue of the sum he had lent me, together with interest at ten per cent., which did not seem excessive, considering that he had no security.

And now, with the utmost anxiety, I looked forward to the time when my poor uncle should be strong enough to tell me, without risk, that history of himself which he had distinctly promised me. Surely it must shed some light on the mystery of my own. This thought, as well as the sense of duty, reconciled me in some measure to the suspension of my life-long search. He would have told me everything then and there, in his warm gratitude for my undertaking; but I durst not let him. He was already fatigued with so much talking, and when the stimulus of the fresh air was gone, he suffered a serious relapse.

CHAPTER III.

On the following Monday, my poor uncle being rather better again, I set off for London, as had been determined, and arrived there late in the afternoon. It had been proposed to send a servant with me, but I had been too long accustomed to independence, and also had reasons of my own for refusing. I was to receive, on the morrow, an account, by telegraph, of my patient's health and spirits, and promised to give, in return, some tidings of myself. Mrs. Shelfer had not been apprised of my coming, because she would have been sure to tell Miss Isola, whom, as well as her brother, I wished to take by surprise. Dear Isola had often inquired about my family, but only knew that I was an orphan, much reduced in the world, poor, and all alone. Much as I loved her, I knew quite well that she could not keep a secret, and whenever she teased me about my "iron mask," I retorted upon her that she had first to discover the secret of her own home.

As we rushed towards the mighty city, what a flush was in my cheeks, what a flutter in my heart! Whom might I not see even upon the platform, or, at any rate, in the streets, and, poverty being removed, what obstacle could there be between us? Not that I intended to resign myself to affection, and lead a life of softness, until I had discharged to the utmost my duty to the dead. Yet some sort of pledge might pass--some surety there might be, that neither of us would feel thereafter quite alone in the world. But how could I tell that he even cared about me? Well, I had a strong suspicion. In some things the eyes are the best detective police. Only I had always been so unlucky. Was it not too good luck for me ever to be true?

Mrs. Shelfer's door was opened at my knock, not by her own little bustling self, nor even by shock-headed and sly "Charley," but by a short stout man of affable self-importance, with a semi-Jewish face, and a confidential air. He had a pot of porter in one hand and a paper-roll in the other, a greasy hat on his head, and one leg of his trousers had lost the lower half. Upon learning my name and object, he took no notice whatever of me, but put up his paper-roll for a trumpet, and shouted along the passage, "Balaam, here's a kick! I'm bothered if it's all lies, after all. Never dreamed the old gal could tell a word of truth. Had a higher opinion of her. Blowed if the young woman herself ain't come!"

"Easy there, Balak"--the mouth of the speaker was full--"keep the door, I tell you. Never gets a bit of time to my victuals. She's up to a plant, I doubt. Just let me have a squint at her." Out came another man with a like appearance and air, and a blade-bone in his hand, whereat he continued to gnaw throughout the interview. It was indeed a squint with which he favoured me, and neither of them would move for me to pass.

"Pray what is the meaning of all this?" I asked, in my grandest manner. "Surely I have not mistaken the house I lived in. This, I believe, is Mrs. Shelfer's house?"

Instead of answering me, they closed the door enough to put the slide-chain on, leaving me still outside, where, with boiling indignation, I heard myself discussed; the cabman looking on with an experienced grin.

"Well, Balaam, now, and what do you think of that party?"

"Uncommon fine young gal, and doosed mannersome too; but it don't follow, for all that, that the thing is on the square, you know. Have she got any luggage, Balak?"

"No, mate. And that looks fishy, now one come to think on it. Stop, let me have another look."

"No; leave that to me. Slip the chain out, Balak: and keep your foot behind the door. She can't push us both in without assault and battery."

To my shame and indignation, I was subjected to another critical cross-fire from half drunken eyes. I turned my back and stamped in my vexation; the cabman gave me an approving nod. This little act of mine was so unmistakably genuine, and displayed such very nice embroidery--I do like a tasteful petticoat--that the hard heart of Balaam was softened; at the same moment a brilliant idea stole through his cautious mind.

"Stop now, Balak, put your foot there. She can't push us both in, I believe; leastways not without battery and contempt of court. Now what do you think of this?"--And he whispered to his grimy friend.

"Well, that beats all I ever heer'd on. Let you alone for brains, Balaam, and me for muscle and pluck!"

"Now, young lady," began Balaam in a diplomatic tone, "me and my mate here be in a constitution of trust, or else you may take your oath, and never a pervarication, we never would keep an agreeable young female"--here he gave me two ogles intended for one--"on the flinty stones so long; only we can't say if you mean honest, and there be such a many bad ones going, and we've got a leary file inside. Now listen to what I say. There's a dog as big as a lion in the room as you calls yourn; and he do show his teeth, and no mistake. We be afeared to show our noses there, even at the command of dooty. You can hear him growling now like all the Strand and Fleet Street; and my mate Balak here leave half his breeches behind him, saving your presence, Miss, and lucky to get off so. Now if so be you undertakes, honour bright, to march straight into that front room, my mate and self have concluded to let you in."

"Of course I will," said I, smiling at their terrors. So I paid the cabman, took up my little bag, and ran right up the stairs. Balaam and Balak feared to come round the corner. "You must unlock the door, Miss," cried one of them, "we was forced to lock him in."

"Oh Judy, my darling Judy, my own pet love of a Judy." He let me say no more; his paws were on my shoulders, and I was in a shower-bath of kisses. In the ecstasy of my joy, I forgot all about the two men and their mysterious doings, and flung myself down on a chair, while Judy, out of his mind with delight, even tried to sit on my lap. He whinnied, and cried, and laughed, and yelled, and could find no vent for his feelings, until he threw his great head back and told all in a wow-wow, that must have been heard in Oxford Street. A little familiar knock, and Mrs. Shelfer appeared, looking rather better than ever.

"Why, dear Mrs. Shelfer, how glad I am to see you! And you look much younger, I declare!"

"And, Miss, you do look bootiful, bootiful, my good friend! Splendid things,"--I was dressed a little better, but still in sombre colours--"splendid, Miss Vaughan, and how you becomes 'em to be sure! Talk of Miss Idols after that, why it's the Queen to a gipsy! And pray, Miss, if I may make so bold, what did you give for this? it beats my sarcenet dress, I do believe."

"Nothing, Mrs. Shelfer, only a little kiss."

"Gracious me, Miss, then you've been and got engaged, and to a lord at least. I heard you were come into your great fortune at last; more than all Middlesex they tell me, Regency Park and all! And that poor straight-legged young man, as come here every day to see Judy, and to ask for you."

"Now, Mrs. Shelfer, don't talk nonsense,"--my heart was jumping, but I did not want her to see it. "I only hope you haven't said a word to him about these foolish reports."

"Me, Miss! Do you think I would now?"

"Yes; I know by your face you have. You can't cheat me, Mrs. Shelfer. Never mind, if you have not mentioned my name." It never struck me that Conrad would be frightened at my money.

"No, never, Miss, as I hope to be saved." And she crossed herself, which I had never seen her do.

"Come, Mrs. Shelfer, now; I've got some pretty little trifles for you in this bag."

She jumped with pleasure; she was so fond of knick-knacks: then she put her fingers on her lips and went to the door and listened. Presently she came back with a mysterious air.

"Pray, Miss, as you are so very kind, excuse my taking the liberty, but would you mind giving Judy the bag in his paws? no fear of them getting it there."

"Why, what on earth is the matter? Why didn't you let me in? Who are those nasty men?"

"Oh, it's nothing, Miss; nothing at all to speak of: only they knocks my sticks so in making the inwentory, and the one they made last time, and the time before, would do every bit as well. But they charges for it, every time, the rogues--and they dare to put the chairs down lackered and American cloth, good, morocco as ever was, and as if Miss Minto--"

"Now, Mrs. Shelfer, tell me in two words what it means. Is it a sale?"

"No, no, Miss, I should hope not; only an execution, and them two men are the bailiffs; civil tongues enough, and very good judges of porter and periwinkles. They're the ones as come last time; but I'd sooner have the old ones, jolly fellows they were, and knew how to wink both eyes. But that cross-eyed thief--"

"And have they got my things, Mrs. Shelfer?"

"No, Miss; only what few was in the bedroom; they daren't come here for Judy. It was as much as their lives were worth. If I had known they was coming, I'd have had him at the front door, but they locked him in as soon as he got a piece out of the other fellow's leg. Bless me, how he did holloa!"

"Do you mean to say, Mrs. Shelfer, that they have taken possession of my things in my bedroom?"

"To be sure, Miss. I said they was yours, and of course they wouldn't believe me, and the folding door was shut, but Judy would have broken it down only they put the bedstead again it. Gracious me! I never see a dog take on so in all my life! He was like a roaring lion."

"I should rather hope so. Giudice, I commend you; and I've a great mind to let you out, and what is more, I will if they don't give me back my things. Surely, Mrs. Shelfer, they have no right to my property."

"Well, so I say, Miss; because it isn't for the landlord; but they won't believe they are yours."

"If they don't believe me pretty soon, Giudice shall convince them. He is a judge you know, and I've no idea of robbery any more than he has. But who is doing all this, and why do you seem so unconcerned about it? I should cry my eyes out, I am sure."

"Bless your pretty heart, Miss; this makes the fifteenth time I've had them here in the last four years. At first I was terribly put out, and made myself a figure crying; but now I only think it's company, and they drink as if they was, that's certain. You must have seen the inwentories, Miss, round the candles lots of times. Only one thing they does that don't strike me as wery honourable, though it's law I b'lieve; they charges me, and wery high too, for eating up my victuals, and they will have meat four times a day. Why, that Balak, him with his breeches gone--"

"Who put them in, Mrs. Shelfer, and how much is it for?"

"Oh, it's one of Charley's bills or notes, of course. Quinlan holds it, him as keeps "the little dust-pan," down Maiden Lane, and Charley says that all he got for it was ten shillings and a waggon-load of water-cresses. Now they'll be here directly, Miss, with you to keep the dog in. Excuse me, Miss, I see you have got one of them new wide things as go all round and up--capital things, I must have one before they come again. And could you manage to sit upon the sofa, Miss, and the three best chairs in your petticoat, with the tea-poy on your lap?"

"What on earth do you mean, Mrs. Shelfer?"

"Why, Miss, they can't lay hold of any article in use, I believe, and you have got so much room in your things."

"Do you suppose I intend to let them come here, for a moment? Now let me look at my bedroom. Come, Judy."

"Oh, Miss, they did have such a hunt here for Charley's double-barrel gun; a regular beauty it is, and that big rogue Quinlan is after it. They know it all round this neighbourhood, it was made by a famous maker, Joe something, I b'lieve, and the best he ever made; it was poor Miss Minto's brother's; and they shan't have it, not one of 'em. I'd sooner shoot them with it. I keeps it always in the safest place I knows on, and twice a year I see that it don't get rusty."

"What safe place do you keep it in?"

She put her little mouth up to my ear, and her little hand up to her mouth, and whispered--

"At the broker's, Miss, in Barbican. He has had it now six years. It's in for a quarter its value, but that's all the better for me: I have less to pay for keeping it, and I carries the ticket night and day in my bosom. And do you know, my good friend, they thought they had got it just now; they got a key that fitted that box of yours, that you always locked so carefully, and they made sure that was it; ha, ha, how I laughed at them when they opened it!"

"What! have they dared to open my mahogany box?" It was the repository of my precious relics.

"To be sure they did, Miss, and they found such curious things there! A lovely thing all set with jewels, they said, a baggonet fit for the Duke of Wellington, and plaster shapes like a cobbler's last, and coloured paper with queer letters on it, and a piece of long black hair, and a plan with distances on it--Lor, Miss, what on earth is the matter? Water! water! You're like death--Balaam! Balak!"

"Stop, Mrs. Shelfer"--I had fallen on the bed--"I would not for ten thousand pounds have had that box exposed to those low ruffians, ransacked, and even catalogued. If I can punish them I will; and you too, you low, miserly, meddling, inquisitive old crone."

She cared for nothing--though afterwards she told me she never saw such eyes in her life--until I luckily called her an "old crone." At that, she fell back upon the towel-horse, and sobbed with both hands over her eyes, as if her heart would break. I had pierced her in the tenderest point--her age.

I did not feel sorry for her at all for at least two minutes, but let her cry away. "Serves her right," I thought. Even if she could not have stopped them from opening that box of mine, at any rate she had no right to gossip about it, and enjoy it all, as she evidently had done. Furthermore, I knew well that she had always been on the tingle to learn the contents of that box, and many a time I had baffled her. Now she had triumphed thoroughly, and I should not have been female if I had calmly allowed it. But seeing her great distress (through all of which she talked, with sobs for affirmations), I began to think what a pity it was; then to wonder whether she deserved it all; next, to believe that she had done no harm; lastly, to feel that I had been a brute. Thereupon I rushed to coax and kiss her, wiped away her tears with my own lawn handkerchief--the feel of which consoled her, for the edge was lace--and begged her pardon fifty times in a thousand foolish words. Finally she was quite set up again by this:

"I tell you, my dear Patty, when I come to your age, when I am five and thirty"--she was fifty-two at least--"I shall fully deserve to be called an old woman for this; and much older I shall look, there is no doubt, than you do."

"Right, my good friend, you are quite right there"--this expression showed me that she herself was right.--"Why the young man from the butcher's, he said to me this morning, and beautiful black hair reminded me of yours, Miss, all stuck together with the fat from off the kidneys--"

"Come, Mrs. Shelfer, let me see about my box."

"To be sure, to be sure, my dear Miss Vaughan; but what do you think he said? 'Now, William John,' says I, 'a good steak mind, a tender juicy steak, for the gentleman visitors here'--Balaam, Miss, and Balak, if you please,--'does like good juicy meat.' 'Mrs. Shelfer, ma'am,' he says, a bowing with his tray like that, 'you shall have a steak, ma'am, as fresh and as juicy as yourself.' Now wasn't that pretty, my good friend?"

"Beautiful, Mrs. Shelfer. But see about my box."

"Surely, surely, Miss Vaughan. But it was very pretty, like a valentine, don't you think it was now?"

"Where is it?"

"Downstairs, Miss, in my little parlour."

"Then send it up at once, by one of the men."

Presently Balaam came up, looking askance at Judy, and with the mahogany box under his right arm. He touched his dirty hat, for Mrs. Shelfer had filled him by this time with the wonders of my wealth, and then he looked doubtfully, and with sorrow, at his burden.

"Put it here if you please," and I pointed to some chairs, "the dog will not touch you while I am here. Now what is the amount of this execution?"

"Debt fifteen pounds, Miss; expenses up to five o'clock, four pound ten."

"Here is the money. Now give me a receipt."

"No, Miss! You don't mean to pay all!"

"Of course, I do."

"Then, Miss, I beg your pardon, but I can't allow you. I has a duty to my employer, and I has a duty to the public too, not forgetting Mrs. Shelfer, and Charley an old friend, and all so handsome in the way of victuals. And I'm sure she wouldn't wish you to be cheated, Miss. Pay ten pounds for the debt, Miss, and that's a deal more than it cost them or they expects to get. 'Twixt you and me, Miss, every stick of this here furniture is in a dozen bills of sale already; and we comes here more for practice like, than for anything else."

In short, I paid 10*l.* for the debt, and 4*l.* for the expenses: whereupon Balaam looked at me with a most impressive and confidential glance.

"Now, Miss, you won't think me rude; but you have come down so handsome, I can tell you something as you may like to know. I've seed the very moral of that sword of yours before."

"Are you certain? Pray where was it?" I trembled with excitement.

"It was in a place in Somers-town, Miss; where I made a levy, some eight year agone."

"What was the name of the people?"

"Dallyhorse, or Jellycorse, or something of the sort. Foreigners they was, and they had only just come to this country. But I can tell you the name more shipshape from the books. Ah, the very moral of it; only there warn't no serpent."

"Do you know what has become of them?"

"No that I don't, and don't want to come across them again. A mean set of mongrel parlywoos; I got starved amost. But I did hear they was riding the high horse now, and something about court."

"Are you quite sure that the weapon was exactly like this? Look at this again."

"Miss, I can take my oath it was the fellow pea, all but the little snake, and he ain't a fixture, I don't believe. I would have sworn it was the very same, only you tells me not. I noticed it most particular; for I never see one like it, though I have had a sight of foreign weapons in my hands ere now. And the gent had got it put away so; we come across it only through a cat as happened to be confined--"

"And what became of it? Did your employer have it?"

"Not he, Miss. When the gent found we had got it, he was put out and no mistake; though he sham not. Away he goes and gets the money somehow, and has us all away in no time."

"How many were there in the family?"

"Well, let me see. They was only living in lodgings, and had but half the house. There was Dallyhorse himself, and a queer-looking lady, and some children, I don't know how many children, for they kept them out of the way; and a nice young woman as did the cooking for them, and precious little it was."

"What was his profession? And who was his creditor?'

"I don't know. They called him an artist I think, but he look to me more like a sailor. It was a boarding-house bill, as I was on him for. Rum-tempered fellow. I thought he would have stuck me when I got his sword thing. A tallish man he was, slight build, and active, and such black eyes."

"Now, Balaam, if you can trace that man, and find out where he is living now, I will give you two hundred pounds. Here's ten pounds for you as an earnest."

Balaam was so amazed, that he almost looked straight at me.

"Please, Miss, may I tell Balak? I shan't be happy if I doesn't. We always works together, and it wouldn't be on the square like."

"Was he with you then? And can he keep a secret?"

"Yes, Miss, he was with me, and I'd trust him with a gallows secret. I can't do no good without him."

"Then, certainly you may tell him; but not while in this house. Here is my country address, that you may know who you act for. Keep clear of the Police. Keep the whole matter to yourselves. In two days, I leave London; if you discover nothing in that time, write to me here, and I will take good care to have the letters forwarded. Do nothing, but find out that one thing, and when I have verified it, I will pay you the two hundred pounds."

"Would you mind, Miss, putting it on paper?"

"Yes: for many reasons, I will not write it down. But you are at liberty to inquire who I am, and whether I am likely to disgrace my word."

After taking his address, "Balaam Levison, Dove Court, Chancery Lane," I allowed him to depart, and heard him pause on every stair, to ponder this strange matter.

Presently Mr. Shelfer came home, and was delighted to see the bailiffs; and the pleasure being mutual, and my cash burning to be quenched, a most hilarious evening was the natural result. My health was drunk, as I could hear too plainly, to unfathomable depths: and comic songs from three loud organs, provided with patent nasal stops, with even Patty's treble pipe audible in the chorus, broke from time to time the tenour of my sad and lonely thoughts.

CHAPTER IV.

The bailiff's discovery, and the pursuit commenced thereon, appeared to me so important, that in reply to the message received the next morning--that my uncle was much the same, and longing for my return--I sent word that my journey was put off until the day after the morrow. This allowed me one day more for tidings from my new scouts, as to the success of their efforts. I was very sorry to disappoint my poor sick uncle, but it seemed still worse to run away all in the dark.

The next thing I did was to arrange with Mrs. Shelfer about the money I had paid for her. It was not the money I cared for, but I had other views. Although she was politely thankful, I perceived that she thought it a very bad job indeed, and a most romantic transaction. Thirty per cent. was the very largest dividend she had ever intended to pay. But the plan which I proposed was so much for her benefit, while it suited me, who otherwise must have lost the money, that it almost recovered her from the shock of having paid a debt. The plan was simply this, that she should reserve my rooms for me, airing and cleaning them duly, and always keeping the bed in a fit state to be slept on at an hour's notice. My previous rent had been twelve shillings a week, the utmost I could afford out of my narrow income; attendance, and linen, and other troubles being now dispensed with, I thought it fair to allow her ten shillings off her debt to me, for every week I should so retain the rooms. The 4*l.* for the expenses of the execution I forgave her altogether; inasmuch as I had paid without consulting her. Directly my payment should be exhausted, to wit in twenty weeks, I would send her a further sum, if I still required the rooms.

She was delighted with this arrangement, which in fact enabled her to have her "sticks" all to herself, to pet them and talk to them every day, and even to clean them, if such a freak of destruction ever should enter her brain. She could use the sitting-room for her own pleasure and pride, as much as ever she chose, so long as it always was ready for me; and already visions were passing before her mind's eye, of letting the parlour downstairs with the onion-room for its dormitory. To me the arrangement was very convenient, as affording a fixed and familiar resort in London, and a pivot of ready communication. Nor was it a small consolation to feel that I still retained a stronghold in the neighbourhood of dear friends.

All this being comfortably settled, Giudice and I went forth to pay our visit in Lucas Street. The whole of that street we found so utterly changed in appearance by a vigorous onset of painters, grainers, and decorators, that it was not easy to know the house we were in quest of. Even the numbers on the doors, which had been illegible, or very nearly so, had now been re-arranged and painted over again upon the fashionable and very sensible mode of marking odd numerals on one side, and even ones on the other. Finding myself in a difficulty, and the houses all alike as the central peas of a pod, I trusted to Judy's delicate nose, and rang the bell of the door at which he halted. Then he drew back, and trembled, and crouched upon the pavement, to wait for my return. As I heard the tinkle, my heart began to flutter: who could tell what new phase of my life might begin with that little pull? After some delay, poor old Cora came, looking as weird and woebegone as ever--fierce would have been that look to any one but me. I knew that I held her by my magic gordit, like the slave of the lamp. After imploring in some mumbled words (which I interpreted only by knowledge of her desire) gracious leave to kiss that potent charm, she led me into the breakfast-parlour, where I found sweet Isola in a passionate flood of tears.

At sight of me, her beautiful smile broke through them, and her quick deep sobs spent themselves in kisses.

"Oh, I am so gug-gug-glad, my own dear Cla-Cla-Clara; and I won't cuc-cuc-cry one bit more, the moment I can stop."

She put her arms around me, and her head upon my breast, as if I had been, at the very least, her brother.

"My pretty dear, what is it all about?"

I had never seen her look so lovely as now, her violet eyes brimming with liquid brightness, the velvet of her cheeks deepened to rich carmine, and the only thing that sweet face ever wanted, the expression of earnest feeling, now radiant through the whole.

"Why, dear, I ought not to tell you; but I must tell somebody, or my heart will break."

Here she pressed her little hand on that pure unfissured casket, where sorrow was as yet an undreamed-of robber.

"You know, dear, it's all about papa and my darling Conny. The only trouble I ever have, but a very great one, big enough and too big for two little folk of my size. Half an hour ago, I went in suddenly to get a book upon the politico-economical science, the very one papa is lecturing about so beautifully; and I did not even know that Conny was in the house. There papa was, white as death with passion; and Conrad with his eyes like coals of sparkling fire; and what do you suppose my papa called his own son Conny?"

"Don't tell me, if it's anything bad. I can't bear it, Isola."

"Oh, I knew you were fond of him, and I am so glad!"

This she said in such an artless way--as if Conrad and I were two dolls which she meant to put in one doll's house--that instead of colouring, I actually laughed.

"Oh, but I must tell you, Clara: it's right for you to know; one of the leading principles of political economy--"

"Don't talk to me of that stuff."

"Well, I won't; because I see that you don't understand it. But he actually called him--and his voice came from a depth, like an Artesian well--he called our darling Conny--"

"What?" And in my passion, I flung off her hand, and stood up.

"A low bastard, a renegade hound, a scandal to his country--and then he even said Rimbecco."

She pronounced the last word almost with a scream, as an insult beyond forgiveness. What it meant I did not ask, I had heard enough already.

"I must leave this house. Where is your brother Conrad?"

"Gone, I believe, to inquire for you. Nothing but that composes him. I wish he would never come here. And he was ordered not to. But it is about some business. Oh, he never will come again." And she began to cry at the thought of the very thing she had wished for.

"Neither will I come again. Where is your father now?"

"Up at his lumbering cabinet, where he always consoles himself, whenever he is put out. But if you are going, dear child, do let me come with you. I shall cry till I die here, all by myself: and Pappy never cares about me, when he is in his black dudgeon."

In a few minutes we left the rude unpleasant house, and even Judy seemed relieved to get away from the door. By the time we reached Mrs. Shelfer's, Idols was in capital spirits again, and pressed me for some account of the wonderful wealth, and the grand house she had heard of. No doubt this rumour had found its way through Ann Maples.

"And the great Lord--what's his name, dear Donna? I wouldn't believe a word of it; though I'm sure you are a deal too good for all the house of peers. But Conny did; and wasn't he in a way? But he ought to be very glad you know-- wish you every blessing, as they say in the plays; and a peer is the very highest blessing to an Englishwoman. But one thing I am quite resolved on: Judy belongs to me now, don't you, lovely Judy?"

"No," said the judicious, "I belong to Clara."

"Though Conny pretends, since he was left at your place, that he belongs to him. Now I will give him to you; and so will Conny too. You can afford to keep him now, and I can't, he does eat such a lot; and he does not care a pin for me, but he loves you with all his heart."

"How do you know he does?" I was not attending much, but thinking of some one else.

"Why, can't you see that he does, how he wags his tail every time you even look at him? But I hope poor Conny is here. I should think he would stop, when he finds *darling Clara* come back."

I had jumped to that hope long ago, before we even left Lucas Street, and that had something to do with my walking so fast.

No, he was not there, he had not been there to-day. It was my turn now to cry; what might he not have done, after that fearful insult, and from his own father too?

The tears, which I confided to no one except the wooden-legged blackbird--for Giudice would have made such a fuss about them--were still upon my cheeks, when I heard the well-known step--not half so elastic as usual. I fled into my bedroom, and pushed the boxes about, to make a goodly noise, and to account for the colour in my face. Then out I came at the side-door, and ran downstairs perversely, though I knew that Conrad and Isola were in my sitting-room.

But this first-rate manoeuvre only outwitted its author, for Isola ran down after me, and sent me upstairs alone. All my little nonsense vanished the moment I looked in Conrad's face. His healthy brown complexion was faded to an opal white; beneath his eyes such dark blue rims, that I thought he had spectacles on; and on either cheek a round red spot was burning. So shocked I was, that when he took my hand, I turned my face away and smothered down a sob. I felt that I had no right to be so fresh and blooming. Nor was it only in health that the contrast between us lay. I was dressed with unusual care, having fidgeted all the morning, and with my utmost taste. Poor Conrad was in his working clothes, full of marble dust, tumbled, threadbare, and even in need of mending; his hair swept anyhow, and his hands not over-lately washed. Yet, for all that, he was as clearly a gentleman, as I was a lady.

Not so would he have been arrayed, I fancy, had he thought to see neat Clara. And yet, who knows? "I trust that you will excuse me," he began to say, "but such things have happened lately--you will not account me rude--I had no sense at all of this great pleasure."

"I fear you have not been very happy." I knew not what to say, or how to keep my voice clear.

"Yes," he replied, "as happy as I deserve. It serves me aright for esteeming so much of myself, before that I do anything. But I will win my way"--and his own proud glance flashed out--"and we shall see how many will scorn me then."

"No one in the world can scorn you," I said very softly, and my voice thrilled through him.

"Ah, you are always kind and gentle:"--am I though, thought I--"but I will no more fatigue you with my different lot in life. I am told that some great nobleman has won you for his own. Perhaps you will give me an order."

His throat was swelling with these bitter words, and he looked at his dusty clothes. Somewhat rude I thought him, but I knew not half his troubles.

"Whoever told you that, has made a great mistake. I am engaged to no one. Your sister knows me better." And I turned away to the window. For a minute he said nothing; but I could hear his heart beat. Stedfastly I looked at the cheesemonger's shop. Oh for a flower, or something on the balcony!

Presently he came round the corner of the sofa. Without being rude, I could not help turning round.

His face was much, much, brighter, and his eyes more kind.

"Have I said any harm--I would not for the world--I knew not it was harm."

"No harm," I said, "to think so ill of me! To believe, for a single moment, that because I am not so poor, I would go and forsake--at least, I mean, forget--any one I cared for!"

"Can I ever hope, if I serve you all my life, that you will ever care for me?"

"Don't you know I do?" And I burst into my violent flood.

When I came to myself, both his arms were round me, and I was looking up at his poor sick face, my hair quite full of marble chips, and he was telling me with glad tears in his eyes, which he never took from mine, how he cared for nothing now, not for all the world, not for glory or fur shame, so long as I only loved him.

"With all my heart and soul," I whispered, "him and no one else whatever, whether in life or death."

All the folly we went through I am not going to repeat, though I remember well every atom of it. Let the wise their wisdom keep, we are babes and sucklings. Neither of us had ever loved before, or ever meant to love again, except of course each other, and that should be for ever.

"One thing I must tell you, my own sweet love, and yet I fear to do it. But you are not like other girls. There is no one like you, nor has there ever been. I think you will not scorn me for another's fault."

"Of course I won't, my own pet Conny. What is this awful thing?"

"I am an illegitimate son."

One moment I sprang from him; the next I despised myself. But in spite of all my troubles, there still lurked in my heart the narrow pride of birth. Down to the earth it fell beneath the foot of true love, and I kissed away from his eyes the mingled reproach and sorrow, assuring him that at least he should have a legitimate wife.

To make amends, I leaned upon him one moment, and put my hand on his shoulder, and let him play awhile with the dark shower of my hair.

"Darling Conny, you have told me yours, now you shall hear my secret. Only promise me you will give tit for tat. You say you loved me ever since you saw me first; then you must have loved your Clara when you saved her life."

"What do you mean, my Clara? Those low ruffians in the Park were not going to kill you."

"No, dearest; I don't mean that at all. But there's a kiss for that, I have owed it you ever since. But what I mean no kisses can repay; no, nor a life of love. You saved a life worth fifty of my own."

Some dark alarm was growing in his eyes, on which I gazed with vague increasing terror.

"Why, dearest, it is nothing. Only your own Clara is not Clara Valence; you must call her 'Clara Vaughan.'"

With actual violence he thrust me from his arms, and stood staring at me, while I trembled from head to foot; his face was one scarlet flame.

"And pray, Sir, what harm have I done? Am I to suppose that you"--special emphasis meant for illegitimacy--"that you are ashamed of my father and me?"

"Yes, I am. Accursed low licentious race! If you knew what you have done, you would tear your heart out rather than give it to me."

"Thank you--I feel obliged--my heart indeed--to a bastard. Take back your ring if you please; kindly restore me mine. May I trouble you for room enough to go by?"

And I swept out of the room, and through the side-door into my bed-room, where I crouched in a corner, with both hands on my heart, and the whole world gone away. "Mad!" I heard him cry, "yes, I must go mad at last!" Away he rushed from the house, and I fell upon the bed, and lay in fits till midnight.

CHAPTER V.

I believe that my heart would have burst, if they had not cut my stays; and how I wished it had. When I came back to my unlucky self, there was something shivery cold in the forehead wave of my hair. Was it Conrad's finger? I put up my hand to dash it away, and caught a fine fat leech. Dr. Franks was sitting by me, holding a basin and a sponge.

"That's the last of them, my dear child. Don't disturb him. He is doing his duty by you."

"His duty! Was it his duty to say such fearful things? To break my heart with every word! Ashamed of me--ashamed of my darling father! Low and licentious! What have I done? what have I done? Oh, it I only knew what harm I have ever done!"

"No harm, my poor dear, no harm in the world; let me bathe your pretty face. Come now, you shan't cry another drop. What is to become of the beautiful eyes I was so proud of saving?"

"Oh, I wish you hadn't, how I wish you hadn't. Dr. Franks, I have no father, and no mother, and no one in all the world to love me, and I was just getting so nice and happy again, so proud of myself, and so much prouder of him, and I began to think how glad my own dear father would be; and, Dr. Franks, I did love him so, with all my heart, perhaps it's not very large, but with every morsel and atom of my heart--and now, now I must hate him as much as ever I can. Oh let me go home, do let me go home, where my father and mother are buried." And I rose in the bed to start, and the candles glimmered in my eyes.

"Please to go out of the room, every one please to go; and don't let Isola come. I can't bear the sight of her now. It won't take me long to dress, and I don't want any luggage; and, Mrs. Shelfer, please to go for a cab: and I shan't want the rooms any more, and it does not matter a bit about any letters. I'll tell my father everything when I see him, and then perhaps he'll tell me what harm it is I have done. Why don't you go, when you see I want to get up?'

"Don't you see, my dear child, we are going? Only you must take this glass of wine first, to prepare you for your long journey. Will you take it now, while we fetch the cab?"

"Yes, anything, anything: I don't care what it is. Only let me get ready."

And I drank, without even tasting it, a glass of some dark liquid, which saved me from wandering further either in mind or body.

When I awoke, it was broad noon once more, and Dr. Franks was sitting by me with one of my hands in his. "Magnificent constitution," I thought I heard him mutter, "glorious constitution." What good was it to me? At the foot of the bed, sat Isola crying terribly. Slowly I remembered all my great disaster, but saw it only through a dull gray veil. The power of the opiate was still upon my brain. But a cold dead pain lay heavy on my heart, and always seemed to want a heavy hand upon it. After he had given me a reviving draught, Dr. Franks perceived that I wished to speak to Isola, and accordingly withdrew.

Poor Isola came slowly and sat beside my pillow, doubting whether she should dare to take my hand. Therefore I took hers, drew her face towards me, and covered it with kisses. Isola had done no harm to me whatever, and I felt it something to have even her to love. She was overcome with affectionate surprise.

"Oh, Clara dearest, I am so very glad to find you love me still. I feared that you would never care for me again. What is it all about, dear, if you are well enough to tell me, what is all this dreadful misery about?"

"That is the very thing I want to learn from you, dear. Surely you must know better far than I do."

I would not even ask her what had become of Conrad.

"No, I don't dear. I don't know at all. All I know is there must have been some dreadful quarrel between you and Conrad. I must tell you, dear, I was so anxious about something you can guess, that I stole up to the door soon after he came in; and you were so intent upon the window, that you never even saw me put the door ajar; and then I heard him tell you how very much he loved you, and I was so glad. And then I thought it was not quite fair of me, and I knew all I wanted, so I ran downstairs again. And the next thing I heard was your bedroom door bang and then Conny dashed out the house, and Judy came down to me looking very sorrowful. And I ran up to you, and here I found you shrieking so, and rolling, and clutching at the bedclothes, and I was so frightened I could not even move. And then Judy came and made such a dreadful howling, and Mrs. Shelfer ran straight off for the doctor, and I poured the water in the decanter over you, and I can't tell any more."

"But surely, darling, you have been home since that?"

"Oh yes; when Dr. Franks came, and you were a little better, he would make me go home, because he did not want two patients, he said; and his eldest daughter, such a nice girl, came with me; and my papa didn't even know that I had been out of the house. He was still upstairs, brooding over his relics, and all the sixth form at the College had to go to dinner without their lectures; but I do believe the stupid girls were glad."

"And did you hear--no, it doesn't matter."

"No, I never heard what became of Conrad. No doubt he went back to his favourite chip, chipping. He has got a splendid thing he is full of now, and it prevents his sleeping; something or other very horrible from Dante, and the leading figure is modelled after you. I have seen the drawings, and he has got you exactly."

"How gratifying to be sure! I will ask you no more questions. Pray let me know when I am for sale; though I should call it a work of illegitimate art."

My eyes were on her face, but she showed no consciousness whatever, which she must have done had she known the fact referred to, for she was quick of perception, and open as the day. I was angry with myself for the low and bootless sneer, which was pretty certain to be conveyed to her brother.

"Now I will delay no longer. Let me speak to Dr. Franks. I shall go this afternoon."

Poor Isola turned pale; she had looked upon the occurrence as only a lover's quarrel, sure to be set right in a day or two. She could not harbour any great resentment long, and forgot that I could.

"Don't talk so, dear; and you so very weak! it would be sure to kill you. And what will Conny think? You must not go, at any rate, till you have been to see him."

"I go to him! I hope to see him never more until I charge him in another world with this bitter wrong. No, no more if you please; I will not hear his name again. How can he be your brother? Darling Idols, I never shall forget you. Take this, my pet, and think of me sometimes, for you will never see me more."

I gave her an emerald ring, set with lovely pearls, small types of herself. It was not the one I had reclaimed from her brother, that was a plain keeper.

"Oh Clara, Clara, don't say that, whatever you do, because I know you will keep to it, you are so shamefully obstinate. And I never loved any one in the world like you; no, not even Conny."

"And not even your father or mother?"

"No, not half so much. I like Pappy very well when he is good and kind, but that is not very often now"--the poor little thing's eyes filled again with tears,--"and as for my mother, I never even saw her; she died when I was born."

"And I love you too, my sweet, best of all the world--now. Nevertheless, we must part."

"And never see each other? I don't call that loving. Tell me why: do tell me why. There seems some horrid mystery about every one I love."

And she was overcome with grief. She had not been, like me, apprenticed young to trouble.

"Darling, I will write to you sometimes. You can come here for the letters. I will have no secrets any more from you; but you must never attempt to write to me--only send your name on a bit of paper when my letters go."

"But why on earth mayn't I write to you, Clara dear?"

"I can't tell you why. Only I cannot bear it." The truth was I could never have borne to read about her brother. So all that was settled, and I said good-bye with plenty of bitter crying. As for Balaam and Balak, from whom I expected tidings, and George Cutting, whom I had thought it right to send for--I had not the heart to attend to any of them. Dr. Franks had done his utmost to oppose my sudden journey, but I told him truly that I should go mad if I stopped there any longer. I could not bear the mere sight of the room where I had been, in the height of delicious joy, so trampled upon and outraged. My brain was burning, and my heart was aching for the only spot on earth where true love could be found, the spot where lay my father and my mother.

Seeing how the fever of the mind was kindling, the doctor, like a good physician, knew that the best plan was to indulge, and so allay it. Yet he begged me, if I had any regard for him, not to travel all alone while in that dangerous state. With most unlooked-for and unmerited kindness, he even sent his eldest daughter, at an hour's notice, to see me home in safety.

The last farewell was said to Judy, whom I would not take away, greatly as I loved him still; and he received most stringent orders first to conduct dear Isola home, and then to go to his old quarters at the livery stables. Apparently he acquiesced, though with wistful glances; but at Paddington, as I was getting the tickets, to my amazement in he rushed, upset a couple of porters, and demanded his ticket too. Under the circumstances there was nothing for it, except to let him go with us, or to lose the train. So his ticket was taken, and he dashed into the dog-box with an enthusiasm which earned him a hard knock on the head.

CHAPTER VI.

Annie Franks was exactly as Isola had described her, "such a nice girl." Kind-hearted like her father, truthful, ladylike, and sensitive; retiring too, and humble-minded, with a well of mute romance in the shadow of her heart, a wave of which she would not for the world display. The only vent she ever allowed this most expansive element was novel-reading, or a little quiet hero-worship. Her greatest happiness was to sit upon a lonely bank, and read a slashing curtel-axe and gramercy romance, with lots of high-born ladies in it, and lots of moonlight love. If history got hard thumps among them, and chronology, like an unwound clock, was right but twice in twenty-four, simple Annie smiled no less, so long as the summer sun flashed duly on pennon, helm, and gonfalon, and she could see bright cavalcades winding through the greenwood shade. In "coat and waistcoat" novels her soul took no delight. Not a shilling would she squeeze from her little beaded purse for all the quicksilver of Dickens, or the frosted gold[#] of Thackeray. Yet she was not by any means what fast young ladies call a "spooney;" she had plenty of common sense upon the things of daily life, plenty of general information, and no lack of gentle self-respect.

[#] "Ice-tempered steel" I had written. But alas, the great author is dead, and they say that his kind heart was grieved by nothing so much as the charge of Cynicism. If he were a Cynic, would that we all were dogs!--"[Greek: *Kynòs ómmat' echôn, kradíen d' eláphoio.*]"--C.V. 1864.

Now she was wending through an upland meet for gray-clad reverie, where she might dream for days and days, and none but silly deer intrude. As we passed along in the gloaming of the May, through bosomed lawn and bosky dell, with lilac plumes for cavaliers, and hawthorn sweeps for ladies' trains, the soft gray eyes of Annie ceased at last to watch me, and her thoughts were in costume of Chevy Chase or Crecy.

By reason of the message sent the day before, no one in the house expected me; so we stole in quietly, lest my uncle should be alarmed, and I requested Gregory, tipsy Bob's successor, to bring Jane to meet us, in my own little room. Annie being installed there, to her great delight, and allowed free boot of "Marry, Sir knight," and "Now by my halidame," I went to see my poor dear uncle, who by this time was prepared for my visit. Very weak he seemed, and nervous, and more rejoiced at my return than even I had expected. To me also it was warm comfort in my cold pride-ailment to be with one of my own kin, whom none could well disparage. There was a dignity about him, an air of lofty birth, which my own darling father had been too genial to support. Soon I perceived from my uncle's manner, that something had happened since my departure to add to his uneasiness. But he offered no explanation and I did not like to ask him. He in turn perceived the heavy dark despondency, which, in spite of all my efforts, would at times betray itself. Pride and indignation supported me, when I began to think, but then I could not always think, whereas I could always feel. Moreover, pride and indignation are, in almost every case, props that carry barbs. In a word, though I would scorn the love-lorn maiden's part, it was sad for me to know that I could never love again.

With a father's tenderness, he feebly drew my head to his trembling breast, and asked me in a tearful whisper what had happened to me. But I was too proud to tell him. Oh that I had not been! What misery might have been spared to many. But all the time my head lay there, I was on fire with shame and agony, thinking of the breast on which my hair had last been shed.

"Now, good nurse Clara," he said at last with a poor attempt at playfulness, "I shall have no more confidence in your professional skill, unless you wheel me forth to-morrow with a cheerful face. You are tired to-night, my love, and so should I have been, if you had not come home. To-morrow you shall tell me why you came so suddenly and saved me a day of longing. And to-morrow, if I am strong enough, I will tell you a little history, which may be lost, like many a great one, unless it is quickly told. Stop--one cup of tea, dear, and how proud I am to pour it out for you--and then I will not keep you from a livelier friend. To-morrow, you must introduce me. I still like pretty girls, and you should have brought that lovely Isola with you. I can't think why you didn't. She would have been most welcome."

"Come, uncle, I shall be jealous. The young lady I have brought is quite pretty enough for you."

He sighed at some remembrance, and then asked abruptly,

"Do you mean to sleep, my darling, in the little room to-night?" His voice shook so, while he asked this question, that I was quite certain something had alarmed him. The little room was the one I had occupied between the main corridor and his present bedroom. It was meant for an ante-room, not a sleeping chamber; but I had brought my little iron bedstead thither.

"To be sure I do, dear uncle; do you suppose, because I have been off duty, that I mean to be cashiered? Only one thing I must tell you; I have brought home with me one of the very best friends I ever had. You have heard me talk of Giudice. I cannot bear the thought of parting with him to-night, he will cry so dreadfully in the strange stables; and in London he always slept on the mat outside my door. May I have him in the lobby, uncle, you will never hear him move, and he never snores except just after dinner?"

"To be sure, my pet; I would not part you for the world. God bless you, my own child, and keep your true heart lighter."

If I had been really his own child, he could not have been more loving to me, than he had now become.

After giving Annie Franks her tea, which she was far too deep in tournament to drink, I paid a visit to Mrs. Fletcher's room, and learned from her that nothing, so far as she knew, had happened to disturb my uncle: Mrs. Daldy had not been near the house, and there was a rumour afloat that she had been called to take part in a revival meeting near Swansea. So after introducing Judy, who was a dreadful dog for jam, and having him admired almost as much as he ought to be, I returned to Annie, and found her in high delight with everything and everybody, and most of all with her tapestry-writer. Leaving her at last under Tilly's care, Judy and I were making off for our sleeping quarters, when truant Matilda followed me down the passage hastily.

"Oh, Miss, please, Miss, I want to tell you something, and I did not like to name it before that nice young lady, because I am sure she is timid like."

Matilda looked not timid like, but terrified exceedingly, as she stared on every side with her candle guttering.

"Hold your candle up, Matilda; and tell me what it is."

By this time we were in the main passage, "corridor" they called it, and could see all down it by the faint light of some oil-lamps, to the oriel window at the farther end, whereon the moon (now nearly full again) was shining.

"Why, Miss, the ghost was walking last night, and the night before."

"Nonsense, Matilda. Don't be so absurd."

"It's true, Miss. True as you stand there. Pale gray it is this time, and so tall, and the face as white as ashes." And a shiver ran through Tilly, at her own description--"You know, Miss, it's the time of year, and she always walks three nights together, from the big east window to this end and back again. So please to lock your door, Miss, and bolt it too inside."

"Well done, Tilly! Does any one intend to wait up for the ghost? What time does it come?"

"One o'clock, Miss, as punctual as a time-piece. But could you suppose, Miss, any one would dare to wait up and see it?"

"Then how have they seen it, in the name of folly?"

"Why, Miss, I'll tell you. One of the carriage-horses got an inflammation in his eyes, and the farrier give orders to have it sponged never more than three hours between, and so William Edwards, the head-groom if you please, Miss"--Tilly curtseyed here, because this was her legitimate sweetheart--"he stops up till one o'clock to see to it, and then Job Leyson goes instead. So William come in, Miss, on Monday night, to go to bed, please, Miss, and he took the short cut, not that he were allowed, Miss, or would think of taking a liberty on no account whatever, but he were that sleepy he didn't know the way to bed, so he went across the corridor for the short cut from the kitchen gallery to the servants' passage; and there he saw--he hadn't any light, Miss, and the lamps all out--Goodness me! Whatever was that? Did you hear it, Miss?"

"Yes, and see it, Tilly; it's a daddy in your candle. Go on, Tilly, will you. Am I to stop here all night and get as bad as you are?"

"There William Edwards, a man who never swears or drinks, there he saw all in the dark, coming so stately down the corridor, as if it hadn't room enough, with one arm up like this, a tall pale melancholy ghost, and he knew it was the lady who was wronged and killed, when the great wars was, Miss, two hundred year agone."

"Well, Tilly, and did he speak to it?"

"He was that frightened, Miss, he could not move or speak; but he fell again the wall in the side-passage, with his eyes coming out of his head, and his hair up like my wicker-broom. And then she vanished away, and he got to bed, and did perspire so, they was forced to wring the blankets."

"Capital, Tilly! And who saw her the next night?"

"Why that nincompoop Job Leyson, Miss. Our William was a deal too wise to go that way any more, but he tell Job Leyson, and he a foolish empty fellow, perhaps you know, Miss. 'Ho,' says Job, 'I often hear tell of her, to-night I'll have a peep.' So last night when William went to bed on the servants' side, down comes Job and takes the front way, pretty impudent of him I think. And, Miss, I don't know what he see, I never says much to him; but there they found him in the saddle-room, at five o'clock this morning, with his heels up on a rack, and his head down in the bucket, and never a bit of sponge had come near the poor mare's eye."

"Oh, thank you, Tilly. Perhaps you had better snuff your candle. No ghost will have much chance that comes near my Judy." And with that I went to bed, tired of such nonsense.

An hour of deep sleep from pure weariness both of mind and body, and I awoke with every fibre full of nervous life. The moon was high in the south-east, and three narrow stripes of lozenged light fell upon the old oak floor. Although my uncle had left the gable where the windows faced the setting sun, he still kept to the western wing. The house, which was built in the reign of Henry the Eighth, covered the site and in some parts embodied the relics of a much more ancient structure. The plan was very simple, at least as regarded the upstair rooms. From east to west ran one long corridor, crossed at right angles, in the centre and near the ends, by three gable passages. Although there were so many servants, not half the rooms were occupied: all the best bedrooms had been empty many a year. No festivities had filled them since my father's days. Gloom and terror still hung over the eastern part, where he had been so foully murdered. In most of the downstair windows along the front of the house, the rickety lattice of diamond panes had been replaced by clear plate-glass, but the old hall, and the corridor, and some of the gable windows still retained their gorgeous tints and heraldry.

As the shadows of the mullions stole upon my counterpane, there began to creep across my mind uneasy inklings of the ghost. A less imaginative man than William Edwards, I who had often enjoyed his escort, knew well there could not be. As for Job Leyson I could not tell with what creative powers his mind might be endowed; but--to judge from physiognomy--a light ring snaffle would hold them.

Thinking, with less and less complacence, of this apparition story, and the red legend which lay beneath it, for the spectral lady was believed to be a certain Beatrice Vaughan, daughter of the Cavalier who perceived the moss-light, and heiress of the house 200 years ago--thinking of this, I say, with more and more of flutter, I sat up in the bed and listened. My uncle's thick irregular breathing, the play of an ivy-leaf on the mullion, the half-hour struck by the turret-clock, were all the sounds I heard; except that my heart, so listless and desponding, was re-asserting some right to throb for its own safety. With my hand upon it, I listened for another minute, resolving if I heard nothing more to make a great nest in the pillows--I always want three at least--and shut both ears to destiny. But there came, before the minute passed, a low, long, hollow sound, an echo of trembling expectation. In a moment I leaped from the bed; though I had never heard it before, I knew it could only be the bloodhound's cautious warning.

I flung a long cloak round me, gathered close my hair, hurried velvet slippers on, locked my uncle in, and quietly opened the outer door. There stood Giudice in the moonlight, with his head towards the far east window, his ears laid back, his crest erect, and in his throat a gurgling sound, a growl suppressed by wonder. He never turned to look at me, nor even wagged his tail, but watched and waited grimly. I laid my hand upon him, and then glided down the corridor, avoiding the moonlight patches. Giudice followed, like my shadow, never a foot behind me, his tread as stealthy as a cat's. Before I reached the oriel window where the broad light fell, something told me to draw aside and watch. I withdrew, and Giudice with me, into the dark entrance to my father's room. Here we would see what came. Scarcely had I been there ten throbs of the heart, when between me and the central light, where the moonbeams fell askance, rose a tall gray figure. I am not quite a coward, for a woman at least, but every drop of blood within me at that sight stood still. Even Giudice trembled, and his growl was hushed, and every hair upon him bristled as he crouched into my cloak. Slowly the form was rising, like a corpse raised from a coffin by the loose end of the winding-sheet. I could not speak, I could not move, much less could I think. With a silent stately walk, or glide--for no feet could I see--the figure came towards the embrasure where we lurked. Ashy white the face was, large the eyes and hollow, all the hair fell down the back, the form was tall and graceful, one arm was lifted as in appeal, to heaven, and the shroud drooped from it, the other lay across the breast. The colour of the shroud was gray, pale, unearthly gray. For one moment as it passed, I kept my teeth from chattering. Giudice crawled one step before me, with his mind made up for death. Back the blood leaped to my heart, as the apparition glided slowly down the corridor without sigh or footfall.

What to do I knew not; my feet were now unrooted from the ground. Should I fly into my father's death-room? No; I was afraid. To stay where I was seemed best, but how could I see it come back, as I knew it would? Another such suspension of my life, and all, I felt, would be over.

Suddenly, while still the figure was receding in the distance, I saw a great change in the bloodhound. He strode into the corridor, and began to follow. At the same time, the deep gurgle in his throat revived. In a moment, it flashed through me that he had smelt the ghost to be a thing of flesh and blood. It might be my father's murderer. At any rate it had entered as he must have done. Close behind the dog I stole after the spectral figure. The supernatural horror fled; all my life was in my veins. What became of me I cared not, I who was so wretched. Almost to the end, that gliding form preceded us, then turned down a flight of steps leading to the basement. Triple resolution gushed through me at this; this was the spot where the ghost was known to turn, and glide back through the corridor. When it had descended about half-way down the staircase, where the steps were on the turn and narrow, standing at the head I distinctly heard a flop, as of a slipper-heel dropping from the foot, and then caught up again. What ghost was likely to want slippers? And what mortal presence need I fear, with Judy at my side? Keeping him behind me by a gentle touch, I hurried down the stairs. Luckily, I stopped before I turned the corner, for a gleam came up the passage; the ghost had struck a lucifer.

It was a dark and narrow passage, proof to any moon-light, and the spectre lost no time in lighting a small lamp, to find the study door; I mean my uncle's private study, where he kept his papers. The lamp was of peculiar shape, very small, and fitted with three reflectors, to throw the light in converging planes.

Still remaining in deep shadow, I saw the person--ghost no longer--produce a key, open the study door and enter. Then an attempt was made to lock the door from the inside, but--as I knew by the sound--the false key would not work that way, and the door was only closed. Whispering into Judy's ear, that if he dared to move--for his honest wrath at these burglarious doings could scarcely be controlled--I would make a ghost of him next day, I left him in the passage, and softly followed the intruder. First I looked through the key-hole; the room was very dark and full of heavy furniture; I could see nothing; but must risk the chance. So I slipped in noiselessly and closed the door behind me. With the ghostly apparel thrown aside, and a mask laid on an ebony desk, stood intently occupied at the large bureau, which I had once so longed to search, my arch-enemy, Mrs. Daldy. I was not at all surprised, having felt long since that it could be no other. Sitting upon a stiff-backed velvet chair, in the shadow of an oaken bookcase--crouch I would not for her--I waited to see what she would do. Already the folding-doors of the large bureau were open; their creaking had drowned the noise of my entry. Before her was exposed a multitude of drawers. All the visible doors she had probably explored on the previous nights, as well as the other repositories of various kinds which the room contained. Her search was narrowed now to one particular part of this bureau.

The folding-doors were very large, and richly inlaid with arabesques and scroll-work of satin-wood and ebony: all the inside was fitted and adorned with ivory pillars, small alcoves containing baby mirrors, flights of chequered steps, and other quaint devices, besides the more business-like and useful sliding trays. With the lamp-light flashing on it, it looked like a palace for the Queen of Dolls--a place for puppet ceremony and pleasure. Every drawer was faced with marquetrie, every little door had panels of shagreen. In short, the whole thing would have been the pride of any shop in Wardour Street, when that street was itself. Having never seen it open till now, I was quite astonished, though I don't know how often my father had promised to show it to me on my very next birthday, if I were good. Probably I was never good enough.

Without any hesitation, Mrs. Daldy pressed a fan, or slide, of cedar-wood, in the right corner of the cabinet; the slide sunk into a groove, and disclosed two deep, but narrow drawers; these she pulled out from their boxes, and laid aside; they were full of papers, which she no doubt had already examined. Then she placed the diminutive lamp on one of the doll steps, and produced from her pocket three or four little tools. Before commencing with these, she probed and pressed the partition between the sockets of those two drawers, in every imaginable way--a last attempt to find the countersign of some private nook, which had defied her the night before.

At length, with a low cry of impatience, she seized a small, thin chisel, and a bottle of clear liquid: with the one she softened the buhl veneer upon the partition's face, and with the other she removed it. Then, after a little unscrewing, she carefully prized away the stop of cedar-wood, while I admired her workman-like proceedings (so far as they were visible to me), and the graceful action of the arms she was so proud of. Her shoulder came rather in my way, but I got a glimpse of the narrow, vertical opening, where the cedar-stop had been. She drew a long breath of delight and pride, then thrust a wire-crook into this opening, and hooked forth two thin and closely-fastened packets. Eagerly she looked at them; they were what she wanted. No doubt she knew their contents; her object was to get hold of them. Having placed them carefully in her bosom, she prepared for a little more joiner's work, to restore what she had dismantled. Her dexterity was so pleasing, that I let her proceed for a while. She soon refixed the cedar-stop, tapping it in the most knowing way with the handle of the screw-driver, then she screwed it tightly, and spread the wood with some liquid cement to carry the veneer. She had mislaid the narrow strip of tortoise-shell and brass, and was looking for it on the chequered steps, when I called aloud:

"Shall I show you where you put it, Mrs. Daldy? But where on earth did you learn your trade?"

Never was amazement written more strongly on any human face. If the ghost had frightened me, I now had my full revenge. She dropped the bottle of cement, and it rolled on the cabinet steps; she turned, with her face as white as the mask, and glared round the room, for I was still concealed in the recess. I thought she would have blown out the lamp, but she had not presence of mind enough: otherwise among all that furniture it would not have been easy to catch her; and she knew nothing of my sentinel at the door.

After some quiet enjoyment of her terror, I came forth, and met her fairly.

"What, Clara Vaughan! Is it possible? I thought you were in London."

"Is it possible that I have found a Christian, so truly earnest about her soul, so yearning over the unregenerate, committing a black robbery in the dead of night? Is this what you call a wholesome conviction of sin?"

Low exultation I confess: but the highest blood in the land, if it were blood, could scarcely have forborne it: for how I abhorred that hypocrite!

For a time she knew not what to do or say, but glared at me without much Christian feeling. Then she tried to carry it off in a grandly superior style. She drew herself up, and looked as if I were not worth reasoning with.

"Perhaps you are young enough to imagine, that because appearances are at this moment peculiar--"

"Thank you: there is no need to inquire into the state of my mind. Be kind enough to restore those packets which you have stolen."

"Indeed! I am perfectly amazed at your audacity. What I have belongs to me righteously, and a stronger hand than yours is required to rob me." She grasped her chisel, and stood in a menacing attitude. I answered her very quietly, and without approaching nearer.

"If I wish to see you torn in pieces, I have only to raise my hand. Giudice!" And I gave a peculiar whistle thoroughly known to my dog. He leaped against the door, forced the worn catch from the guard, and stood at my side, with his great eyes flashing and his fangs laid bare. Mrs. Daldy jumped to the other side of the table, and seized a heavy chair.

"My dear child, my dear girl, I believe you are right after all. It is so hard to judge--for God's sake keep him back--so hard to judge when one's own rights are in question. The old unregenerate tendencies--"

"Will lodge you in Gloucester jail to-morrow. Once more those papers--or--" and I looked at Giudice and began to raise my hand. His eyes were on it, and he gathered himself for the spring like a cannon recoiling. In the height of her terror, she tore her dress open and flung me the packets across the end of the table. I examined and fixed them to Judy's collar. Then we both advanced, and penned her up in a corner. It was so delightful to see her for once in her native meanness, despoiled of her cant and phylactery, like a Pharisee under an oil-press. She fell on her knees and implored me, in plain earnest English for once, to let her go. She appealed to my self-interest, and offered me partnership in her schemes; whereby alone I could regain the birthright of which I had been so heinously robbed. I only asked if she could reveal the mystery of my father's death. She could not tell me anything, or she would have jumped at the chance. At last I promised to let her go, if she would show me the secret entrance under the oriel window. It was not for her own sake I released her, but to avoid the scandal and painful excitement which her trial must have created. When she departed, now thoroughly crestfallen, I followed her out of the house by the secret passage, wherein she had stored a few of her stage-properties. Giudice, whom, for fear of treachery, I kept at my side all the time, showed his great teeth in the moonlight, and almost challenged my right to let her go. After taking the packets from him, I gave him a sheepskin mat under the window there, and left him on guard; although there was little chance of another attempt being made, while the papers were in my keeping. Her mask and spectral drapery remained with me, as trophies of this my ghostly adventure.

CHAPTER VII.

Next day when I showed my uncle the two sealed packets which I had rescued, and told him all that had happened, at first he was overcome with terror and amazement. His illness seemed to have banished all his satirical humour, and that disdainful apathy which is the negative form of philosophy. He took the parcels with a trembling hand, and began to examine the seals.

"All safe," he said at last, "all safe, to my surprise. Dear child, I owe you more than life this time. You have defeated my worst enemy. To your care only will I commit these papers, one of which, I hope will soon be of little value. It is my will; and by it your father's estates are restored to you, while the money which I have saved by my own care and frugality is divided into two portions, one for you, and the other, upon certain events, for that worthless Mrs. Daldy. This must be altered at once. When you have heard my story, you may read the will, if you like. Indeed I wish you to do so, because it will prove that in spite of all our estrangement, I have meant all along to act justly towards you. But that you may understand things properly, I will tell you my strange history. Only one thing you must promise before I begin."

"What is it, uncle dear?"

"That you will forgive me for my one great error. Although it was the cause of your dear father's death."

I could not answer, for a minute. Then I took his hand and kissed it, as he turned his face away.

"My darling, I am not quite strong enough now after all you have been telling me. Although I had dark suspicions yesterday that some plot was in action; for I had observed that things in the study were not as I had left them; and I had other reasons too. But take me, my precious child, to the sunny bank this afternoon, and please God, I will at least begin my tale."

I begged him in vain to defer it: there was a weight upon his mind, he said, which he must unload. So in the early afternoon, I wheeled him gently to the sheltered nook. There, with the breezes way-lost among new streets of verdure, tall laburnum dangling chains of gold around us, and Giudice stretching out his paws in sunny yawns of glory, I listened to my uncle's tale, and was too young to understand the sigh which introduced it. How few may tell the story of their lives without remembering how they played with life! Alas the die thrown once for all, but left to roll unwatched, and lie uncounted!

Though I cannot tell the story in his impressive way, I will try to repeat it, so far as my memory serves, in his words, and with his feelings. Solemnly and sadly fell the history from his lips, for his mind from first to last was burdened with the knowledge that the end was nigh at hand, that nothing now remained, except to wait with resignation the impending blow.

STORY OF EDGAR VAUGHAN.

"I have always been, as you know, of a roving unsocial nature. My father being dead before I was born, and my mother having married again before I could walk, there was little to counteract my centrifugal tendencies. I seemed to belong to neither family; though I always clung to the Vaughans, and disliked the Daldys. The trustees of my mother's settlement were my virtual guardians; for all the Vaughan estates being most strictly entailed, my father had nothing to dispose of, and therefore had made no will. My mother's settlement comprised only personal estate, for no power had been reserved under the entail to create any charges upon the land. The mortgages, of which no doubt you have heard, as paid off by your father, were encumbrances of long standing.

"The estates, I need not tell you, were shamefully mismanaged, during your father's long minority. An agent was appointed under the Court of Chancery, and an indolent rogue he was. Meanwhile your father and myself went through the usual course of education, no difference being made in that respect between us. Although we were only half-brothers, we were strongly attached to each other, especially after a thorough drubbing which your good papa found it his duty to administer to me at Eton. It did me a world of good; before that, I had rather despised him for the gentleness of his nature. At Oxford, after your father had left, I kept aloof both from the great convivial and from the thinly peopled reading set, and lived very much by myself. Soon as the humorous doings, whose humour culminates in the title 'lectures,' soon as these were over, I was away from the freckled stones, punting lazily on the Cherwell, with French and Italian novels; or lounging among the gipseys on the steppes of Cowley. Hall I never frequented, but dined at some distant tavern, and spent the evening, and often the night till Tom-curfew, in riding through the lonely lanes towards Otmoor, Aston Common, or Stanlake. It was strange that I never fell in love, for I had plenty of small adventures, and fell in with several pretty girls, but never one I cared for. Gazing on the wreck I am, it is no conceit to say that in those times I was considered remarkably good-looking. Of course I was not popular; that I never cared for; but nobody had reason to dislike me. I affected no peculiarity, gave myself no airs, behaved politely to all who took the trouble to address me; and the world, which I neither defied nor courted, followed its custom in such cases, and let me have my way.

"At Lincoln's Inn, my life was much the same, except that wherries succeeded punts, and evening rides were exchanged for moonlight walks in the park. It was reported at home, as it is of most men who are called to the Bar, that I was likely to do great things. There never was a chance of it. Setting aside the question of ability, I had no application, no love of the law, no idea whatever of touting; and still more fatal defect, my lonely habits were darkening into a shy dislike of my species.

"You have heard that I was extravagant. As regards my early career, the charge is quite untrue. Money, I confess, was never much in my thoughts, nor did I ever attempt to buy things below their value; but my wants were so few, and my mode of life so ungenial, that I never exceeded the moderate sum allotted to me as a younger son. Afterwards this was otherwise, and for excellent reasons.

"During the height of the London season I was always most restless and misanthropic. Not that I looked with envy on the frivolous dust of fashion, and clouds of sham around me; but that I felt myself lowered as an Englishman by the cringing, the falsehood, the small babooneries, which we call 'society.' I longed to be, if I could but afford it, where men have more manly self-respect, and women more true womanhood.

"Your parents were married, my darling Clara, at the end of December, 1826, six years before your birth. Upon that occasion, your dear father, the only man in the world for whom I cared a fig, made me a very handsome present. In fact he gave me a thousand pounds. He would have given me a much larger sum, for he was a most liberal man, but the estates had suffered from long mismanagement, and were seriously encumbered. I do not hesitate to say that the gross income of this property is now double what it was when your father succeeded to it, and the net income more than quadruple. During the four years which elapsed between that event and his marriage, he had devoted all he could spare to the clearance of encumbrances and therefore, as I said, the present he made me was a most generous one. More than this, he invited and pressed me to come and live on the estate, and offered to set me up in a farm which I might hold from him on most advantageous terms. Upon my refusal, he even begged me to accept, at a most liberal salary, the stewardship of the property, and the superintendence of great improvements, which he meant to effect. I remember, as if it were yesterday, the very words he used. He took my hand in his, and with that genial racy smile, which very few could resist,

"'Come, Ned,' he cried, 'there are but two of us; there's room for both in the old nest; and you are big enough to thrash me now.'"

At the sweet recollection of his Eton drubbing, as he called it, my poor uncle's eyes grew moist.

"So you see, my child, instead of grudging your father the property, I had every reason to love and revere him. However, I refused this as well as the other offer; but I accepted his present, and invested it rather luckily. After spending a pleasant month at home--as I always called it--I returned to London early in April, 1827. There are no two minds alike, any more than there are two bodies; and yet how little variety exists in polite society! Surely it were more reasonable to wedge the infant face into a jelly-mould, to flute its ears and cheeks like collared head, and grow the nose and lips and eyebrows into rosettes and grapes and acorns, than to bow and cramp and squeeze a million minds into one set model. Yet here I find men all alike, Dane and Saxon, Celt and Norman, like those who walk where snow is deep, or Alpine travellers lashed to a rope, trudging each in other's footprint, swinging all their arms in time, looking neither right nor left, and so on through life's pilgrimage, a file some million deep. Who went first they do not know, why they follow they cannot tell, what it leads to they never ask. I was marked and scorned at once, because I dared to adopt a hat that did not scalp me in half-an hour, and a cravat that did not throttle me; and even had the hardihood to dine when I felt hungry. How often I longed for a land of freedom and common sense, where it is no disgrace to carry a barrel of oysters, or shake hands with a tradesman. I know what you are smiling at, Clara. You are thinking to yourself, 'how different you are now, my good uncle; and wern't you a little inconsistent in sanctioning all this livery humbug here?' Yes, I am different now. I am older and wiser than to expect to wipe away with my coat-sleeve the oxide of many centuries. As for the livery, it makes them happy: it is an Englishman's uniform. And I have seen and suffered so bitterly from the violence of an untamed race, that I admire less what I used to call the unlassoed arch of the human neck. I have seen a coarse line somewhere,

"'And freedom made a deal too free with me,'

which expresses briefly the moral of my life. However, at the time I speak of, nursing perhaps a younger son's bias against the social laws, and fresh from the true simplicity and unaffected warmth of your father's character and the gentle sweetness of your mother's, I could not sit on the spikes of fashion's hackney coach, as becomes a poor Briton, till the driver whips behind. Finding of course that no one cared whether I sat there or not, and that all I got at the side of the road was pea-shots from cads in the dickey, I did what thousands have done before me, and will probably do again, I voted my fellow-Britons a parcel of drivelling slaves, and longed to be out of the gang. Perhaps I should never have made my escape, for like most of my class, I spent all my energy in small eccentricity, if it had not been for what we idlers entitle the force of circumstances. At a time when my life was flowing on calmly enough though babbling against its banks, it came suddenly on an event which drove it into another and rougher channel.

"Early one afternoon in the month of April, 1829, I launched my little boat from the Temple-stairs, where I kept it, and feeling more than usually saturnine and moody, resolved on a long expedition. So I victualled my ship like Robinson Crusoe, and took some wraps and coverings. It was then slack water, just at the height of the flood. I meant to have gone to Richmond, but being far too indolent to struggle against the tide, I yielded to nature's good pleasure, and pulled away down stream. In a few minutes a rapid ebb tide was running, and I made up my mind to go with it as far as ever it chose, and to return with the flood whenever that pleased to meet me.

"After rowing steadily for several hours, I found myself a long way past my customary Cape Turn-again. With a strong ebb tide as well as a land-fresh in the river, I had got beyond Barking Reach, and as far as the Dagenham marshes. Here some muddy creeks, pills, and sluggish channels wind and welter among the ooze-lands on the north side of the Thames. All around them stretches and fades away a dreary flat monotonous waste; no dot of a house, no jot of a tree, to vary the dead expanse; except that by the river-side one or two low cabooses, more like hoys than houses, are grounded among the slime. This, so far as my memory serves, was the state of these Essex marshes in the year 1829: how it is now I cannot say.

"It was high time for me to turn: row as I would, I could hardly get back to my haven by midnight. Outrigger skiffs were not yet known; and an oarsman could not glide along at the rate of ten miles an hour. Just as I was working round, a steam packet, which had been moored a short way below, crippled perhaps in her engines, now at the turn of the tide passed up, and was quickly out of sight. As she passed me I hailed for a tow-rope; but either they could not hear, or they did not choose to notice me. There was nothing for it but to bend my back to the oars, and keep a sharp look out. Presently the flood began to make strongly up the river, and I gave way with a will, my paddles bending and the water gleaming in the early starlight. It was a lonely and melancholy scene. The gray mist returning from some marshy excursion, and hugging the warm sea-water, floated along in dull folds, with a white flaw of steam here and there curdling over the current. Not a ship, not a barge was in sight; no voice of men or low of cattle broke the foggy silence: but the wash of the stream on its sludgy marge, or on some honey-combed mooring-post, surged every now and then betwixt the jerks of my rowlocks. The loneliness and the sadness harmonised with my sombre mind. All is transient, all is selfish, all is a flux of melancholy. If we toss and dance we are only boats adrift; we are nothing more than crazy tide-posts, if we be philosophers.

"Suddenly a clear loud cry broke my vacant musings. It startled me so that I caught a crab, ceased rowing, and gazed around. At first I could not tell whence it came, till my boat, with the way she had on her, shot round a low spit of the Essex shore, which from the curve of the river I was nearing rapidly. Louder and louder the cry was twice repeated, and I heard in the still spring evening the oaths of men and the scuffling of feet. Within fifty yards of me was an ill-looking house, made of battens, and raised on piles above high water mark. A tattered sign hung on a pole, and a causeway led to the steps. While I was hesitating, two figures crossed a lattice window, as if in violent struggle, and a heavy crash resounded. Three strong strokes of my oars, and the keel grated on the causeway. Out I leaped with the boat-hook, threw the painter over a post, and rushed up the slimy jetty, and the narrow wooden steps. The door was fastened, I pushed it with all my force, but in vain. One faint scream reached my ears, as of some one at length overpowered. Swinging the boat-hook with both hands, I struck the old door with the butt, and broke it open. In the lower room there was no one, but a moaning and trampling sounded over head. Upstairs I ran, and into the room where the villany was doing. A poor girl lay on the floor at the last gasp of exhaustion. Two ruffians with a rope were bending over her. Down went one, at a blow of my boat-hook, flat beside his victim: the other leaped at my throat. I saw and soon felt that he was a powerful man, but in those days I was no cripple. We were most evenly matched. I wrenched his hand from my throat, but twice he got me under him, twice I writhed from his grasp like a python from a tiger's jaw. Clutched and locked in each other's arms, in vain we tugged to get room for a blow. Throttle, and gripe, and roll--which should be first insensible? An accident gave me the mastery. For a moment we lay face to face, glaring at each other, drawing the strangled breath, loosing the deadly grip, panting, throbbing, and watching. My boat-hook lay on the floor, my enemy spied and made a sudden dash at it. Instead of withholding, I jobbed him towards it with all my might, and as he raised it, the point entered one of his eyes. With a yell of pain and fury, he sank beneath me insensible. Shaking and quaking all over after the desperate struggle, I bound him and his mate, hand and foot, with the twisted tarry junk, which they had meant for the maiden.

"At length I had time to look round. On a low truckle bed at the end of the long dark room, in which a ship-lamp was burning, there lay an elderly lady in a perfect stupor of fright and illness. Upon the floor with her head thrown back against the timbers, and her black eyes wide open and fixed on me, sat a girl of remarkable beauty, though her cheeks were as white as death. A magnificent ring, for which she had fought most desperately, was wrenched from its place on her finger and hung over the opal nail, for her hands were clenched, and her arms quite stiff, in the swoon of utter exhaustion. Both ladies were in deep mourning.

"For the rest a few words will suffice. The poor ladies revived at last, after chafing of hands and sprinkling, and told me where to find the woman of the house, who had been locked up in another room by her husband and brother. There was no one else on the premises. How came the ladies there, what was their destination, and why were they so outraged? They were on their return to London from the Continent, being called home by tidings of death, and had sailed from Antwerp two days and a-half before, in the steamer which I had seen lying to. Steamers were then heavy lumbering things, and all that time Mrs. Green and her daughter had been knocking about on a pecky sea. No wonder that the poor mother had cried out feebly, to be landed anywhere, anywhere in the world, where things would leave off going round. And before they came to that tedious halt in the river, fair Adelaide, who had enjoyed her meals throughout, renewed and completed her poor mamma's excavation, by inquiring calmly with her mouth full of pickled pork, where the peas-pudding was. Now too Miss Adelaide soon recovered from her fearful battle for honour and life. She was what is called now-a-days a girl of "splendid organisation." If she had not been so, she would have lain ere now with her mother at the bottom of Barking Reach. The two scoundrels of that lonesome hostelry had been ordered to send to Barking for a conveyance. But they only pretended to do so; for they had cast foul covetous eyes on the wealth of their unknown guests and on brave Adelaide's beauty. Beyond a doubt both ladies would have been murdered, but for the gallant resistance, the vigour, and presence of mind of Adelaide.

"Having restored their watches, and scattered trinkets, and led the poor things from the scene of the combat, I was quite at a loss for means to convey them home. Barking was a long way off, and the marshy track unknown to me, and not likely to be found in the dark. Moreover, there must be some hazard in leaving them still in that villanous den, no matter how their cowardly foes might be bound. At last, and with great difficulty, I embarked the two ladies in my shallop, and wrapped them warmly from the night air; then after relashing my prisoners, and locking them up in separate rooms, and the woman downstairs, I pulled away stoutly for Woolwich. Here I obtained a carriage, and started my convoy for London, and then returned with two policemen to the "Old Row Barge," as the low caboose was called. But both our birds were flown, as I was inclined to expect. Most likely the woman had contrived to get out, and release them. At any rate the "Old Row Barge" had no crew, and the deserters had set it on fire. The flames, as we rowed away, after vainly searching the marshes, cast a lurid glow on the mud-banks, and on the slackening tide; a true type it was of what soon befell me--the burning of my caboose. The two men were caught long afterwards by the Thames Police, and transported for life on a conviction for river piracy. At least, I was told that they were the men."

"And of course, dear uncle, you fell deeply in love with the beautiful Adelaide Green."

"Of course, my dear, a young lady would conclude so. But at present I must not talk any more." I had several times tried to stop him. "And what I have next to relate is matter of deeper feeling. By Jove, to think how I battled with that strong man! And now your little fist, Clara, would floor me altogether."

He sighed, and I sighed for him. Then I thought of Mr. Shelfer, and gloried in my prowess, as I wheeled my uncle home.

CHAPTER VIII.

My uncle's tale, as repeated here, will no more be broken either by my interruptions, which were frequent enough, or by his own pauses, but will be presented in a continuous form.

STORY OF EDGAR VAUGHAN.

"On the following day, when I called at the house in Bloomsbury--then a fashionable neighbourhood--to which I had been directed, I was met at the threshold, with power and warmth, by Peter Green himself, an old acquaintance of mine, who proved to be Adelaide's brother. My nature had been too reserved for me to be friendly with him at College, but I had liked him much better than any one else, because he was so decided and straight-forward. The meeting rather surprised me, for Green is not a rare name, and so it had never occurred to me to ask the weary Adelaide whether she knew one Peter Green, a first-class man of Christchurch. Peter, who was a most hearty fellow, and full, like his sister, of animal life, overpowered me with the weight of his gratitude, which I did not at all desire or deserve. As, in spite of your rash conclusion, my romantic Clara, I did not fall in love with Adelaide, who besides her pithsome health and vigour was in many respects astray from my fair ideal, and more than all, was engaged long ago to the giver of the sapphire ring, I need not enlarge upon my friendship with Peter Green, whom I now began to like in real earnest.

Young as he was, his father's recent death had placed him at the head of a leading mercantile house, Green, Vowler, and Green, of Little Distaff Lane. And young as he was--not more than seven-and-twenty--his manners were formed, and his character and opinions fixed, as if he had seen all the ways, and taken stock of the sentiments of all the civilised world. Present to him any complexity, any conflict of probabilities, any maze whose ins and outs were abroad half over the universe, and if the question were practical, he would see what to do in a moment; if it were theoretical, he would quietly move it aside. I have known many learned judges sum up a case most lucidly, blow away all the verbiage, sweep aside all the false issues, balance the contradictions, illuminate all the obscurities, and finally lift from its matrix, and lay in the colourless sunlight the virgin truth, without either dross or polish. All this Peter Green seemed to have done in a moment, without any effort, without any reasoning process; not jumping at his conclusion, but making it fly to him. He possessed what an ancient writer, once highly esteemed at Oxford, entitles the "wit universal," which confers and comprises the "wit of details." For this power when applied to a practical purpose, a great historian employs a happy expression not welcomed by our language; he calls it the power to "pontoon the emergency." Excuse my harsh translation, perhaps it is better than paraphrase.

With all these business qualities, my friend was as merry and unpretentious a man as ever made a bad joke, or laughed at another fellow's; liberal also, warm-hearted, and not sarcastic. In a word, he was a genuine specimen of the noble English merchant, who has done more to raise this country in the esteem of the world than would a thousand Nelsons or Wellingtons.

Now this man discerned at a glance the wretched defects of my nature and position. An active mind like his could never believe in the possibility of being happy without occupation. And by occupation he meant, not the chasing of butterflies, or maundering after foxes, but real honest Anglo-Saxon work; work that strings the muscles, or knits the hemispheres of the brain. And work he would himself, ay, and with all his energies. Not the man was he to tap the table with his pipe, and cry out, "Bravo, Altiora! A little more gin if you please, and chalk it down to the Strike;" but he was the man to throw off his coat, and pitch into the matter before him without many words, though with plenty of thought. Now, this man, feeling deeply indebted to me, and beginning to like me as my apathy and reserve went to pieces before his energy, this man, I say, cast about for some method of making me useful and happy. Wonderfully swift as he was in pouncing upon the right thing, I believe it took him at least five minutes to find out the proper course for an impracticable fellow like me. And when he had found this out, it took even him a week to draw the snail out of his hole. Years of agreeable indolence, and calm objective indifference, seldom ruffled except at fashionable snobbery, had made of me not a Sybarite, or a supercilious censor, much less a waiter on fortune, but a contemplative islander, a Haytian who had been once to Spain, and would henceforth be satisfied with the view of her caravels. But my Adelantado was a man of gold and iron. Green, Vowler, and Green were largely concerned in the oil and dried fruit business. They had ransacked the olive districts of continental Europe, and found the price going up and the quality going down, so they wanted now to open another oil vein.

Peter Green observing my love of uncultured freedom, the only subject on which I ever grew warm and rapturous, espied the way to relieve me of some nonsense, give my slow life a fillip, and perhaps--oh climax--open a lucrative connexion. He knew, for he seemed to know everything done or undone by commerce, that there was a glorious island rich in jewels and marble and every dower of nature, and above all teeming with olives, lemons, and grapes, and citrons; and that this gifted island still remained a stranger, through French and Genoese ignorance, to our London trade. This was the island libelled by Seneca, idolised by its natives, drenched with more blood than all the plains of Emathia, yet mother of heroes and conquerors of the world--if that be any credit--in a single word, Corsica. Once or twice indeed our countrymen have attempted to shake hands with this noble race, so ruined by narrow tradition; and in the end we shall doubtless succeed, as we always do; but the grain of the Corsican is almost as stubborn as our own. In fact the staple is much the same, the fabric is very different. Bold they are, and manly, simple, generous, and most hospitable, lovers too of their country beyond all other nations; but-- oh fatal ignorance--industry to them is drudgery; and labour is an outrage. Worse than all is the fiend of the island, the cursed Blood-revenge.

"Just the place for you, Vaughan," said the indomitable Peter, "every one there as dignified as an eagle after stealing a lamb. No institutions to speak of, but the natural one of Vendetta, splendid equality, majestic manhood, lots of true womanhood, and it does all the work that is done, which isn't saying much. Why, my dear Quixotic, the land of Sampiero and Paoli, and where Rousseau was to legislate, only he proved too lazy,--is not that the jockey for you? After all these levees and masquerades that you so much delight in--you need not scowl like a bandit; it is only because they don't want you, you are just the same as the rest, or why do you notice the nonsense?--after all this London frippery, Monte Kotondo will be a fresh oyster after devil'd biscuits."

"True enough, my friend: but an oyster to be swallowed shell and all."

"Well, is not that just what you want? Lime is good for squeamishness. And more than that, you are just the man we want. You can talk Italian with excellent opera style and sentiment; and you won't be long till you fraternise with the Corsicans. Perhaps they will drive out the French, who don't know what to do with it, and make you their king like Theodore of Neuhoff; and then you proclaim free trade restricted to the navy of Green, Vowler, and Green. But in sober earnest, think of it, my dear Vaughan. Anything is better than this cynic indolence. Some of your views will be corrected, and all enlarged by travel. A common sentiment. Yes, the very thing you are short of. All your expenses we pay of course, and give you an honest salary; and all we ask of you is to explore more than a tourist would; and to send us a plain description of everything. You have plenty of observation; make it useful instead of a torment to you. We know well enough the great gifts of that island, but we want to know how they lie, and how we may best get at them."

"Then you would expect me to make commercial arrangements?"

Peter laughed outright. "I should rather fancy not. Somewhat queer ones they would be. Platonic no doubt, and panisic, but not altogether adapted to double entry."

"Then in fact I am to go as a committee of inquiry."

"I have told you all we want. If you make any friends all the better; but that we leave to yourself. Perhaps you'll grow sociable there. Though the Corsican does not sing, 'We won't go home till morning,' and be going home all the time."

"And how long would my engagement last?"

"Till you have thoroughly traversed the country, if you stick to it so long; and then if you quit yourself well, we should commission you for Sardinia. What an opening for an idle man, though it would soon kill me--so little to do. But you may cut it short when you like. Plenty of our people would jump at such an offer; but for a country like that we must have a thorough gentleman. A coarse-mannered bagman would very soon secure the contents of a fusil. He would be kissing the Corsican girls, who are wonderfully lovely they say, and their lovers amazingly jealous; and every man carries a gun. A timid man they despise, an insolent man they shoot; and most of our fellows are one or the other, or both. But will you undertake it? Yes, or no, on the spot. And I ask you to say 'yes' as a special favour to me."

"Then of course I say yes. When shall I go?"

"To-morrow, if you like. Next month if you prefer it. We can give you introductions. There is no real danger for a thorough gentleman, or you should not go for all the olives in Europe. Mind we want a particular sort, very long and taper--Virgil's 'Ray,' in fact. You shall have a sample of it. As yet we know but one district of Italy where it grows, but have got scent of it in Corsica. Glorious fellows they are, if half that I hear is true, glorious fellows but for their laziness, and that ---- Vendetta."

To be brief, I received very clear instructions in writing, and was off for Bonifazio the following week, in a small swift yacht of my own, a luxury to which I had always aspired, and which I could now for a time afford. But before I went, your poor father, Clara, protested most strongly against the scheme, and even came to London in the vain hope of dissuading me. He had some deep presentiment that it would end darkly, and so indeed it did.

"Ned," said he once more, "there are only two of us, and my dear wife is very delicate. I have been at Genoa, where those islanders are well known, and even there they are rarely spoken of but with a cold shudder. They are a splendid race, I believe, great heroes and all that, but they shoot a man with no more compunction than they shoot a muffro. I implore you, my dear brother, not to risk the last of our family, where blood flows as freely as water. And your temper, you know, is not the best in the world. Don't go, my dear fellow, don't go. I shall have to come and avenge you, and I don't understand Vendetta."

Ah, me! If I had only listened to him. And yet, I don't know. After a pleasant voyage we reached the magnificent island, about the middle of May. My intention was to skirt round it from the southern extremity, taking the western side first, and touching at every anchorage, whence I would make incursions, and return to my little cutter, as the most convenient head-quarters. Of course I should have to rough it; but what young man would think twice of that, with an adventurous life before him?

I will not weary you, my dear child, with a long description of Corsica. It is a land which combines all the softness and the majesty, all the wealth and barrenness, all the smile and menace of all the world beside. I could talk of it by the hour; but you want to know what I did, and was done to, more than what I saw. From the awful rock of Bonifazio, the streets where men should have no elbows, and the tower of Torrione, along the fantastic coast which looks as if time were a giant rabbit, we traced the blue and spur-vexed sea, now edged with white, and now with gray, and now with glowing red, until we reached that paradise of heaven, the garden of Balagna.

CHAPTER IX.

STORY OF EDGAR VAUGHAN.

Let me hold myself. Weak as I am and crippled by premature old age, not the shortness of my breath, not the numbness of my heart, not even the palsy of my frame, can quench or check the fire rekindled by the mere name of that heavenly valley. To live there only half a minute is worth a day of English life. Life--it is a space to measure, not by pendulum or clock-hand, not by our own strides to and fro (the ordnance scale of the million), not even by the rolling sun, and nature's hail and farewell; but by the well-spring of ourselves, the fount of thought and feeling. Every single breath I draw of this living air--air the bride of earth our sire, wedded to him by God Creator, air whose mother-milk we fight for in clusters baulking one another--every breath I draw dances with a buoyant virtue, sucked, in any other land, but from mountain nipples. Bright air of a rosy blue, where northern eyes are dazed with beauty, where every flower cuts stars of light, and every cloud is sunshine's step; can even lovers parted thus believe themselves divided? Every rock has its myrtle favour, every tree its clematis wreath; under the cistus and oleander hides the pink to lace its bodice, watched by the pansy's sprightly eye. Lavishly, as children's bubbles, hover overhead oranges, and citrons, lemons, almonds, figs, varied by the blushing peach and the purpling grape. Far behind, and leaning forth the swarthy bosom of the mountain, whose white head leans on the heaven, are ranks on ranks of glaucous olive, giants of a green old age dashed with silver gray. And oh, the fragrance under foot, the tribute of the ground, which Corsica's great son--as we men measure greatness--pined for in the barren isle, where the iron of his selfishness entered his own soul.

These are said to be the largest olive-trees in the world, and of the very best varieties. Heaps upon heaps the rich fruit lies at the foot of the glorious tree; nature is too bountiful for man to heed her gifts. For this district of Balagna, and that of Nebbio further north, my attention had been especially bespoken by my shrewd and sagacious friend. Therefore and by reason of the charms around me, here I resolved to pass the summer; so my vessel was laid up at Calvi, and being quartered in Belgodere at a little Inn--"locanda" it should be called, but I hate interlarding--I addressed myself right heartily to business and to pleasure.

First I had to study the grand Palladian gift. Unless old Seneca was, as the Corsicans say, a great liar, he cannot have been the author of that epigram which declares this land a stranger to the peaceful boon. It is impossible to believe that a country so adapted to that tree, so often colonized by cultured races, can have been so long ungifted with its staff of life. The island itself in that same epigram is utterly mis-described.

As regards the inhabitants, the first line of the well-known couplet is verified by ages; to the second it does not plead guilty now, and probably never did.

"Law the first revenge. Law the second to live by robbery.

Law the third to lie. The fourth to deny any Gods."

The Corsicans, on the contrary, have always been famous for candour, whose very soul is truth, and for superstition, the wen or hump of religion. For my own part, loving not that unprincipled[#] fellow hard labour, towards whom these noble islanders entertain a like antipathy, and loving much any freedom not hostile to my own, I got on with the natives admirably, for a certain time. Time had reconciled me to their custom of carrying, instead of cane or umbrella, long double-barrelled guns, whose muzzle they afford the stranger full opportunity of inspecting. First-rate marksmen are they, but they sling their guns at hap-hazard on their backs, and cheek to jowl we come upon the cold metal at the corner of the narrow streets. Tall and powerful men they are, especially the mountaineers; with all the Spaniard's dignity and the Italian's native grace. The women are lithe, erect, and beautifully formed, with a swan-like carriage, and a free and courteous bearing, such as very few of our high-born damsels own.

[#] "Labor improbus" of Virgil.

The olive-growers frankly gave me all their little information about that tree whose typical virtues they have never cared to learn. The variety chiefly grown, or rather which chiefly grows itself, is one they call the Genoese. The owners afford them very little culture, and many are too idle even to collect the fruit. There are said to be ten million olive-trees in the island; at least they were reckoned up to that number by order of the Government; then the enumerators grew tired, and left off counting. Whatever number there is might easily be tripled, if any one had the energy to graft the oleasters, with which the hills are covered. There is also the Saracen olive, and the Sabine, the latter perhaps the Regia of Columella, Raggiaria of Cæsalpinus, and Radius of Virgil. However, though not unlike my sample fruit, it was not quite identical, and as my employers wanted a very special sort for very special qualities, I was as far from my object as ever.

One magnificent summer evening, as I rode along the mountain side near the village of Speloncato, suddenly the track turned sharply into a wooded dingle. Steeped in the dream of nature's beauty, I was thinking of nothing at all, as becomes a true Corsican, when I received a sharpish knock in the eye. Something fell and lodged in my capacious beard. Smarting from the pain. I caught it, and not being able to see clearly, took it at first for a spent and dropping bullet. But when my eyes had ceased to water, I found in my hand a half-grown olive of the very kind I had so long been seeking. I drew forth some of my London specimens which had been chemically treated to prevent their shrivelling, and compared it narrowly. Yes, there could be no doubt; the same pyriform curve, the same bulge near the peduncle, the same violet lines in the skin, and when cut open, the same granulation and nucleus. I was truly delighted, at length I should be of some real service; at least if there were many trees here of this most rare variety. By riding up the dingle, I soon ascertained that it was planted with trees of this sort only, gray old trees of a different habit from any other olive. Afterwards I found that it requires a different soil, and a different aspect. Full speed I galloped back to the hamlet of Speloncato, and inquired for the owner of this olive Eldorado. Signor Dezio Della Croce, owner of all this lovely slope, and of large estates extending as far as the road to Corte; in fact the chief proprietor of the neighbourhood. He was, said the peasant with some pride, a true descendant of the great race of Cinarca, foremost in the island annals for a thousand years, and of whom was the famous Giudice Della Rocca, Count and Judge of Corsica, six hundred years ago."

At the sound of his name, Giudice opened his great sleepy eyes, and pricked his ears: I promised not to interrupt, but he gave no such pledge.

"Let the Cinarchesi blood go for its full value; but it was worth something to the Della Croce to be descended also from the Tuscan Malaspina; for the lands of those great Marquises were now in the possession of the Signor Dezio. And the Signor had such a daughter, a young maiden. Ah, Madonna! The loveliest girl in Corsica. And the vine-dresser crossed himself. As I listened to all this information, I began to look through my unused credentials, which I always carried. It struck me that this name of Della Croce was quite familiar to me, though I knew not how, until a letter in the sprawling hand of young Laurence Daldy fell out from among Peter's crabbed characters. Laurence Daldy, my mother's younger son, was now in full career, as a pigeon and a Guardsman, spending at full gallop his dead father's money. These Daldys were of Italian origin, the true name being D'Aldis, which after some years of English life they had naturalised into Daldy. And now I recollected that when we Vaughan boys scorned them as ignoble sons of commerce, they used to brag about their kinship to the ancient Della Croce.

Riding up the forest hill, on whose western bluff stands boldly the gray old tower of the Malaspinas, I began of course to make forecasts about the character of my host. My host I knew he needs must be, for Corsica is of all the world the most hospitable spot. Although by this time well acquainted with the simple island habits, I could not but expect to find a man of stateliness and surroundings, of stiffness and some arrogance. Now the sun was setting, and the western fire from off the sea glanced in spears of reddening gold into the solemn timeworn keep. All things looked majestic, but a deal too lonely. Where was I to apply, how was I to get in? The narrow doorway overhung with the wreck of some portcullis, was blocked instead with a sort of mantlet like the Roman Vinea; the loopholes on the ground-tier were boarded almost to the top, the high windows, such as they were, had their rough shutters closed. Everything betokened a state of siege and fear. Two or three magnificent chesnuts, which must have commanded the front of the tower, had been cut down and added to the defences of the approach. Over these I managed at last to leap my horse, who was by no means a perfect hunter; and there I halted at a loss how to proceed. I had been long enough in Corsica to know, even without a certain ominous gleam from a loophole, and the view in transverse section of a large double-barrelled gun, that the owner of this old mansion was now in the pleasant state of Vendetta.

Expecting every moment to be shot, and nothing said about it, I waved my letter, as a white flag, furiously above my head. Presently that frightful muzzle was withdrawn, and the slide pushed back, to reconnoitre me at leisure. I tried, for the first time in my life, to look like a real Briton; my Corsican ambition was already on the wane. So I sat my horse, and waited; and what came was worth a thousand years of waiting.

Round the bastion of the tower, under the rich magnolia bloom, towards me glided through the rosy shadow the loveliest being that ever moved outside the gates of heaven. She seemed not to walk but waft along, like the pearly Nautilus. A pink mandile of lightest gauze lit the sable of her clustering hair, and wreathing round her graceful head deepened the tinge of the nestling cheeks. The lithe faldetta of white cashmere, thrown hastily over the shoulders, half concealed the flowing curves of the slender supple form, half betrayed them as it followed every facile motion. But when she smiled--oh, Clara, I would have leaped from her father's tower, or into the black caves of the Restonica, for one smile of hers. The dark-fringed lustre of her eyes seemed to dance with golden joy, trusting, hoping, loving all things, pleasure pleased at pleasing. And the gleesome arch of her laughing lips, that never shaped evil word! Oh, my Lily, my own Lily, I shall see you soon again.

My dear Clara, I ought to know better. I am ashamed of myself. And after so many years! But at the first glance of Fiordalisa, my fate was fixed for this life and the other. I never had loved before. I never had cared to look at a girl; in fact I despised them all. Now I paid for that contemptuous folly. Loving at one glance, loving once, for all, for ever, my heart stood still like the focus of a hurricane; my speech and every power but that of vision failed me. I dared not try to leave the saddle, such a trembling took me.

It was a visitation unknown in our foggy plains, scoffed at by our prosy race, but known full well in Southern climes, as the sunstroke of love. My own darling--I can call her nothing less--my own delicious darling was quite startled at me. Whether she had a like visitation in a milder form, is more than I can say; but I hope with all my heart she had; for then, as the Southern tale recites, God placed her hand in mine.

How I got my horse tied up, how I followed her through the side entrance, and returned her father's greeting, I have not the least idea; all I know is that she smiled, and I wanted nothing more. But I could not bear to see her in the true Homeric fashion still maintained in Corsica, waiting on us like a common servant, with her beautiful arched feet glancing under the brown pelone, and her tapering white arms laid demurely on her bosom; then at her father's signal how she flew for the purple grapes or the fragrant broccio! But do what she would, it seemed to become her more than all she had done before. As that form of love and elegance flitted through the simple room, and those lustrous heavenly eyes beamed with hospitable warmth, Signor Dezio Della Croce, careworn man with beard of snow, seemed at times no little proud of his sweet and only child, but was too proud to show his pride. As for me, he must have thought that I spoke very poor Italian.

END OF VOL. II.

BOOK III. (*continued*).
CHAPTER X.

STORY OF EDGAR VAUGHAN.

Child Clara, for your own dear sake, as well as mine and my sweet love's, I will not dwell on that tempestuous time. If you cannot comprehend it without words, no words will enable you. If you can, and I fear you do, no more words are wanted; and, as an old man weary of the world, I know not whether to envy or to pity you.

Hither and thither I was flung, to the zenith star of ecstasy or the nadir gulf of agony, according as my idol pet chose to smile or frown. Though she was no silly child, but a girl of mind and feeling, she had a store, I must confess, of clouds as well as dazzling sunlight in the empyrean of her eyes. Her nature, like my love, was full of Southern passion. It is like the air they breathe, the beauty they behold. One minute of such love compresses in a thunder flood all the slow emotions stealing through the drought-scrimped channel, where we dredge for gold deposits, through ten years of Saxon courtship. Instead of Lily-bloom, she should have been called the Passion-flower.

My life, my soul--how weak our English words are--she loved me from the first, I can take my oath she did, although her glory was too great for her to own it yet, though now and then her marvellous eyes proved traitors. Sometimes when she was racking me most, feigning even, with those eyes cast down, her pellucid fingers point to point, and her little foot tapping the orchid bloom, feigning, I say, in cold blood, to reckon her noble lovers-- long names all and horribly hateful to me--suddenly, while I trembled, and scowled like a true-born Briton, suddenly up would leap the silky drooping lashes, and a spring of soft electric light would flutter through them to the very core of my heart.

As for me, I abandoned myself. I made no pretence of waiting a moment. I flung my heart wide open to her, and if she would not come in, desert it should be for ever.

She did come. That life-blood of my soul came in, and would and could live nowhere else for ever.

It was done like this. One August evening, when the sun was sinking, and the air was full of warmth and wooing sounds, the cicale waking from his early nap, the muffro leaping for the first dew-drop, the love-birds whispering in the tamarind leaves, Fiordalisa sat with me, under a giant cork-tree on the western slope. The tower was still in Vendetta siege, and the grave and reverend Signor knew better than to come out, when the Sbirri were gone to the town. Lily-bloom was sitting by me in a mass of flowers; her light mandile was laid by, that her glorious hair might catch the first waft of the evening breeze. All down her snow-white shoulders fell the labyrinth of tresses, twined by me with red Tacsonia, and two pale carnations. Her form was pillowed in rich fern, that feathered round her waist; of all the fronds and plumes and stems, not one so taper, light, and rich as that. The bloom upon her cheeks was deepened by my playing with her hair, and her soft large eyes were beaming with delicious wonder.

We knew, as well as He who made us, that we loved one another. None who did not love for ever could interchange such looks. Suddenly, and without a word, in an ecstasy of admiration, I passed my left arm round her little waist, drew her close to me--she was very near before--and looking full into her wondrous eyes, found no protest but a thrill of light; then tried her lips and met her whole heart there. Darling, how she kissed me! No English girl can do it. And then the terror of her maiden thoughts. The recollection of her high-born pride, and higher because God-born innocence. How she wept, and blushed, and trembled; trembled, blushed, and wept again; and then vouchsafed one more entrancing kiss, to atone for the unwitting treason. Even thus I would not be content. I wanted words as well.

"Do you love me, my own Lily, with every atom of your heart?"

"I have not left one drop of blood for all the world besides."

And it was true. And so it was with me. I told her father that same night. And now in the heaven of gladness and wild pleasure, beyond all dreams of earth, opened the hell of my wickedness and crime; which but for mercy and long repentance would sever me from my Lily in the world to come. To some the crime may seem a light one, to me it is a most atrocious sin, enhanced tenfold by its awful consequences.

By my crime, I do not mean my sinful adoration, as cold men may call it, of a fellow mortal. Nature has no time to waste, and unless she meant my Lily to be worshipped, she would not have lavished all her skill in making her so divine. No, I mean my black deceit, in passing for my brother. Oh, Clara, don't go from me.

Like many another ruinous sin, it was committed without thought, or rather without deliberation. No scheme was laid, not even the least intention cherished; but the moment brought it, and the temptation was too great. Who could have that loving pet gazing at him so, and not sell his soul almost to win her to his arms?

Laurence Daldy was a lazy ass. I do not want to shift my blame to him, but merely state a fact. If he had not been a lazy ass, your father would be living now--ay, and my Fiordalisa. When he chose, he could write very good Italian, and a clear, round hand, and oh, rare accomplishment for an officer, he could even spell. But his letter to Signor Dezio, scrawled betwixt two games of pool, was a perfect magpie's nest of careless zigzag, wattles, and sand slap-dash. In those days a hasty writer used to flick his work with sand, which stanched but did not dry the ink. The result was often a grimy dabble, like a child's face blotched with blackberries.

Lily and I had quite arranged how we should present ourselves. Like two children we rehearsed it under the twilight trees. "And then, you know," my sweet love whispered, "I shall give you a regular kiss beneath the dear father's beard, and you will see what an effect it will have. Thence he will learn, oh sweetest mine, that there is no help for it; because we Corsican girls are so chary of our lips."

"Are you indeed, my beautiful Lily? I must teach you liberality, to me, and to me alone."

"Sweetest mine," she always called me from the moment she confessed her love; and so, no doubt, she is calling me now in heaven.

The curtain hung in heavy folds across the narrow doorway of the long dark room. The hospitable board was gay with wine and dainty fruit, melons, figs, and peaches, plums of golden and purple hue, pomegranates, pomi d'oro, green almonds, apricots, and muscatels from the ladders of Cape Corso. Through them and upon them played the mellow light from a single lamp, with dancing lustres round it. All the rest of the room was dark. At the head of the table sat Signor Dezio Della Croce, waiting for his guest and daughter. Posted high at the end window on a ledge of rough-hewn board, stood the ancient warder, who had lived for fifty years among them, and whose great fusil commanded the only approach to the castle.

As we entered timidly, the maiden's right hand on my neck, my left arm round her ductile waist, our other hands clasped firmly, I glanced toward that noxious sentinel.

"Never mind him, sweetest mine. Don't believe that he is there. Grandpapa, I call him, and he knows all my secrets."

Signor Dezio looked amazed, as we glided towards him. His life had been one series of crushing blows from heaven. Three brave sons had been barbarously murdered in Vendetta, and his graceful loving wife had broken her heart and died. The sole hope of his house, his petling Fiordalisa, though she called herself a woman and was full sixteen, he looked upon her still in his trouble-torn chronology, as only ripe enough to be dandled on his lap. Still he called her his "Ninnina," and sang nannas to her, as he had been obliged to do after her mother's death.

As he sat there, too astonished to smile, or frown, or say a word, Lily dropped upon her knees before him, as a Grecian maiden would. We English are not supple-jointed; but for Lily's sake, I could not stand beside her. Then she placed her soft right hand in the centre of my hard palm, flung the other arm round my neck, and with her eyes upon her father's, gave me a long affectionate kiss. This done, she drew her father's head down, and kissed his snow-white beard. Now, she told me, after this, any father who is obdurate, must according to institution blame himself and no one else, if harm befall the maiden.

All this time, I spoke not, and thought of nothing except to screen my Lily. Signor Dezio kept a stately silence, but the tears were in his eyes, and the long white beard was quivering. Lily bent her head, and waited for his words.

"Mother of God! My little child, what are you thinking of?"

"Only thinking of being married, father."

"And set another Vendetta afoot, and be killed yourself! Signor"--turning haughtily to me--"this lady is betrothed, from her early infancy, to her cousin Lepardo Della Croce."

"Oh, I hate him," cried Fiordalisa, clasping her hands piteously. "Ah, Madonna, I hate him so; and thank our Lady, no one has seen him for six years. He is dead no doubt in some Cannibal Island. Saints of mercy, keep him. I saw it in the Spalla, in the Shepherd's Spalla, and I saw my own love there, the eve before he came."

"Grace of Holy Mary! Who read the Spalla for you?"

"The hoary goatherd from Ghidazzo." And up sprang Fiordalisa, flew to an inner room, and fetched from the dark niche in the wall the box of holy relics. With these she knelt before her father, and placed her right hand on the box.

"My child, it is not needful. I believe you without an oath. Never yet have you passed the boundary of truth."

The old chief bowed his head in thought. He had lost his last surviving son by neglecting the Spalla's decree. The Spalla is the shoulder blade of a goat, polished, and used for divination; upon it had been read Sampiero's death, and the destiny of Napoleon. The old man who had forecast the latter was still alive, and of immense renown, and traversed the island now like an ancient prophet. He was the hoary goatherd of Ghidazzo.

Lily saw that she was conquering; she leaped upon her father's knee and hugged him; and her triumph was complete. While she wept upon his breast, and told him all her little tale, and whispered in his ear, and while he kissed, and comforted her, and thought of her dear mother, I rushed out and leaped the Vinea, and wept beneath the olive-trees.

At last the old man rose and called me, he durst not venture from the door; but he did what was far better, he sent my own love after me. At length when we returned, and we found cause not to hurry,--

"Signor Vogheno," he began, "I have observed you well. I am a man of very keen observation"--Lily's eyes gave me a twinkle full of fun--"or I should not be alive this moment. I have observed you, sir, and I approve your character. I cannot say as much, sir, of all the Englishmen I have been privileged to meet. There is about them very much of the nature of a dog. Forgive me, sir; pray interrupt me not. I only judge by what I have seen. God forbid that I should say so to you, while you were my guest. Now you are one of my family, and entitled to the result of my observations. Of the little island itself I know nothing at all, though I am informed that its institutions are of a barbarous character."

"Vendetta for instance," was on my lips, but Lily's glance just saved it. And I thought of his three brave sons.

"But, Signor beloved, you are different from them; indeed you have the nobility of the Corsican nature. And what is most of all, my little child has fixed her heart upon you. But she is very young, sir, quite a child you see." I saw nothing of the sort, but a blooming maiden figure, growing lovelier every day. Poor Lily dropped her long eyelashes, and smiled through a glowing blush. So blushed Lavinia under the eyes of Turnus.

"This darling child is now the heiress to these lands of mine. And if her cousin Lepardo, whose death she has seen on the Spalla, be indeed removed from us, she is the very last of all the Della Croce. I cannot easily read the billet of your brother. He does not write good Corsican of our side of the mountains, but some outlandish Tuscan. There is something first which I cannot well decipher, and then I see your name Signor Valentine Vogheno, and that you are the lord of very large estates, in some district called Gloisterio?" He looked at me inquiringly.

Instead of explaining that I was only the brother of the great Signor Valentino, I bowed, alas I bowed with a hot flush on my cheeks. What could it matter, and why should I interrupt him, if he chose to deceive himself? Lily charmed away all hesitation, by clapping her little hands, and crying, "Sweetest mine, I am so glad."

"Then, upon two conditions I will give you my daughter. The first, that you leave this island, and do not see our Lily, write to, or even hear from her, for a period of six months. If she has not outgrown her love, she will then be almost old enough to wed. I mean, of course, if Lepardo does not appear. The other condition is that you shall promise on the holy relics, and you as well, my flower, never to part with these old estates, but keep them for Lily while she lives, and transmit them to her second child."

A load of terror was off my heart--I thought he was going to bind me to the accursed Vendetta. Even for my Lily, I could hardly have taken that pledge. So I assented readily to the last stipulation, though it was based upon a virtual lie of mine. But with Lily's eyes upon me, brimming as they were with tears at the first condition, and her round arms trembling to enfold me, could I stick at anything short of downright murder? The first proviso I fought against in vain. Even Lily coaxed and cried, without any good effect.

When at last we yielded to the stern decree, the venerable father, as we knelt before him, joined our hands together, and poured a blessing on us, which I did not lack. He had given me my blessing.

After this we sat down to supper, and the trusty musketeer, who had watched the whole scene grimly, and without hearing all, knew what the result was, he, I say, upon his perch began to improvise, or haply to adapt, and sing to a childish air, some little verses upon the glad occasion. Having exhausted his stock, down he leaped without permission, and drank our health in a bumper of Luri wine.

Lily was now in due course of promotion. No longer was she the handmaid, whose eyes created and rejoiced in countless mistakes of mine. Now she was sitting by my side, as she had good right to be, and was lost in pretty raptures at my gallant attentions. They were very nice, she owned, but thoroughly un-Corsican. How I wished her father and the old fusileer away!

CHAPTER XI.

"Six long months to be away from Lily! And perhaps forget her, and find some lovelier maiden."

"By Lily's side, all maids are burdocks. And yet what if I do?"

She showed a small stiletto toy with a cross upon the handle, and ground her pearly teeth together.

"Will it be for me, or her?"

"Both; and Lily afterwards."

"Oh you wholesale little murderer! Three great kisses directly, one for every murder."

"Only if you promise, on the relics, never to look twice at a pretty maiden."

And so we spent the precious time,--ten days allowed me to prepare my yacht--in talking utter nonsense, and conning fifty foolish schemes, to make us seem together. I was for departing at once, that the period might begin to run; but Lily was for keeping me to the last possible moment, and of course she had her way. It was fixed that I should sail on the 10th day of September. My little boat, now called the "Lily flower," was brought from Calvi, and moored in a secluded cove, where my love could see it from her bedroom window. It was no longer Corsican law that I should live in the castle. The privileges of a guest were gone; and the rigorous code of suitorship began. But to me and my own darling it made very little difference. I never left Vendetta tower, as I lightly named it, until my pet was ordered off to bed; and every morn I climbed the heights, after a long swim in the sapphire ripple, and met my own sweet Lily sparkling from the dew of her early toilet. How she loved me, how I loved her; which more than other let angels say; for we could not decide. That ancient Corsican her father, albeit little versed in books, was as upright and downright a gentleman as ever knew when his presence was not required. Therefore he took my word of honour for his Lily's safety; and left her to her own sweet will; and her sweet will was to spend with me all her waking hours. For her as yet there was no fear of the blood-avenger. According to their etiquette they cannot shoot the daughter, until they have shot the father. As to the sons the restriction does not hold. The feud we were concerned in had lasted now 120 years, and cost the lives of 130 people. It lay between the ancient races of Della Croce, and De Gentili, and owed its origin to the discovery of a dead mule on the road to church. The question was which family should be exterminated first. For many years the house of Della Croce had been in the ascendant, having produced a long succession of good shots and clever bushmen. At one time all the hopes of the De Gentili hung upon one infant life, which was not thought worth the taking. Fatal error-- that one life had proved a mighty trump. One after one the Della Croce fell before that original artist, who invented a patent method of trunking himself in olive bark and firing from a knot-hole. Many a story Lily told me of his devilish wiles; and in those stories I rejoiced, because she clung around my neck, and trembled so that I must hold her. Happily now this olive-branch was dead, having received his death-wound while he administered one to Lily's youngest brother. Ever since that, the feud had languished, and strict etiquette required that the Della Croce should perpetrate the next murder. But her father, said my

Lily, with her sweet head on my breast and her soft eyes full of fire, her father did not seem to care even to shoot the cousin of the man who had shot her brothers.

Darling Lily, my blood runs cold, even with your beauty in my arms, to hear you talk of murder so. Own pet, I shall change you. You heaven meant for love, and softness, and delight: human devilry has tainted even you. It was not an easy task to change her. Of all human passions revenge is far the strongest. Clara, how your eyes flash. You ought to have been a Corsican. It was not an easy task; but love loves difficulties. In my ten short days of delicious wretchedness, almost I taught Fiordalisa to despise revenge. And what do you think availed me most? Not the Bible. No, her mind and soul were swathed by Popery in the rags of too many saints. What helped me most, and the only thing that helped me at all, except caresses, was the broad and free expanse of the ever changing sea. Her nature was all poetry, her throbbing breast an Idyl. Upon my little quarter-deck I had a cushioned niche for her, and there we sat and steered ourselves while the sailors slept below. Alone upon the crystal world, pledged for life or death together, drinking deepest draughts of passion and thirsting still for more, what cared we for petty hatreds, we whose all in all was love? How she listened as I spoke, how her large eyes grew enlarged.

At last those eyes, pure wells of love, were troubled with hot tears. The fatal day was come. Tokens we had interchanged, myriad vows, and countless pledges, which even love could scarce remember. With all the passion of her race, and all the fervour of the clime, she bared her beautiful round arm, the part that lay most near the heart and touched it with the keen stiletto, then she threw her breast on mine, and I laid the crimsoned ivory on my lips. How the devil--excuse me, Clara--how the devil I got away, only phlegmatic Englishmen can tell. No Frenchman, or Italian, would have left that heavenly darling so. We put it off to the last moment, till it was quite dangerous to pass the rocky jaws. As my bad luck would have it, there was a purpling sunset breeze. My own love on the furthest point, her white feet in the water, growing smaller and smaller yet, and standing upon tiptoe to be seen for another yard; my own darling love of ages, she loosed her black hair down her snowy vest, for me to know her from the rocks behind; then she waved and waved her sweet palm hat, fragrant of my Lily,--I had kissed every single inch of it,--until she thought I could not see her; and then, as my telescope showed me, back she fell upon a ledge of rocks, and I could see or fancy her delicious bosom heaving to the fury of her tears. We glided past the cavern mouth, and the silver beach beyond it, whence we had often watched the sunset; and then a beetling crag took from me the last view of Lily.

However long the schoolboy may have bled from some big coward's bullying, or the sway of the rustling birch and the bosky thrill that follows, however sore he may have wept while hung head-downwards through the midnight hours, with a tallow candle between his teeth, or in the pang of nouns heteroclite and brachycatalectic dinners; yet despite these minor ills, his fond heart turns through after life to the scene of foot-ball and I-spy, to the days when he could jump or eat any mortal thing. And so it is with bygone love. Even the times of separation or of bitter quarrel, the aching heart whereon the keepsake lies, the spasms of jealousy, the tenterhooks of doubt; remembrance looks upon them all as treasures of a golden age.

Over the darkening sea, we bore away for Sardinia. Hours and hours, I gazed upon the cushions, where my own pet darling used to lean and love me. To me they were fairer than all the stars, or the phosphorescent sea. From time to time our Corsican pilot kept himself awake, by chanting to strangely mournful airs some of the voceros or dirges, the burden of many ages in that lamenting land. Fit home for Rachel, Niobe, or Cassandra, where half a million gallant beings, twice the number of the present population, have fallen victims to the blood-revenge. So Corsican historians tell; a thousand violent deaths each year, for the last five centuries. Sometimes the avenger waits for half a lifetime, lurking till his moment comes. Before his victim has ceased to quiver, or the shot to ring down the rocky pass, he is off for the bush or the mountains, and leads thenceforth a bandit's life.

They tell me, Clara, that things are better now, and this black stain on a chivalrous race is being purged by Christian civilization. Be it as it may, I love the island of my Lily still; and hope, please God, to see it once more, before I go to her.

Banished though I was, for the present, from the only place I cared for, it seemed still greater severance to go further than I could help. Therefore instead of returning to England, I spent the winter in cruising along the western coast of Italy, and the south of Spain; and coasted back to Genoa. To Seville, and other places famed for beautiful women, I made especial trips, to search for any fit to compare with my own maiden. Of course I knew none could be found; but it gave me some employment, and bitter pleasure, to observe how inferior were all. To my eyes, bright with one sweet image, no other form had grace enough to be fit pillow for my charmer's foot. How I longed and yearned for some fresh token of her: all her little gifts I carried ever in my bosom, but never let another's eyes rest one moment on them. Not even would I tell my friends one word about my love; it seemed as if it would grow common by being talked about. To Peter Green I wrote, resigning my commission, although I did not tell him that I had found the olives. No, friend Peter, those olives are much too near my Lily; and I won't have you or any other stranger there. I know she would not look at you; still I would rather have you a thousand miles away. Free trade, if you like, when I have made my fortune; which by the bye is somewhat the maxim of that school. My fortune, not in olives, oil, or even guineas-- all that rubbish you are welcome to--but my fortune where my heart and soul are all invested, and now, no more my fortune, but my certain fate in Lily.

At length and at last my calendar--like a homesick pair at school, we had made one for each other, thanking God that it was not a leap-year--my calendar so often counted, so punctually erased, began to yield and totter to the stubborn sap of time. My patience long ago had yielded, my blood was in a fever. Another thing began to yield, alas it was my money. Green, Vowler, and Green had behaved most liberally; but of course the expenses of my vessel had been heavy on me; and now my salary had ceased. Peter Green wrote to me in the kindest and most handsome manner, pressing me, if tired (as he concluded) of those murderous Corsicans, to accept another engagement in Sardinia. Even without imparting my last discovery, I had done good service to the firm. I smiled at the idea of my being weary of Corsicans: even now the mere word sends a warm tide to my heart.

It was not for the beauty of the scene, or the works of art, that I remained in Genoa; but because it was the likeliest place to see the Negro's head. As we lay at the end of the mole, my glass commanded all that entered; and every lugger or xebec that bore the sacred emblem--off my little dingy pushed from our raking stern, and with one man, now my friend because a thorough Corsican, I boarded her, at all hazards of imprisonment; and craved for tidings of the sacred land. Although, of course, I would not show the nest of all my thoughts, yet by beating about the bush, I got some scraps of news. The great Signor was flourishing, and had harvested an enormous crop of olives: his lovely daughter, now becoming the glory of the island, had been ill of something like marsh-fever, but was now as blooming as the roses. They did say, but the captain could not at all believe it, that she had been betrothed to some foreign olive-merchant. What disgrace! The highest blood and the sweetest maid in Corsica, to be betrayed to an oilman! Plenty of other news I gathered--the good people are great gossips--but this was all I cared for. Meanwhile your father, Clara dear, replied most warmly to my letter, sending me a sum on loan, which quite relieved me from cheese-paring. And now the wind was in the north, and it was almost time to start for the arms of Lily. If I waited any longer, I should be too mad to bear the voyage. At the break of day we left the magnificent harbour, and the cold wind from the maritime Alps chilled all but the fire of love. Up and down the little deck, up and down all day and night; sleep I never would again, until I touched my Lily. On the evening of the 8th of March, we were near Cape Corso; next day we coasted down the west to the lively breeze of spring, and so upon the 9th we moored to the tongue of Calvi. At midnight we were under way, and when the sun could reach the sea over the snowy peaks, we glided past the mountain crescent that looks on the Balagna. In the early morning still, when the dew was floating, we rounded the gray headland of Signor Dezio's cove, and I climbed along the bowsprit to glance beyond the corner.

What is that white dress I see fluttering at the water's edge? Whose is that red-striped mandile tossed on high and caught again? And there the flag-staff I erected, with my colours flying! Only one such shape on earth--only two such arms--out with the boat or I must swim, or run the yacht ashore. The boat has been towing alongside for the last six hours: Lily can't wait for the boat any more than I can. From rock to rock she is leaping; which is the nearest one? Into the water she runs, then away in blushing terror--she forgot all about the other men. But I know where to find her, she has dropped her little shoe, she must be in my grotto.

There I press her to my heart of hearts, trembling, weeping, laughing, all unable to get close enough to me.

"Sweetest mine, ten thousand times, I have been so wretched." Her voice is like a silver bell.

"My own, I am so glad to hear it. But how well you look!"

If she were lovely when I left her, what shall I call her now? There is not one atom of her but is pure perfection. I hold her from me for one moment, to take in all her beauties. She has a most delicious fragrance that steals upon my senses. Toilet bottles she never heard of; what she has is nature's gift, and unperceived except by love. I have often told her of it, but she won't believe it. It is not your breath, you darling; your breath is only violets; it comes from every fibre of you, even from your hair; it is as when the wind has kissed a lily of the valley.

The ancient Signor being a man of very keen observation, did not delay our wedding any longer than could be helped. That evening we hauled down the family fusileer, gave him a goblet of wine, and sent him about his business: for one night we would take our chance even of Vendetta. At supper-time the Signor was in wonderful spirits, and drank our health with many praises of our constancy and obedience. One little fact he mentioned worth a thousand propinations; his daughter's fever had been cured by some chance news of me. He even went away to fetch a bottle of choicest Rogliano, when he saw how I was fidgetting to get my arm round Lily. Then after making his re-entrance, with due clumsiness at the door, he quite disgraced himself, while drawing the cork, by even winking at me, as he said abruptly,

"Fiordalisa, when would you like to be married?"

My Lily blushed, I must confess, but did not fence with the question.

"As soon as ever you please, papa. That is, if my love wishes it." But she would not look at me to ask. In the porch she whispered to me, that it was only from her terror of the bad Lepardo coming. Did the loving creature fancy that I would believe it?

Once more we sailed together over the amethyst sea; she was as fond of the water as a true-born Briton. In her thoughts and glances was infinite variety. None could ever guess the next thing she would say. Thoroughly I knew her heart, because I lived therein, and sweeter lodgings never man was blessed with. But of her mind she veiled as yet the maiden delicacies, strictly as she would the glowing riches of her figure. What amazed me more than all, was that while most Corsican girls are of the nut-brown order, no sun ever burned the snowy skin of Lily: she always looked so clear and clean, as if it were impossible for anything to stain her. Clara, you are always talking of your lovely Isola. I wonder where she got her name: it is no stranger to me. Something in your description of her reminds me of my Lily. I long to see the girl: and you must have some reason for so obstinately preventing me.

CHAPTER XII.

Though Lily and I were most desirous to keep things as quiet as possible, by this time our engagement was talked of in every house of the Balagna. That paternal fusileer and my merry yachtsmen, although they looked the other way whenever we approached, would not permit the flower of Corsica, as she was now proclaimed, to blush with me unseen. My sailors attended to her far more than to their business, and would have leaped into the water for one smile of Lily.

It is the fashion of the island to make a wedding jubilee; and the Signor was anxious to outdo all that had ever been done. We, absorbed in one another, did our best to disappoint him; but he scorned the notion of any private marriage. I never shall forget how he knit his silver brows when I made a last attempt to bring him to our views. "Signor Vogheno, to me you appear to forget whose daughter it is that loves you. Perhaps in your remote, but well regarded island maidens may be stolen before their fathers can look round. Indeed, I have heard that they leap over a broomstick. That is not the custom here. Fiordalisa Della Croce is my only child--the child of my old age; and not altogether one to be ashamed of. I can afford to be hospitable, and I mean to be so."

The Corsicans are a most excitable race, and, when affronted, seem to lash their sides as they talk. By the time the good Signor had finished his speech, every hair of his beard was curling with indignation. But his daughter sprang into his arms and kissed away the tempest, and promised, if it must be so, to make herself one mass of gold and coral. So the Parolanti, or mediators, were invoked; an armistice for a week was signed, and honour pledged on either side. Free and haughty was the step of the Signor Dezio as he set forth for the town to order everything he could see; and very wroth again he was, because I would not postpone the day for him to get a shipload of trumpery from Marseilles. This time I was resolved to have my way. Besides the fervour of my passion and my dread of accidents, the one thing of all others I detest is to be stared at anywhere. And it is far worse to be stared at by a foreign race. The Corsicans are gentlemen by nature, but they could not be expected to regard without some curiosity the lucky stranger who had won their Lily.

I will not weary you, as I myself was wearied, with all the ceremonies of the wedding-day. All I wanted was my bride, and she wanted none but me: yet we could not help being touched by the hearty good-will of the commune. The fame of Lily's beauty had spread even to Sardinia, and many a handsome woman came to measure her own thereby. Clever as they are at such things, not one of them could find a blemish or defect in Lily, and our fair Balagnese told them to go home and break their mirrors.

It was a sweet spring morning, and amid a fearful din of guns and trumpets, mandolins and fiddles, I waited with a nervous smile under the triumphal arch in front of my fictitious house. A sham house had been made of boards, and boughs, and flowers, because it is most essential that the bride should be introduced to the bridegroom's dwelling. Here I was to receive the procession, which at last appeared. First came fifty well-armed youths, crowned with leaves and ribbons; then four-and-twenty maidens dressed alike, singing and scattering flowers, and then a boy of noble birth, mounted on a pony, and carrying the freno, symbol of many scions. None of them I looked at; only for my Lily. On a noble snow-white palfrey, decked from head to foot with flowers, her father walking at her side, came the bloom, the flower, the lily of them all, arrayed in clear white muslin, self-possessed, and smiling. One glorious wreath was round her head; it was her own black hair by her own sweet fingers twined with sprigs of myrtle. A sash, or fazoletto, of violet transparent crape, looped at the crown of her head, fell over the shy lift of her bosom, parting like a sunset cloud, where the boddice opened below the pear-like waist. To me she looked like a white coralline rising through an amethyst sea. Behind her came the authorities of the commune. The sham keys were already hanging at her slender zone. It was my place to lift her down and introduce her formally. This I did with excellent grace, feeling the weight of eyes upon me. But when I got her inside, I spoiled the folds of the fazoletto. I heard the old man shouting, "Who are ye gallant sons of the mountain, who have carried off my daughter? To me, indeed, ye seem to be brave and noble men, yet have ye taken her rather after the manner of bandits. Know ye not that she is the fairest flower that ever was reared in Corsica?"

"Yes, old fellow, I know that well enough; and that's the very reason why I have got her here." One more virgin kiss, and with Lily on my arm, forth I sally to respond.

"Friends we are, who claim some hospitality. We have plucked the fairest flower on all the strands of Corsica, and we bear her to the priest, fit offering for Madonna."

"Bide on, my noble friends; then come and enjoy my feast."

No more delay. The maids have got all they can do to keep in front of us with their flowers. The armed youths stand on either side at the entrance to the church. The tapers are already lit, the passage up the little church is strewed with flowering myrtle. Lily, holding her veil around her, walks hand in hand with me.

Fiordalisa Della Croce now is Lily Vaughan; amidst a world of shouting, shooting, and cornamusas, we are led to the banqueting-room; there they seat us in two chairs, and a fine fat baby is placed on Lily's lap, to remind her of her duties. She dandles it, and kisses it as if she understood the business, and then presents it with a cap of corals and gay ribbons. Now Lily Vaughan throws off her fazoletto, and gives me for a keepsake the myrtles in her hair. Then all who can claim kin with her, to the fortieth generation, hurry up and press her hand, and wish the good old wish. "Long life and growing pleasure, sons like him, and daughters like yourself."

After the banquet, we were free to go, having first led off the ballo in the Cerca dance. Thank God, my Lily is at last my own; she falls upon my bosom weary and delighted. Clara, remember this: the little church in which we were married is called St. Katharine's on the cliff; and I signed the record in my proper name, Edgar Malins Vaughan: the Malins, very likely, they did not know from Valentine, for I always wrote it with a flourish at the end. The Signor, with all his friends, escorted us to the limits of his domain; there we bade them heartily farewell, and they returned to renew the feast. My little yacht was in the bay, and we saw the boat push off to fetch us as had been arranged. We were to sail for Girolata, where the Signor had a country-house, lonely enough even for two such lovers. Three or four hours would take us thither, and the sun was still in the heavens. As no one now could see us, Lily performed a little dance for my especial delight. How beaming she looked, how full of spirits, now all the worry was over. Then she tripped roguishly at my side to the winding rocky steps that lead to St. Katharine's cove. The cove was like a well scooped in the giant cliffs. As we descended the steep and narrow stairs, my Lily trembled on my arm. The house and all the merry-makers were out of sight and hearing. Of course we stopped every now and then, for the boat could not be at the landing yet, and we had much to tell each other.

As we stepped upon the beach, and under the eaves of a jutting rock, a tall man stood before us. His eyes and beard were black as jet, and he wore the loose dress of a Southern seaman. Three sailors, unmistakeably English, were smoking and playing cards in the corner shade of the cliff. Lily started violently, turned pale, and clung to me, but faced the intruder bravely. He was quite amazed at her beauty, I at his insolent gaze.

"Fiordalisa Della Croce," he said with a pure Tuscan accent, "behold me! I am come to claim you."

He actually laid his small, but muscular hand upon my Lily's shoulder. She leaped back as from a snake. I knew it must be Lepardo.

"Sir," I said, as calmly as I could, "oblige me by allowing my wife to pass."

The sneering, supercilious look which he hardly deigned to spare me, was honest, compared to his foul stare at her.

"Signor, she is too beautiful. I must have my rights. Come for her when I am tired, if any can tire of her."

And he thrust his filthy, hairy lips under my own pet's hat. My muscles leaped, and my soul was in the blow. Down he went like a flail, and I thought he was stunned for an hour; but while I was bearing my pet to the boat, which now was close to the beach, up he leaped, and rushed at me with a dagger--a dagger like one which you know. I did not see him, but Lily did over my shoulder; she sprang from my arms and flung herself between us. He thrust her aside, and leaped at me like a panther, aiming straight at my heart. How he missed me I cannot tell, but think it was through Lily. Before he recovered, I closed with him, wrested away the weapon and flung it far into the sea. But one main thing I omitted; I ought to have stunned him thoroughly. Into the boat with Lily--I caught up an oar, and away we dashed. The three English sailors were running up. As a wave took the boat about, one of them grasped the stern; down on his knuckles crashed my oar, and with a curse he let go. All right, all clear, off for the yacht for your lives. I would show fight, for my blood is up, but what would become of Lily? And we are but three against four, and none of us have arms.

Meanwhile, that black Italian, I can never call him a Corsican, sneaked away to a tuft of sea-grass for his double-barrelled fusil. Bowing with all my might, I saw him examine the priming, lay his red cap on a rock, and the glistening gun on the cap, and, closing one eye, take steady aim, not at me, but at Lily. Poor Lily sat on the thwart at my side, faintly staring with terror. No time to think; oar and all I dashed in front of my darling. A ping in the air, a jar on my wrist, a slight blow on my breast, and at my feet dropped the bullet. It had passed through the tough ash handle. Down, Lily, down, for God's sake; he is firing the other barrel. I flung her down in the bilge water; the brute cannot see her now. Not quite so easily off. Up a steep rock he climbed like a cat, the cursed gun still in his hand. He won fifty feet of vantage, and commanded the whole of the boat. We were not eighty yards away. There he coolly levelled at my prostrate Lily. I had grey hairs next morning. Forward, I threw myself, over my wife; me he might kill if he chose. One lurch of the boat--a short sea was running--and my darling's head was shown. He saw his chance and fired. Thank God, he had too little powder in; my own love is untouched. The ball fell short of Lily, and passed through my left foot, in at the sole and out below the instep. Luckily I had retained my dancing shoes, or my thick boots would have kept the ball in my foot. The brute could not see that he had hit any one, and he cursed us in choice Italian.

Poor Lily had quite swooned away, and knew nothing of my wound. Over the side of the yacht I lifted her myself, standing upon one leg. No one else should touch her. So furious I was with that cold-blooded miscreant, that if I could only have walked, I would have returned to fight him. My men, too, were quite up for it. But when Lily came to herself, and threw her arms round me and wept, and thanked God and her saints, I found my foot quite soaked in a pool of blood, and stiffening. Poor little dear! what a fuss she did make about it! I would have borne ten times the pain for the smiles and tears she gave me. One thing was certain--under the mercy of God, we owed our lives to each other, and held them henceforth in common.

As, with a flowing sheet, we doubled the craggy point, concealed close under the rocks we saw a low and snake-like vessel, of the felucca build. She was banked for three pair of sweeps, and looked a thorough rover. This was, of course, Lepardo's boat. We now bore away for Ajaccio, dear Lily having implored me not to think of Girolata, where no medical aid could anyhow be procured. Moreover, she wanted to fly from that dark Lepardo; and I am quite willing to own that, despite my delicious nursing, I was not ambitious to stand as target again during our honeymoon.

CHAPTER XIII.

At first I thought a great deal more of the pain than the danger of my wound; but when I showed it to the French surgeon at Ajaccio, he surprised me by shrugging his shoulders formidably, and declaring that it was the good God if I kept my foot. Being of a somewhat sceptical turn, I thought at first that he only wanted to gild the frame of his work; but when I began to consider it, I found that he was quite right. The fact was, that I had thought much more of my bride than of my metatarsals. Two of these were splintered where the bullet passed between them, and it was a question whether it had not been poisoned. Many of the mountaineers are skilled in deadly drugs, and use them rarely for the bowl, not so rarely for the sword and gun.

At one time there were symptoms even of mortification, and my wife, who waited hand and foot upon me, joined the surgeon in imploring me to submit to amputation.

"Sweetest mine! do you suppose that I shall love you any the less because you walk on crutches, and all through your love of me? And what other difference can it make to either of us? I shall cry a great deal at first, for I love your little toe-nails more than I do my own eyes; but, darling, we shall get over it."

As she loved my toes so much, I resolved to keep them, if it was only for her sake; and, after a narrow crisis, my foot began to get better. To her care and tenderness I owed my recovery, far more than to the skill of the clever surgeon. Six months elapsed before I could walk again, and our little yacht was sent to Calvi to explain the long delay. Fond as I was of the "Lily-flower," I was anxious now to sell her; but my darling nurse, although she knew before our marriage that I was not a wealthy man, would not listen to the scheme at all; for the doctor ordered me, as I grew stronger, to be constantly on the water.

"Not by any means, my own, will we sell our little love-boat. I should cry after it like a baby; and another thing, far more important, you can bear no motion except on board our *Lily*. Papa has got great heaps of money, and he never can refuse me anything when I coax in earnest."

Conscious as I was of my vile deceit, I would rather have died than apply to Signor Dezio, albeit I am quite sure that he would soon have forgiven me. So I wrote again to my good-natured brother and banker, and told him all that had happened, but begged him not to impart it even to your mother. I have strong reason for suspecting that he did not conceal it from her; but as I never alluded to the subject before her, she was too much a lady ever to lead me towards it. My motive for this reserve was at first some ill-defined terror lest my fraud upon Signor Dezio should come to light prematurely. Also I hate to be talked about among people whom I despise. Afterwards, as you will perceive, I had other and far more cogent reasons.

I need not say that your father--dear Clara, I ought to love you, if only on his account!--your father wrote me a kind and most warm-hearted letter, accompanied by a most handsome gift--no loan this time, but a wedding-gift, and a very noble one. Also he pressed me to come home with my bride the moment I could endure the voyage. Ah! if I had only obeyed him, not Lily and Henry, but myself would have been the victim.

We returned as soon as possible to Vendetta tower, and found the good Signor in excellent spirits, delighted to see his sweet daughter again, and still more delighted by hope of a little successor to the gray walls and the olive groves. When this hope was realized, and a lusty young grandson was laid in his arms, he became so wild in his glory, that he went about boasting all over the commune, feasting all who came near him, forgetting the very name of the blood-revenge. Many a time we reminded and implored him to be more careful. He replied, that his life was of no importance now; he had come to his haven among his own dear ones, and was crowning the old ship with flowers. Moreover, he knew that the De' Gentili were of a nobler spirit than to shed the blood of a gray-haired man, when institution did not very loudly demand it. And so I believe they were.

Alas! the poor old man!--a thorough and true gentleman as one need wish to see--choleric albeit, and not too wide of mind; but his heart was in the right place, and made of the right material, and easy enough to get at. He was free to confess his own failings, and could feel for a man who was tempted. Deeply thankful I am that, before his white beard was laid low, I acknowledged to him my offence, and obtained his hearty forgiveness. Little Henry was on his lap, going off into smiles of sleep, with his mother's soft finger in his mouth. At first my confession quite took the poor Signor aback; for I did not attempt to gloss the dishonour of what I had done; but I told him truly that the meanness was not in my nature, and although I had won my pet Lily, the road ran through hemlock and wormwood. And now I perceived how uncalled-for and stupid the fraud had been.

When the old man recovered a little from the shock caused by the dishonesty--towards which recovery the tears of his daughter and the smiles of his grandson contributed--he was really glad to find that I was not a landed Signor. He rubbed his hands and twitched his beard with delight, for now his little Enrico would never be taken away to the barbarous English island. Was he not rightful successor to the lands of the Della Croce? and what more could he possibly want? What could he care for the property in Gloisterio? However, he made us promise that if the present remarkable baby, Master Henry Vaughan, should ever enjoy the property in the unpronounceable county, Lily's second child, if she had one, should take the Corsican lordships; for his great fear was, that the Malaspina and Della Croce estates should become a servient tenement to the frozen fields of the North. To express and ensure his wishes, he had a deed-poll prepared according to his own fancy, read it to us and some witnesses, then signed, sealed, and enrolled it. This was one of the documents which you, my brave Clara, rescued from that vile, stealthy ghost.

And now, for a short time, we enjoyed deep, quiet, delicious happiness. The crime which had haunted me was confessed and forgiven. Amply possessed of the means, and even the abundance of life, I was blessed with strong health again, and freedom among the free. Richest and best of all blessings, I had a sweet, most lovely, and most loving wife, and loved her once and for all. No more beautiful vision has any poet imagined than young Lily Vaughan sitting under the vine-leaves, her form more exquisite than ever, her soft-eyed infant in her lap wondering at his mother's beauty, while her own deep-lustred eyes carried to her husband's, without the trouble of thinking, all that flowed into her heart--joy at belonging to him, hope of bliss to come, fear of over-happiness, pride in all the three of us, and shame at feeling proud. Then a gay coquettish glance, as quick youth warms the veins, and some humorous thought occurs, a tickle for the baby, and a feint of cold-shouldering me. But, jealous as I was, desperately jealous, for my love was more passionate than ever, I can honourably state that Lily's one and only trial to arouse my jealousy was an ignominious failure, recoiling only on the person of the dear designer. However exacting little Harry might be, I never grudged him his double share of attention. In the first place I looked upon him as a piece of me, still holding on; and, in the next place, I knew that all he laid claim to was only a loan to him, and belonged in fee simple to his father.

At this time I wrote to my brother again, announcing the birth of our boy, and that we had made him his namesake; dispensing, too, with all further reserve on the subject of our marriage. This letter was never delivered to your dear father. That much I know, for certain; and at one time I strongly suspected that our cold-blooded, crafty foe contrived to intercept it. But no; if he had, he would have known better afterwards.

After that cowardly onslaught upon my bride and myself, I had of course learned all I could of the history of this Lepardo. He was the only son of the Signor's only brother, but very little was known of him in the neighbourhood, as he came from Vescovato on the east side of the island. He was said to have great abilities and very great perseverance, and under the guardianship of his uncle had been intended and partly educated for the French Bar. But his disposition was most headstrong and sullen; and at an early age he displayed a ferocity unusual even in a Corsican. Neither had he the great redeeming trait of the islanders, I mean their noble patriotism. One good quality, however, he did possess, and that was fidelity to his word. With one of the contradictions so common in human nature, he would even be false in order to be true: that is, he would be treacherous wherever he was unpledged, if it assisted him towards a purpose to which he was committed. While he was yet a boy, his intended career was cut short by an act of horrible violence. He disliked all the lower animals, horses and mules especially; and one day he was detected by a master of the Paoli College, screaming, and yelling at, and lashing, from a safe distance, a poor little pony whom he had tied to a fence. The master, an elderly man, very humane and benevolent, rebuked him in the most cutting manner, and called him a low coward. The young villain ran off, with his eyes flashing fire, procured a stiletto, and stabbed the poor man in the back. Then he leaped on the horse he had been ill-treating, and pricking him with the dagger, rode away furiously in the direction of Bastia. The pursuers could not trace him through the wild mountain district, but it was believed that he reached the town and took refuge in an English brig, which was lying off the harbour, and sailed for Genoa that evening. The pony was found dead, lying by the roadside with the brute's dagger in its throat. No wonder Lily, who told me all this, with true Corsican rage in her eyes, no wonder my Lily hated him. Even as a little girl, for she was but ten years old when he disappeared, she always felt a strong repugnance towards him. He was about six years older than Fiordalisa, and four years younger than I; so when he shot at Lily, he must have been three-and-twenty. It was reported that after his disappearance he took to a sea-faring life, and made himself very useful, by his knowledge of languages, in the English merchant service. Quarrelling with his employers, he was said to have resorted to smuggling in the Levant, if not to downright piracy.

Clara, for reasons I cannot explain, I wish you to follow my story step by step in its order, noting each landing-place. To do this with advantage, you must have the dates carved upon each of the latter: therefore I beg you to copy them as you pass.

I arrived in Corsica, as you heard, during the month of May, 1829. On the 12th of August in that same year I first beheld my Lily. That day I remember, beside other reasons, because I had wondered, as I rode idly along, whether my brother was opening his usual Highland campaign, and whether he would like to shoot the muffrone. Lily and I were married on the 21st of March, 1830, when I was twenty-seven years old: and our little Henry first saw the light on the 24th of December following, more than two years before your birth. Your father having no children as yet, I looked upon my Harry as heir presumptive to these estates. Although your birth appeared to divest him of the heirship, it has since, through causes then unknown to me, proved otherwise; and if he were living now, he would in strict law be entitled to this property after my death. But if he were alive, he never should have an inch of it, that is if I could prevent it; because in strict righteousness all belongs to you. And now I hold the property in fee simple, under an Act which abolishes fines and recoveries; for I have suffered so much from remorse, ever since your dear mother's death, that even before you saved my life, dearest child, I enrolled a deed in Chancery, which gives me disposing powers; and as I think you know, I made thereupon a will devising the lands to you. This also was one of the documents you caught that vile hypocrite stealing.

To return to the old Signor. He was now as happy as the day was long, and desirous, as an old man often is, to set on foot noteworthy schemes, which might survive his time. Of this desire I took advantage to inoculate him with some English views. It was rather late to learn another catechism, at threescore years and five; but a green old age was his, hale and hearty as could be. "Why should all those noble olives shed, and rot upon the ground, all those grapes of divers colours be of no more use than rainbows? Why should all the dazzling marbles slumber in the quarry, the porphyry of Molo, the verde antique of Orezza, the Parian of Cassaconi, the serpentine near Bastia, and the garnets of Vizzavona--nay even the matchless white alabaster--

"Mother of our Lord, I have got such pretty stuff in my cavern on the gulf of Porto. Some one told me it was the very finest alabaster. But then it would require cutting out." The last thought seemed a poser.

"Well, father"--so I called him now--"when Harry has finished his tooth, suppose we go all together in the yacht and see it."

And so we did; and it was worth a voyage all the way from London only to look at it. Pillars of snow, pellucid, and fancifully veined, like a glacier shot with sea-weed; clean-working moreover, and tough, and of even texture, as I proved to my Lily's delight. There is now a small piece in the drawer of my walnut-wood desk. But I took home a square block with me, and under my wife's most original criticisms, worked it into a rough resemblance of the baby Henry. Perhaps I have a natural turn for sculpture, perhaps it was a wife's flattery; but at any rate the young mother was so charmed with it, that in one of her pensive moments she even made me promise, that if she died soon and alone, I would have the little recumbent figure laid upon her breast.

Meanwhile the Signor was gayer than ever: he told us to have no anxiety about anything less than a score of children; to such effect would he work his great olive grounds, quarries, and vineyards. Some ingenious plan he formed, which delighted him hugely, but was past my comprehension. As fast as he quarried his alabaster, he would plant young vines in the holes, and every one knew how the vine delighted to run away over the rocks. So at once he must set off for Corte, the central town of the island, to procure a large stock of tools well-tempered in the Restonica. That turbulent little river possesses a magic power. Its water is said to purify steel so highly that it never can rust again. I have even heard that the cutlers of Northern Italy import it, for the purpose of annealing their choicest productions. For my part, little as I knew of commerce, I strongly recommended that arrangements for shipping and selling the alabaster should be made, before it was quarried. But the Signor scorned the idea.

Having in prospect all the riches of Croesus, and in possession enough to make us happy, and having worked, as we thought, uncommonly hard, we all four indulged in a tour through Sicily and Italy, proposing to visit and criticise the principal marble quarries. By the time we had done all this and enjoyed it thoroughly--dear me, how my wife was admired in the sculptor's studio!--and by the time we had fallen to work again, surveyed and geologised all the estates, taken, or rather listened to, long earfuls of advice, settled all our plans summarily over the Rogliano, and reopened them all the next morning, by this time, I say, nearly three years of bliss had slipped by, since my recovery from the lingering wound; and it was now the summer of 1833. My loving wife was twenty years old, and we were looking forward to the birth of a brother or sister for Harry. Meanwhile we had heard of your birth, which delighted us all, especially my Lily. She used to talk, in the fond way mothers discover, to Harry, now gravely perched up on a stool, about his little sweetheart away in the dark north country.

It was in the month of July 1833 that the Signor found he could no longer postpone his visit to Corte. Alone he would go, riding his favourite jennet, as sure-footed as a mule, and as hardy as a mustang. Behind him he slung his trusty fusil, with both barrels loaded, for he had to traverse a desert and mountainous district haunted by banditti. He was to travel through by-ways to Novella, and so on to the bridge where the roads from Calvi and Bastia meet, put up in rude quarters there for the night, and follow the steep descent to the town of Corte next day. In vain we begged him to take some escort, or at least to let me go with him. No, I must stop to guard the Lily and the little snow-drop; could he possibly take me at such a time from home, and did I think a Della Croce was afraid of bandits? It was a Monday morning when he left the tower, and he would be back on Saturday in good time for supper. He kissed and blessed his Lily, and the little snow-drop as he called young Harry, who cried at his departure; and then he gave me too an earnest trembling blessing. By this time he and I had come to love each other, as a father and a son.

I went with him quite to the borders of the commune; and there, in a mountain defile, I lit for him his cigar. With some dark foreboding, I waited till I saw him reach and pass the gap at the summit of the rise. There he turned in the saddle to wave his last adieu, and his beard, like a white cloud, floated on the morning sky.

CHAPTER XIV.

On the Saturday night, an excellent supper was ready: the Signor's own particular plate was at the head of the table, and by it gleamed, in a portly bottle, his favourite Rogliano. Little Harry, who could say anything he was told, and knew right well what was good, or at least what tasted good--that beloved child was allowed to stop up, that grandpapa might kiss him; this was a sovereign specific, believed in the nursery creed, to ensure sweet sleep for both.

That silver beard never kissed the chubby cheek again. All night we waited and wondered: Harry was sent to bed roaring; no grandpapa appeared. The olives rustled at midnight, and out I ran; the doors creaked afterwards, and I opened them, all in vain; the sound of hoofs came up the valley before the break of day; but no step or voice of man, no bark of his favourite mountain hound, no neigh of the jennet to her sleepy brother-horses.

All Sunday we remained in terrible uneasiness, trying to cheer each other with a hundred assurances that the dear old man must have turned aside to see an ancient friend living now at Prato. When Monday morning came, but brought no tidings of him, I set off, amid a shower of tears, to seek the beloved father. The old fusileer was left on guard, and I took two young and active men, well acquainted with the mountain passes. All well mounted, and well armed, we purposed to ride hard, and search the track quite up to the town of Corte. There, if indeed he had ever arrived, we should be sure to hear of him. But it proved unnecessary to go so far from home.

Along that dreary mountain road, often no more than a shepherd's walk difficult to descry, we found no token of any traveller either living or dead, until we came to the Ponte Leccia, where the main roads meet. Here our fears were doubled, and the last hope nearly quenched; for on asking at the shepherd's hut, where Signor Dezio meant to put up, we found that he had slept there on the Friday night, as he was returning from the town. The shepherd's wife, who had known him for years, assured us that he was in wonderful spirits and health, insisted upon her supping with them--which is contrary to Corsican usage--and boasted much of the great things he would do, and still more of his beautiful grandson. His goatskin wallet was full of sample tools, which were to astonish his English son, and he had a toy gun no bigger than the tail of a dog, with which he intended to teach the baby to shoot. Telling us all these little things, and showing us her presents, the poor woman cried at the thought of what must have happened to him. Right early on Saturday morning he set off, as impatient as a child, to see his beloved ones again, and exhibit all his treasures. For love of the Della Croce her husband had groomed the mare thoroughly, and she neighed merrily down the hill at thought of her stable friends. Moreover, the shepherd's wife told us that there had been in those parts no bandit worth the name, since the death of the great Teodoro, king of the mountains, whose baby still received tribute.

After resting our horses awhile, with heavy hearts we began to retrace our steps through that awful wilderness. Instead of keeping together, as we had done in the morning, we now rode in parallel lines, right and left of the desert track, wherever the ground permitted it. All this district is very barren and rugged, and the way winds up and down, often along the brink of crags, or through narrow mountain gorges. The desolation and loneliness grew more oppressive, as the shadows lengthened.

We had thoroughly searched two-thirds of the distance homeward, and had crossed some granite heights whence the sea was visible; the sun was low over Cape Bevellata, and the vapours from the marsh were crouching at the mountain's foot. Here as I rode to the left of my two companions, I heard the faint bay of a dog far down a deep ravine, that trended leftward from our course. Putting my jaded animal to his utmost speed, I made for the hollow which echoed the dismal sound--a feeble bark prolonged into a painful howl. Turning the corner sharply I scared two monstrous vultures, who were hovering over and craning at a dog. The dog so gaunt and starved, that at every bark the ribs seemed bursting the skin, still was fighting past despair with his loathsome enemies. He stood across the breast of the noble Signor Dezio. There lay that gallant cavalier, stark and rigid, with his eyes wide open, and his white beard tipped with crimson. There he lay upon his back, his kingly head against a rock, his left hand on his clotted breast and glued thereto with blood; his right hand hung beside his chin whence it had slipped in death, and in it still securely grasped was a trinket newly made, containing a little sheaf of the baby's flossy hair tied with a black wisp of the mother's. The poor old man had dragged himself thither to die, and died with that keepsake on his lips. The fatal shot had been fired from above, and passed completely through his body. It pierced his lungs, and I believe that he felt little pain, but gasped his simple life away. Near him was his wallet, with the tools still in it; I think he had been playing with the toy gun when he received the wound; at any rate it lay separate from the rest, and at the old man's side.

Examining by the waning light, with icy awe upon me, the scene of this damned atrocity, I found that the hoary traveller must have dismounted here, to eat his frugal dinner. A horn cup and a crust of bread were on a rocky shelf, and a little spring welled down the dingle, with the mark of the dog's feet here and there. The craven foe had been sneaking along behind, and took advantage of the old man's position, as he sat upon a stone to make certain of him from the granite loophole. We found the very place where the murderer must have crouched, but the cliff-side kept no footprint. The victim's gun was gone, and so was the Spanish mare: no other robbery seemed to have been committed.

This glen led to a shorter but more difficult track towards home, which the Signor, in his impatience, must have resolved to try. Reverently we laid him on the freshest horse; while I with the faithful mountain dog on my saddle--for he was too exhausted to walk--rode on to break the melancholy news, and send assistance back.

To break bad news--the phrase is a failure, the attempt it implies a much worse one. Lily knew all in a moment, and in her delicate state she received so appalling a shock, that for a week she lay on the very threshold of death. At the end of that time, and three days after the old man's funeral--at which for his daughter's sake I allowed no wailings or voceros--a lively little girl was born, who seemed to be none the worse for her mother's bitter sufferings. Her innocent caresses, or some baby doings optimised by her mother--though even as a new-born babe she seemed a most loving creature--all those soft endearing ways, which I could not understand, did more to bring my Lily's spirit back than even my fond attentions.

But as yet, though able to walk again, and nurse her child, whom she would not commit to another, my wife remained in a fearfully sensitive and tremulous condition. The creak of a door, the sound of a foot, the rustle of the wind--and she, so brave and proud of yore, started like a cicale, and shook like a forest shadow. In everything she feared the ambush of that sleuth cold-blooded reptile, on whom alone, truly or not God knows, she charged the blood of her venerable father. But still she had the comfort of a husband's love, a husband even fonder than when the flowers fell on his path; and still she had the joy of watching, with a mother's tender insight, the budding promise of two sweet infants. Infants I call them, why Master Harry was now a thorough chatterbox! With all this love around her, she by far the loveliest, the pride and glory of all, was sure to find her comfort soon upon the breast of time, even as small Lily found it in her own sweet bosom. Deeply and long we mourned that ancient Signor, chivalrous and true gentleman, counsellor of all things. Every day we missed him; but could talk of it more as time flowed on. Rogliano had no sparkle, Luri not the tint of old: never could I pour out either from his favourite flagon, without a thought of him who taught us the proper way to do it; who ought to be teaching us still, but was lying foully murdered in his lonely grave at St. Katharine's on the Cliff.

We had done our utmost to avenge him: soon as I could leave my wife, I had scoured all the neighbourhood. The Sbirri too had done their best, but discovered nothing. Brave fellows they are, when it comes to fighting, but very poor detectives. Only two things we heard that seemed at all significant. One of these was that a Spanish jennet, like the Signor's favourite "Marana," but dreadfully jaded and nearly starved, had been sold on the Friday after the murder, being the very day of the funeral, at the town of Porto Vecchio on the south-eastern coast. I sent my coxswain Petro, an intelligent and trusty Corsican, to follow up this clue; for I durst not leave my wife as yet. Petro discovered the man who had bought the mare, and re-purchased her from him, as I had directed: but the description of the first seller did not tally with my recollections of Lepardo. However, it proved to be the true Marana; and glad she was to get home once more.

The other report, that seemed to bear upon the bloody mystery, was that a swift felucca, flush-built and banked for triple sweeps, had been seen lying close in shore near point Girolata, during the early part of the week in which the Signor left home. And it was even said that two Maltese sailors, belonging to this felucca, had encamped on shore in a lonely place near Otta, and were likely to be found there still.

Lily being stronger now, I determined to follow this last clue myself; and so I put the little yacht into commission again, and manned her with Calvi men, for all my English crew had been dismissed long ago. Leaving my wife and children under the care of the old fusileer, away I sailed from St. Katharine's, intending to return in three days' time. All this coast I now knew thoroughly, and Otta was not far beyond the poor Signor's cave of alabaster. It is a wild and desert region, far away from any frequented road, and little visited except by outlaws.

We found no trace of any tent, no sign of any landing, and an aged fisherman, whom we met, declared that no felucca or vessel of any sort had lately been near the bay. I began to fear that, for some dark purpose, I had been beguiled from home, and despatched upon a fool's errand. The dreary coast was still the home of solitude, the alabaster cave untouched since our pic-nic survey; the marks of which were undisturbed except by wind and weather. So I crowded sail, and hurried back to St. Katharine's, with a strange weight on my heart. To add to my vexation, a strong north wind set in, and smartly as our cutter sailed, we were forced to run off the land. When at last we made the cove, it was unsafe for the yacht to anchor, and so I was compelled to send her on to Calvi.

It was nearly midnight on the 2d of October, when Petro and myself plodded up the wooded hill on which the old tower stands. Weary and dispirited, though glowing every now and then with the thought of all my darlings, in vain I called myself a fool for fearing where no fear was. When we reached the brow of the hill, my vague alarm was doubled. The rude oil-lamps that marked the entrance, why were they unlighted? I had especially ordered that they should be kindled every night, and Lily had promised to see to it herself. No challenge from the watchman, no click of the musket hammer, even the vinea was not in its place. In vain we knocked and knocked at the old chesnut doors; no one answered, no one came to open. None of the loopholes showed a light; the house was dark and silent as the ivy. Wild with terror I ran to the little side-door, whence first my Lily met me. This too was locked, or fastened somehow; and only the echo of my knock was heard. Petro and I caught up a great bough of ilex, which myself had lopped last week, rushed at the door with the butt, and broke it in with one blow. Shrieking for Lily, Lily, I flew from room to room, tumbling over the furniture, blundering at the doorways. No voice of wife, no cry of child, no answer of domestic; all as silent as if ten fathoms under water.

Having dashed through every room, I turned to rush off to the hamlet, when my foot struck something--something soft and yielding; was it a sack or bolster? I stooped to feel it; it was Lily, laid out, stiff and cold Dead, my Lily dead! Oh, God can never mean it; would He let me love her so?

For all intents of actual life, for all that we are made for, for all the soul's loan of this world, I died that very moment; and yet a mad life burned within me, the flare of hope that will not die. How I forced her clenched hands open, bowed her rigid arms around me, threw myself upon her, breathed between her lips and listened, tore her simple dress asunder and laid my cheek upon her heart; feeling not a single throb, flooded her cold breast with tears, and lay insensible awhile. Then, as if awaking, felt that she was with me, but somehow not as usual; called her all our names of love, and believed we were in heaven. But there stood Petro with a light, sobbing, and how his beard shook!--What right had he in heaven? Would they let him in without shaving? I rose to order him out; when he restored my wits awhile by pointing with his finger.

"Look, look, Signor! She is not dead, I saw her eyelid tremble."

Wide she opened those glorious eyes, looked at me with no love in them, shuddered, and closed them again.

Mad with rapture, I caught her up, sent Petro headlong lamp and all, and kissed her enough to kill her. She was not dead, my Lily, my pet of eternal ages. There she fell trembling, fluttering, nestling in my arms, her pale cheek on my breast, her white hand on my shoulder; then frightened at her nest shrunk back, and gazed with unutterable reproach, where love like the fallen lamp was flickering: then clung to me once more, as if she ought to hate, but could not yet help loving. She died the next morning. Clara, I can't tell you any more now.

CHAPTER XV.

Before my own and only love departed, she knew, thank God, she knew as well as I did, that I had never wronged her pure and true affection. But it was long before I learned what had so distressed her. Though she appeared quite sensible, and looked at me, every now and then, with the same reproachful harrowing gaze, it seemed to me ages, it must have been hours, before she could frame her thoughts in words. In an agony of suspense for her, for our children, for our love, I could hardly repress my impatience even at her debility. Many a time she opened her trembling lips, but the words died on them. At last I caught her meaning from a few broken sentences.

"How could he do it? How could he so betray her? And his own Lily that loved him so--no, she must not be Lily any more, she was only Fiordalisa Della Croce. How could he come and pretend to love her, and pretend to marry her, when all the while he had a young wife at home in England? Never would she have believed it but for the proofs, the proofs that hateful man had shown her. How could he shame his own love so, and his children, and the aged father--there was no hope for her but to die--to die and never see him more; and then perhaps he would be sorry, for he must care about her a little."

Then she burst into such a torrent of tears, and pressed both hands on her bounding heart, and grew white with terror. Then as the palpitation passed, she looked at me and knew me, and crept close to me, forgetting all the evil,--and seemed to sleep awhile. Of course I saw what it was; dazed as I was and wild at her sorrow and danger, I slowly perceived what it was. The serpent-like foe had been there, and had hissed in her ear what he thought to be true--that I had done her a dastard's wrong; had won her passionate maiden love, and defiled her by a sham marriage, while my lawful wife was living.

When once I knew my supposed offence, it did not take long to explain the murderer's error, an error which had sprung from my own deceit. But my children, where are my children, Lily?

In her ecstatic joy, she could not think for the moment even of her children; but pressed me to her tumultuous heart, as if I were all she wanted. Then she began to revile herself, for daring to believe any ill of her noble husband.

"And even if it had been true, which you know it never could be, dear,--I must have forgiven you, sweetest darling, because you couldn't have helped it, you did love me so, didn't you?"

This sweet womanly logic, you, Clara, may comprehend--But where are the children, my Lily?

"Oh, in bed I suppose, dear: let me get up, we must go and kiss the darlings. When I first came in, I could not bear to go near them, poor pets; but now--Oh my heart, holy Madonna, my heart!"

She leaped up as if she were shot, and a choking sound rose in her throat.. Her fresh youth fought hard in the clutches of death. "Oh save me, my own husband, save me. Hold me tighter; I cannot die yet. So young and so happy with you. It is gone; but the next pang is death. Hold me so till it comes again. God bless you, my own for ever. You will find me in heaven, won't you? You can never forget your own Lily."

Her large eyes rested on mine, as they did when she first owned her love; and her soul seemed trying to spring into the breast of mine. Closer to me she clung, but with less and less of strength. Her smooth, clear cheek was on mine, her exhausted heart on my wild one. I felt its last throb, as the death-pang came, and she tried to kiss me to show that it was not violent. Frantic, I opened my lips, and received the last breath of hers.

The crush of its anguish her heart might have borne, but not the rebound of its joy.

Her body, the fairest the sun ever saw, was laid beside her father's in the little churchyard at St. Katharine's, with the toy baby on her breast; her soul, the most loving and playful that ever the angels visited, is still in attendance upon me, and mourns until mine rejoins it.

You have heard my greatest but not my only distress. For more than three months, my reason forsook me utterly. I recognised no one, not even myself, but sought high and low for my Lily. At night I used to wander forth and search among the olive-trees, where we so often roved: sometimes the form I knew so well would seem to flit before me, tempting me on from bole to bole, and stretching vain hands towards me. Then as I seemed to have overtaken and brought to bay her coyness, with a faint shriek she would vanish into hazy air. Probably I owed these visions to capricious memory, gleaming upon old hexameters of the Eton clink. True from false I knew not, neither cared to know: everything I did seemed to be done in sleep, with all the world around me gone to sleep as well. One vague recollection I retain of going somewhere, to do something that made me creep with cold. This must have been the funeral of my lost one; when the Corsicans, as I am told, fled from my ghastly stare, and would only stand behind me. They are a superstitious race, and they feared the "evil eye."

All the time I was in this state, faithful Petro waited on me, and watched me like a father. He sent for his wife, old Marcantonia, who was famed for her knowledge of herbs and her power over the witches, who now beyond all doubt had gotten me in possession. Decoctions manifold she gave me at the turn of the moon, and hung me all over with amulets, till I rang like a peal of cracked bells. In spite of all these sovereign charms, Lepardo might at any time have murdered me, if he had thought me happy enough to deserve it. Perhaps he was in some other land, making sure of my children's lives.

Poor helpless darlings, all that was left me of my Lily, as yet I did not know that even they were taken. Petro told me afterwards that I had asked for them once or twice, in a vacant wondering manner, but had been quite content with some illusory answer.

It was my Lily, and no one else, who brought me back to conscious life. What I am about to tell may seem to you a feeble brain's chimera; and so it would appear to me, if related by another. But though my body was exhausted by unsleeping sorrow, under whose strain the mental chords had yielded, yet I assure you that what befell me did not flow from but swept aside both these enervations.

It is the Corsican's belief, that those whom he has deeply mourned, and desolately missed, are allowed to hover near him in the silent night. Then sometimes, when he is sleeping, they will touch his lids and say, "Weep no more, beloved one: in all, except thy sorrow, we are blessed as thou couldst wish." Or sometimes, if the parting be of still more tender sort, (as between two lovers, or a newly wedded couple) in the depth of darkness when the lone survivor cannot sleep for trouble, appears the lost one at the chamber door, holds it open, and calls softly; "Dearest, come; for I as well am lonely." Having thrice implored, it waves its cerements like an angel's wing, and awaits the answer. Answer not, if you wish to live; however the sweet voice thrills your heart, however that heart is breaking. But if you truly wish to die, and hope is quenched in memory; make answer to the well-known voice. Within three days you will be dead, and flit beside the invoking shadow.

Perhaps old Marcantonia had warned me of this appeal, and begged me to keep silence, which for my children's sake I was bound to do. All I know is that one night towards the end of January, I lay awake as usual, thinking--if a mind distempered thus can think--of my own sweet Lily. All the evening I had sought her among the olive-trees, and at St. Katharine's Church, and even on the sad sea-shore by the moaning of the waves. Now the winter moon was high, and through the embrasured window, the far churchyard that held my wife, and the silver sea beyond it, glimmered like the curtain of another world. Sitting up in the widowed bed, with one hand on my aching forehead--for now I breathed perpetual headache--I called in question that old church of one gay wedding and two dark funerals. Was there any such church at all; was it not a dream of moonlight and the phantom love?

Even as I sat gazing now, so on many a moonlight night sat my Lily gazing with me, whispering of her father's grave, and looking for it in the shrouded distance. Her little hand used to quiver in mine, as she declared she had found it; and her dark eyes had so wondrous a gift of sight, that I never would dare to deny, though I could not quite believe it. Had she not in the happy days, when we roamed on the beach together, waiting for the yacht and pretending to seek shells, had she not then told me the stripes and colours of the sailors' caps, and even the names of the men on deck, when I could hardly see their figures?

Ah, could she tell my own name now, could she descry me from that shore which mocks the range of telescope, and the highest lens of thought; was she permitted one glimpse of him from whom in life she could hardly bear to withdraw those gentle eyes? Answer me, my own, in life and death my own one; tell me that you watch and love me, though it be but now and then, and not enough to break the by-laws of the disembodied world.

Calmly as I now repeat it, but in a low melodious tone, sweeter than any mortal's voice, a tone that dwelt I knew not where, like the sighing of the night-wind, came this answer to me:

"True love, for our children's sake, and mine who watch and love you still, quit this grief, the spirit's grave. All your sorrow still is mine, and would you vex your darling, when you cannot comfort her? Though you see me now no more, I am with you more than ever; I am your image and your shadow. At every sigh of yours, I shiver; your smiles are all my sunshine. Let me feel some sunshine, sweetest; you know how I used to love it, and as yet you have sent me none. I shall look for some to-morrow. Lo I, for ever yours, am smiling on you now."

And a golden light, richer than any sunbeam, rippled through the room. I knew the soft gleam like the sunset on a harvest-field. It was my Lily's smile. A glow of warmth was shed on me, and I fell at once into a deep and dreamless sleep. You, my child, who have never known such loss--pray God you never may--very likely you regard all this incident as a dream. Be it so: if it were a dream, Lily's angel brought it.

CHAPTER XVI.

The next day I was a different man. All my energy had returned, and all my reasoning power; but not, thank God, the rigour of my mind, the petty contempt of my fellow-men. Nothing is more hard to strip than that coat of flinty closeness formed upon Deucalion's offcast in the petrifying well of self. Though I have done my utmost, and prayed of late for help in doing it, never have I quite scaled off this accursed deposit. This it was that so estranged your warm nature, Clara; a nature essentially like your father's, but never allowed free scope. You could not tell the reason, children never can; but somehow it made you shiver to be in contact with me.

Petro and Marcantonia would have been astonished at my sudden change, but they had lately dosed me with some narcotic herb, procured, by a special expedition, from the Monte Rotondo, and esteemed a perfect Stregomastix; so of course the worthy pair expected my recovery. No longer did they attempt to conceal from me the truth as to my poor infants, who had been carried off on the day of my return. What I learned of the great calamity, which then befell me, was this.

Towards sunset, my dear wife, with her usual fondness, went forth to look for the little yacht returning from the gulf of Porto. Our darling Harry, then in his third year, was with her, and the young nurse from Muro. Lily sat upon the cliff, watching a sail far in the offing, probably our vessel. Then as she turned towards the tower, a man from the shrubbery stood before her, and called her by her maiden name. She knew her cousin Lepardo, and supposed that he was come to kill her. Nevertheless she asked him proudly how he dared to insult her so, in the presence of her child and servant. He answered that it was her name, and she was entitled to no other. Then he promised not to harm her, if she would send the maid away, for he had important things to speak of. And thereupon he laid before her documents and letters.

Meanwhile the tower was surrounded by his comrades; but they durst not enter, for the trusty fusileer kept the one approach up the steep hillside; and his grandson, a brave boy, stood at the loop-hole with him. The maid, however, with her little charge, was allowed to pass, and she joined the two other women in weak preparations for defence. The period of attack had been chosen skilfully. So simple and patriarchal is the Corsican mode of life, that very few servants are kept, even by men of the highest station; and those few are not servants in our sense of the word. It happened this night that the only two men employed upon the premises, beside the old fusileer, had been sent into the town for things wherewith to welcome me.

However, the faithful gunner, with his eye along the barrels, kept the foe at bay, and seemed likely to keep them there, until the return of the men; while his sturdy grandson split his red cheeks at the warder's conch. But they little knew their enemy. Lepardo Della Croce was not to be baulked by an old man and a boy. At the narrow entrance a lady's dress came fluttering in the brisk north wind. Poor Lily tottered across the line of fire, her life she never thought of; what use to live after all that she had heard? Close behind her, and in the dusk invisible past her wind-tossed drapery, stole her scoundrel cousin; whom, like trees set in a row, or feather-edged boards seen lengthwise, a score of lithe and active sailors followed. No chance for the marksman; like tiles they overlapped one another, and poor Lily, upright in her outraged pride, covered the stooping graduated file. French and English, Moorish and Maltese, a motley band as ever swore, they burst into a hearty laugh at the old gunner's predicament, the moment they had passed his range. All within was at their mercy. True he kept the main gate still, and all the doors were barred; but gates and doors were lubber's holes for seamen such as they. Up the ivy they clambered, along the chestnut branches, or the mere coignes of the granite, and into the house they poured at every loop-hole and window. One thing must be said in their favour--they did very little mischief. They were kept thoroughly under command, and a wave of their captain's hand drove them anywhither. All he wanted was possession of my children, and of some valuable property which he claimed in right of his father.

Having secured both objects, he ordered his men to depart, allowing them only to carry what wine and provisions they found. But the three domestics, and the ancient sentinel and his boy, were bound hand and foot, and concealed in a cave on the beach, to prevent any stir in the neighbouring hamlet. Poor Lily was left where she fell, to recover or not, as might be. My own darling was not insulted or touched; the men were afraid, and Lepardo too proud to outrage one of his kin. Moreover, his word was pledged; and they say that he always keeps it. Soon after dark the robbers set sail, and slipped away down the coast, before that strong north wind which had so baffled me. But for me a letter was left, full of triumph and contumely. It was addressed to "Valentine Vaughan, the Englishman;" "Signor Valentine" was the title conferred on me by the fusileer, and adopted by the neighbourhood. To my surprise that letter was written in English, and English as good as a foreigner ever indites: I can repeat it word for word:--

"SIR,--I am reluctant to obtrude good counsel, but with the obtuseness of your nation you are prone to the undervaluing of others. It is my privilege to amend this error, while meekly I revindicate my own neglected rights. From me you have stolen my bride and my good inheritance, and in a manner which the persons unversed in human nature would be inclined to characterise as dastardly and dissolute. Furthermore, you have rendered the heiress of the noblest house in Corsica a common Englishman's adulteress. If I had heard this on the day of your mocking marriage, not the poor victim but you, you, would have been my direction. Now I will punish you more gradually, and longer, as you deserve. Your unhappy adulteress knows the perfidy of your treachery, and your two poor bastards shall take refuge with me. The inquiry with respect to my drowning them to-night is dependent upon the stars. But if I shall spare them, as I may, because they cannot come between me and my property, I will teach them, when they are old enough, to despise and loathe your name. They shall know that in the stead of a father's love they have only had a vagabond's lust, and they shall know how you seduced and then slew their mother; for death, in my humble opinion, appears in her face to-night. Although she has betrayed me, I am regretful for her: but to you who have disgraced my name and plundered me, as a man of liberal and exalted views I grant a contemptuous forbearance; so long, that is to say, as you remain unhappy, which the wicked ought to be. Of one thing, however, I bid you to take admonishment. If I hear that you ever forget this episode of debauchery, and return to your English wife and property, no house, no castle that ever was edified, shall protect you from my dagger. Remember the one thing, as your proverb tells, I am slow and sure.

LEPARDO DELLA CROCE."

CHAPTER XVII.

Instead of enraging or maddening me, as the writer perhaps expected, this execrable letter did me a great deal of good. I determined to lower that insufferable arrogance; and brought all my thoughts to bear upon one definite object, the recovery of my darlings and the punishment of that murderer. I did not believe that he had destroyed them, or was likely to do so; for had not their mother's spirit referred to them as living?

Without delay, my yacht was prepared for a lengthened cruise; the tower committed to Marcantonia and the gray sentinel; and with Petro for my skipper, I sailed on the following day. Alas, the three months now elapsed during my delirium, had they not like the sea itself closed across the track? All the neighbours knew was this, the felucca had passed Point Girolata, and had been seen in the early morning, standing away due south. All the villagers, and even the men from the mountain, thronged the shore as I embarked, and there invoked Madonna's blessing on poor Signor Valentine, so basely robbed of wife and children.

When we had rounded Girolata, we bore away due south, and in less than fifteen hours made the Sardinian shore in the gulf of Asinara. Here we coasted along the curve, inquiring at every likely place whether any such vessel had been sighted as that which we were seeking. But we could learn nothing of her until we were off the Gypsum Cape; where some fishermen told us, that at or about the time we spoke of, a swift felucca, built and manned exactly as we had described, glided by them and bore up for the town of Alghero. We too bore up for Alghero, and soon discovered that the roving vessel had undoubtedly been there: even Lepardo, the captain, was described by the keen Sardinians. But she had only lain to for a few hours, and cleared again for Cagliari. For Cagliari we made sail as hard as the sticks could carry, and arrived there on the fourth day from Cape Girolata.

The pirates, if such they were, had offered their vessel for sale at Cagliari; but, failing of a satisfactory price had sailed away again, and after much trouble I found out that their destination was Valetta. To Valetta also we followed, feeling like a new boy at school who is mystified by the experts--innocent of much Greek themselves--with a game which means in English, "send the fool on further."

When at length we reach the Maltese capital--where I was not sorry to hear once more my native tongue--we found the felucca snugly moored near the "Merchant's Yard," and being refitted as a pleasure-boat for a wealthy Englishman. This gentleman knew a good deal about ships, but not quite enough. Pleased with the graceful lines and clean run of the felucca, he had given nearly twice her value for her; as he soon perceived when the ship-carpenters set to work. He was in the vein to afford all possible information, being thoroughly furious with the condemnable pirates--as he called them, without the weakness of the composite verb--who had robbed him so shamefully of his money. He told me that my children had been ashore, and Harry was much admired and kissed in the Floriana. One thing the sailors did which would have surprised a man unacquainted with the Corsicans, or perhaps I should say the islanders of the Mediterranean. They decked my little babe with flowers and ribands, and bore her in procession to the church of St. John of Jerusalem; and there they had her baptized, for Lepardo had found out that she had never undergone the ceremony. I was anxious to see the record, but was not allowed to do so; therefore I do not know what the little darling's name is, if she be still alive: but they told me that the surname entered was not Vaughan, but Della Croce. It was said that the sailors had become very fond of her, the little creature being very sweet-tempered and happy, and a pleasing novelty to them. Very likely they named her after their own felucca.

The crew being now dispersed, some to their homes, and some on board ships which had sailed, I was thrown completely off the scent. All I could learn, at a house which they had frequented, was that Lepardo, the commander, had long ago left the island. Whither, or in what ship, he had sailed, they could not or would not tell me: he had always plenty of money, they said, and he spent it like a prince. But Petro, who was a much better ferret than I, discovered, or seemed to have done so, that the kidnapper and murderer had taken passage for Naples. My heart fell when I heard it; almost as easily might I have tracked him in London. At Naples I had spent a month, and knew the lying ingenuity, the laziness in all but lies, of its swarming thousands. However, the little yacht was again put under way, and, after a tedious passage, we saw the Queen of cities. Here, as I expected, the pursuit was baffled.

I will not weary you with my wanderings, off more often than on the track, up and down the Mediterranean, and sometimes far inland. If I marked them on a map, however large the scale, you would have what children call a crinkly crankly puzzle, like Lancashire in Bradshaw. Once, indeed, I rested at the ancient tower, near my Lily's grave, which I always visited twice in every year. I have some vague idea, now in my old age, that though we Vaughans detest any display of feeling--except indeed at times when the heart is too big for the skin--we are in substance, without knowing it, a most romantic race. Whether we are that, or not, is matter of small moment; one thing is quite certain, we are strutted well and stable. We are not quick of reception, but we are most retentive. Never was there man of us who ever loved a woman and cast her off through weariness; never was there woman of our house who played the jilt, when once she had passed the pledge of love. And after all I have seen of the world, and through my dark misfortune few men have seen more, it is my set conclusion that strong tenacity is the foremost of all the virtues. My enemy has it, I freely own, and through all his wickedness it saves him from being contemptible.

For a time, as I said before, I paused from my continual search, and abode in the old gray tower. That search now appeared so hopeless, that I was half inclined to believe no better policy could be found than this. Some day or other the robber would surely return and lay claim to the lands of the Della Croce. At present he durst not do it, while under the ban of piracy and the suspicion of his uncle's murder. Moreover, I thought it my duty to see to the welfare of my children's property. Under the deed-poll of the old Signor, his friend at Prato and myself were trustees and guardians. But I could not live there long: it was too painful for me to sit alone in the desolate rooms where my children ought to be toddling, or to wander through the shrubberies and among the untended flowers, every one of them whispering "Lily." Formerly I had admired and loved that peculiar stillness, that rich deep eloquent solitude, which mantles in bucolic gray the lawns and glades of Corsica. But when I so admired and loved, I was a happy man, a man who had affection near him, and could warm himself when he pleased. Now though I had no friends or friendship, neither cared for any, solitude struck me to the bones, because it seemed my destiny.

After striving for half a year to do my duty as a hermit Signor, I found myself, one dreary morning, fingering my pistols gloomily, and fitting a small bullet into my ear. My thumb caught in the guard of the Signor's locket, and jerked it up my waistcoat. It was the same which the poor old man had pressed to his dying lips. There was Lily's hair and Harry's, and a tiny wisp of down since added, belonging to baby--name unknown. Looking at them and seeing how Lily's bound them together and to me, I felt ashamed of my cowardly gloom, and resolved to quit myself like a man in my duty towards the three. I rode at once to Prato, and persuaded Count Gaffori to come and live at the tower. Like his old friend the Signor, he had only himself and his lovely daughter to think of; but unlike Signor Dezio he had lost nearly all his paternal property, through political troubles. Therefore it was for him no little comfort and advantage to be placed at the head of a household again, and restored to some worldly importance. Nevertheless, his sense of honour was so nice and exacting, that I thought I should never succeed in bringing him to my views; and indeed I must have failed but for his daughter's assistance. A very sweet elegant girl she was, and she had been a great friend of my Lily's. If I could ever have loved again, I should have loved that maiden: but the thing was impossible.

The old Count promised to come and settle at Veduta tower--which name, in light days, I had corrupted into "Vendetta"--and living there to assume the management of the estates, in trust for my lost infants, as soon as his arrangements could be made. I saw nothing that need have delayed him a day; however, he declared that he must have a month to get ready, and he was plainly a man whom nature meant not to be pushed. So I employed the interval in having my dear old "Lilyflower" overhauled at Marseilles, coppered, and thoroughly painted. I could not bear to alter our little love-boat, as my darling called it, even in outward appearance; but like our love she had laboured through many a tempest; unlike it, she needed repairs. However, I saved from the painter's brush our favourite quarter-deck bench, whereon through the moonlight watches my Lily seemed still to recline.

And so my life for some years wandered on, a worthless, unsettled, forlorn existence, only refreshed at intervals by return to the scenes of past happiness. If I had really wronged Lepardo Della Croce, he could hardly have wished for a better revenge. But in truth I had never wronged him. Even if I had never come near his betrothed, it is quite certain she would not have accepted him. And he, by his own desertion, had left her free to choose.

Late in the autumn of 1812, when I had abandoned all hope of ever recovering my little ones, except by one of those eddies of Providence, which we men call accidents, and in which I place my confidence to this hour, at that season, I say, I landed at Gibraltar, being wind-bound in the straits. We were making for Lisbon, where I was to ship some English watches, guns, and fine cutlery for Ajaccio. What a loss of rank for the "Lilyflower," to turn her into a trading smack! Well, I could not see it so; and I am sure her late mistress, who with all her sweet romance was an excellent hand at a bargain, would have thought it far more below my dignity for me to sponge on our children. There was plenty of money in hand at Veduta tower; but having retired from stewardship, I did not feel myself justified in drawing upon my children. Therefore, and for the sake of the large acquaintance and great opportunities gained, I had renewed my connection with the firm of Green, Vowler, and Green. Somehow, I could not bear to revisit the shores of England; otherwise I am sure that with the knowledge I now possessed of the Mediterranean ports, and a house of such standing and enterprise to back me, I should quickly have made my fortune. My vessel, moreover, was much too small for the fruit-trade, even if I could have lowered her to an uncleanly freight; but she was just the craft for valuable goods in small compass. I knew the Corsican fondness for arms and first-rate cutlery; and the tools the poor Signor Dezio meant to astonish me with, certainly did astonish me by their wonderful badness. True, the material was good, but all the waters of the Restonica will not convert a hammer into a handsaw. Although hardware was not at all in his line of business, Peter Green most kindly undertook to send me a cargo of first-rate Sheffield and Birmingham goods, by a return fruit-schooner. These, consigned to his Lisbon agent, I could fetch away, as I pleased, or wanted them. Having arranged with a shrewd merchant of Ajaccio to take my goods wholesale, and save the dignity of all the Vogheni from haggling, I had already made six trips, and in spite of the most tyrannical douane perhaps in all the world, I as a Corsican, importing goods in a Corsican bottom, had cleared very nearly three hundred per cent. on my outlay. We were now on our seventh voyage, to reship the last of the second English consignment, when a violent gale from the west met us right in the teeth, and we were forced to bear up for the anchorage. A first-rate sea-boat the "Lilyflower" was, although she had been built for racing, and for two or three years had beaten all competitors, whenever there was wind enough for a cat to stand on the sheets.

But one hot June day she got beaten in a floating match, when the lightest bung went fastest, and her prig of a "noble owner" sold her in disgust, and built a thing that drew as much water as a nautilus. In her he was happily upset, and could hardly find a sheet of paper to hold on by. Knowing some little about yachts, from my pool and reach experiences, I bought the famous racing cutter at about a quarter her value; and even in these, her olden days, she could exhibit her taffrail to the smartest fruit-clipper--the name was then just invented--that ever raced for the Monument. Her register was fifty tons, but she carried eighty.

Landing at Gibraltar, I kept clear of my countrymen, not that I dislike them, but because-- well I cannot tell why; and strolled away to the Spanish and Moorish quarters.

It was a windy evening, and in front of a low refreshment house some sailors and Spanish girls were dancing. A squabble arose among them; something I think it was about a young girl's dress. Knives were drawn, and two men were stabbed in less than the time I am speaking. I just saved the life of one, just saved it by half an inch. A fine-looking Spaniard lay under a Moor, who had tripped him up in their quick way. The point of the knife had flashed through the Spaniard's shirt and his flesh was cut, before the swing of my stick-- upwards luckily--had jerked the Moor off his body. If I had struck downwards, or a millionth part of a second later, the blade would have stood in the heart. But I knew those fellows by this time. The Moor lay senseless from the quick upper-cut on his temples, and the knife was quivering where the impulse had failed it.

Now if Petro and I held deliberate choice--"proairesis" Oxford calls it--not to be turned into knife-sheaths, our only chance of developing into action that undeniable process of "nous," was to be found in the policy, vulgarly called "cut and run." At a shrill signal, from ship and from shore, the Moors came swarming silently and swiftly. Their yellow slippers and coffee-coloured legs seemed set upon springs by excitement. Some of the Spaniards stood bravely by us, and with their aid we hurried the wounded man into our boat, and pushed off just in time. Unlike the Corsican peasants, our pursuers carried no fire-arms, and before they could get any, we were at safe distance.

Having sent for an English surgeon, we kept the poor sailor on board the yacht, until he was quite out of danger. We Britons are not, as a general rule, an over-grateful race; we hate to be under an obligation, and too often illustrate the great philosopher's saying, that the doer feels more good will than the receiver of a kindness. Moreover, the Spaniards, in the neighbourhood of the Rock, could hardly be expected to love us, even if we were accustomed, which it is needless to say we are not, to treat them with decent courtesy. Therefore I was surprised at the deep and warm gratitude of this wounded man. A thing that enhanced his debt to me--for life, in my opinion, is very little to owe--was that he loved a young girl, the one over whom they had quarrelled, and he was about to marry her. Discovering who I was, for he knew nothing of me at first, he saw that he could be of no little service to me. The only obstacle was a solemn oath; but from this, he believed, he could soon obtain release. With an Englishman's honest and honourable repugnance to any breach of faith, I was long reluctant to encourage this absolution. But the thought of my helpless children, robbed of their inheritance, and, still worse, of a father's love, and dependant on the caprice of a superstitious villain, this, and the recollection of my desolating wrongs, overpowered all scruples. And is it not a wiser course, and more truly Christian, to port the helm than to cross the bows of another man's religion, at any rate so long as it be Christian also, though frogged in a pensioner's coat?

Being duly absolved--for which he would not allow me to pay--the Spanish sailor told me all he knew. He had been Lepardo's mate, on many a smuggling run, and in many an act of piracy off the coast of Barbary. But he had never liked his captain, no one ever did; though all the crew admired him as the cleverest man in the world. After the felucca was sold and her crew dispersed, the mate had followed for a while the fortunes of Lepardo. He told me things about him which I knew not how to believe. However, I will not repeat them, because they do not seem to bear upon my story. The name of my little girl he could not remember, for he was not at the christening, and she was always called the baby. Being a good-natured man he took kindly to the children, and told me anecdotes of them which brought the tears to my eyes.

After two or three months spent at Naples, they all left suddenly for Palermo, on account, as the mate believed, of my unexpected arrival; and here he lost sight of his commander, for tired by this time of an idle life, and seeing no chance of any more roving adventures, he accepted a berth in a brig bound for the Piræus, and now after many shifts and changes was first mate of a fruit vessel sailing from Zante to London. The most important part to me of all his communication was that, on their previous voyage, they had carried to England Lepardo Della Croce and my two dear children. That murderer and kidnapper had taken the lead in some conspiracy against the government of the Two Sicilies, and through the treachery of an accomplice had been obliged to fly for his life. Disguising himself he contrived to reach Gibraltar, and took refuge on English ground. He was now very poor and in great distress, but still clung to the children, of whom he appeared to be fond, and who believed him to be their father. The "Duo Brachiones" touching there, as usual, for supplies, Lepardo met his old mate ashore; and begged for a passage to England. They took him to London, and there of course lost sight of him. He was greatly altered, the mate said, from the Lepardo of old. Morose and reserved he had always been; but now misfortune had covered him with a skin-deep philosophy. But his eyes contracted and sparkled as of yore, whenever my name was mentioned; and the mate knew what his intention was, in case he should find me a happy man. The simple mate was still more surprised at the alteration in my children; as pretty a pair, he said, as ever he set eyes on. But they were kept most jealously from the notice of the crew, and even from their ancient friend's attentions; they were never allowed to be on the deck, except when the berths were being cleaned. They seemed to fear their reputed father, a great deal more than they loved him.

Upon hearing this last particular I seized the mate by the hand, and felt something rise in my throat: I was so delighted to learn that the pirate had not succeeded in carrying nature by boarding. The next day I left Petro to see to the hardware business--to which we were bound by charter--while I set sail in the "Duo Brachiones" for the arms of my darling little ones.

CHAPTER XVIII.

They put me in the very hammock where that murderer of all my happiness had slept, and no wonder that I could find no rest there. Soon as I knew the reason, I was allowed to change, and crept into the little berth where my innocent pets had lain in each other's arms. Here I slept much better than a king, for I even fancied that it smelt of Lily. If little Lily, as she shall be called, whatever the rogues have christened her, if my little beauty--for that I am sure she must be--ever comes to light, when I am in my grave, remember one thing, Clara, you will find her breath and general fragrance just as her mother's were. Such things are hereditary, especially among women.

After a long and stormy passage, and a fortnight spent in repairing at Bordeaux, we passed the familiar Essex marshes by night, and were off the Custom House by the last day of the year. When that tedious work was over--talk as we please of the douane, our own is as bad as most of them--feeling quite out of my latitude, and not a bit like an Englishman, I betook myself to a tavern near London Bridge. There everything seemed new, and I could not walk the streets without yawing into the wrong tide. But one old London custom held its ground with time. Papers a week and a fortnight old still strayed about in the coffee-room. Being told that the journals of that day were "in hand," as they always are, I took up a weekly paper of some ten days back to yawn over it till supper time. It was too late for me to think of disturbing Peter Green by a sudden arrival, and so I had ordered a bed at this hotel.

The weekly gazette in my hand was one of those which use the shears with diligence and method. Under the heading "Provincial News," I found the following paragraph:--

"SEASONABLE BENEVOLENCE.--We understand that in these times of severe and unmerited pressure upon the agricultural interest--the true back-bone of old England--the head of one of our most ancient and respected county families has announced his intention of remitting to all his tenantry no less than twenty per cent. upon their rentals. He has also bespoken a lavish and most princely repast--shall we say dinner--to be provided on Christmas eve for every man, woman, and child upon his large domain. When we announce that mine host of the Elephant is to be major domo, and our respected townsman George Jenkins, who purchased as our readers are aware the gold medal ox at Smithfield, is to cater for the occasion, need we say anything more? At the risk of gratuitous insult to the intelligence of the county, we must subjoin that the honoured gentleman to whom we allude is Henry Valentine Vaughan, Esquire, of Vaughan Park. Is not such a man, the representative of time-honoured sentiments, and who to a distinguished degree adds the experience of continental travel, is not such a man, we ask, a thousand times fitter to express in the Senate the opinions and wishes of this great county, than the scion, we had almost said spawn, of the Manchester mushrooms, whom a Castle that shall be nameless is attempting to foist on the county? We pause for a reply.--*Gloucester Argus*."

My dear brother's distinguished degree was that of B.A. after a narrow escape from pluck. Clara, don't look offended. Your father had very good abilities, but spent most of his Oxford time in pigeon matches at the Weirs, and expeditions to Bagley wood, which later in life he would have looked upon as felonious.

This paltry puff would never have been reprinted by a London journal of eminence and influence, but for the suggestion at the end, which happened just to hit the sentiments of the more exalted editor. Now this weekly paper was sure to circulate among refugees from the continent, by reason of its well-known antipathy towards them; and there happened to be in this very number a violent tirade against our Government for displaying what we delight to call the mighty Ægis of England. I saw the danger at once, and my heart turned sick within me. My gay and harmless brother in the midst of his Christmas rejoicings, and a stealthy murderer creeping perhaps at that very moment towards him.

But even if it were so, was there not some chance of Lepardo discovering his mistake, when in the neighbourhood where the Vaughans were so well known? Yes, some chance there was, but very little. Bound upon such an errand he would not dare to show himself, or to make any inquiries, even if they seemed needful. And the mention by that cursed gossip of what he called "continental travel"--your father's wedding tour--would banish all doubt of identity, had any been entertained. Even supposing that cold-blooded fiend should meet my poor brother, face to face, in the open daylight, it was not likely that he would be undeceived. Lepardo and I had met only once, and then in hot encounter. My brother was like me in figure, in face, and in voice; and though I was somewhat taller and much darker of complexion, the former difference would not attract attention, unless we stood side by side; the latter would of course be attributed to the effects of climate. From the gamekeeper's evidence, I am now inclined to believe that Lepardo, while lurking in the lower coppice, among the holly bushes, must have cast his evil eyes on your poor father's face, and convinced himself that he beheld his enemy.

Flurried and frightened, I looked at the date of the paper. It was twelve days old. Possibly I might yet be in time, for most likely the murderer would set out on foot, according to Corsican practice, with the travel-stone bound on his knee. Even if he had travelled in modern fashion, he would probably lurk and lie in ambush about the house, enduring hunger and cold and privation, until his moment came. Could I leave for Gloucester that night? No, the last train would have started, before I could get to Paddington. So I resolved to go by the morning express, which would take me to Gloucester by middle day.

After a sleepless night, I was up betimes in the morning, and went through the form of breakfast while the cab was sent for. Presently a waiter came in with the morning papers, the papers of New Year's-day, 1843. What I saw and what my feelings were, you, my poor child, can too well imagine. That day I could not bear to go. It was cowardly of me, and perhaps unmanly; but I could not face your mother's grief and the desolate household. Therefore I persuaded myself that I had discharged my duty, by visiting all the London police stations, and leaving the best description I could give of Lepardo. The following day I left London, and arrived, as perhaps you remember, long after dark, and during a heavy fall of snow. There at the very threshold I began amiss with you, for I outraged your childish pride by mistaking you for the housekeeper's daughter. With a well-born child's high self-esteem, and making no allowance for the dim light, you believed it to be a sham intended to mortify you; and it poisoned your heart towards me. But you were wholly mistaken. My mind was full of your mother and of the terrible blow to her; to you, whom I had never seen, and scarcely even heard of, I never gave a thought; except the mistaken one that you were not old enough to be sensible of your loss. Little did I imagine what a fount of resolute will, and deep feeling, found a vent in the kicks and screams of the large-eyed minnikin, that would not be ordered away.

You are entitled, Clara, to know all that I have done towards the discovery of your father's assassin, and all that I can tell to aid your own pursuit. The hair found in your mother's grasp was beyond a doubt Lepardo's; that laid upon your father's bosom was, of course, my Lily's. It was to show that her supposed seduction had been expiated. The one thing that most surprised me was that the murderer left no token, no symbol of himself. In a Vendetta murder they almost always do, as a mark of triumph and a gage to the victim's family. Hence I believed that Signor Dezio was not killed in Vendetta, but by his nephew for gain. How Lepardo got into the house I have no idea, or rather I had none, until you told me of the secret passage, and Mrs. Daldy's entrance. Till then I always thought that he had clambered up, as he did at Veduta tower. But unless there was a traitor in the household, he must have been there more than once, to have known so well your father's sleeping room.

It would have been waste of time for me to concern myself about the county police. That body of well-conducted navvies--Lepardo would have outwitted them, when he was five years old. Neither did I meddle with the coroner and his jury, but left them to their own devices and indigenous intellect. These displayed themselves in much puzzle-headed cross-questioning, sagacious looks, and nods, and winks of acute reservation. It was, as most often it is, a bulldog after a hare. Lepardo might safely have been in the midst of them, asked for a chair, and made suggestions. as "amicus curiæ."

But with the London police it was somewhat different. They showed some little acumen, but their fundamental error is this--they pride themselves on their intelligence. No man of any real depth ever does such a thing as this. He knows very well that whatever he is, there are half a million more so; that the age of exceptional intellects expired, at least in this country, with Mr. Edmund Burke, and is not likely to rise from the dead. Now we are all pretty much good useful clods on a level: education, like all good husbandry, tends to pulverisation; and if the collective produce is greater, let us be at once thankful and humble.

The London police, being proud of their intelligence, declared that there could be no doubt about their catching the criminal. They laughed at my belief that he might walk through the midst of them, while they would touch their hats to him, and beg him to look after his handkerchief. At one time, I think, they were really on his track, and I went to London, and stayed there, and did my best to help them. But they were all too late; Lepardo, if he it were, had left for Paris the week before. To Paris I followed, but found no trace of him there. Then I went on to Corsica, thinking it likely that he would return to his old piratical ways. Moreover, I wanted to see how my children's estates were managed, and to revisit St. Katharine's.

All was calm and peaceful. Lily's grave and her father's were blended in one rich herbage. There all the bloom of my life was drooping, like the yellow mountain-rose, whence if a single flower be plucked, all the other blossoms fall.

Count Gaffori received me kindly. His daughter was married and had two children, who played where Lily's boy and girl should by rights be playing. I could not bear it, and came away, having nothing now to care for. Wherever I went the world seemed much of a muchness to me; and to my own misfortunes the blood of my brother was added. I found the "Lilyflower" still under worthy Petro, and returned in her to England, and she still is mine. Petro would not come; he was too true a Corsican to leave the beloved island now his hair was grey. So I set him up at Calvi with a vessel of his own, and now and then I receive a letter from good Marcantonia. They have promised to watch for the reappearance of our fearful enemy; and Petro has sworn to shoot him, if ever he gets a chance.

After my return to England, I set to work with all my energy to improve this property. In this, if in nothing else, I have thoroughly succeeded. Much opposition I had to encounter; for the tenants regarded me as a mere interloper, and their hearts were with you and your mother. When I call them together to-morrow, as I intend to do, abandon all my right, title, and interest, and declare you their Signora, it is my firm belief that they will hardly think me worth cursing before they worship you. This old retainership is a thing to be proud and yet ashamed of. It is a folly that makes one glory in being a fool. Why, after you left for Devonshire (much, as you know, against my will), I could not ride out without being insulted, and even the boys called me "Jonathan Wild." But this was due, in some measure, to your father's gay geniality, and hearty good-will to all men, contrasted with my satiric and moody reserve. Neither were your youth, and sex, and helplessness, lost upon that chivalrous being--if he only knew his chivalry--the sturdy English yeoman.

Why did I let you go? Well, I believe it was one of the many mistakes of my life; but I had a number of reasons, though personal dislike of you was not, as you thought, one of them. No, my child, I have never disliked you; not even on the night when you came and denounced me, with the dagger in your hand. I must indeed have been worse than I am, if I could have nourished ill-will against a young thing, whom I had made an orphan. By some instinct, you knew from the first that the deed was mine, although I was not the doer. I would have loved you, if you would have let me, my heart yearned so over children. But of my reason for letting you go, the chiefest perhaps--setting aside that I could not stop you--was this consideration. For years I had longed, and craved in my heart of hearts, to tell your mother all, and obtain her gentle forgiveness. But any allusion--no matter how veiled and mantled--to the story of her loss threw her, as you know well, into a most peculiar state, wherein all the powers of mind and body seemed to be quite suspended. With a man's usual roughness of prescription for the more delicate sex, I believed firmly that total change of living, and air, and place, and habits, would relax this wonderful closure, secure my forgiveness, and re-establish her health. The shock I received at her death was almost as terrible as when my brother died. When I stood beside you at her grave, I was come with the full intention of telling you all my story, and begging you to return with me, and live once more in your father's house. But your behaviour to me was so cold and contemptuous, that I forgot my crushing debt to you; and humiliation became, for the moment, impossible. I meant, however, to have written to you that evening, before you should leave the village; but (as you now are aware) that very evening, I was smitten helpless. Partially recovering, after months of illness, I was deeply distressed to find that you had left your good friends in Devonshire, and were gone, my informants could not say whither. Neither had I learned your whereabouts up to the time of my last illness, when I was making inquiries, of which your enemy reaped the benefit. For the rest, you know that I never meant to rob you of your inheritance, though bigoted nonsense enables me. To-morrow, please God, I will put it out of my power to do so. Mrs. Daldy's motive you have long since perceived. Failing my children, and the attainted Lepardo, her son is the heir to all the lands of the Della Croce. She has held me much in her power, by her knowledge of parts of my history. Henry's baptismal entry, as well as that of my marriage, was in the packet she stole. One word more, my darling--and from an old man, who has wandered and suffered much, you will not think it impertinent. Leave your revenge to God. In His way--which we call wonderful, because the steps are unseen--He will accomplish it for you, as righteousness demands. Any interference of ours is a worm-cast in His avenue. Though I am stricken and dying, He, if so pleases Him, will bring me my children before I die, that I may bless Him, and tell my Lily."

I fell upon the old man's neck--old he was, though not in years--and as I wept I kissed him. How could I have wronged him so, and how could I keep myself from loving one so long unhappy? If sorrow be the sponge of sin, his fault was wiped away.

CLARA VAUGHAN

BOOK V.

CHAPTER I.

At this time and place, I, Clara Vaughan, leap from the pillion of my Uncle's pensive mule, and am upon the curb-stone of my own strange life again. How I wandered with him through the olive groves of Corsica, how I wept for his loving Lily, that ancient Signor, and the stolen babes; and how, beyond the vomito of words, I loathed that fiend who had injured whom or what most I know not, unless it were his own soul, if he had any, and for God's sake I hope he had--all this, though I am too weak of language, will, perhaps, be understood.

To myself I would hardly confess the interest I could not discard in the pure and constant love of that impassioned pair; for what had I any longer to do with Pyramus and Thisbe? No more of love for me. You will not see me droop, and fret, and turn to a mossy green. No nonsense of that sort for me: I have a loop at either side entitled self-respect, which will keep my skirt from draggling. Neither will I rush into the opposite extreme, pronounce all love a bubble because my own has burst, take to low-necked dresses, and admire cats more than babies. No; I am only eighteen, not yet eighteen and a half; I have loved with all my heart, and a free true heart it is, albeit a hot and haughty one; if it be despised, outraged, and made nothing of, though I can never transfer, I will not turn it sour. The world is every whit as fair, children are quite as pretty, flowers have as rich a scent, and goodness as pure a charm, as if that silly maiden Clara had not leaped before she looked. And yet how I wish that I could only think so.

Before I go on with my tale, I must recur to one or two little matters, that everything may be as clear as it lies in my power to make it. For although I am but a "female," as Inspector Cutting observed, I am doing my best to make everything as clear as if told by a male.

In the first place then, when my Uncle had recovered from the exertion of telling his tale, I acquainted him with my discovery of the letters upon the bed-hangings. They confirmed his account of the fearful Vendetta usages, and explained the point which had been to him most mysterious.

Secondly, as to the anonymous letter which had led me first to London; like the detective policeman, he now attached but little importance to it. He had done his best, at the time, to trace the writer and follow the clue, if there were any. But he had met with no success. His reason for passing it on to me, was that he hoped to create some diversion of my thought, some break in the clouds of my sorrow.

Next, to show the full meaning of Mrs. Daldy's manoeuvres. Through her connexion--which she had carefully cultivated, when it began to seem worth her while--with her husband's kindred near Genoa, she had learned some portions of my poor Uncle's history; for, as he himself observed, the islanders are much addicted to gossip, as indeed all islanders are, and continentals too for that matter, especially in hot climates. Now there is no lack of intercourse between the Balagna and Genoa. Of course our chastened hypocrite made the most of her knowledge in a hundred ways, and by her sham sympathy and pretended aid--for up to the time of his illness the desolate father still sought and sought--she even secured some little influence over her brother-in-law. How often is it so: though we know people to be false, we do not believe, when our hearts are concerned, that they are so false to us. Moreover, when she found him shattered in body and mind by paralysis, she commenced an active bombardment, pulling out the tompions from every gun of mock religion. But, as in her treatment of me, she displayed, in spite of all her experience and trials, a sad ignorance of unregenerate human nature. My Uncle was not the man, palsied or no, to be terrified by a Calvinist: and he knew too much of her early days, and certain doings at Baden, to identify her at present with the angel that stands in the sun. And this prison-eyed mole made another mistake. Not content with one good gallery, she must needs work two runs, side by side, in a very mealy soil. The result was of course that they ran into one, and she had to dig her way out. If she had worked, heart and soul, for my Uncle's money only, which he rightly regarded as his own, and at his own disposal, I believe she might have got most of it. At any rate, under the will which I caught her carrying off, she was to take half of the large sum which he had laid by; I mean if his children did not come to light, and prove their legitimacy. But twenty-five thousand pounds would be nothing to her dear son, who had inherited his father's extravagance, or to herself, who loved high play. Therefore, believing me out of the field, she began to plot for the Vaughan estate as well, and furthermore for the magnificent property in Corsica. Of the Vaughan estates she had no chance--albeit she had the impudence to propose a compromise with me--of Veduta tower she had some prospect, if the right heirs, the poor children, should never appear, or establish their claim, and if she could procure the outlawry of Lepardo.

Believing my Uncle to be dying by inches, she made a bold stroke for possession of the most important documents; and, but for Giudice and me, no doubt she would have succeeded. But she had dashed far out of her depth, and had little chance now of reaching the coveted land. I hope she felt that everything was ordered for her good.

Another point which seems to require some explanation, is the discovery by the assassin of the secret entrance, an access quite unknown to the family, the servants, or any other person, except, at a later time, Mrs. Daldy. The house, as I said before, was built upon the site and partly embodied the fabric of a still more ancient structure. Probably these narrow stairs, now enclosed in the basement of the eastern wall, had saved many a ripe priest from reeling, in the time of the Plantagenets. They led, I think, from the ancient chapel, long since destroyed, to the chaplain's room, and perhaps had been reopened secretly during the great rebellion, when the Vaughans were in hot trouble. Beatrice Vaughan, the cavalier's child, who was now supposed to begin her ghost walk at the eastern window, glided probably down this staircase, when, as the legend relates, she escaped mysteriously from the house, in her father's absence, roused the tenants, and surprised the Roundhead garrison in their beds. The house was soon retaken, and Beatrice, in her youthful beauty, given up to the brutal soldiers. She snapped a pistol at the Puritan officer, and flew like a bird along this corridor. At the end, while trying perhaps to draw the old oak slide--though nothing was said of this--she was caught by the gloating fanatics, and stabbed herself on the spot rather than yield to dishonour. The poor maiden's tomb is in the church, not far from the chancel arch, with some lines of quaint Latin upon it. Her lover, Sir William Desborough, slit that Puritan officer's nose and cut off both his ears. I wonder that he let him off so lightly; but perhaps it was all he was worth. Major Cecil Vaughan married again, and the direct line was re-established.

The chapel well, as it was called, dark and overhung with ivy, was a spring of limpid icy crystal, spanned by and forming a deep alcove in the ancient chapel wall, which, partly for its sake, and partly as a buttress for the east end of the house, had been left still standing. This old well had long time been disused, hiding, as it did, in a wild and neglected corner out of sight from the terrace walk; and the gardeners, who found the pump less troublesome, had condemned the water as too cold for their plants. The mouth, with its tangled veil of ivy and periwinkle, was also masked by a pile of the chapel ruins, now dignified with the name of a rockwork. Some steps of jagged stone led through the low black archway to the crouching water, which was so clear that it seemed to doubt which was itself and which was stone.

This peaceful, cold, unruffled well, formed the antechamber to the murderer's passage. For on the right-hand side, not to be seen in the darkness, and the sublustrous confusion, by any common eye, was a small niche and footing-place not a yard above the water. It needed some nerve and vigour to spring from the lowest stepping-stone sideways to this scarcely visible ledge. None, of the few whose eyes were good enough to espy it, would be tempted to hazard the leap, unless they knew or suspected that the facing would yield to the foot, that it was in fact a small door purposely coloured and jointed like the slimy green of the masonry. In this well the murderer must have lurked; and he might have done so from one year's end to another. There with the craft of his devilish race--my Uncle may admire them, but not I--and with their wonderful powers of sight, he must have found this entrance, and rejoiced in his hellish heart.

As for Mrs. Daldy, she found it out at the other end, most likely. Unless my memory fails me, I spoke long ago of some boards which sounded hollow to the ring of my childish knuckles. These were in the skirting--if that be the proper name for it--under the centre of the great oriel window. The oak slides, when pressed from below, ran in a groove with but little noise, and without much force being used: but it required some strength to move them on the side of the corridor. It was the sound of these sliding boards which had first drawn Judy's notice: but as they were in deep shadow, I neither perceived the opening, nor gave him the opportunity. That woman would never have dreamed of the thing, if she had not surprised me one day when I was prying about there; she must have returned alone, and being, as we have seen, a superior cabinet-maker, discovered the secret which baffled me. As I did not want Judy to catch cold by watching there any longer, I had this horrible passage walled up at either end, and built across in the middle.

Having thus made good my arrears, I am at liberty to proceed. When my Uncle had paused from his many sorrows, which he did with a mellow dignity not yet understood by me; and when I, in the fervour of youth, had offered much comfort kindly received, but far better let alone, I asked him for one thing only:--the most minute and accurate description he could give of that Lepardo Della Croce. His answer was as follows:--

"My dear, I have seen him once only, and that more than twenty years ago, and in an interview of some excitement"--I should think so indeed, when one tried to kill the other--"but I will describe him to the best of my recollection. He is rather a tall man, at least of about my own height, but more lightly built than myself. His hands and feet are remarkably small and elegant. His face is of the true Italian type, a keen oval with a straight nose, and plenty of width between the eyes, which are large and very dark. His forehead is not massive, but well-formed, and much whiter than the rest of his face. The expression of his countenance is that of shrewdness and versatility, with a quickness eager to save both you and himself from the trouble of completing your sentence. But all this is common enough. One thing I saw, or fancied, which is not quite so common. As I dealt him that blow with my fist, my eyes for one flash met his, and his leaped towards one another, as if he had a strong cast in them. Before that, and afterwards too, there was no appearance of any distortion: if there were any at that moment, it arose from the start of terror or fury jerking the muscles awry. His voice is flexible and persuasive, and soft as a serpent-charmer's. I think he must be a most arrogant man; profoundly convinced of his own abilities, but seldom caring to vindicate them. Just the man to get on in the world, if he were only what is called respectable. Just the man to break a woman's heart, and crush the spirit of a meek and humble child. Ah, I would forgive him his sins against me, though not his wrongs towards you, if I could only learn that he had been kind to my children."

This description dwelt on my mind for days and days of thinking. It did not altogether apply to the man whom I had observed so closely at the meeting of the conspirators. That man was of middle height, and though his face was oval, there was scarcely the average width between the eyes. And he did not seem to me like an arrogant man, cold except when excited; but rather of a hasty, impassioned nature, sure to do its utmost in trifles. Could it be that I had watched and hated the wrong man? It might be so; and it was not unlikely that Mr. Cutting himself knew not which was the guilty one. Like most of the London policemen--my Uncle had taught me this--he was too proud of his sagacity to be in truth very sagacious. Experience he had, and all that; but he would not have done in Paris. The real depth, that goes below, and yet allows for the depth of another, must be in the nature, can rarely exist in a small one, and in a large one is seldom worked but for theoretical purposes. Therefore shallow men overreach in daily life, and fancy they have blinded those who know them thoroughly, and know themselves as well.

So far as my experience goes, large-natured men abhor cunning so much, that they fear to work the depth of their own intelligence, because it seems akin to it. So they are cheated every day, as a strong man yields to the push of a child; and the fools who cheat them chuckle in the idea that they have done it by fine sagacity, and without the victim's knowledge.

CHAPTER II.

At my earnest entreaty, the idea of assembling the tenants especially was allowed to drop, and I was to be inducted at the Midsummer dinner, which was very near at hand. A deed had been prepared by the London solicitors, reciting the facts and assuring all the estate to me, as my father's proper heiress. My Uncle also desired to settle upon me all the personal property, except a sum of 10,000*l.*, which he would reserve for his children, to enable them, if ever they should be found, to establish their claims in Corsica: then if the son obtained his rights, his sister was to have the money with all expenditure made good by him. But I would not hear of it. It would have made me a rogue. By his skill and economy, my Uncle, during the nine years of his management, had saved more than 50,000*l.* from the proceeds of the estate. But he had added at least an equal amount to the value of the land, by carrying out most judiciously the improvements begun by my father; and the whole was now considered the best-managed estate in Gloucestershire.

Therefore, when he abandoned his legal right, in the most honourable manner, it would have been horribly shabby and unlike a Vaughan, to hold him accountable for the back rents. I begged him to leave the whole of it for the benefit of his poor children, requesting only, and unnecessarily, that the hypocrite might not have sixpence. Another thing I entreated, that he would prolong his guardianship, and stewardship, if his health allowed it, until I should be of age, that is to say, for two years and a half. Seeing how earnestly I desired it, he undertook to do so, though he made the promise with a melancholy smile, adding that he hoped his children would be found ere then, if he was to see them at all.

When the rent-dinner was over, and the glasses had been replaced, my Uncle, who had not been there as usual, led me into the great old hall. Feeble as he was, he entered with a grace and courtesy not always to be discovered in the mien of princes. The supper--as the farmers called it--had not begun till six o'clock; and now the evening sunshine glanced through the western window, and between the bunches of stoning grapes into the narrow doorway, stealing in from the Vinery with sandals of leafy pattern. The hall was decked with roses, no other flower but roses; yet who could want any other, when every known rose was there? Even the bright yellow blossoms of the Corsican rock-rose, a plant so sensitive that to steal one flower is to kill all the rest. From time out of mind, some feudal custom of tenure by the rose had been handed down in our family.

All the guests rose as we passed, which made me rather nervous, albeit I knew every one of them from my childhood up. Then my Uncle, leaning on me, spoke a few words from the step, plain and simple words without flourish or pretence. What he said was known long since, and had been thoroughly discussed in every house of the village. He finished by setting me in the black oak chair of state--which he had never used--and presenting me with a rose; then he turned round and proposed my health. When I took the rose, an exquisite crested moss, kissed it and placed it in my bosom, according to the usage, such a shout arose, such an English hurrah, that it must have echoed to the other bank of the distant Severn. At first I was quite frightened, then I burst into tears as I thought of him whose chair I sat in, whose memory still was echoing in that mighty shout. It was not only love of right, or sympathy with a helpless girl, that moved those honest bosoms, but the remembrance of him who had been so pleasant to them, humble, kind and just, in one word, a gentleman.

But as they came up, one by one, and begged to take my hand, and wished me joy and long life with all their hearts, I found that I was right in one thing; I knew them better than my Uncle did. Instead of being rude or cold to him, as he expected, they almost overwhelmed him with praise and admiration. But all this I must not dwell on, for my story hurries hence, and its path is not through roses.

Annie Franks, who still was with us, and did not mean to go until she had finished all the Froissart novels, and such a dear good girl she was, that we hoped they would last for ever, Annie Franks brought me next day two letters of aspect strange to "good society." One I knew at a glance to be from Tossil's Barton, though the flourishes were amazing, and the lead-pencil lines rubbed out. The other, a work of far less ambition and industry, was an utter stranger; so of course I took it first. Nevertheless, I will treat of it last, because it opens the stormy era.

Dear Sally's gossip is not to be served up whole. Even if it were interesting to others as to me, my space permits no dalliance with farm-yards, no idyls of Timothy Badcock, nay, nor even the stern iambics of Ebenezer Dawe. Only to be just and clear, I may not slur it all. The direction was remarkable. The farmer was always afraid of not being duly explicit, for he believed that letters were delivered throughout England as in the parish of Trentisoe; where all, except those for the parson and Tossil's Barton farm, were set upside down in the window at Pewter Will's, the most public-house in the place. The idea was ingenious, and, I believe, original--having been suggested by the Queen's boy, whose head Mrs. Huxtable punched. It was that no one could read the name upside down, except the owner of the name and therefore of the letter. Sound or not, I cannot say, having had no experience; but there was this to be said for it, that no one would try the puzzle who did not expect a letter, unless indeed he were of precocious genius, and from that Trentisoe was quite safe.

Upon the present "papper-scrawl," after a long description of me, patronymical, local, and personal, the following injunctions and menaces were added, "Not be stuck tops I turve I on no account in no public house. She be in her own house now again, thank God and dang them as turned her out I say, so mind you carr it there. A deal of money there be in it, and no fear of Joe because he knows it, and there lives a man in Gloucestershire knows me well by the name of Thomas Henwood. Best look sharp I say. I be up to every one of you. John Huxtable his name, no mark this time. God save the queen."

So the farmer had actually learned to write, although as yet to a strictly limited extent. Of course he had not written any of the above except his name; but that was his, and did him credit, though it nearly described a circle.

After the warmest congratulations and returning the five-pound note, which I had sent for interest, with an indignant inquiry from father whether I took him for a Jew, and after several anecdotes and some histories of butter sold at Ilfracombe market, Sally proceeded thus:

"Now what do you think, Miss Clara dear? No you never would guess as long as you live--father are going to London town, and me, and Jack, and Beany Dawe. None of us have slept two grunts of a pig, ever since it were made up, only father, and he always sleep without turning. Now mind if I tell you all about it, you must not tell again, Miss Clara, because there is ever so much money upon it, and we do hear they have put it on some London paper and no business of theirs. Two great gentlefolks, the greatest of any about these parts, have been and made up a bet for my father to wrestle along with a great big chap as they calls the North Country champion. Seems as some great Northern lord was boasting in London one dinner-time, Speaker's dinner they called it because there were a deaf and dumb dinner next day, this here great lord was telling up as how Sam Richardson were the strongest man in the world. So our Sir Arthur spake up for Devonshire, and laid him a quart-pot full of sovereigns as he would find a better man in the West country. And so I don't know the rights of it, nor father nor mother either, but it was made up atwixt them that Farmer Huxtable, that's my father, Miss, should try this great North country chap at the time of the great Xabition--you never showed me the way to spell it, Miss, so I go by the light of nature, as you used to say, Miss--and should take best of three falls for 200*l.* a side. That will be 400*l.* for us, when father gets it, and all his expenses paid, and they say the other folk won't allow no kicking, so he must be a soft-shelled chap; but father feel no call to hurt him, if so be he can help it. Mother don't want father to go, but he say he be bound for the honour of old Devonshire, or maybe they will take a man not good enough to make a standard.

And please, Miss, when we brings home the money, I be to go to Miss Bowden's, in Boutport Street, and our Jack to be put to a day-school not more than six miles away, and then I hope he know himself, and look higher than that minx of a Tabby Badcock. What do you think, Miss Clara, you would never believe it I know, but only a week ago last Tuesday I come sudden round the corner, and catched her a kissing of our Jack in the shed there by the shoot. And after all you taught her, Miss! Jack he ran away, as red as mangawazzle, but that brazen slut, there she stand with her legs out, as innocent as a picture. Never a word I said, but with no more to do I put her head in the calves' stommick as we makes the cheese with, in a bucket handy. It would have done you good to see her Miss, she did cry so hard, and she smell of it for a week, and it cure our Jack, up to Sunday anyhow. Mother come out at the noise, but her see that she deserve it, and the runnet was no account, except for the pigs, because it were gone by. I hope she know her manners now and her spear in life with her sheep's eyes, and not come trying to catch any of my family.

Well, Miss Clara please, father want mother to go; but no, say she, "with all they"--she ought to have said "them" Miss, now hadn't she ought?--"with all they young pigs, and the brown cow expecting every day, and Suke no head at all, and all the chillers and little Clara"--she call her "Clara" now, Miss,--"why farmer what be thinking of?" Then father rub the nose of him, you know the way he do it, Miss, and he say, "I must have some one. London be such a wicked place." Mother look up very sharp at that, and say quite peart, "take your daughter, farmer Huxtable, if you wants to be kept respectable." So I be to go Miss; and go I wouldn't without Jack and leave him along of that sly cat Tabby, and her got sweet again now; besides I want him to choose a knife I promised him, same as he saw to Coom one time, if he wouldn't let Tabby kiss him with seven blades and a corkscrew, and I'll give eighteen pence for it, that I will. And Beany Dawe must go to show us the way about, and see as they doesn't cheat us, because his father was once to London town, and told him a power about it.

If you please, Miss Clara, father be put in training as they call it in these parts, all the same as a horse. He run up and down Breakneck hill, with the best bed on his back, nine times every day, and he don't drink no cider, no nor beer, nor gin and water, and mother hardly know him, he be come so clear in the skin; but he say his hand shake still from the time I taught him to write, and please, Miss, what do you think of the way he is going to sign this? I can't get him to put his thumb right, no nor his middle finger, and he stick his elbow out every bit as bad as Tabby, and he say he like the pot-hooks over the fire best, but for all that I believe I shall make a scholard of him, particular when he give up wrestling, which he have sworn to do if he throw this Cumberland chap, and stick to his Bible and Prayer-book.

Please, Miss, not to be offended, but excuse us asking if you like to see the great wrestling. Father say no, it would not be fitty, and that be the worst of being a gentlefolk; but mother say what harm, and she be sure the farmer do it twice as well with you there, and you shall have the best seat in the place next to the two judges, and such a pretty handkerchief they sent down all spotted the same as a Guernsey cow, how the people in church did stare at me, and you shall have two of the best, Miss, but I am afraid it be making too bold; but you never see any wrestling, Miss, and I am sure you would enjoy it so. It take place in the copandhagen fields, next Saturday week. Do come, Miss Clara dear, it will do you so much good, and you see father, and me, and Jack, and Beany Dawe."

I need recount no more of poor Sally's soft persuasions. The other letter was of a different vein:--

"HONOURED Miss,--Balak and me after a deal of trouble and labouring night and day and throwing up our vacation has at last succeeded in finding you knows who. Personal interview will oblige, earliest inconvenience. No more at present not being safe on paper, from your most obedient servants and suitors

BALAAM AND BALAK--you knows who.--

Poscrip.--Balak says a sharp young lady quite sure to know what is right, but for fear of accidents please a little of the ready will oblige, large families both of us has and it do take a deal of beer more than our proper vacation no one would guess unless they was to try and bad beer too a deal of it. For self and partner.--BALAAM."

CHAPTER III.

When my Uncle saw that letter, he declared that he would go to London with me. No power on earth should prevent him. Not even his self-willed Clara. It was not revenge he wanted: even though it were for his innocent brother, whose wrongs he could not pardon. No, if the small-minded wretch who had spent his life in destroying a fellow-creature's, if that contemptible miscreant lay at his feet to-morrow, he would not plant foot upon him; but forgive him heartily, if he had the grace to desire it. But for his children,--for them he must go to London. Only let him see them once before he died. No torpid limbs for him. Who said he was old--and he only forty-seven?

One thing seemed rather strange to me. He longed, yearned I should say, to look upon his little Lily even more than on the child he knew, his son, his first-born Harry. "Why, Clara," he used to say, "she is nearly as old as you, and you are a full-grown girl. On the 21st of this month"--it was now July--"she will be eighteen; I can hardly believe it. I wonder what she is like. Most likely she takes after her lovely mother. No doubt of it, I should say. Don't you think so, Clara?"

"Of course, Uncle," I would reply, knowing nothing at all about it, "of course she does. How I should like to see her."

Perhaps fifty times a day, he would ask for my opinion, and I would deliver it firmly, perhaps in the very same words and without a shade of misgiving; and though of no value whatever, it seemed to comfort him every time. But the prolonged excitement, and the stress of imagination exerted on Lily junior, told upon him rapidly in his worn and weak condition. Longing for his company, assistance, and advice, I waited from day to day, even at the risk of leaving Balaam and Balak without good beer. All this time, my imagination was busy with weak surmises, faint suspicions, and tangled recollections.

At last, I could delay no longer. Tuesday was the latest day I could consent to wait for, and on the Monday my Uncle was more nervous and weak than ever. It was too plain that he must not attempt the journey, and that the long suspense was impairing his feeble health. So for once I showed some decision--which seemed to have failed me of late--without telling him any more about it, I got everything ready, and appeared at his bedroom door, only to say "Good bye." Annie Franks, who was going with me, for a short visit to her father, hung back in some amazement, doubting whether she had any right to be there, and dragged off her legs by the coil of my strong will. My poor Uncle seemed quite taken aback; but as it could not be helped, he speedily made up his mind to it. "The carriage was at the door;" which announcement to English minds precludes all further argument.

"Good bye, Uncle dear," I cried, as cheerily as I could, "I shall be back by the end of the week and bring your Lily with me. Give me a good kiss for her, and now another for myself."

He was sitting up in the bed, with a Cashmere dressing-gown on, and poring over some relics of olden time.

"Good bye, my darling, and don't be long away. They have robbed me enough already."

After giving Judy the strictest orders, I hurried off in fear and hope, doubtful whether I ought to go. Annie lingered and gave him a kiss, for she was very fond of him. He whispered something about me, which I did not stop to hear, for I wanted to leave him in good spirits.

After a rapid journey, I saw dear Annie safe in the arms of her father and mother, and found Mrs. Shelfer at home, and in capital spirits, all the birds, &c. well, and no distress in the house. Charley was doing wonders, wonders, my good friend, sticking to his work, yes, yes, and not inside the public house for the best part of the week. Leastways so he said, and it would not do to contradict him. And she really did believe there were only three bills over-due!

My little rooms were snug and quiet, and the dust not more than half an inch thick. Mrs. Shelfer used to say that dusting furniture was the worst thing in the world to wear it out. According to her theory, the dust excluded the air, especially from the joints, and prevented the fly-blows coming. However, I made her come up and furbish, while I went out to post a letter for Messrs. Balaam and Balak, requesting them to visit me in the morning.

When things were set to rights a little, and air, which Mrs. Shelfer hated, flowed in from either balcony, I bought a fine crab and some Sally Lunns, and begged for the pleasure of my landlady's company at tea. This she gladly gave me, for the little woman loved nothing better than sucking the hairy legs of a crab. But she was so overcome by the rumours of my wealth, that she even feared to eject the pieces in her ordinary manner, and the front rail of her chair was like the beam of a balance. Infinitely rather would I be poor myself, than have people ceremonious to me because I am not poor; and to tell the honest truth, I believe there is a vein of very low blood in me, which blushes at the sense of riches and position. Why should I have every luxury, that is if I choose to have it, while men and women of a thousand times my mind, and soul, and heart, spend their precious lives in earning the value of their coffins?

This thought has wearied many a mind of pure aerial flight, compared whereto my weak departures are but the hops of a flea; so I lose the imago, but catch the larva, upon the nettle, practice. Mrs. Shelfer is soon at ease; and we talk of the price of cat's meat, and how dear sausages are, and laugh--myself with sorrow--over the bygone days, when dripping played the role of butter, and Judy would not take a bone because he thought I wanted it.

Then we talk over the news. Miss Idols had been there, bless her sweet face, yes, ever so many times, to look for letters, or to hear tidings of me. But she was not one bit like herself. She never teased the poor little woman now; the poor little woman wished very much she would. Oh, I should hardly know her. She did not know which bird it was that had the wooden leg, and had forgotten the difference between a meal-worm and a lob. And she did not care which way she rubbed the ears of the marmoset. Mrs. Shelfer believed, but for the world it must not be told again, that Isola was deeply in love, unrequited love, perhaps one of the weteranarian gents. They did say they had some stuff as would lead a girl like a horse. But whatever it was, Mrs. Shelfer only knew that she could not get at the rights of it. Girls had grown so cunning now-a-days, what with the great supernatural exhibition, and the hats they had taken to wear flat on the tops of their heads, not at all what they used to be when she and Charley were young. Then a young woman was not afraid of showing what her neck was like; now she tucked it in cotton wool like a canary's egg. And what were they the better, sly minxes? She saw enough of it in the Square garden, and them showing their little sisters' legs for patterns of their own, oh fie!"

"Come, Mrs. Shelfer, no scandal, if you please. What news of your Uncle John?"

"Ah, Miss, you must ask the sharks, and the lobsters, and the big sea-serpent. They do say, down at Wapping, that the ship was cast away among the cannibal islands, and the people ate a policeman, and he upon his promotion. What a pity, what a pity! And his coat four and sixpence a yard, ready shrunk! But them natives is outrageous."

"Nonsense, Patty, I don't believe a word of it. Sailors are dreadful story-tellers, ever since the days of Sindbad. Has any one besides Miss Isola, Mrs. Elton, or any one, been here to ask for me?"

"No, Miss, Mr. Conrad never come after the day you served him so dreadful; and Miss Idols say he went back and spoiled 300*l.* worth of work; but that great lady with the red plush breeches, and the pink silk stockings, and the baker's shop in their hair, she been here twice last week, and left a letter for you. And Balaam been here several times, and Balak along of him; but I banged the door on them both, now I hear they be out of the business, and a nice young man set up who don't bother about the gun."

"Lady Cranberry's letter may lie there, and go back the next time Ann Maples comes. But the bailiffs I must see. If they come to-morrow, let them in immediately. And how are all my friends at the Mews?"

Her reply would fill a chapter, so I will not enter upon it, but go to bed and miss the sound of dear Judy's tail at the door. In the first course of my dreams, Mr. Shelfer passed on his bedward road, having politely taken his shoes off at the bottom of the stairs; in doing which he made at least three times the noise his shodden feet would have inflicted.

In the morning I took my old walk round the Square, and then sat down and tried to be patient until the bailiffs should come. Of course I did not mean to go to my darling Isola, nor even to let her know that I was so near at hand, although my heart was burning to see her sweet face again. I even kept away from the window, though I wanted to watch for the bailiffs, and strictly ordered Mrs. Shelfer not to tell her, if she should call, a word about my being there. However, it was all in vain. Mr. Shelfer went out after breakfast to his play-work in the Square, and the smell of his pipe invaded my little room. I think he must have left the front door open; at any rate I heard, all of a sudden, a quick patter of running feet, and such a crying and sobbing, and Mrs. Shelfer hurrying out to meet it.

"You can't, Miss, you can't indeed--not for a thousand pounds. The rooms are let, I tell you, and you can't go up. Oh dear, oh dear, whatever am I to do?"

"Patty, I *will* go up. I don't care who's there. My heart is breaking, and I *will* die on my darling's bed. If you stand there, I'll push you. Out of the way, I tell you." And up flew Idols, in a perfect mess of tears. What could I do but fly to meet her, and hug my only pet? What with her passion of grief, and sudden joy, at seeing me, she fainted away in my arms. I got her somehow to the sofa, and kissed her into her senses again. When she came to herself, and felt sure it was not a dream, she nestled into my bosom, as if I had been her husband, and stole long glances at me to see whether I was offended. Her pretty cloak lay on the floor, and her hat beneath the table. For a long time she sobbed and trembled so that she could not say a word, while I kept on whispering such vain words as these:

"Never mind, my pet. There, you have cried enough. Tell your own dear Clara who has dared to vex you."

To see that sweet child's misery, I felt in such a rage, I could have boxed her enemy's ears. But I never thought that it was more than a child's vexation. At last, after drinking a tumblerful of water, and giving room to her palpitating heart, she contrived to tell me her trouble.

"Why, dear, you know my pappy--pappy I used to call him--he is not my papa at all, he says himself he is not; and that is not the worst of it, for I could do well enough without him, he is always so dreadfully cross, and doesn't care for me one bit. I could do without him very well, if I had a proper papa, or if my father was dead and had loved me before he died; but now I have no father at all, and never had any in the world; I am only an outcast, an abandoned-- Oh, Clara, will you promise to forgive me, and love me all the same?"

"To be sure I will, my dearest. I am sure, you have done no harm. And even if you have been led astray--"

She looked at me with quick pride flashing through her abasement, and she took her arm off my shoulder.

"No, you have quite mistaken me. Do you think I would sit here and kiss you, if I were a wicked girl? But who am I to be indignant at anything now? He told me--are you sure the door is shut?--he told me, with a sneer, that I was a base-born child, and he used a worse word than that."

She fell away from me, her cheeks all crimson with shame, and her long eyelashes drooping heavily on them. I caught her to my heart: poor wronged one, was she a whit less pure? I seemed to love her the better, for her great misfortune. Of course, I had guessed it long ago, from what her brother told me.

"And who is your father, my pretty? Any father must be a fool who would not be proud of you."

"Oh, Clara, the worst of it is that I have not the least idea. But from something that hard man said, I believe he was an Englishman. I think I could have got everything from him, he was so beside himself; but when he told me that dreadful thing, and said that my father had lied to my mother and ruined her, I felt so sick that I could not speak, till he turned me out of the house, and struck me as I went."

"What?"

"Yes, he turned me out of the house, and gave me the blow of disgrace, and said I should never look on his face again. He had won his revenge--I cannot tell what he meant, for I never harmed him--and now I might follow my mother, and take to--I can't repeat it, but it was worse than death. No fear of my starving, he said, with this poor face of mine. And so I was going to Conny, dear Conny; I think he knew it all long ago, but could not bear to tell me. And I sat on some steps in a lonely place, for I did not know how to walk, and I prayed to see you and die: then old Cora came after me, and even she was crying, and she gave me all her money, and a morsel of the true cross, and told me to come here first, for Conny was out of town, and she would come to see me at dark; and perhaps the Professor would take me back when his rage was over. Do you think I would ever go? And after what he told me to do!"

Such depth of loathing and scorn in those gentle violet eyes, and her playful face for the moment so haughtily wild and implacable--Clara Vaughan, in her stately rancour, seemed an iceberg by a volcano.

I saw that it was the moment for learning all that she knew; and the time for scruples was past.

"Isola, tell me all you have heard, about this dastard bully?"

"I know very little; he has taken good care of that. I only know that he did most horrible things to unfortunate cats and dogs. It made me shudder to touch him at one time. But he gave that up I believe. But there is some dark and fearful mystery, which my brother has found out; that is if he be my brother. How can I tell even that? Whatever the discovery was, it made such a change in him, that he cared for nothing afterwards, until he saw you, Clara. I am not very sharp, you know, though I have learned so much, that perhaps you think I am."

"My darling, I never thought such a thing for a moment."

"Oh, I am very glad. At any rate I like to talk as if I was clever. And some people say I am. But, clever or stupid, I am almost certain that Conny found out only half the secret; and then on the day when he came of age, that man told him the rest, either for his own purposes, or holy Madonna knows why."

"When was your brother of age?"

"Last Christmas Eve. Don't you remember what I told you at the school of design that day?"

"And when is your birthday, Isola?"

"I am sure I don't know, but somewhere about Midsummer. They never told Conny when his was, but he knew it somehow. Come, he is clever now, Clara, though you don't think I am. Isn't he now? Tell the truth."

"I am thinking of far more important matters than your rude brother's ability. Whence did you come to England and when?"

This was quite a shot in the dark. But I had long suspected that they were of Southern race.

"I am sure I don't know. I was quite a child at the time, and the subject has been interdicted; but I think we came from Italy, and at least ten years ago."

"And your brother speaks Italian more readily than English. Can you tell me anything more?"

"Nothing. Only I know that old Cora is a Corsican: she boasts of it every night, when she comes to see me in bed, although she has been forbidden. But what does she care--she asks--for this dirty little English island? And she sits by my bed, and sings droning songs, which I hardly understand; but she says they are beautiful nannas."

How my heart was beating, at every simple sentence. None of this had I heard before, because she durst not tell it.

"Any other questions, Donna?" She was recovering her spirits, as girls always do by talking. "Why, my darling, you ought to have a wig. You beat all the senior sophists."

"Yes. Now come and kiss me. Kiss me for a pledge that you will never leave me. I am rich again now: you can't tell how rich I am, and nothing to do with my money, and nobody likely to share it. If you were my own sister, I could not love you more; and most likely I should not love you a quarter as much. And my Uncle longs to see you so. You shall come and live with me, and we'll be two old maids together. Now promise, darling, promise. Kiss me, and seal the bargain."

"Clara, I would rather be your servant than the queen of the world. Only promise first that you will never scold me. I cannot bear being scolded. I never used to be; and it will turn all my hair gray."

"I will promise never to scold you, unless you run away."

She swept back her beautiful hair, threw her arms round my neck, looked in my eyes with a well-spring of love, and kissed me. Oh, traitorous Clara, it was not the kiss--deeply as I loved her--but the evidence I wanted. I knew that with her ardent nature she would breathe her soul upon me. The exquisite fragrance of her breath was like the wind stealing over violets. I had noticed it often before. My last weak doubt was scattered; yet I played with her and myself, one sweet moment longer.

"Darling, what scent do you use? What is it you wash your teeth with?"

"Nothing but water, Clara; what makes you ask in that way?"

"And the perfume in your hair--what is it? Oh, you little Rimmel!"

"Nothing at all, Donna. I never use anything scented. Not even Eau de Cologne. I hate all the stuff they sell."

"How very odd! Why, I could have declared that your lips and your hair were sprinkled with extract of violets."

"Oh, now I know what you mean. I never perceive it myself, but numbers of people have fancied that I use artificial perfume. But that man--oh, what shall I call him? And only this morning I called him 'pappy'--he always accounts for everything, you know; and he said it was hered--herod--I can't say it now, the long English word, but I could at college--no matter, it means something in the family. My mother, he said, was so well known to possess it, that she had an Italian name among the servants for it; though her real name was quite a different flower. Clara, why do you look at me so? And what are you crying for?"

"Because, my own darling dear, I have not loved you for nothing. You are my own flesh and blood. You are my own cousin, I tell you, my dear Uncle's daughter; and your name is Lily Vaughan."

She drew her arms from me, and leaped up from the sofa; she was so amazed and frightened. She looked at me most sadly, believing that I was mad; then she fainted again, and fell back into my arms.

When I had brought her round, and propped her up with a pillow--for cushions were very scarce--the strain of the mind being over, my brain began to whirl so that I could neither think nor act. For a long time I could not have enough of kissing and hugging Idols. I played with her hair, as if I had been her lover; and then patted and caressed her, as if she had been my baby. And had I no thought of another, who ought to be doing all this to me? Yes, I fear that it lay in the depth of my heart, stronger than maid's love of maiden, or even than my delight at the joy coming to my Uncle.

Then I hated myself for my selfishness, and caught up my Lily and rubbed her, and made her understand things. I flung a decanter of water over both her and myself, which saved us from hysterics.

Poor little thing! She was not like me. Strong Passion was a stranger to her, and she fell before his blow. I had fought with him so long, that I met him like a prize-fighter, and countered at every stroke. Up ran Mrs. Shelfer, in the height and crest of the wave, when backwards or forwards, crying or laughing, hung on a puff of wind. She came with a commonplace motive; she thought we were playing at cricket with her beloved sticks. Her arrival made a diversion, though it had no other effect, for I walked the little thing out, and locked the door behind her.

Then I got my darling new cousin into my arms, and kissed her, and marched her about the room, and made her show her Vaughan instep. Excuse the petty nonsense--what women are quite free from it?--but for many generations our feet have been arched and pointed: of course it does not matter; still I was glad that hers were of the true Vaughan pattern. Then, as she so hated all the stuffs they sell, I showered over her an entire bottle of the very best Eau de Cologne. It was a bit of bullying; but all girls of high spirit are bullies. And it made her eyes water so dreadfully, that she cried as hard as I did.

CHAPTER IV.

It must be owned that my evidence at present was very shadowy. Yet to myself I seemed slow of hand for not having grasped it before. To the mind there was nothing conclusive, to the heart all was irresistible. I have not set down a quarter of the thoughts that now dawned upon me; and it would be waste of time to recount them, when actual proof is forthcoming. And poor Idols gave me small chance of thinking clearly, in the turbulent flood of her questions.

"And are you quite sure, quite certain, Clara darling, that I have a lawful father, one who is not ashamed of me, and was not ashamed of my mother! And why did he never come for me? And do you think he will love me? And is dear Conrad my own brother? I don't seem to understand half that you have told me."

At length I knelt down, and thanked God--rather late in the day, I must own--for His wonderful guidance to me. While doing so, and remembering, as I always did then, my mother--revealed in sudden light I saw the justice of God's Providence. Long as I had groped and groped, with red revenge my leading star, no breath of love or mercy cheering the abrupt steps of a fatalist, so long had He vouchsafed to send me check and warning, more than guidance. By loss of wealth and dearest friends, by blindness and desertion, and the crushing blow to maiden's pride when her heart is flung back in her face, by sad hours of watching and weeping over the bed of sickness, by the history of another's wrongs-- worse than my own, and yet forgiven--by all these means, and perhaps no less by the growth of the mind, and wider views of life, the spirit, once so indomitable, had learned to bow to its Maker. Stooping thus it saw the path, which stiff-necked pride could not descry. Not first and sole, as it would have been two years since, but side by side with softer thoughts, came the strong belief that now God had revealed to me the man who slew my father. And what humiliation to all my boasted destiny! I had grasped the hand that did the deed, smiled to the eyes that glared upon it, laughed at the sallies of the mind that shaped it. Enough of this; ere it go too hard with Christian feeling. My bosom heaves, my throat swells, and my eyes flash as of old.

Before I had time to resolve what next to do (for Isola would not let me think), we had another interruption. That girl had a most ill-regulated and illogical mind. And the fault was fundamental. If the lovely senior sophist had ever got her degree, and worn the gown of a Maiden of Arts, it could only have come by favour, after the manner of kissing. Her enthymems were quick enough, and a great deal too quick I believe; but as for their reduction or eduction into syllogisms--we might as well expect her to make a telescope out of her boot-tags. And now at once she expected, and would not give me room for a word, that I should minutely detail in two sentences, with marginal annotations, and footnotes, queries, conjectures, and various readings, all incorporated into the text, everything that had ever, anywhere, or by any means, befallen her "genuine father." Not being Thucydidean enough to omit the key-word in the sentence, and mash ten thoughts into one verb, I could not meet the emergency; and my dear cousin lost her patience, which was always a very small parcel.

"At any rate, Clara, tell me one thing clearly. Are you quite certain that Conny and I are not--not--"

"Not base-born," I said--why be mawkish in Oscan-English, when Saxon is to be had?--"No, my darling, you are as lawful as I, your cousin Clara. We Vaughans are a passionate race, but we never make wrecks of women, and scoundrels of ourselves. That we leave for Corsicans, and people brought up to lies."

The sneer was most unjust, and dreadfully unkind, but far too natural for me, so long pent in, to resist it. I saw that I had grieved my pet, so I begged her pardon, and reviled myself, till all was right again. Then suddenly she leaped up and cried, with her hand upon her bounding heart--every look and gesture must have been like her mother's.

"Let me go now, Clara. What am I thinking of? Let me start at once. And you say my own father is very ill. He will die without seeing me. On with your things, while I run to the cab-stand. I have money enough for both."

She wrenched at the door-handle in her hurry, forgetting that I had locked it; rich colour leaped into her cheeks, and her features and form seemed to dance, like a flickering flame, with excitement. No wonder her mother had loved, and been loved, with such power of passion.

"Idols, take it easily, or I won't let you go at all. I rather fancy, we must have some evidence, before my Uncle owns a little chit picked up in London. He is a clever and cautious man, and will expect something more convincing than your beautiful eyes and sweet breath. Do you expect, you impetuous jumper, that he will know you by instinct?"

Poor little thing, how her face fell, and how the roses faded out of it! That look of hers went to my heart; but I knew what the mother had died of, and feared lest her image and picture should perish in the same manner. So I said again:

"Did you suppose, my dear, that your father would know you by instinct?"

"Well, perhaps I did, Clara; if I thought about it at all. I am sure I should know him so."

At this moment, two heavy knocks, like a postman's, but not so quick, sounded through the house. I knew what they meant, one was Balaam, the other was Balak. Isola clung to me, and turned pale; she thought it was some one pursuing her. I told her hastily whom I expected, and sent her to Mrs. Shelfer's room. My heart beat high, when with many a scrape and bow, the worthy but not ornamental pair sidled heavily into the room.

To my greetings they answered me never a word; but Balaam stood solemnly at the end of the little table, and beckoned to his partner to fasten the door. This being done with some pantomime, which meant "By your leave, if you please, Miss," the two men, who looked none the leaner for their arduous exertions, stood side by side before me. Tired of this nonsense I exclaimed impatiently,

"Be quick, if you please; what is it you have found out?"

Balaam winked at Balak, and receiving a ponderous nod, began to digest it leisurely.

"Have you brought me to London for nothing? What do you mean by all this mummery? I shall ring the bell in a moment, and have you both shown out."

Balaam's tongue revolved in his mouth, but burst not the bonds of speech, and he tried to look straight at both windows,--till my hand was on the bell-pull.

"Balak, I told you so. Lor, how much better it be for you to take my advice, than for me to take yourn! Balak said, Miss, as we come along, the young lady would be sure to know what was right, and turn up handsome afore she asked us nothing. Now, says I, that ain't the carakter of my experience, the women most always wants--"

"Here, quick, how much do you want, before I know what you have to tell?"

Here a long interchange of signals took place, and even whispering behind a hat.

"Well, Miss, I say ten, and that quite enough till you has time to judge. But Balak say nothing under twenty, considering all the beer, and some of it country brewers'--"

"Your advice is better than Balak's; I agree with you on that point; and I will take it in preference. Here are ten pounds." He looked rather taken aback, but could not well get out of it. Balak smiled grimly at him.

"If what you tell me proves really valuable, I will give you a cheque for another ninety ere long, and the residue hereafter: but not another farthing, if you keep me in this suspense. Do I look likely to cheat people of your class?"

"No, Miss, we hopes not; nor of any other class, I dare say. Still there be so many rogues in the world--"

"You have taken my money; speak on."

What they told me at wearisome length, and with puzzling divergence, and quantities of self-praise, need not occupy many lines. They had traced the Jelly-corses, as they called Della Croce, from Somers Town to Lisson Grove, where they stayed but a very short time, Lepardo Della Croce, under some fictitious name, giving lessons in French, Spanish, and Italian, at schools in Portland Town and St. John's Wood. But he only seemed to play with his work, though he never broke any engagement to which he really pledged himself. He was always reserved and silent, accepted no invitations, and gathered his real subsistence by night at chess-clubs and billiard-rooms, where his skill was unequalled. His only friends were Italian refugees, his only diversion the vivisection of animals. It must have been about this time that he saw the newspaper paragraph, and did what he did to me. Then he changed his name again, and lived awhile in Kensington; he had been in London years before, and seemed to know it well. Here a nobleman, whom he had taught some new device at billiards, took him up and introduced him to a higher class of pupils, and obtained him some back-door palace appointment. He dubbed himself "Professor," and started as Dr. Ross. But still he missed the excitement and change of his once adventurous life, and several times he broke loose, and left his household, for weeks and months together. Then the two lovely children, whom all admired but none were allowed to notice, were attended wherever they went, by a dark-browed Italian woman. Suddenly they all left Kensington, and went to live at Ball's Pond; the reason being some threatened exposure of the Professor's cat-skinning propensities. His love of vivisection had become the master-passion, and he would gratify it at all hazards. There is to some natures a strange fascination in the horrible cruelties perpetrated under the name of science. Through its influence he even relaxed his strict reserve a little, and formed the acquaintance of a gentleman connected with the college at Camden Town; to which suburb after a while he removed, because he found it impossible to pursue his inhuman researches under his own roof comfortably. Here, by means of his new ally, who could not help admiring his infinitely superior skill, he was appointed lecturer at several schools for young ladies, where smatterings of science were dealt in. And now he was highly respected by people who did not know him, and idolised by young ladies too clever to care for pet parsons. Of course he became conceited; for his nature was but a shallow one, and his cunning, though sharp and poisonous, had no solid barb at the end. So he sneered, and grimaced, and sniggered, and before an ignorant audience made learned men stammer and stutter, amazed at his bold assumptions, and too honest and large of mind to suspect them, at short notice.

But the skill of his hands was genuine, and his power of sight most wonderful. I have since been told--though I do not believe it possible--that he once withdrew and bottled nearly half the lungs of a dog, tubercular after distemper, while the poor sufferer still gasped on, and tried to lick his face. Oh that I were a man! How can I hear such things and not swear? All animals, except one, hated him by instinct. The only one, not sagacious enough to know him, was his fellow-man. Men, or at any rate women, thought him a handsome, lively, playful, and brilliant being. And yet, upon the honour of a lady I declare--let those who know nothing of honour despise it as an after-thought--that when he first entered my room, in his graceful and elegant way, there ran through me such a shudder as first turns the leaves towards autumn, such a chill of the spinal marrow as makes the aura of epilepsy.

Darling Judy hated him from every bristle of his body, not only through instinct, but for certain excellent reasons. The monster's most intimate friend was a gallant Polish patriot, who had sacrificed all for his country, and lived here in dignified poverty. This gentleman and his wife could only afford one luxury; and that, by denying themselves many a little comfort. They had the finest dog in London, one who had saved his master's life from the squat-nosed sons of the Czar. This glorious fellow, of Maltese family, was the father of my Giudice--whom in his puppy days the Polish exile gave to Conrad and pretty girl Isola. Slowski, now an ancient dog, had a wen behind his shoulder, which grew and grew until the Professor could scarcely keep his hands from it. But he knew that any operation, in so severe a case, was nearly sure to kill a dog so old and weather-beaten. The owner too knew this, and would not have it meddled with. Lepardo Della Croce swore at last that he would taste no food until he had traced the roots of that wen. Judy, then a pretty pup, gambolled into the room and saw his poor papa--but I will not describe what a dog cannot even bear to think of. Poor Slowski died that night, and the Pole knocked down the surviving brute, who shot him next day upon Hampstead Heath. However, the gentleman slowly recovered; but during his illness the frenzied wife overstepped the bounds of honour--according to their ideas; she took advantage of Cora, in the absence of Lepardo, and learned some of his previous crimes, by practising on the poor woman's superstition. Then she found, through the firm of Green, Vowler, and Green, that my Uncle was still alive, traced out the history of the atrocious deed, and wrote the letter which had brought me to London. Soon afterwards, when her husband recovered, she was sorry for what she had done, and opened her lips on the subject no more; at least in this country, which they soon forsook for America.

In this brief epitome, I have told, for the purpose of saving trouble, a great deal more than I learned at the time, a great deal more than Balaam and Balak would have found out in a twelvemonth. But it makes no difference: for my conclusions and actions were just the same as they would have been, if I had known all the above. "And so you see, Miss"--was Balaam's peroration--"we have had a downy cove to deal with, for all his furious temper. Lor now, I never believe any Bobby would have discovered him; but we has ways, Miss, what with the carpets and the sofys, and always knowing the best pump at the bar, gentlemen of our profession has ways that no Peeler would ever dream of. And now, Miss, the ink is on the table, and both of us wishes you joy--didn't you say so, Balak?--if you only think we has earned that cheque for 90*l.*, and the rest, please God, when the gentleman feel Jack Ketch."

"You shall have the money soon, if not now. For I believe you have deserved it. But I must trouble you first to write down briefly what you have told me, and to sign it in full. It is not for myself. I remember every word. It is for the satisfaction of a gentleman who cannot see you."

Balaam and Balak looked very blank, and declared it would take them a week to write out half they had told me. This objection I soon removed, by offering to make an abstract of it, which I could do from memory, and then let them read and sign it. By this time they were both afflicted with thirst, which I sent them away to quench, while I drew up a rough deposition. But first I called darling Idols, and told her that now I had evidence which would satisfy even a sceptical father.

"And surely, my pet, you yourself must have something; some relic, or token, to help us."

"No, cousin Clara, I can't think of anything, except this little charm, which has been round my neck for years, and which I have shown you before: but I fear it is not uncommon. He took it away from me once, but I managed to steal it back again."

The charm was a piece of chalcedony, ground into some resemblance which I could not recognise then, and very highly polished. She said it had been her brother Conrad's, and he had given it to her; hearing which I ceased to examine it.

Presently the bailiffs returned, in very high spirits indeed, and ready to sign almost anything. But I took good care to inform them that, however hard they had laboured, I had made the discovery before them; which they said was permiscuous, and not to be thought nothing of. All the forms being quickly despatched, I found a few minutes to think what was next to be done.

It is too late in my journey for dalliance and embarrassment with the heavy luggage of motives, and the bandboxes of reflections, when we are past the last station, and flying to our terminus: enough that I resolved to take poor little Isola home at once to the house at Vaughan St. Mary, and the arms of her longing father, that he might see her before he died. I hoped he might live for years, but I feared he might die to-morrow; so hangs over every one's mind that fatal third stroke of paralysis. Her own entreaties and coaxing told much upon my resolution; if none could resist her when happy, who could withstand her distress? So Balaam and Balak were ordered most strictly to watch that demon's abode, and at any risk give him in charge if he made attempt at departure. To ensure due vigilance, I reclaimed the 90*l.* cheque, and gave one payable three days afterwards. They grumbled and did not like it; but in the course of all my rough usage, I had learned one great maxim--Never trust, beyond the length of a cork, any man who is slave to the bottle.

CHAPTER V.

Eager as Isola was to see her true father at last, she pressed me strongly to call at her brother's lodgings on our way to Paddington, and take him with us if possible; or at any rate learn where he was, and how long he would be absent. But I refused to do anything of the kind. Though not half so proud as of old, I could not quite stoop to that. "You know, dear," she continued, "Conny will think it unfair of me to get such a start of him with the real good Papa; and it would be so much nicer to have him there to help. And I am terribly frightened, though of course you can't understand it."

"Isola, no more nonsense. For your sake, and my poor Uncle's, I would do anything honest and proper: but neither can I travel with your brother Conrad, nor can I go near his lodgings. I am not quite reduced to that, however I am trampled on."

"But, darling, they need not see you. And you know he has made some wonderful mistake."

Of course I knew it, and told myself so fifty times in a minute; but it was a likely thing that I would tell his sister so.

"He has, indeed, a very grave mistake, if he ever thinks I will forgive him. No mistake ever made by man can be pleaded for what he has done. Even if he believed, by some excess of absurdity, that my father had murdered his, instead of his murdering mine (which was much nearer the mark), would even that justify his rudeness, low rudeness, and personal violence to a lady? What he did I never told you; and he, I should hope, was too much ashamed to speak of it: why he actually pushed me; thrust me, Clara Vaughan, away from him, till I almost fell on the floor!"

"Oh, Donna, how your eyes flash! And you call me excitable! Let me put your hair back. There now, give me a kiss. I am so sorry for Conny. He loves you with all his heart, and you look as if you could kill him. But no doubt the new good papa will put every thing to rights."

"Will he indeed? Let us go and see."

We got to Paddington just in time to catch the two o'clock train, having telegraphed first to my Uncle that I was coming to take his advice, before doing anything more. This was true, so far as it went, and as much of the truth as I then dared to administer. This message was sent, not for the sake of finding the carriage at Gloucester, but in order to break the suddenness of our arrival. Through all my joy I dreaded what was to come, and knew not how to manage it. Idols talked fast enough all the way down the line. As yet she had seen scarcely anything of our quiet, rich English scenery; and although the Great Western exhibits it rather flatly, some parts there are, below Swindon, which fill the mind with content. But our minds could not be so filled, being full of excitement already. Near Stroud poor Idols was in the greatest ecstasy, and expected me to know the owner of every pretty meadow.

But after we entered my Uncle's carriage--or mine, I suppose, it should now be called--dear Isola fell away into the deepest silence. She stored her wonder inwardly, nor showed the sweet depths of her eyes, until she sprang out at the foot of the old stone steps, trodden by so many hundreds of her ancestors. Then she looked up at the long gray house, with the dusk of July around it, and bats of three varieties flitting about the gables; and I saw beneath her dark eye-lashes the tremulous light of a tear.

After leading my sweet new cousin--whom everybody stared at, and who feared to look at the pavement--to my own snug quarters, I left her there under kind Mrs. Fletcher's charge, and ran to my Uncle's favourite room. Already my breath was short, and my heart up and down with excitement, and I had but the presence of mind to know that I was sure to make a mistake of it. I saw a great change in him, even since the Monday; but he was the first to speak.

"My dear child, kiss me again. You are nearly as tall as I am, since my upright ways have departed. From the moment you went away, I have done nothing but miss you, every hour and every minute; and last night I slept never a single wink. Let us give it up, my darling. God has sent you to me to make up for both daughter and son."

"Well, Uncle, that's all very fine, but I doubt it strongly." I was forced to be flippant a little, for fear of breaking down. "It is my firm belief that proud Clara will still have to wash at the pump."

He knew what I meant; it was an old tale, in our neighbourhood, of a nobleman's second wife who would not allow her step-children even the use of a yellow basin.

"What! do you mean to say"--and he began to tremble exceedingly--"that you have found any trace, any clue even, to my poor darlings?"

"Yes, thank God, I have. Oh, Uncle, I am so glad!" And I threw myself into his arms: his head fell heavily on my shoulder, and I felt that I had been too sudden. He could not speak, but fetched one long sob. I parted his white hair, and looked at him as if in surprise at his hastiness.

"Dear Uncle, we must not be certain yet. I mean that I have found something, or fancy I have found something, which--which--I mean if properly followed up--may lead in time--but you know how sanguine I am."

"Clara, you are playing with me. It is a mistake to do so. I cannot bear it, child. But the sudden shock I can bear. Let me know all at once. Are they alive or dead?"

"Alive, I think, dear Uncle; and I hope to find them soon, if you will calmly advise me."

"You have found them. No more fencing. I know it by your eyes. All the truth this moment, unless you wish to kill me."

He stood up as if to seize me, for I had withdrawn from his grasp, but his poor legs would not carry him; so I was obliged to seize him instead. He fell sideways on a chair, and vainly tried to speak; but his eyes never faltered from mine.

"Dearest Uncle, I tell you the truth. Of course I cannot be certain yet, and it won't do to make a mistake; and so I want more evidence."

"I want no more. Only let me see them." He spoke very slowly, and the muscles of his face twitched at every word.

"Now, keep your mind calm and clear, to help me, my dear Uncle; for I know not what to do. Have you anything, any tokens at all, of their beloved mother?"

My object was to divert his mind, for I saw the approach of coma, and now trembled more than he did.

With a feeble smile at the folly of my question, after such a love as his, he answered in great exhaustion,

"Take the key from my neck. You know the large black box in--in--"

Here his chin fell on his breast, and he could not lift the key, but his eyes still shone with intelligence, and followed me everywhere. Ribbon and all I took the key, and rang the bell for Jane, the most careful and kind of nurses. I ordered her, in a whisper, to give my Uncle a glass of very strong brandy and water, if she could get him to swallow it; and away I ran upstairs, hoping to relieve him. Then suddenly it struck me that I had no right to open that box, without the presence of a competent witness. I knew at once what box it was, from the constant anxiety my poor Uncle had shown about it. Who had such right to be my witness as his darling daughter? So back I flew to my own rooms, and dragged the bewildered Isola down the broad corridor. The poor little thing was frightened so that she could hardly breathe. I had no especial object in opening that old box, at that particular moment, much as I had often longed to know what its contents were. My presence of mind was lost, and all I could think of was, that I might find something there to break that awful suspension of life, so likely to end in death.

The box was in a panelled closet by the head of my Uncle's bed. When I handed Idols the light to hold, she took it as if in a dream; her cheeks were as white and transparent as the wax, and she held the candle so that a hot flake splashed on my neck. The lock of the long box turned most easily, and the hinges moved without creaking: most likely it had been pored over every day, for many years. The lid was arched and hollow, with straps of faded web inside it.

In beautiful order, so fair that I hardly dared to touch them, lay the clothes and trinkets, the letters and little relics, the gloves and pocket-handkerchiefs, the fairy slippers, the wedding-dress, the coquettish veil, and saucy hat of the dead. I am not over sensitive, thank God, or I should not be living now; but the sight of those things upset me more than any distress of my own. The small parcels of silver paper, screwed at the end and pinned in the middle, the pins put stupidly as men always put them, the light gay dresses made for some sweet figure, folded with such care, and yet quite out of the plaits, and labelled with the dates when last the dear one wore them, even a withered fern-wreath and a sprig of shrivelled myrtle--I could not thrust my commonplace hands into these holy treasures; if I could I should never deserve to be myself so remembered. But one thing struck me, as thoughts profane always strike us crookedly; if the poor lady could have been wept to life again, how much better would she have found all her things arranged, than she had ever kept them! That is to say if she resembled her wondering and crying daughter, who knelt down and wanted to kiss every article in the box. Her little white hands were as busy as mice among them; and long-drawn sobs were tumbled with interjections.

"Now, my dearest Idols, you must not disturb these things. Your father will be so vexed."

Would he though?--said I to myself--not if he knew whose hand it was that did it. She paid no attention to me.

"Now just put back that silver knife, with the bit of peach-skin upon it: and leave the stone as it was."

To my surprise she began to suck the stone, which her mother perhaps had sucked, eighteen years ago. Inside the paper was written, "Knife and peach-stone found in my Lily's pocket. The stone was meant for me to set. I will plant it, when I have found her children. E.V., January, 1834."

"Now, you foolish child, you are really too bad." And with that I gave her a little push. In her heedless way, she fell almost into the box, and her light form lay amongst her mother's dresses. A sudden thought flashed across me.

"Isola, off with that nasty dark frock!"

"Nasty, indeed, Clara! Why you said this morning how very pretty it was."

"What has that to do with it? Pull it off, or I'll tear it. Now, out with the other arm."

In a moment or two, I had all her beauty gleaming in white before me; and carefully taking from the box a frock of pale blue silk, I lifted it over her head, and drew her dimpled arms through the sleeves; then I fixed it in front with the turquoise buttons, and buckled the slender zone. Her blue eyes looked on in amazement, like violets at a snow-storm. Then I led her to the mirror, and proud as we both had always been of her beauty, the same thought struck us now. I saw it in the mirror, by the toss of her pointed chin and the coy bend of her neck: she saw it there as clearly, by the flash of my tear-bright eyes. Neither of us had ever seen that loveliest of all girls look half so lovely before. The glow of pride and beauty's glory mantled in her cheeks; and her eyes were softly beaming down the avenue of lashes, from clearest depths of azure. I never saw such eyes as she had, among all our English beauties. Some perhaps are as fine of colour, and as liquid, though not so lustrous: but the exquisite arch of the upper lid, and the rich short fringe of the lower, cast a tremulous light and shade, which dull Anglo-Saxons feel not. Like moonbeams playing through a mantled bridge.

The dress fitted her exactly. It had been made for a slender, buoyant figure, as graceful and pure as a snow-wreath, yet full of warm motion and richness. Indeed, I must confess, that, although correct enough for the time and clime of the owner, it showed too much of the lifting snow for our conceptions of maidenhood: so I drew a gauzy scarf--perhaps a true *fazoletto*--over the velvet slope of the shoulders, and imprisoned it in the valley. This being nicely arranged, I hung her chalcedony charm from her neck, and fastened it to her waist-band. Then I caught up her clustering hair, nearly as thick and long as my own, after the Corsican fashion, snooded it close in ripples with a pink and white-striped mandile, and told her to love herself in the glass, while I ran off to the hot-house for a truss of Stephanotis. This, with a glossy sprig of Gardenia leaves to back it, I fastened cleverly into the clear mandile, on the curve of her elegant head, and my darling was complete. Then I kissed her sweet lips, and admired her, more than she admired herself.

"Clara, it does not matter how much trouble you take; you can't make me look a quarter so well as you do."

"Not quite so tall, my darling, nor anything like so naughty; but a thousand times more lovely."

"Well, I wish I could think so. I am always longing to change with you."

"Don't talk nonsense, my pretty; if I were a man I should die for you. Now I glory in you as a Vaughan. Come along."

I led her through the gallery and to the door of her father's room, before she had time to think. She did not know but what I was taking her back to my own rooms, along another passage. At the sick man's door I left her, while I went in to see how much might be safely ventured.

My Uncle was leaning back in his deep reclining chair, with his weak eyes fixed most eagerly on the door. In vain he strove to hide his disappointment, and to look at me with gratitude. The wandering mind too plainly hoped for something dearer than a brother's child.

Dismissing Jane through the other room, that she might not encounter Isola, I sat down to examine him. The brandy and water had rallied his vital power, but made him hot and feverish. He kissed my hand to atone for some sharp and impatient expressions, and I saw that the moment was favourable.

"Uncle dear, what will you say to me? I have brought you another new visitor, the loveliest girl in London. You know her well by name. You have often longed to see my sweet darling Isola. And she wants to see you so much. Only you must promise me one thing honourably. Be gay and sprightly with her; she is timid in this old house."

"My dear, I can't see her to-night. You don't mean that of course. Give her my best apologies. You say she is very sweet-tempered; I am sure she will excuse me."

"If she would, I will not. Nor would you excuse her, if you knew whom she resembles."

"What do you mean? Have you locked my box again?"

"Yes, and here is the key. I found a portrait of a lady"--I had not shown this to my cousin--"very like beautiful Isola."

He began to tremble again, so I thought the quicker the better. Placing the lamp-shade so that a dim light fell on the door, I ran out to fetch his daughter.

"Now, don't be a baby, Isola. Remember how ill he is. Keep as much in the shadow as possible; and if he should guess who you are, pretend not to care a bit for him."

"I will try my very best, Clara. But I don't think I can do that."

She shook so much that I was obliged to support her, as she had supported me that evening when first we met. Stiffly I brought her in, and began to introduce her, holding her back all the time.

"Uncle Edgar, this is my dearest friend, of whom you have heard so often, Miss Isola"--Ross I could not say. "Why, Uncle--why, Idols, darling--"

It was all in vain; I might as well have spared my devices. From the moment she crossed the threshold, his eyes had been leaping towards her. The paralysed man bounded forward, as if with galvanic life. His daughter met him as wildly. "My Lily, my Lily," was all he could sob, "my own Lily come from the grave!" With a father's strength he clasped her, and her dark locks were showered with silver. As for tears--but I left them together when I had seen both safe on the sofa.

CHAPTER VI.

To our surprise and delight, the genuine Papa, instead of being worse the next day, looked more like himself than he had done at any time since the fever. But in spite of added importance, and the sense of parental dignity, he sat hand in hand with his beautiful daughter by the hour together, playing with her cheeks and hair, as little girls do with dollies. And all the time he was talking to her about her darling mother, and made her answer him in Italian, and made her kiss him every other minute; and found out a thousand times, as a novelty every time, that she was the very image and model of her mother, and yet he was not sure that her smile was quite so sweet; then to make up for depreciation he needs must kiss her again, and say, yes, he thought it was, though it was quite impossible for any other to be so--and thus they went on, till I thought there never would be an end of it; albeit I did my utmost to keep away from them both.

Knowing that I was in their way, and feeling rather out of spirits, I went my old accustomed round of places, sacred in my memory to a certain father and mother of my own. How long I wept at their simple graves, how I knelt to their God and mine, thanking Him from my desolate heart for the light now shed upon me, and how I prayed that they might both be looking down on me now and craving heavenly guidance for me through the peril yet to come--these, and the rest of my doings there, cannot well be told except to the ears of orphans. The clouds of an overcast existence seemed to be opening rapidly, and though they could never disclose my sun and moon again, some happiness it was to know even how those had set. And more than all, the foul aspersion upon my father's memory, which all the while I scorned it so, had lain heavily on my thoughts, this was now proved liar's spittle, and my sweet darling father had offended not even a villain. A thousand times I implored his pardon for the splash having ever descended upon the hem of my garment, though shaken off straight-way with loathing.

In the midst of my dreamy thoughts, and while I sat between the two low headstones, upon the very spot where I hope my own head may lie, the tremulous beauty of the Golden Thuja, which I had planted there, was pushed aside too carelessly, and something far more beautiful planted itself in front. It was my cousin Lily. I have been strictly forbidden ever to call her "Isola," or even "Idols," again, as savouring of the evil one. Lily Vaughan was beaming with young delight and happiness: the fresh west country air, sweet from the tropic gulf-stream, had crowned the April of her cheeks with a June of roses.

"Oh, Donna, I am so glad I have found you at last. What makes you run away from me and my Papa? I have lost my way all over the world. What a lovely world it is, Donna!"

"Don't call me that name here. Do you not see where you stand?"

She glanced at the headstones engraved with initials and dates, and at once understood it all. For a long time she was silent, a long time I mean for her; and her soft eyes glistened at once with awe and pity. At last, she crept close to me, looked at the ground, and whispered with a deep sigh:

"How you must hate me, Clara."

"Hate you, my darling! What for?"

"Oh, because I have got such a dear Papa, and you have none at all. And much worse than that, because--because--oh, I don't know how to tell you."

"Tell me all you mean. Let there be no misunderstanding between us."

"Because my mother and my father seem somehow to have killed--though I am sure they would rather have killed themselves--your poor papa and mamma." And she leaned on my mother's headstone, and sobbed till I feared for her heart.

I put my arm around her waist, drew her towards me, and sat on my father's grave, with his niece upon my lap.

"Dearest, I could not be the child of those who sleep beneath us, if it were in my nature now to feel as you imagine. Years ago, I might have done so; though I hope not even then. Orphan as I am and helpless, already I perceive that I have not lived for nothing. My father, I believe, my mother, I am sure, would have laid down life with pleasure to see me led from wayward childhood even to what I am. Oh, Lily, you can't think how they loved me." And at the tender memory, came tears, the voice of silence.

Lily said not a word, but gathered and plaited a wreath of flowers, wherewith, as in a nuptial tie, she bound the white headstones together--anything so as not to disturb me just then. Even that trifle, a graceful idea born of her Southern origin, even that for the moment touched me deeply. Times there are when our souls seem to have taken hot baths in the springs of memory, and every pore of them is open.

"Darling Lily, come--how proud they would have been of you--come and kiss me in this presence, and promise that, whatever happens, none shall ever thrust cold hands between your heart and mine. That we will bear, and trust, and love; nor, if a shadow steals between us, blink it till the substance follows, but be frank and open--the very breath of friendship--and when doubt begins to grow, for the devil is sure to sow it, have it plucked away at once, each by the other's hand. Kiss me, dear; your weakness is that you are not so outspoken as I am. Never let me vex you, without knowing it."

The innocent creature kissed me, and promised solemnly.

"Oh, Clara," she cried, "how on earth did you find it out? Sometimes you have vexed me dreadfully, for you don't care much what you say; but I always thought it was my fault, and I never told you of it. But it never made me love you a single bit the less."

"Yes, it did for the moment, though you may soon have forgiven it. But a love which is always undergoing forgiveness, is like glass steeped in water, you may cut it in two with a pair of common scissors."

"Well, I should like to see the scissors that would cut me away from you. I'll have a great piece off your hair, Clara, if you talk such nonsense. Now come; my father wants you."

"Have you told him?"

"Yes, everything about dear Conny and you; and he says you are a noble girl, but uncommonly thick-headed about your own concerns, though as quick as lightning for others. Now, I won't have you look so pale; let us run and get some colour. See, I'll get first to that tree."

"Will you indeed?" I won the race by a yard, and was glad that the exercise made excuse for the quick rise of my bosom. After all that had happened, I would not have her imagine that I still cared for her brother. Like a girl all over, she said not another word, determined that I should begin it.

"Let us walk faster, Lily, if my Uncle wishes to see me."

"No, there is plenty of time. It will do him good to sleep a little."

"Oh, then it is nothing important. I rather feared that it might be."

"Don't be at all afraid, darling. He wants to show you how nicely he made the Chalcedony Spalla that used to be round my neck. He made it for my mother, in remembrance of something."

"Oh, nothing more than that. I thought you spoke of something--at least you seemed to imply--"

"Nothing that you need blush about, nor stammer either, proud Donna. You know you proved to me yesterday, when we were in the cab, that you did not care for Conny any more than you did for a flake of London soot, which happened to come in at the window, and fall upon your glove. And you were kind enough to compare him to that individual smut."

"Oh, Judy, Judy," I cried, as the dog came bounding to meet us--"darling Judy, you love Clara, if nobody else has sense enough."

And half an hour ago, Lily and I in dramatic language, vowed eternal affection!

"Oh, Clara, darling Clara, don't you know that I was in fun? I thought you were so clever. And now to see you sobbing over that great muff of a dog! Judy, I hate you, get out of the way"--the judicious would not stir--"take your great hulking paws from cousin Clara's neck. There then, make the most of that! Oh, I have hurt my hand so, and he is only wagging his tail. But I am so delighted, my own pet, that you love poor Conny still."

"And pray, who said I did?"

"Nobody, only me. All dear Papa said was this, that there was a great mistake, and he soon perceived what it was; and I asked him to take my opinion about it, because I was a senior sophist. And he pretended not to know what a senior sophist was. And I told him it was my degree, not from that man, you know, but fairly earned at the College; though they did have the impudence to say that the Professors were going to pluck me, until I gave them a smile."

"True enough, no doubt. But I know all that long ago. What more did my Uncle say?"

"That he would tell you his opinion, but he would rather not talk about it to me. And he could not bear me to go out, for fear I should be stolen again. And I do believe he has had me watched all the way. Here I come, Pappy; large as life you see, and three times as natural."

"Yes, my own treasure, three times as natural to me, as my life has been without you. But wheel me indoors, young maidens. No other man in the world has such a pair of horses. I want to talk to Clara, in my own room alone. Lily, go to Mrs. Fletcher, I can't have you roving about so." Lily obeyed him instantly.

"Wait one minute, Uncle dear; I want to go and fetch something."

I ran to my own rooms, and found the deed of gift, which had not been returned to the lawyers. This I took to his study and placed it in his hands.

"What is the matter, Clara? Have you turned conveyancer, and detected some informality?"

"No, dearest Uncle. But I want you to cancel this. I cannot allow you so to rob your children."

I will not say what he called me in his surprise and delight. It seemed to me quite uncalled for; I had only done what my conscience told me was just. But as for accepting my offer-- he would not hear of it twice. "Darling, it would be wrong. It would be downright robbery; and no plea whatever for it, on the score of paternal duty. You are the proper heir, the child of the elder son, the true representative of our ancient family. All the rest is a quibble and quirk, of which, even without your countless benefits, I never intended to take advantage. And my children are, by the mother's side, of a family older even than ours--so far as that nonsense goes--and are heirs to wealth compared to which--if it only be rightly worked--these Vaughan estates are nothing. All I ask you is to do a thing which I am sure you would do without asking--to assist them, if what I have left them is spent before they prove their claims. Here is a letter to Count Gaffori; that excellent man is still alive; and here are the certificates, and my own brief deposition, which I have begged a neighbouring magistrate to come to-day and attest; here is my Lily's Spalla, and perhaps other relics are in my son's possession. Lastly, here are two more letters, one to my old friend Peter Green, who has now much influence in that part of Corsica, the other to James McGregor, once my messmate at Lincoln's Inn, now an acute and rising Counsel, and a leading authority upon municipal law. Take all these, my darling, if you will so far oblige me; for I fear my lovely daughter--isn't she lovely, Clara?"

"The loveliest girl in all the world; and what is far more important, the sweetest, and the best."

"Yes, if you had searched the kingdom, you could not have brought me such another love. But ah! you should have seen her mother! However, I fear the sweet pet is a little careless and random, as her father used to be. At any rate, I prefer entrusting this great budget to your brave and honest hands; at least until my son comes here to claim it. The deposition you shall have, when attested."

"But, Uncle, surely you had better keep it all yourself. No fear of Mrs. Daldy now."

"No, my darling; but these things must not be buried with me."

There was something in his eyes which made me start with terror. But he smiled so sweetly that my terror fled.

"And now, my child, about yourself. Though you have found me another daughter, I look upon you as the eldest; and I venture to speak to you, as a father would. Is it as my Lily tells me? Is it true--God grant it may be--that you love my son, my Lily's son, Henry Conrad? Why don't you answer me, darling? Tell the truth like a real Vaughan. Surely you are not ashamed of him." And he laid his hand on my head. My tears fell fast; and my heart was in a tempest.

"Yes, Uncle," at last I answered, frightened for his suspense, and looking him full in the face, "Yes, Uncle, I do--I mean at least I did--love him very much at one time."

"With all your heart, as we Vaughans love; with all your heart, poor darling?"

"Yes, Uncle," I sobbed, in bitter humiliation; "none of my heart is left me."

"Thank God! what blest news for his mother! My Harry is the happiest fellow alive."

"But, Uncle, he does not think so, he--he--doesn't perceive his blessedness." A flash of my old self-irony came even through my anguish.

"Oh, I have heard all that. But surely you know the absurd mistake he made."

"Indeed, I cannot guess it. Is it my place to do that?"

"Of course it is; when you are in the light, and he is all in the dark. Whom did that kidnapper believe himself to have murdered?"

"You, Uncle, of course."

"And whose child then does he suppose you to be; if he heard of your existence, as he is sure to have done?"

"Merciful God, I see it all! And how bitterly I have wronged him, my own noble Conrad!"

My poor weak Uncle had to manage me, all by himself, in my terrible hysterics. Frightened as he was, for he never before had to deal in that way with a nature resembling mine, he would not even ring for help, lest I should betray my secret to other ears than his own. When at last I came to myself, he kissed me tenderly, and said:

"My poor dear child, remember--when you may be glad to think of it--that whether I see my noble boy or not, I shall die now in perfect happiness. Noble he must be, or Clara could not love him. It would have been the pet scheme of my heart, if I could have had a voice in it. And here it is done without me! How often have I longed and yearned that he could only see you, as you waited day and night by my pestilential bed, that he could only know the tale of your troubles and devotion. At my death, the generation so visited from heaven expires; and you three darlings start anew, with all things in your favour. Now mind that the good old Signor's directions are complied with, and that Harry, if he lives here, abandons the Corsican property to his sister Lily. Promise me this, my Clara."

"Of course I will, dear Uncle--I mean, so far as my influence goes. And he will then be bound to do so under the deed-poll, if I understood you aright. But perhaps he has quite forgotten me now."

"Of course he thinks himself bound to avoid you. But I have written to set him right, and to bring him as soon as possible. And now about--about that horrible--"

"Ah, yes. If I had the right, I would even let him go. My feeling has changed from fierce hatred to utter contempt. And surely his vengeance is satisfied now."

"No, Clara. It will flame more wildly than ever the moment he learns his mistake, and my final triumph over him. Has he any idea where our Lily is?"

"As yet, he can have none. If old Cora went to Albert Street last evening, she would learn nothing from Mrs. Shelfer, I took care of that, except that Lily had been there, and was gone again. The old woman does not speak English enough to attempt to cross-examine. She loves poor Lily, I know, but will be satisfied with the belief that the child had gone to her brother's. And as for that monster, even if he relents, he will be too proud to inquire."

"What had my poor child done, that the brute turned her out, and struck her?"

"Nothing, I believe, beyond defending her brother Conrad, as she always did. I suppose I may call him 'Conrad,' Uncle?"

"Yes, my dear, it is his true name, chosen by his mother. Where are you going so hastily?"

"To London at once. For your sake, Uncle dear, I must not think of sparing him. I must have him in custody to-night. I would have avoided it, if I could for a thousand reasons; but there is no alternative."

"Yes there is. In two days I shall be beyond his reach. Don't ask me what I mean. To-day is Thursday. Promise only to let him go free till Saturday."

"I will. But I must go to London. I cannot rest quiet here."

My Uncle's face brightened beautifully. And he took my hand in his.

"I know what you mean, my darling. You intend to discover my Harry, for fear of any mishap. I will let you go, dear; though the house seems empty without you, its truthful and graceful mistress. But you must not go alone. It is not right for a beautiful girl, however self-possessed and dignified, especially one of your station, to rove about unattended."

"Only one man ever insulted me, Uncle, I mean in a serious way, and he never did it again."

"It does not matter. The example is bad, and all men are not gentlemen. Mrs. Fletcher shall go with you, and our pretty Lily keep house. But I have an especial reason, and a most powerful one, for wishing that you should be here. Don't go till to-morrow, my darling; I am so well to-day, and I must see you once at your own table, with my daughter and me for your guests."

"Oh, Uncle, I hope so a thousand times. I will stop till the morning, if you have set your heart upon it."

"I have indeed. You may go in the morning by the first train, and be back to-morrow night. Will you promise?"

Though I could not understand his motive, and he was pleased to conceal it, I promised all he asked. Then I told him all the story of Conrad and the accident, how he saved my mother's life and mine, with the courage and skill of a true-born mountaineer. My Uncle was moved to tears, not only at the gallantry of his son, but also by the joy of discovering that all the obligations lay not upon one side. I also wept at finding that Lily had never heard of it. Conrad's lofty nature scorned to narrate its own achievements. When, after that adventure, he discovered who we were, he avoided us because he believed that his father had slain mine. It was not till a later date, when he became of age--as the Corsicans reckon manhood[#]--that Lepardo Della Croce told him all he knew of his history, dwelt on the foul shame wrought to the Della Croce by his bigamist father, and tried in vain to force on him the awful oath of Vendetta. The youth had too much English blood in his heart to accept the black inheritance. Thenceforth he could not bear the sight of the man who had killed, as they both supposed, his father, although, in his wrath for his mother's wrongs and his own, he would not resent the deed. What marvel then that he spurned me, and was maddened with himself, at finding that he, the illegitimate, was in love with me, his legitimate sister? But now, we are only half-cousins, and nature has never misled us.

[#] *i.e.* the age of twenty.

All that evening, my Uncle was in the most glorious spirits, and I am not sure that Lily and I were very far behind him. He played us all sorts of boyish tricks, and we made reprisals with girlish ones, till Lily's joyous laughter rang halfway clown the corridor. I had dressed her with especial care, and she did look such a love! But it was all too sudden, and far too sweet to last. My Uncle indeed seemed quite beside himself, more gladsome than nature allows us to be with impunity. Then the vein dried all of a sudden, and the mind flowed the opposite way. He made his beautiful daughter, who, though not much of a sophist, had a soul that thrilled to music, he made her play the soft Corsican airs, that seem to weep as they breathe, and which she had learned from old Cora. He knew them all; how well he knew them, his face turned from the light betrayed. The depth of melodious sadness, the touch of some nervine chord, which knew not its own existence, and starts to be known and appreciated, as might an unconscious poet, and more than all the trembling spread of the feelers of the heart, these are the proofs of nature's presence in music or in poetry.

Then he begged me to play some of the sweet and simple melodies of Wales. These he declared, and I had already perceived it, these were born of the self-same spirit, though not so highly intensified, as the Corsican romances.

Finally, he told us many a moving tale of his Lily; tales a man is loth to tell to those with whom he expects to live. How she was loved, and how she seemed to love everybody, and pretty answers she made to those who praised her beauty, and more than words or kisses, the loving things she did, the elegance of self-denial, and the innocence of merit.

That night, that memorable night, we stayed up more than two hours over his proper time for going to bed. He seemed so sad to part, that I could not bear to hurry him. One thing he told me which I was glad to hear.

"Clara, darling, I have taken a liberty with your house. This afternoon, I wrote by the London post, for Annie Franks to come back again to-morrow, if she will, as an especial favour to me."

I was rather surprised; but answered him warmly, and in all truth:

"Dear Uncle, you know that I love her; and I cannot see too much of the few whom I really love."

Then, as I was to start at six o'clock in the morning, he wished me "Good bye," in a solemn manner, which seemed to me quite uncalled for. He drew my young face to his own, so marked by sorrow and illness, looked into my eyes as if I were to remember something, then held me in his trembling embrace, and kissed me long and fondly.

"God in heaven bless you, darling, for all you have done to me and mine."

"*Mine*, you should say, dear Uncle. I count them now my own."

His daughter took him away, with her white arms thrown around him. For now she slept in the closet next to his room, where I had so long been quartered.

CHAPTER VII.

In the early morning, I was off for London, taking Mrs. Fletcher with me, much against my will, because she seemed to cumber me both in thought and action. Between the door and the avenue, I looked from the open carriage--I hate to be shut up in summer--at the dear old house. Lily had got up to breakfast with me, in spite of my prohibition; and she was going with us as far as the lodge, to have a nice walk back. To my great surprise I saw my poor Uncle, standing at his open window, wrapped in a dressing-gown. He kissed his hand and waved me his last farewell. I leaped on the seat to reply, and then scolded him with my glove. Half in play and half in sorrow, he mocked my lively gestures, and the morning breeze lifted his silver hair, as he wafted me the last kiss. I told Lily to scold him well, with my very best love, and she asked me in the most ladylike manner, if I saw any green in her eye. The girl had picked up a great deal of slang among the fair collegians. Mrs. Fletcher looked sadly shocked; so I said, to reassure her: "You know, Mrs. Fletcher, we must make allowances for young ladies who come from college."

"To be sure, Miss Vaughan, to be sure we must," she replied with her most sagacious air: and at Gloucester she whispered to the coachman, "John, the villain that stole Miss Lily sent her to Oxford, in a young gentleman's clothes, and she took a very high degree: but don't say a word about it." "Not by any means, ma'am," answered John, with a grin. Nevertheless, it found its way over the house, and the result was that all the girls came to Lily about their sweethearts.

I mention this trifling incident only to show how little I thought that I then saw the last of my Uncle.

At Paddington we met Annie Franks taking her ticket for Gloucester, and looking most bright and blooming, with a grand pocket in her cloak, made to hold a three-volumed novel. I had only time for a few words with her, in which I commended my Uncle to her especial attention, as she had ten times my cousin's experience. Then I went with her to the down-platform, and saw her get into the carriage, and gave her the last of my sandwiches, while a cruel guard made her turn out her new pocket, insisting that she must have a little dog concealed there. I laughed at the poor little dear, as crimson with mortification she showed before all the gentlemen the triple fluted bulk, and the guard read out, more in amazement than rudeness, "Sir Ingomar of the Red Hand; or, The Knight of St. Valentine, and the Paynim Lady." The gentlemen were gentlemen, and tried very hard not to smile; but the way the guard scratched his head was a great deal too much for them. "Dog's ears, anyhow," cried he, trying to escape with a joke. I drew her out of the carriage, with tears in her soft gray eyes, and put her into another, where Sir Ingomar was unknown, and might spur on at pleasure. Then the smiles returned to her shy and innocent face, and she put her head to the window, and whispered gently to me:

"Any strawberries left, dear?"

"I should think so, Annie. The best of them all, the British Queens, are just coming in. And such a crop of grapes!"

Annie's conception of perfect bliss was to sit upon a shady bank, "the breeze just fanning her delicate cheek," with a cabbage-leaf full of strawberries by her, and a cut-and-thrust novel upon her lap. Off she went with a lovely smile, foreseeing all these delights.

From Paddington we drove straightway to the lodgings of Conrad Vaughan. As we jolted along the New-road, which always has more holes in it than any other street in London, I lost my wits in a tumult of thick tempestuous thought. What would Conny say to see me, me the haughty Clara, coming all impatiently even in quest of him? Would it not have been far better, far more like an English maiden, to wait, and wait, and wear the soul out, rather than to run the risk of mis-interpretation? True, it was for his father's sake, to save him from deadly peril, and to make his happiness complete; but might not all have been done by messenger, as well as by me in person? So at least might fancy those who did not know our enemy. Worst of all, and cloudiest thought, that filled the eyes every time it came,--would he love me still? Would not the strong revulsion, that must have torn him in two, when he dashed his hand on his forehead, and forgot even man's forbearance, would not, must not this have snapped all the delicate roots of love? I could not tell. Of man's heart I know nothing; but I felt that with me, a woman, such a horrible thing would create only longing to make amends.

"Mrs. Fletcher, how is my hair?"

"Lovely, my pretty child"--she always called me so from habit when no one else was present--"you look your very best; and I'd like to see them that could--talk to me of Lilies indeed, when our Miss Clara--"

"No smuts on my nose, Mrs. Fletcher, I hope? I never feel sure, in London. You don't know London, you see."

"No, my pretty, as clean as a whistle, and as clear as the voice of a May-bird, every atom of you. There's no such complexion nowhere out of Gloshire or in it: and its all along of the brimstone and treacle I give you, when you was small. Talk to me of Lilies--why I see three great butter spots, as big as the point of a needle, and I know by the make of her boot that her little toe turn over; and what's more than that--"

"Mrs. Fletcher, I won't hear a word of it. As to her little toe, I can most solemnly declare that you are wrong altogether; for I have seen her naked foot, and a lovelier one never was--"

"Take yours out of the way, Miss. But--"

"But-- here we are; and you have made my cheeks quite red! I shall be ashamed to be seen."

However, it did not matter; for there was no one there to see me. Conrad was gone to Paris; he had quitted London quite suddenly, and there was a letter left for his sister, which the girl forgot to post, till she thought it was too late. And he said very likely he should go on to Italy; and they were not to keep the rooms, if they had a chance of letting them, only to put away the things he had left, in the cupboard. So I took the letter, directed "Miss Isola Ross," but I did not dare to open it, much as I longed to do so. Having enclosed it in a new envelope, and posted it in the nearest letter-box, with a heavy heart I re-entered the cab, and went on to Mrs. Shelfer's.

Mrs. Shelfer was of course surprised to see me so soon again. Nevertheless she was all kindness and hospitality, as usual. The residue of her little debt had been long ago released, and now I paid full rent, for I could easily afford it. In answer to my eager inquiries as to what had occurred since Wednesday, the little woman said shortly:

"Nothing at all, Miss, of any account, I thank you. Only Charley threw double size, three times running, and won--"

"I don't mean that, Mrs. Shelfer; I mean, what has happened for me?"

"Nothing, Miss Vaughan; no, nothing to concern a great lady like you: only such a queer lot come, and they seemed to be friends of yours. They ain't gone from here more than half an hour ago."

"Tell me all about them."

"They come and ringed the bell, as modest as could be; and when I went to the door, says they, 'If you please, where be Miss Clara, ma'am?' 'Miss Clara!' says I, 'a set of dressed up trollops like you, come and ask for Miss Clara! She'd Miss Clara you, pretty quick time, I doubt, if she was only here.' 'Us humbly hopes no offence, ma'am,' says the great big man, the biggest man as ever I see without paying, 'only us has come up from the country, ma'am.' 'Up from the country!' says I, 'needn't tell me that, my good giant; any fool can see that. And if you take my advice, you'll clap your hat on, and go down again, and thank God for it.' You see, Miss, he had got his hat off, and he standing out of doors, on the shady side of the street! So what I said seemed to stop him altogether, and he looked as if he wanted to think about it; and I was just a slapping the door in their faces, when the other man, the queerest guy I ever see, a hanging in his clothes like a skiver in a dish-clout, he look full in my face as grave as a heretic parson, and stretch out his skinny arm, and keep time with one foot, while he say or sing,

> "'Ma'am, us be
> here now in this
> Lunnon town,
> And it bain't likely
> as we be going
> down,
> Till us see every
> mortal thing as
> there be for to see,
> And take all the
> change out in a
> thorough-going
> spree.'

Then the big man laugh and clap him on the back; and the little one wink both his eyes, and look to see what I think of it. Then when he see me laugh, he make me such a coorous bow, that what with his--what do they call the plaister, Miss?"

"Diachylon, perhaps you mean, Mrs. Shelfer?"

"Ah, that's the word. What with his strange diaculum, and his dancing altitude, I declare I was a most a going to invite them in: but I recollects, no, no: If Charley gets along of such Reginalds as these, I may stand at the bed-room door and whistle for a week. There's nothing Charley loves so much as a downright Reginald."

Poor simple-minded woman; how little she perceived that she of all the number was by far the most original! And, like most of those who are truly so, she would have taken the imputation as an outrageous insult. Only the sham original glories in being thought queer.

"Well, Mrs. Shelfer, I want to hear the end of it."

"Just what I say, Miss. Yes, yes, no time to spare, and the pudding boiling. So I says, quite sharp, 'What name, my good sir, and will you leave a message? Miss Vaughan is out of town.' 'Wull,' says he, just as I tell you, Miss, 'ony plase you say, ma'am, as Jan Uxtable, and Beany Dawe, and the two beggest of the chillers has doed theirselves the honour of coming to lave their dooty.' Then the little girl look up and she flash her ribbons and say, 'Mr. Huxtable, if you please, ma'am, and Mr. Ebenezer Dawe, and Miss Huxtable, and Master John, has called.' 'Hadn't you better write it down, Miss?' says I, as innocent as possible. 'Do you suppose I can't then?' says she, with such a spitting out of her eyes, and she swinging a new parry sole. 'Just give me a sheet of papper, if you keep such a thing in the house.' 'Plase to excuse the little wanch, ma'am,' says the big man, quite humble, 'us can't hardly make head nor tail of her, since her come to this here Lunnon. If I had only knowed it I'd have had her mother along of me, that I would ees fai, and the coo be her own midwaife. But ony plase you say Jan Uxtable come if they count it dacent hereaway. Threescore acres and five, ma'am, without reckon the Cleeve, and no man have a call, to my mind, to christen himself "Mister" on less than a hundred acres, in Lunnon or out of it.' 'Very well, sir,' I says, for I took to the big man somehow, 'I will deliver your message. Miss Vaughan only went from here of middle day on Wednesday.' 'And tell her please, if she do come back,' says spirity Miss Parrysole, with the tears in her great blue eyes, 'that Sally Huxtable leave her very best love and duty, and hope so much Miss Clara will come to see the great wrestling to-morrow, twelve o'clock, and be early. And they be betting now two to one on the other man, ma'am. But he have no chance, no more than Tim Badcock with father.' 'I be much afeared, ma'am,' says the deep-voiced man, as soft as any bell, 'I be afeared our Sally will be begger by a lanyard nor ever her daddy or her mammy was. But likely it be all for the best.' And with that all four of them crooked their legs to me most polite, and went on round the corner; and after them went a score of boys, that seemed to follow them everywhere. The boys knew all about it, and so did I at last, that it was the great champion wrestling, that is to be to-morrow. Charley have been mad about it going on now two months. And can you please to tell him, Miss, which way to lay his money?"

"To be sure, I can. Let him take every offer of two to one against the Devonshire champion; and if he loses I will make it good to him, upon condition that he gives you everything he wins. Now please to let me have a cup of strong tea."

Having thus got rid of my most talkative friend, and Mrs. Fletcher having started off to buy something, I had time to think a little.

It was nearly two o'clock on the Friday afternoon. Nothing more could be done at present towards recovering Conrad, for he had not even left at his lodgings any Continental address. Possibly his place of sojourn might be revealed in the letter to his sister, posted by my hand: but it was far more likely that he himself knew not, at the time of writing, where he should find quarters. I must have been beside myself with worry and disappointment, when I dropped that letter into Her Majesty's box; for if I returned, as had been arranged, by the express at five o'clock, several hours would be saved in the delivery of its tidings. And, as yet, I little dreamed where I should be at five P.M.

In that little room, whose walls were more relieved than decorated by certain daubs of mine, which even in my narrowest straits I could not bear to part with, because an indulgent critic had found merit in them--a discovery requiring much acumen--here I now sat, gazing fondly, dreaming hazily, yearning strongly for the days gone by, yet only three months old, when I had not a crust or dress till I earned it by my labour. How that pinch enlarged my heart, God only knows, not I. Ah, then I was a happy girl, though I never guessed it. How proudly I walked down the Square, with my black straw bonnet on-- which Idols called the Dowdy,--and my dark plaid shawl around me, the plainest of the plain, yet not prepared to confess myself so quotidian as my dress. Who could tell, in those happy days, who might come, or round what corner, and who could say whether of the twain would look the more accidental? And then the doubt--shall I look or not, better perhaps be intent on the fire-plug, and make him come round again?

But now. Ah me, they have heaped up riches for me, and who shall come to enjoy them?

Just as I was warming to this subject, gushing along in a fine vein of that compassion which alone of soft emotions we find it no duty to wrestle with, I mean of course self-pity--in came Mrs. Fletcher, suddenly, and in anger.

"Well, Miss Clara," she exclaimed, throwing down her parcel, "so this is London, is it?"

"To be sure, Mrs. Fletcher. What objection have you to make to it?"

"No objection, Miss, only this, that if ever I seen a set of countrified folk, the Londoners are them. Why the commonest of our kitchen-maids would be ashamed to talk so broad, and to dress so contemptuous. And here I went half a mile to buy boots, real London-made; and trees all along by the side of the road, and pots on the shelves of the windows. I never, if Gloucester don't look much more like a town."

As Mrs. Fletcher did not tell a story with the Herodotean vivacity of Tim Badcock, I will render her facts in my own unpretending version, premising only that she had taken the farmer and Sally for specimens of the true Cockney; a bit of saltatory reasoning of which she has not heard (and perhaps never will hear) the last. While then the worthy housekeeper was driving a slow but shrewd bargain, in a smart shop by the Broadway, taking the boots to the sunshine, to pick clever holes in the stitching, she observed a diminutive boy, of the genuine shoe-black order, encamping in a bight or back-eddy of pavement, just at the side of the door. This little fellow was uniformed, or rather multi-coloured, in gold, and red, and green. His cap was scarlet, and edged with gold twist; his tunic red, and his apron of very bright green baize. On his cap, and on one shoulder, appeared his number, 32, in figures of brass, an inch and a half in length. Strapped on his back he carried an oblong block of wood, like a great club-foot, and nearly as large as himself. This he deposited, with elaborate fuss, on the curb of the inner pavement, which terraced some inches above the true thoroughfare. A blacking-jar hung at one end of his block; from a drawer below he pulled out three well-worn brushes, and began to hiss and to work away, in double quick time, with both hands, at some boot projected towards him on the delicate foot of fancy. As he grew warm at his work, with one sharp eye all the while looking out for a genial passenger, there slowly came straggling towards him a bevy quite fresh from Arcadia. First, in treble importance walked, impressively rolling and leering around, Hermes, Pan, and the owl of Pallas, combined in one Ebenezer Dawe. His eyes, never too co-operative, roved away upon either side, in quest of intelligence, which they received with a blink that meant, "Pooh, don't I know it?" With occasional jerks of his lank right arm, he was dragging along, like a saw through a knot, the sturdy, tight-buttoned, and close-pronged form of our little Jack. Jack was arrayed in a black wide-awake, with blue ribbons, and a bran-new suit of broad-furrowed corduroy, made of nights by his mother and Suke, and turned out with countless pockets, each having three broad buttons, to foil the London thieves. In one of these pockets, the trouser one I do believe, in spite of all Sally had taught him, he was now chinking, to the creak of the corduroys, his last-abiding halfpence, and lagging heavily on the poet's arm, he cast fond glances at a pile of glorious peg-tops. Sticking her toes into little Jack's heels, to kick anybody that dared to steal him, came my little Sally, all fire, and wonder, and self-assertion, towing her mighty father along, like a grasshopper leading an ox. At times she strove to drag him towards the finery of the windows, and paid very little heed to his placid protestations. "Walk fitty, my dear; walk as you ought to do, my dear. Oh fai! oh fai! Whatever wull they Lunnoners think of Davonsheer, if they zees you agooin on laike this here? There, dang that Beany Dawe; blest if I baint a toornin Poüt too. Coomth of larnin to wraite, I reckon." The farmer's pockets were crammed with circulars, handbills, and puffs of every description, which he received from all who offered, and was saving them all for his wife.

"Clean your boots, my gentleman," cried a little shrill voice; "clean both your boots for a halfpenny. Never say die, Sir; polish 'em bright till the cat at home won't know them. Three-fardings-worth of blacking, and a penny in skill and labour, and all for the laughable sum of one half-penny. Pure satisfaction guaranteed, or the whole of the money returned. Up with your foot, my gentleman!"

The farmer pulled up suddenly, for fear of walking over him, as the boy, despising Beany Dawe, had dashed in between Jack and Sally, and danced before Mr. Huxtable. His brushes were whisking about, like bumble-bees roughly disturbed, and already menaced the drab of the Sunday fustian gaiters.

"Zober now," cried the farmer, who could not believe that he was addressed, having never dreamed, in his most ambitious moments (if any such he had), of ever being called a gentleman, "zober now, wull'e. Where bee'st gooin to, thou little hosebird; be they your Lunnon-town manners? Lat alo-un, I zay; lat alo-un now, wull 'e?"--as the boy got more and more tentative--"Heart alaive, cant e zee, they be my Zunday gaiters? Oh, if my missus wor here! And 'e bain't more nor naine year old! Wull, wull, where ever do 'e goo to schoüll?"

"Hinstitooshun 66. No children or females admitted. Up with your foot, old bloke! Do the young uns and tootor half-price. Just two minutes to spare, till the Dook of Cambridge's turn. Great Exhibition polish, and all to encourage the fine arts."

The good farmer was lost beyond hope, in the multitude of subjects pressed all of a pulp on his slow understanding; nevertheless, he had presence of mind to feel first for his watch and his money, and then for the best pocket-handkerchief stitched into the crown of his hat; meanwhile the boy got hold of one foot, and began to turn up his gaiters. Then Sally and little Jack rushed to the rescue, and Jack punched the boy in the face, while Beany Dawe looked on with a grin of broad experience. But in spite of all aid, the farmer began to collapse before his mosquito enemy; when luckily three giant Life-guards (for a crowd was now collected) opened their mouths, like the ends of a monkey-fur muff, in a round and loud guffaw, with a very coarse sneer at poor Sally. The farmer looked at them in much amazement; then his perplexity went like a cloud, and his face shone with something to do, as he gave Sally his hat to hold. Till now all the mockers had been too small for him anyhow to fall foul of. Ere the echo of laughter was over, the three dandy Lifeguards lay on their backs in the mud, with their striped legs erect in the air, like the rods of a railway surveyor. The crowd fell back headlong, as if from a plunging horse, then laughed at the fallen and with the conqueror. Even the boy was humility multiplied into servility.

"Wutt be up to, arl on 'e?" asked the farmer, replacing his hat; "cas'n none on 'e lat a pacible chap alo-un? And wutt will they chillers think as coom here to get example? Why, Beany, if us had knowed this, us would have brought Bill constable with us, ees fai. Now 'e don't know nothing about it"--he remonstrated with the admiring multitude--"one o' them dree worn't throw handsome laike, ony dree pins, I tull 'e. But us'll do it over again, if he claimeth it. Can't do nothing vitty, zin I laved my missus at home. But her wadn't coom, God knows." These last two remarks were addressed to himself, but the crowd had full benefit of them. "Worn't 'e axing of lave, two or dree minutes agone, little chap with the brisk there, to tend my butts, and tuk it amost wiout axing? Us be bound laike to stap here now till us zees if them 'lisher men feels up for any moor plai. Do as 'e plase, little chap, zoon as Sally hath toorned my best gaiters up, if her bain't too grand in Lunnon."

With bright ribbons fluttering and finery flapping about her, poor Sally knelt down in a moment to work at the muddy fustian: but her father would not allow it, he had only wished to try her; so he caught her up with one hand, and kissed her, and I think, from what Mrs. Fletcher said, he must have given her sixpence at least.

It is needless to say that, although the boy worked with both hands in the most conscientious manner, the farmer's boots defied him. Neats'-foot oil, and tallow, and beeswax held their own against Day and Martin. "Coom, little chap," said Mr. Huxtable, kindly, "thee hast dooed thy very best, but our Zuke will have the laugh of thee. Tache thee perhaps it wull to be zoberer next taime, and not be quite so peart to do a dale more nor thee can do. But thee hast used more ink than ai wud over two copies. Here be a groat for the Exhibition polish."

In this little episode, as will be manifest, Sally has helped me more than Mrs. Fletcher. But now, to return to my narrative.

Almost directly after the housekeeper left me, Patty came trotting in with a large white breakfast-cup full of most powerful tea. I cannot help thinking that the little woman put some brandy in it, or allowed Mrs. Fletcher, who trusted much in that cordial, to do so; but they stoutly deny the charge, and declare that there was only a pinch of gunpowder. Whatever it was, being parched with thirst, I swallowed without tasting it, and the effect upon my jaded brain was immediate and amazing. All self-pity was gone; and self-admiration, and haughty courage succeeded. Was I, Clara Vaughan, who had groped and grubbed for years to find the hole of a blasting snake, and had now got my hand upon it, was I to start back and turn pale at his hiss, and say, "God speed you and polish your skin. Give me your slough for a keepsake?" Would I not rather seize the incarnate devil, trample his spine, and make his tongue sputter in dust? In a moment my cloak and hat were on again; I scarcely looked at the glass, but felt the hot flush on my cheeks, as I lightly skipped down the stairs, and silently left the house. What to do next I knew not, nor asked, but flew headlong before the impulse, to lift and confront--as is my nature--the danger that lay before me. As I glided along, I was conscious of one thing, the people in the street turned in surprise to watch me. As if by instinct, I hurried straight to Lucas Street, my courage mounting higher and higher as I neared the accursed threshold. Balaam and Balak stood at the bar of a tavern which commanded a view of the street, but were much too busy with beer to see me passing so swiftly. Loudly I rang the bell of No. 37; the figures were bright on the door, and looking narrowly, I perceived the old No. 19, more by the lines than the colour.

Old Cora came as usual; but started at seeing me, and turned as pale as death.

"Is your master within?" I could not use his false name.

"Yes, Meesa, but you not see him now."

"Dare you to disobey Our Lady's heart?" And I held my gordit before her. She cowered with one knee on the mat and kissed it; then led me into the presence of Lepardo Della Croce.

CHAPTER VIII.

It was a dark and gloomy room, with three high, narrow windows. Cora departed hastily, frightened at what she had done. In a recess at the farther end, before a chest of black bog-oak, sat the man I sought. The crowning moment of my life was come. All rehearsals went for nothing: the strongest feeling of my heart was scorn, cold, unfathomable scorn. To show myself well, I took off my hat, and advanced in my haughtiest manner.

As he turned his head, I saw that his mood was blacker than the oak before him. Some dark memorials perhaps were there; hastily and heavily he flung down the lid, as I walked with even steps towards him.

"Ah! Miss Valence! The young lady that paints. I feared that you were lost to London; for now-a-days the pursuit of the fine arts requires either genius, or fashion, at any rate the latter most, to be at all remunerative. May I show you the way to the drawing-room? I have not often the honour of receiving visitors here. But I think you know how entirely I am the slave of young ladies, Miss Valence." And he held out his delicate hand.

"Lepardo Della Croce, my name is not Valence. I am Clara Vaughan, the only child of him whom in his sleep you murdered."

He turned not pale, but livid. His jaunty nonsense was gone in a moment. He quailed from my dark eyes, and fell upon a chair. For one minute there he crouched, and dared not meet my gaze; every fibre of his flesh was quivering. It was not shame that cowed him, but the prostration of amazement.

Suddenly he leaped upright, and met me eye to eye. Then I saw that his pupils turned towards each other, as my uncle had described. I neither spoke, nor allowed my gaze to falter. Every nerve and cord of my frame was tense, and rigid, and rooted. To him I must have seemed the embodiment of revenge.

At last he spoke, very slowly, and in words that trembled.

"You have no right to judge me by your English notions. You do not understand me."

"I judge you not at all. God shall judge and smite you. In cold blood you murdered a man who never wronged you."

"What!" he burst forth in a blaze of triumph, "no wrong to steal my lovely bride, and my noble inheritance, to debauch the purest blood of Corsica by a prostitute wedding; no wrong to strike me senseless! Even your nation of policemen would call this rather initiative."

"The man you stole upon in his sleep had never seen or heard of you, had never been in Corsica."

"What?" His teeth struck together like fire-tongs badly jointed, and he could not part them.

"It is true. I regret to inform you that you must go to hell for nothing. You could not even murder the right man."

"Tell me."

"Like a coward as you are, you crawled, and lurked, and lied; you spent what little mind you have in securing a baby's blow, you crouched among old clothes and bed-ticks, and behind the housemaid's flask; and you went away exulting in your bloody soul, over what? the wrong man's murder."

"Can it be?"

"Not only this, but you enriched and brought into high position the man you meant to kill. He became the lord of his half-brother's lands, and now is wealthy and happy, and the children you stole will help him to laugh at your Vendetta."

"Wait a little."

"Cats and small dogs you can carve alive, when a woman has strapped them down for you, and the poor things are trying to lick you. But as for midnight murder, however sound your victims sleep, you have not nerve enough. You quake and quiver so that you know not a dark man from a fair. Clever, don't you think? Particularly for a Professor."

I saw that my contempt was curling round him like a knout; so I gave him a little more of it.

"Of course we could not expect you to meet your foe like a man. Even were you a worthy sample of your sneaking race, you never could do that. Too wholesome memory of the English blow between your quailing eyes. I am pleased to see you fumbling clumsily for your dagger. Who knows but what you are fool enough even to have some self-respect?"

A black tint darted beneath his skin, as if his heart were a cuttle-fish. Had I taken my eyes from him, he would have stabbed me. He fell back against the oak chest. My madness grew with my triumph.

"No. You dare not do it, because I am not asleep. Come, I will give you every chance, Lepardo Della Croce. If you are brave enough to shoot a white-haired man at dinner, surely you have the courage to stab a young girl on the sofa. Here I lie. I will not move. And I defy you to do it."

Quietly I lay and watched him; but as if he were scarcely worth it. He could not take his eyes from mine. He was like a rat before a snake. And all the while, his hand was working on the cross haft of a poniard.

"What more can I do to encourage you? Would you like the curtain to skulk behind?"

And I threw the window-hangings over the foot of the sofa, but so that I held him still in view. Calm as I was, I must have been mad to play with my life so contemptuously. Presently I rose, put back my hair and turned away, as in weariness.

"I fear your appetite is cloyed with the writhings of cats and dogs. Or has murder no relish for you, unless it be in cold blood? But there, I am tired of you: you have so little variety. We will send you back to Corsica, and write 'Rimbecco' on you."

He sprang at me madly, gnashing his teeth, and whirling his stiletto. I faced him just in time, with both hands by my side. Had I raised them, or shown the least sign of fear, my life would have followed my father's then and there.

"Yes," I said, while he paused, with the weapon not a yard from me, "a spirited attempt, considering what you are. But waste of time and trouble. However, I have hit the word which seems to suit your views. Allow me to repeat the agreeable term, 'Rimbecco.'"

I saw in his eyes the flash which shows the momentum given, but his arm fell powerless. He looked even humbly at me.

"Clara Vaughan--"

"Be kind enough to address me properly."

"Miss Vaughan, you must have some powerful reason for wishing to be rid of life." He tried to look piercingly at me.

"You are quite mistaken. It is nothing more than contempt of an abject coward and murderer."

"To you I will make no attempt to justify myself. You could not understand me. Your ways of thought are wholly different."

"I beg leave to hope so. Don't come near me, if you please."

"If I have injured you in ignorance, I will do my best to make amends. What course do you propose?"

"To let you go free, in pity for your abject nature and cowardice. We scorn you too much for anything else."

This seemed to amaze him more than all before. It was plain that he could not believe me. A long silence ensued. Looking at the wily wretch, I began unwittingly to compare, or rather to contrast his noble victim with him. I thought of the deep affliction and misery wrought by his despicable revenge. I thought of his brutal cruelty to the poor creatures God has given us; and a rancour like his own began to move in my troubled heart. It had been there all the while, no doubt, but a larger pressure had stilled it. Watching me intently, he saw the change in my countenance, and as cold disdain grew flushed with anger, my power over him departed. But he did not let me perceive it. I am sure that I might have gone whither and when I pleased, and he would have feared to follow me, if I had only regarded him to the end with no other emotion than scorn.

"Am I to understand," he said at last, "that you intend to do nothing to me?"

"It is not worth our while to hang you. For such a crime any other punishment would be an outrage and a jest. You slew a good and a gentle man; one as brave as you are cowardly. By the same blow you destroyed his wife, who lingered for a few years, pining till she died. Both of these were dear to God. He will avenge them in His good time. Only one thing we shall insist on, that you leave this country immediately, and under a solemn oath never to return to it. One good point you have, I am told--fidelity to your word."

"And if I refuse, what then?"

"Then you die a murderer's death. We have evidence you little dream of."

He had now recovered his presence of mind, and his scoffing manner; and all his plan was formed.

"What a brave young lady you are to come here all alone, and entertaining so low an opinion of the poor Professor."

"The very reason why I scorned precautions." A deep gleam shot through the darkness of his eyes.

"You must indeed despise me, to come here without telling any one!"

"Of course. But I did not mean to come, till my father's spirit led me."

With a shudder he glanced all round the room. Lily was not mistaken when she called him superstitious. Then he tried to sneer it off.

"And did the good Papa, dear to God, undertake to escort you back?" Seeing that I disdained to answer, he continued thus: "You have displayed much graceful and highly-becoming scorn. I, in turn, will exhibit some little contempt of you. You were pleased to say, if my memory serves me, that you had some wonderful evidence. I will furnish you with more, and perhaps what you little dream of. Approach, and examine this box."

He raised the lid of the oaken chest, and propped it with a staple. Quite thrown off my guard for the moment, I began to devour the contents with my eyes. Not many things were in it; but all of them were remarkable. To me they looked like theatrical properties, or materials for disguise. Some of them were faded and tarnished; some were set with a silver cross. My gaze was rivetted on a pair of boots, fixed in a ledge with horse-shoe bays; on the sole of one I perceived a cross of metal inlaid; I drew nearer to see it more closely, when something fell over my head. All down me, and round me, and twisted behind in a tight *tourniquet*, before I could guess what it was. I am not weak, for a girl; but I could no more lift my arms than a swathed mummy can. Neither could I kick, although as a child I had been famous for that accomplishment; if I lifted either foot, I must tumble head-foremost into the box, which was large enough for me to live in. Scream I could, and did, in spite of all my valour, not only from fright, but from pain, for my chest was dreadfully tightened; but before I could scream more than twice, a cloth was passed over my mouth, and knotted behind my neck. So there I stood, a helpless prisoner, in the recess at the end of the oaken ark. A low laugh thrilled in my ears, but the hand on my spine relaxed not; I turned my neck by a violent effort and met the demon's eyes.

"Very pretty you look, young lady, very pretty indeed. I must have a kiss before I have done with you, in spite of all indignation. There is a dress resembling this among the Tartar tribes. Did I hurt your proud, straight nose? If so, accept most humble apologies. I would not injure it for the world; it does express so much scorn. Take care, my child, your eyelashes are coming through the worsted."

Yes. Ignoble confession! I, for whose disdain the world had been too small, was prisoned and helpless in an "anti-macassar," like a fly in a paper cage-trap. The sofa, on which I had lain so grandly defying my enemy, was covered with a stout worsted net, long and very strong: this he had doubled end to end, and flung over my haughty head. I have not patience to recount his paltry, bantering jeers. Contempt is a tool I am used to grasp by the handle only. Be it enough to say that, without releasing me, he rang the bell for Cora, whose greedy eyes glistened when she saw my gordit loose from my bosom, and tangled in the net. Her master allowed her to disengage, and, for the time at least, appropriate it. In return for this, she was, at his pleasure, to stab me if he should order it. By his directions, she tied my ankles together, while he lashed my arms anew, and tightened the muffler over my bleeding lips. I closed my eyes, and prayed; then I made up my mind to die, as many a Vaughan had done, at the hands of a brutal enemy. My last thought was of Conrad, and then my senses forsook me.
CHAPTER IX.

I have a faint recollection of feeling myself swung, and jolted down a number of stairs, and of a cold breeze striking on my face. And doubtless they carried me down; for the room in which I had found my enemy was two floors above the cellarage. When I came to myself, I had no idea where in the world I was. The air was heavy with a most powerful and oppressive smell, a reek and taint as of death and corruption. It made me faint, and I think I must have gone off again. Lifting my head at last, I began to look languidly around. The table, or working-bench, on which I lay, was near the centre of a long and narrow room, gloomy and cold, even in the dog-days, floored with moss-green stone, and far below the ground-level. Those flag-stones, I suppose, were bedded immediately upon the tough blue London clay, that most unconquerable stratum, sullen, damp, and barren. I could only see two windows in the long low room, both upon the same side, horizontally fixed, and several feet from the floor. Heavy iron bars, perpendicularly set, crossed them at narrow intervals, as if it had been the condemned cell in a prison. One of these windows was already darkened with a truss of straw, and sacks over it, placed outside the glass; as is done in Corsica, during Vendetta siege. The technical term is "inceppar le fenestre." Through the other window (which looked up a slide or scoop of brickwork, like a malt-shovel, to the flabby garden behind the house), I saw an arm, the colour and shape of an American herring, very active with a hammer.

I knew that arm at once. Sticking out at the joints, like the spurs of a pear-tree, welted and wired with muscle between them, like the drumstick of a turkey, but flat as if plaited of hide, no friend of mine could claim it, except the Corsican Cora. Deliberately she drove the nails, like a gardener training a tree, paying undue attention to her skinny knuckles; then she lifted the sacks, stooped down and looked in, grimly reconnoitring me. By the slanting light I saw what a horrible place I lay in. Around and under me, on the furrowed timber, were dull plum-coloured blotches, where the slowly trickling blood of many an unlucky dog and cat had curdled; even if there were not any shed from nobler veins. Reaching in a back-handed way towards the jagged margin, I grasped a cold hard cylinder. It was an iron hold-fast, like, but larger than the instrument to be seen in every carpenter's bench, which works in a collared hole, and has a claw for clutching. Under it, no doubt, many a poor live victim had quivered and sobbed in vain. At my head were two square slides, fitted with straps of stout unyielding web. Near them was a rasped iron plane working along a metal bed or groove, with a solid T piece, and a winch to adjust it.

As with morbid observation I surveyed these fiendish devices, and many others which I cannot stop to tell of, I who love almost every creature made by our own Maker, especially those to whom we are lent as Gods, my flesh, I say, began to creep, and my blood to curdle, as if the dissecting knife were already in my diaphragm. Surely those who in full manhood torture His innocent creatures--poor things that cannot plead or weep, but worship the foot that kicks them--surely these, if any, we may without presumption say that He who made will judge. Four brief lines by a modern poet, too well known for me to quote them, express a grand and simple truth, seldom denied, more seldom felt.

But here am I, laid out in this fearful place, perhaps myself a subject for vivisection. No, I am not strapped; even my feet are free. Off the grouted and grimy table I roll with all possible speed, the table where even strong Judy must have lain still as a skeleton. Of skeletons there were plenty ranged around the walls, and other hideous things which I cannot bear to think of. One was a monstrous crocodile, with scales like a shed fir-cone, all reflexed and dry, and ringent lips of leather, and teeth that seemed to look the wrong way, like a daisy-rake over-worked. Another was some pulled-out beast, that never could hit his own joints again--plesiosauri, deinosauri, marsupials, proboscidians--I am sure I cannot tell, having never been at college. I only know that at every one of them I shuddered, and shrugged my shoulders, and wished that he smelled rather nicer. Then there were numbers of things always going up and down, in stuff like clarified syrup, according to the change of temperature, just as leeches do in a pickle-bottle. Snakes as well, and other reptiles streaked like sticks of peppermint, and centipedes, and Rio wrigglers, called I think La Croya. It was enough in that vault-like room, which felt like the scooping of an August iceberg; it was more than enough to strike a chill to the marrow, as of one who sleeps in a bed newly brought from the cellar. But the worst and most horrible thing of all was the core and nucleus of the smell that might be felt, the half-dissected body of a porpoise, leaning on a dozen stout cross-poles. It was enough to make the blood of a dog run cold.

Overpowered by sights and smells, and the fear of mingling with them, I huddled away in a corner, and tried in vain to take my eyes from the only sign of life yet left, the motion of Cora's club-like arm. The poor old woman enjoyed my interest in her work, and when she had finished, she made me a mock salaam, and kissed the pixie's heart. Then, with a grin, she dropped the rough hangings, and left me in ghastly twilight.

As the sacks fell over the window-frame, I lost all presence of mind, all honest indignation, everything but a coward horror, and the shrinking of life from death. With all the strength of my chest and throat, I cast forth, as a cannon discharges, one long, volleyed, agonising shriek. As it rang among the skeletons, and rattled their tissue-less joints, a small square grating in the upper panel of the heavy door swung back, and in the opening appeared the face of Lepardo Della Croce. He lifted his hat with a pleasant air, and addressed me with a smile,

"Ah! now, this I call a pity, a great pity, indeed, Miss Vaughan; but that I always fear the imputation of pedantry, I should call it a bathos. You can hardly be aware that since you made that dreadful noise, you have fallen in my opinion from a Porcia, or an Arria, to a common maid Marian. Fie, fie, it is too disappointing. It saps one's candid faith in the nobility of human nature. But, as I can no longer appeal to your courage or spirit, I must, it appears, address myself to your reason; if, as I am fain to hope, your nerves have not impaired it. Be assured, then, once for all, that it is a vulgar error to exert your sweet voice in so high a key. My little dissecting theatre, though not so perfect as I could wish, particularly in ventilation, is nevertheless so secured from erroneous plebeian sympathy, that all the cats in London might squall away their fabulous nine lives without affecting the tea and muffins of the excellent old ladies who live on either side of us. That noble tabby, on the third shelf right, was a household god at No. 39, until he had the honour of attracting my attention. Breathe not a word about him, if you ever come out. Twice a day, I sent to inquire, with my kindest compliments, whether poor Miss Jenkinson had recovered her darling cat. Meanwhile, by inanition scientifically graduated, I succeeded in absorbing his adipose deposit, and found him one of the kindest subjects I have had the pleasure of manipulating. Be not alarmed, Miss Vaughan; I have no intention of starving you; neither, if you behave with courtesy, will I even dissect you. I only mention these little facts to convince you of our pleasing retirement. The ceiling of your room is six feet below the level of the street, the walls are three feet thick and felted, and the bricks set all as headers, which makes a great difference in conducting power. The windows, as perhaps you have already observed, are secluded from vulgar eyes, and command a very partial view of our own little Eden. Moreover, if by exerting your nobly-developed chest, to an extent which for your sake I affectionately deprecate, you even succeeded at last in producing an undulation--do you remember my lecture upon the conflicting theories of sound?--or a vibration in the tympanum of a neighbour, I fear you would be regarded--it shocks me greatly to think of it--as a cat of rare vocal power, unduly agitated by my feeble pursuit of science. Therefore, let me conclude my friendly counsel in the language of all your theatres--ah! you have no drama now in this country, such poverty of invention--but in the words, which I regret to say, appear from six to a dozen times in every British trugody, Miss Vaughan, 'Be calm.'"

Through all this brutal sneering, I stood resolutely with my back turned to him. Perhaps he thought that I would stoop to supplication. I could have bitten my tongue off for that contemptible shriek; it was such a triumph to him.

"Ah! sulky, I fear; young lady sulky with the poor Professor, who tries to develop her mind. Fie, fie, very small and ungrateful, and not half so grand a study as the attitude of contempt. What a pity poor Conrad was not present an hour ago! How he might have enriched his little book of schemata. Several most magnificent poses. But I fear the poor fellow has taken his last chip. A sad thing, was it not? Why, how you start, Miss Vaughan! Oh, you can show your face at last! And how pale! Well, if eyes could only kill--"

"What is it--I mean be good enough just to go away."

"To be sure I will. I have a little matter on hand which must not be delayed; to leave my carte de visite upon the right man, this time. I cannot sufficiently thank you for your invaluable information. Is that snug little entrance practicable still? Very hospitable people they used to be at Vaughan Park. Fare you well, young lady; I will not keep you in any unnecessary suspense. After my return, I shall arrange for your release; if it can be made compatible with my safety. You will have plenty of food, and much time for meditation. Let your thoughts of me be liberal and kindly. I never injure any one, when I can avoid it. I only regret that the air you breathe will impair, for the while, your roses. But what an opportunity of analysing the gases! Carbonic acid predominant. Do you gratify me by bearing in mind a lecture, at which you were very attentive, on Malaria and Miasma?"

Taunting to the last, and sneering even at himself, as men of the blackest dye of wickedness are very apt to do, he closed the grating carefully, and I heard the ring of the metal cross on the rough stone steps. He had the boots of vengeance on; his errand was stealthy and cold-blooded murder; me, who had never harmed him, he was abandoning perhaps to death, certainly to madness--and yet to his own ideas, all he was doing was right.

Frantic at the horrors around me, and still more so at those impending through my own rash folly, I tore and scratched at the solid door, and flung myself against it, till my nails were broken, and my fingers bleeding, and all my body palpitating with impotent mad fury. In weariness at last and shame at this wild outburst, I sat upon the floor, for I could not touch the operator's stool, and tried to collect my thoughts. Was there any possibility of saving my poor Uncle? It must now be nearly four o'clock on the Friday afternoon, or at least I so computed it. The beautiful watch given me by my Uncle had stopped through my reckless violence, and the breaking of the glass. The hands, as I could barely perceive, stood at a quarter to four. The express-train, by which Mrs. Fletcher and I were to have returned, would leave Paddington at five P.M. and reach Gloucester soon after eight. Lepardo Della Croce would catch it easily, and perhaps would accomplish his foul design that night. My only hope of preventing him lay in his own tenacity of usage. From my Uncle's account, I knew, that on their cursed Vendetta enterprises, a certain pilgrimage on foot is, in many families, regarded as a matter of honour. This usage owes its origin perhaps to some faint trace of mercy, some wish to afford the evil passions one more chance of relenting to the milder reflections of weariness, and the influence of the air. Be that as it may, I believed that the custom was hereditary in the Della Croce family; and if so, the enemy would finish his journey on foot, quitting the train some distance on this side of Gloucester. Therefore if I could contrive to escape in the course of the night, I might yet be in time.

All the rest of the daylight, such as it was, I spent in examining, inch by inch, every part of the loathsome chamber, which was now my dungeon. By this time all my patience, habitual more than natural, had returned, and all my really inborn determination and hope. Surely I had been every bit as badly off before, and had struggled through quite as hopeless a difficulty. If arduous courage and tough perseverance were of any avail, those four walls should not hold me, though they might be three feet thick. So stopping both my nostrils with cotton-wool from a specimen (for the smell was most insufferable), and pinning up my dress, I set to work in earnest. First, I examined the windows: there was nothing to hope from them; I could never loosen a bar, and even if I could, I should only escape from one prison to another, for the garden behind the house was surrounded with high dead walls. Fireplace there was none; the door had already baffled me; could I dig through the party wall, and into the adjoining house? Most likely it was all a falsehood and boast about the thickness, intended perhaps to discourage me from attempting the easiest way. And in so damp a place, the mortar probably would be soft.

So, after searching and groping, ever so long, to find, if possible, one loose brick to begin with, I drew from my pocket a knife, of which I was very proud, "because my father had given it me; and I looked at it wistfully in the dusk, because I feared so to break it. Nothing but the thought that life itself was at stake would ever have induced me to use that beloved knife for work so very unsuitable.

It was a knife of strong but by no means elegant make, shorter in the handle, and squarer in the joints, than the rising generation of knives. Very likely Sheffield of the present day would laugh at it; but like most who laugh, it could not produce the fellow. My father himself had owned it for nearly thirty years, and had treated it with the high respect which an honest knife deserves. From this due regard his daughter had not derogated, and the knife was now as good as when it left the maker's hand. It had never been honed in utter ignorance of proper plane and angle, as nearly all knives are, and by none so often as the professional knife-grinder. I never dared to meddle with it, except on a very mild razor-strap; and all it was allowed to do was to mend my pens--I, Clara Vaughan, hate steel paper-stabbers--and sometimes to cut my pencils.

Now, this true and worshipful knife was to cut bricks and mortar! In my natural affection for it, I hesitated and trembled, and knowing what was to come it closed upon my fingers. Oh, ruthless Atta Nævia! trusty knife, fall to!

Meanwhile old Cora showed at the heavy grating her countenance demiss; to all my eager adjurations, promises, and prayers, she answered not a word, but grimly smiled, like an ancient bird, beyond the reach of chaff. She handed me in a pint of milk, and a loaf of the variety termed in London a "twopenny brick." A red herring on the toasting-fork, dripping with its own unction, was hastily shown, and then withdrawn, and the gordit appeared in its stead; which being done, the experienced dame winked, and regarded me deeply. This meant, "Surrender your legal right in Our Lady's heart, without which I shall have no luck, and I will give you this beautiful fish, hard-roed, and done to a nicety." Ah no, sweet Cora, a good red herring is not to be despised; but who could eat in a reeking hole like this? Once I went, for Judy's sake, being rash and light of step, into the back premises of a highly respectable butcher. Woe is me, what I saw and smelt there was Muscat grapes compared to this.

When Cora had departed, after handing me in a pillow and a blanket of the true work-house texture, and crossing herself with a strange expression, meaning, as I interpreted, "Now keep alive if possible till breakfast time, young woman," I sat me down upon the floor at one end of the room, and began my labours. First. I put on a pair of tan-leather gloves; for small as my vanity is, I do not like my hands to look altogether like a hodman's. Then I removed a strip of the felt with which the wall was covered. It was nearly dark, but I could easily feel the joints between the bricks. The mortar was not very good, but my work was rendered doubly difficult by the bricks being all set cross-wise to the line of the wall; this, I suppose, is what he meant when he described them as "headers." By reason of this arrangement, I had to dig and dig for hours, before I could loosen a single brick; and working all in the dark as I was, I feared every moment to break the stick-blade of my knife. The fingers of my gloves were very soon worn away, and even the palm where the heel of the knife was chafing; nor was it long before my skin was full of weals, and raspy, like the knobs I have seen inside the legs of a horse. At last, to my wonderful delight, one brick began to tremble. In another half-hour, I eased it out most carefully, kissed my trusty blade, now worn almost to a skewer, and with stiff and aching muscles, and the trophy brick upon my lap, fell off into as sound a sleep as ever I was blest with.

CHAPTER X.

When I awoke, the summer dawn was stealing faintly through the barricaded windows. Oh! how I longed for one draught of air, even as London imports it! My head was burning and my eyes distended from the tainted stuff around me, and my hands, and arms, and even shoulders were stiff from over exertion. Languidly regarding the brick I had worked so hard for, and commiserating much the plight of my tender hands, I felt inclined to give it up, till I thought of all at stake. My poor Uncle in deadly peril through my desperate folly; Conrad too, as that murderer implied, in a critical position. My own life also--it might be a week before the monster returned; and I felt sure that I could not live more than three days in that corruption. The oppression was so horrible, especially when I stood up, that I resolved at all hazards to break one of the windows. I had tried to do so the night before, but they were beyond my reach, and I had no stick, for I durst not touch the poles that propped the unlucky porpoise. Now, I had a good missile, and after two or three vain attempts from the closeness of the bars, I hurled the brick-bat through the glass; and, as it raised the sacks a little, I obtained more light, as well as a breath of air. The taint upon the glass, the reek of the deadly gases, even cleared away for a short distance round the fracture.

Cora was fast asleep no doubt, and the crash of the glass did not disturb her; so I fell to again, and worked very hard till breakfast time. If I could only get out by noon, in time for the two o'clock train! When I expected my jailor, I hid away under the porpoise the seven bricks I had removed since daylight--for I could work much faster as the aperture increased--and then I fastened my blanket over the hole. After drinking the milk with some relish--eat I could not in that pestilential den--I returned to my labour, and prepared to attack the second course in the thickness of the wall. By this time I had contrived, with the help of a brick, to extract the hold-fast from the bench, which I could not do the night before; and very useful I found it, both as a hammer and lever. So with rising hopes, I resumed.

Oh, cruel disappointment! The second course was bedded in cement harder than the bricks themselves. Most likely they had formed the outside of the wall, until Lepardo added the nine-inch lining of headers. I was utterly dismayed; and now my beloved knife, which had stood like a hero-martyr all its grinding indignities, broke off short at the haft, and left me helpless and hopeless. And I was getting on so well, and so proud of all I had done. There was nothing for it but a storm of crying. It served me right for ill-treating my dear father's knife so shockingly.

I cried for at least a quarter of an hour, before it occurred to me what a great baby I was. Then, with the tears in my swollen eyes, and sobs that made my net-pressed bosom sore, I began to grope and peer again along the sides of my prison. There was more light now than had hitherto entered, since Cora dropped the curtain. This was partly owing to the position of the sun, and partly to the interposition of the brick. Just opposite that window, on a shelf where lay an old Penguin looking very bilious, I spied the corner of a little box, half covered with tow and moth-eaten feathers. Snatching it eagerly, I found it to be a match-box. But alas, how light! With trembling fingers I pulled it open, for it was one of those that slide. There were three, and only three, fine stout lucifer matches, with the precious blue still on them. But even if they should prove dry enough to kindle, what good would they be to me?

"All the good in the world," said hope, looking towards the door, "if you had shown sense enough, Clara, to fall to at that door, before your knife was broken, you might have cut through it by this time. Now you can't, that is certain; but why shouldn't you burn it down?"

At any rate, I would try; that is, if my matches would only strike fire. I had felt last night a piece of candle on the floor near the crocodile. This I soon laid hands upon; and now for operations. No fear of old Cora smelling the smoke, for she spent all the forenoon, as I knew well, in a little chapel she had established quite at the top of the house; and this being the festival of St. Bottle-imp, she would be twice as devout as usual. As for suffocating myself, that I must take the chance of. Much better to die of curling wood smoke than of these crawling odours.

To give the wood, which was hard and solid, every inclination to burn, I channeled it first in a fan from the bottom with my little pen-blade. Then I cut off the lower half of my precious candle, and smeared the tallow in the shallow grooves I had made. This being done, I broke, with as little noise as possible, some other panes of glass, to admit the air to my fire, procured all the wool and tow that I could reach, and a pile of paper, and steeped them, though it sickened me to do it, in the rank oil from some of the specimens.

All this being ready at hand, I prepared, with a beating heart, to try the matches, on which the whole depended. I had taken the precaution of slipping them just inside my frock, hoping that the warmth of my body might serve to dry them a little. The first, as I rubbed it on the sandpaper, flashed for a moment, but did not kindle; the second just kindled with a sputter, but did not ignite its stick: the third--I was so nervous that I durst not attempt it then; but trembled as I looked at it. I would not even breathe for fear of damping the phosphorus. Perhaps three lives depended on the behaviour of that match. In desperation at last I struck boldly! a broad blue flame leaped upon the air, and in a moment my candle was lighted. In the hollow of my hand I carried it round the room, to search for anything likely to be of service to me. Oh! grand discovery--behind a great tabby cat, I found a bottle containing nearly a pint of naphtha, used, I suppose, for singeing some of the hair off. Now I need not fear, but what I could burn the door down; the only thing to fear was that I should burn myself as well, used the naphtha very cautiously, keeping most of it as a last resource.

Then commending the result to God, I set my candle carefully at the foot of the door, just below the spot where all my little grooves converged. At once the flame ran up them, the naphtha kindling angrily with a spatter and a hiss. The blue light showed in livid ghastliness all the horrors of the chamber. The naphtha was burnt in a moment, it seemed to go off like gunpowder; from a prudent distance I threw more upon it, and soon I had the delight of seeing a steady flame established. The lumps of tallow were burning now, and the wood began to smoulder. Several times I thought that I must be choked by the smoke, till it went in a cloud to the windows, and streamed away under the sacks.

As the fire grew and grew, and required no more feeding, I lay on my face, to get all the air possible, at the further end of the room, where my loose mortar was scattered. I could feel my heart thumping heavily on the pavement, and my breath was shorter and shorter, as much from fear as from smoke. If once I became insensible, or even if I retained my senses but failed to extinguish the fire, nothing more would ever be known or heard of Clara Vaughan; there would be nothing even to hold an inquest upon. I must burn ignobly, in the fat of that dreadful porpoise, and with the crocodile, and all those grinning beasts, so awful in the firelight, making faces at me! Surely it must be time, high time to put it out; that is to say if I could. Once let the flame gather head on the other side of the door, and with my scanty means I never could hope to quench it.

At last, I became so frightened, that I hardly let it burn long enough. It was flaring beautifully, and licking deeper and deeper (with ductile wreathing tongues and jets like a pushing crocus), the channels prepared to tempt it; and now the black wood was reddened, and a strong heat was given out, and the blazes began to roar; when I cast on the centre suddenly my doubled blanket, and propped it there with the pillow. After a few vain efforts, the flames, deprived of air, expired in gray smoke; then I removed the scorched blanket, and let the smouldering proceed.

The charring went on nicely for perhaps a quarter of an hour, and the smell made me think of bonfires and roast potatoes; and I gouged away with the claw of the holdfast, until I saw that, by a vigorous onset, a large piece might be detached; so I stepped back and ran at it with a mighty kick, and with a shower of dust and sparks, a great triangle flew out before my "military heel."

At the risk of setting myself on fire, though gathered in the smallest possible compass for a girl rather full in the chest, I squeezed through the hole in the door, and met face to face old Cora.

She could not speak, but fell back upon the steps, and rolled in fits of terror. I thought her black eyes would have leaped from their sockets; they came out like hat-pegs japanned. Pressed as I was for time, I could not leave her so. I ran up to the pump-trough for water, and put out the fire first, and then poor Cora's hysterics.

I cannot repeat her exclamations, to our ears they are so impious; but the mildest of them were these, as rendered weakly into English.

"Holy Madonna, most sacred mother, take back your blessed heart. Take it back, for the sake of the God that loved you, take it back, and trample on the wicked stomach of her who dared to steal it. You have come through the fires of hell to fetch it, mother of the beloved one, lo I hold it out to you."

I gladly received my poor gordit, and left the old lady, as there was now no danger, to recover her wits at leisure; for I had not a moment to spare.

As I entered Mrs. Shelfer's door, the church clock at the top of the Square was striking twelve. By the two o'clock train I must go, or I might as well have stopped in my dungeon. Though the smoke had purified me a little, I still felt conscious of a nasty clinging smell; but it would have surprised me, if there had been time, when the little woman cried,

"Lor bless my soul, Miss Vaughan, where ever have you been? Why, Mr. Chumps the butcher--"

"The bath in one moment, and all the water in the house. And as I throw my things out, burn them in the garden."

In twenty minutes I was reclad from head to foot, and as sweet as any girl in Gloucestershire; my eyes were bright with energy, and my dripping hair in billows, like a rapid under the pine-trees. I had no time to tell Mrs. Shelfer, who was off her legs with excitement, one word of what had happened, or what I was going to do; but flung on myself another hat and cloak, then her old bonnet and little green shawl on her, dragged her out of the house, and locked the door behind us; for Mrs. Fletcher, after waiting and wondering long about me, was gone to consult Ann Maples. If Mrs. Shelfer's best bonnet was twenty-two years old, her second-best must have been forty-four; at any rate it appeared coeval with herself.

Patty trotted along at my side, wondering what would come next. Her thin little lips were working, and her face was like a kaleidoscope of expressions; but whenever I glanced toward her, she cast her eyes up, with a scared weird look, as if she was watching a ghost through a skylight, and trudged still faster, and muttered, "Yes, yes, Miss Vaughan. Quite right, my good friend; not a moment to lose."

"And pray, Mrs. Shelfer, where do you suppose we are going?"

"Oh, I knows well enough "--with her eyes like corks drawn by distance--"I knowed it all the time. Yes, yes. Let me alone for that. Patty Shelfer wasn't born yesterday. Why only Tuesday was a week--"

"If you guess right, I will tell you."

"Why going to Charley, Miss Vaughan, to be sure. Going for Charley's opinion. And very wise of you too; and what a most every one does; particular when he have money. But how you knowed he were there--"

"Where?"

"At the great wrestling match to be sure. And he wanted to take me; a thing he ain't offered to do fifteen year next oyster-day. No, no, says I, with Miss Vaughan away, and most likely among them resurrectioners--"

Here she cast at me a glance, like a flash of lightning, to see if the hit had told. In a moment I understood all that I had not cared to ask about; why she trembled and shrunk from my hand, why she feared to look at me, and fixed her eyes away so. She believed that I had been burked, and that what she saw walking beside was my spirit come to claim burial. I could not stop to disprove it, any more than I could stop to laugh.

"And his grandfather were a sexton, Miss; and our Charley himself a first-rate hand at the spade."

"Mrs. Shelfer, we are close to the place. Now, listen to what I say. It is not your husband I want, but Farmer Huxtable, whom you saw at the door. Nothing but a question of life and death would bring me among this rabble. No doubt there are many respectable men, but it is no place for a lady. The farmer himself knows that, and has never dared to ask me; though his wife and daughter, in ignorance, have. It is half-past twelve exactly; in a quarter of an hour at the utmost, I must speak to, and what is more, carry off the Devonshire competitor. Your husband is here, and on the Committee, you told me. I expect you to manage it. Go in at once and find him. Stop, here is plenty of money."

In her supreme astonishment, she even dared to look at me. But she feared to take the money, although her eyes glistened at it, for I offered more gold than silver.

"Come back to me at once; I shall not move from here. Mind, if the farmer loses the match through me, I will pay all, and give the money for another."

For once the little woman obeyed me, without discussion. She pushed through a canvass door into the vast marquee, or whatever it ought to be called, and was admitted readily on giving her husband's name. I hung back, but with a sense of the urgency of my case, which turned my shame into pride. Many eyes were on me already of loungers and outsiders. In two or three minutes poor Patty came back, bringing Mr. Shelfer himself, who ever since his ducking had shown me the rose and pink of respect. He even went the length now of removing his pipe from his mouth.

"Very sorry indeed, Miss Vaughan, very sorry, you know. But we darrn't interrupt the men now. Our lives wouldn't be worth it, and they'd kill both the umpires and the referee too you know. Why it's fall for fall, only think of that, Miss Vaughan, it's fall for fall!" And the perspiration stood upon his forehead, and he wanted to run back.

"What do you mean?" In spite of my hurry, I felt deeply interested. How could I help it, loving the farmer so?

"Why, the Great Northern won the first throw by a bit of foul play, a foul stroke altogether, and no back at all, say I, and my eyes is pretty good; however, the umpires give it, and you should see John Huxtable's face, the colour of a scythe-stone; he knew it was unfair you know. And you should see him go in again for the second fall. 'I could ha dooed it,' I hear him say, 'I could ha dooed it aisy, only I wudn't try Abraham, and I wun't nother if can help it now.' None of us knows what he mean, but in he go again, Miss, and three times he throw Sam Richardson clean over his shoulder, and one as fair a back as ever was in sawdust. But the umpires wouldn't give it, till just now he turn him over straight for'ard, just the same as a sod in a spade, and they couldn't get out of that. And now they be just in for the finishing bout, and if you want him, your only way is to come. May be, he'll try Abraham, when he see you. Ah they've catched."

A shout inside proclaimed some crisis; Mr. Shelfer, in his excitement, actually pulled me in without knowing it. Once there, I could not go back; and the scene was a grand and thrilling one.

In the centre of a roped arena, hedged by countless faces, all rigid, flushed, and straining with suspense, stood two mighty forms; the strongest men in England and perhaps in all the world. A loose sack, or jerkin, of the toughest canvass, thrown back clear of the throat, half-sleeved, and open in front, showed the bole of the pollard neck, the solid brawn of the chest, and the cords of the outstretched arm. Stout fustian breeches, belted at waist, and strapped at knee, cased their vast limbs so exactly, yet so easily, that every curve was thew, and every wrinkle sinew. Thin white stockings, flaked with sawdust and looking rather wet, rolled and stood out, like the loops of a mace, with the rampant muscles of the huge calf, and the bulge of the broad foreleg.

As the shout proclaimed, they had caught or clutched; a thing which is done with much fencing and feinting, each foining to get the best grasp. Where I went, or what happened to me, I never noticed at all, so absorbed at once I became in this rare and noble probation of glorious strength, trained skill, and emulous manhood.

Round and round the ring they went, as in musical measure, holding each other at arms' length, pacing warily and in distance, skilfully poised to throw the weight for either attack or defence. Each with his left hand clutched the jerkin of the other, between the neck and shoulder, each kept his right arm lightly bent, and the palm like a butterfly quivering. Neither dared to move his eyes from the pupils of the other; for though they were not built alike, each knew the strength of his fellow. The Northern Champion was at least three inches taller than the Son of Devon, quite as broad in the shoulders and large of limb, but not so thick-set and close-jointed, not quite so stanch in the loins and quarters. But he was longer in the reach, and made the most of that advantage. On his breast he bore the mark of a hug as hard as a bear's; and his face, though a fine and manly one, looked rather savage and spiteful.

The farmer was smiling pleasantly, an honest but anxious smile. For the first time he had met with a man of almost his own power; and on a turn of the heel depended at least four hundred pounds, and what was more than four million to him, the fame of the county that nursed him. Above them hung the champion's belt, not of the west or north, but of England and of the world.

Suddenly, ere I could see how they did it, they had closed in the crowning struggle. Breast to breast, and thigh to thigh, they tugged, and strained, and panted. Nothing though I knew of the matter, I saw that the North-man had won the best hold, and as his huge arms enwrapped my friend, a tremble went through my own frame. The men of the North and their backers saw it, and a loud hurrah pealed forth; deep silence ensued, and every eye was intent. Though giant arms were round him and Titan legs inlocked, never a foot he budged. John Huxtable stood like a buttress. He tried not to throw the other; placed as he was, he durst not; but he made up his mind to stand, and stand he did with a vengeance. In vain the giant jerked and twisted, levered, heaved, and laboured, till his very eyeballs strained; all the result was ropes and bunches in the wide-spread Devonshire calves, and a tightening of the clench that threatened to crush the Northern ribs. As well might a coiling snake expect to uproot an oak.

As this exertion of grand stability lasted and outlasted, shouts arose and rang alike from friend and foe, from north, and west, and east; even I could not help clapping my feeble hands. But the trial was nearly over. The assailant's strength was ebbing; I could hear him gasp for breath under the fearful pressure. By great address he had won that hold, and made sure of victory from it, it had never failed before; but to use a Devonshire word, the farmer was too "stuggy." Now, the latter watched his time, and his motive power waxed as the other's waned. At length he lifted him bodily off his legs, and cast him flat on his back. A flat and perfectly level cast, as ever pancake crackled at. Thunders of applause broke forth, and scarcely could I keep quiet.

With amazement the farmer espied me as he was bowing on all sides, and amid the tumult and uproar that shook the canvass like a lark's wing, he ran across the ring full speed. Then he stopped short, remembering his laboured and unpresentable plight, and he would have blushed, if he had not been as red as fire already. None of such nonsense for me. I called him by name, took his hand, and with all my heart congratulated.

"But, farmer, I want you immediately, on a matter of life and death." Beany Dawe and the children came, but I only stopped to kiss Sally, and motioned them all away. "If you remember your promise to me, get ready for a journey in a moment, and run all the way to my lodgings. We must leave London, at two o'clock, to save my Uncle's life."

Mr. Huxtable looked astounded, and his understanding, unlike his legs, for the moment was carried away. Meanwhile up came Sally again, caught hold of my hand, and silently implored for some little notice, if only of her costume, violet, indigo, blue, green, yellow, orange and red. I could only kiss her again.

"Oh do come, farmer Huxtable, do come at once, I entreat you; or I must go alone and helpless."

"That you shan't, my dearie, dang Jan Uxtable for a girt lout."

"Please, sir, I am sent to tell you that the umpires gives it no fall, and you must play again."

The man looked abased by his errand; even he knew better. In my hurry I had paid no attention to the ominous hissing and hooting around a knot of men on the benches at the end.

The farmer's face I shall never forget; as he slowly gathered the truth, it became majestic with honest indignation. A strong man's wrath at deceit and foul play sat upon it, like a king on his throne.

"For the chillers--" he stammered at last--"ony for the poor chiller's sake--else I'd never stand it, danged if I wud, Miss Clara; it make a man feel like a rogue and a cheat himself."

Then, with all the power of his mighty voice he shouted, so that every fold of the canvass shook, and every heart thrilled fearfully:

"Men of Lunnon, if men you be, no chap can have fair play with you. It be all along of your swindling bets about things you don't know nothing of. You offered me five hunder pound, afore ever here I come, to sell my back to the Northman. A good honest man he be, and the best cross-buttock as ever I met with; but a set of rogues and cowards that's what you be; and no sport can live with you. As for your danged belt, I wun't have it, no tino, it wud be a disgrace to the family; it shan't never go along side the Devonshire and Cornwall leather. But I'll throw your man over again, and any six of you to once as plases."

Then, thorough gentleman as he was, he apologized to me for his honest anger, and for having drawn all eyes upon me, as there I stood at his side.

"But never fear about the time, Miss Clara, I won't kape you two minutes. I'll give him Abraham's staylace this time. They have a drove me to it, as us hasn't a moment to spare."

Proudly he stepped into the ring again, and again the North Country giant, looking rather ashamed, confronted him. No fencing or feinting this time; but the Devonshire wrestler, appealing thus to the public,

"Now look here, Lunnoners, wull e, and zee if this here be a back," rushed straight at his antagonist, grappled him in some peculiar manner, seemed to get round his back, and then spun him up over his own left shoulder, in such a way that he twirled in the air and came down dead on his spine. Dead indeed he appeared to be, and a dozen surgeons came forward, in the midst of a horrible silence, and some were preparing to bleed him, when the farmer moved them aside; he knew that the poor man was only stunned by concussion of the spine. Awhile he knelt over him sadly, with the tears in his own brave eyes:

"I wudn't have doed it, lad; indade and indade I wudn't, ony they forced me to it; and you didn't say nought agin them. It be all fair enough, but it do hoort so tarble. That there trick was invented by a better man nor I be, and it be karled 'Abraham Cann's staylace.' I'll show e how to do it, if ever us mates again. Now tak the belt, man, tak it--" he leaped up, and tore it down, with very little respect, "I resigns it over to you; zimth they arl wants you to have it and you be a better man nor deserves it. And I'll never wrastle no more; Jan Uxtable's time be over. Give us your hond, old chap. We two never mate again, unless you comes down our wai, and us han't got a man to bate e, now I be off the play. There be dacent zider and bakkon to Tossil's Barton Farm. Give us your hond like a man, there be no ill will atween us, for this here little skumdoover." Perhaps he meant skirmish and manoeuvre, all in one. Sam Richardson, slowly recovering, put out his great hand, all white and clammy, and John Huxtable took it tenderly, amid such uproarious cheering, that I expected the tent on our heads. Even Shelfer's sharp eyes had a drop of moisture in them. As for Beany Dawe, he flung to the winds all dithyrambic gravity, and chanted and danced incoherently, Cassandra and Chorus in one; while Sally Huxtable blotted all her rainbow in heavy drops.

Hundreds of pipes were smashed, even the Stoic Shelfer's, in the rush to get at the farmer; but he parted the crowd right and left, as I might part willow-sprays, and came at once to me. Whether by his aid, or by the sympathies of the multitude, I am sure I cannot tell, but I found myself in a cab, with Sally at my side, and Mrs. Shelfer on the box, and the farmer's face at the window.

"Twenty minutes, Miss, I'll be there, raddy to go where you plases. It bain't quite one o'clock yet. I must put myself dacent like, avore I can go with you, Miss; and git the money for the sake of them poor chiller, if so be they Lunnoners be honest enough to pai. Jan Uxtable never come to Lunnon town no more."

With thousands of people hurraing, we set off full gallop for Albert Street.

CHAPTER XI.

At the door we found Mrs. Fletcher just returned from Lady Cranberry's, and eager to say a great deal which could not now be listened to. Having proved the speed of our horse, I begged the cabman to wait for a quarter of an hour, and then take us to Paddington at any fare he pleased, so long as he drove full gallop. This suited his views very nicely, and knowing Mr. Shelfer, as every one in London does--so at least I am forced to believe--he fain would have kept me ten minutes of the fifteen, to tell of Charley's knowingness, how he had kept it all dark as could be, you see, Miss, and had won three hundred and twenty-five pounds, without reckoning the odd money, Miss--

"Reckon it then, Mr. Cabman," and I ran upstairs full speed, after telling Mrs. Shelfer the sum, lest she should be cheated.

In five minutes I was ready, and came out of my bedroom into the sitting-room, with my hat in one hand, and a little bag in the other; and there, instead of Mrs. Fletcher, I found, whom?--Conrad!

Very pale and ill he looked, so unlike himself that I was shocked, and instead of leaping to him, fell upon a chair. He mistook me, and approached very slowly, but with his dear old smile: how my heart beat, how I longed to be in his arms; but they looked too weak to hold me.

"Oh, Miss Vaughan, I know everything. Will you ever forgive me?"

"Never, my own darling, while you call me that. Forgive you indeed! Can I ever forgive myself, for the evil I have thought of you? How very ill you look! Come and let me kiss you well."

But instead of my doing that, he had to do it for me; for I was quite beaten at last, and fainted away in his arms. By this folly five minutes were lost; and I had so much to say to him, and more to think of than twenty such heads could hold. But he seemed to think that it must be all right, so long as he had me there.

"Oh, Conny," I said through my tears at last, "my own pet Conny, come with me. Your father is in such danger."

"Life of my heart, I will follow you by the very next train. This one I cannot go by."

I could wait for no explanation, and he seemed inclined to give none. Perhaps this was the reason that he spent all the time in kissing me; which, much as I enjoyed it, would have done quite as well at leisure. Be that as it may, there was no time to talk about it; he said it did his lips good, and I believe it did, they were so pale at first, and now so fine a red. Suddenly in the midst of it, a great voice was heard from the passage:

"Why now, what ever be us to do with the chillers?"

Out I ran, with my hair down as usual, and a great flush in my cheeks, but I did not let any one see me.

"Leave them here, to be sure, leave them here, Mr. Huxtable. They shall have my rooms; and in all London they would not find such a hostess as Mrs. Shelfer."

There was no time to consider it. The throat of hurry is large, and gulps almost any suggestion. Away we went full gallop; the farmer was on the box,--how the driver found room I can't say,--Mrs. Fletcher and I inside, all consulting her watch every minute. Across the Regent's Park, scattering the tame wild ducks, past Marylebone Church, and the Yorkshire Stingo, and Edgware Road--we saved it by just two minutes. Although I had taken his ticket, the farmer would not come with us, but went in a second-class carriage.

"They blue featherbeds trimmed with pig's tails, is too good for the likes of I, Miss Clara; and I should be afeared all the wai that the Missus was rating of me for my leg-room. I paid parlour price coming up, and went in the kitchen waggons, because it zim'd only fair, as I takes such a dale of room."

I knew that none ever could turn him from what he considered just, and therefore allowed him to ride where he pleased. But a dozen times I thought we should have lost him on the way; for at every station, where the train stopped, he made a point of coming to our window, which he had marked with a piece of chalk, and "humbly axing our pardon, but was we all right and no fire? He couldn't think what they wanted, not he, with tempting God Almighty fast." Not fast enough for me, I told him every time; whereupon he put on his hat with a sigh, and said he supposed I was born to it. And yet all the time he seemed to consider that he was protecting me somehow, and once he called me his dearie, to the great surprise of the other passengers, and the horror of Mrs. Fletcher; seeing which he repented hastily, and "Miss Vaughan'd" me three times in a sentence, with a hot flush on his forehead. At Swindon, where we changed carriages, he pulled out very mysteriously from an inner breast-pocket a little sack tied with whipcord, and in which, I do believe, the simple soul had deposited all his hard-earned prize-money. Then he led us to the counter, proud to show that he had been there before, and earnestly begged for the honour of treating us to a drop of somewhat. His countenance fell so on my refusal, that I was fain to cancel it, and to drink at his expense a glass of iced sherry and water; while Mrs. Fletcher, with much persuasion and simpering, and for the sake of her poor inside, that had been so long her enemy, ventured on a "wee wee thimbleful of Cognac." The farmer himself, much abashed at the splendour around him, which he told me, in a whisper, beat Pewter Will's out and out, and even the "Fortescue Arms," would not call for anything, until I insisted upon it; being hard pressed he asked at last, hoping no offence of the lady, for a pint of second cider. The young woman turned up her nose, but I soon made her turn it down again, and fetch him, as the nearest thing, a bottle of sparkling perry.

As always happens, when one is in a great hurry, the train was an hour behind its time, and the setting sun was casting gold upon the old cathedral--to my mind one of the lightest and grandest buildings in England, though the farmer prefers that squat and heavy Norman thing at Exeter--when we glided smoothly and swiftly into the Gloucester Station. I fully intended to have sent an electric message from London, not for the sake of the carriage, which mattered nothing, but to warn my dear uncle; at Paddington, however, we found no time to do it, and so stupid I was that I never once thought of telegraphing from Swindon. To make up by over alacrity, in a case of far less importance, I went to the office at Gloucester, and sent this message to Tiverton, then the nearest Station to Exmoor--"Farmer has won, and got the money. Clara Vaughan to Mrs. Huxtable." The amazement of the farmer, I cannot stop to describe.

No time was lost by doing this, for I had ordered a pair of horses, and they were being put to. Then, stimulating the driver, we dashed off for Vaughan St. Mary. Anxious as I was, and wretched at the thought of what we might find, so exhausted was my frame by the thaumatrope of the last six-and-thirty hours, that I fell fast asleep, and woke not until we came to the lodge. Old Whitehead came out, hat in hand, and whispered something into Mrs. Fletcher's ear. That good old lady had been worrying me dreadfully about her jams, for the weather was so hot, she was sure all the fruit would be over, &c., none of which could I listen to now. As Whitehead spoke, I saw through my half-open lashes that she started violently; but she would not tell me what it was, and I did not want to intrude on secrets that might be between them. The farmer also diverted attention by calling from the box, as we wound into the avenue, "Dear heart alaive; this bate all the sojers as ever I see, Miss Clara, or even the melisher to Coom. Why, arl thiccy treeses must a growed so a puppose, just over again one another, and arl of a bigness too. Wull, wull! Coachman, was ever you to Davonsheer?"

I do believe those men of Devon see nothing they admire, without thinking at once of their county.

At the front door, the butler met us, which surprised me rather, as being below his dignity. He was a trusty old servant, who had been under Thomas Henwood, and had come back to his place since the general turn-out of the household. Now he looked very grave and sad, and instead of leading me on, drew me aside in the hall. It was getting dark, and the fire in the west was dying. Great plumes of asparagus--shame it was to cut them--waved under the ancient mantel-piece.

"Bad news it is, Miss Clara"--they all seemed to call me that--"very bad news indeed, Miss. But I hope you was prepared for it."

"What do you mean?"

"Why, haven't you heard about poor master's death?"

"Dead, my dear uncle dead! Do you mean to say"--I could not finish the sentence.

"No, Miss, only to-day, and not as you thinks; no fit at all, nor paralyatic stroke. He went off quiet as a lamb, as near as could be three o'clock. He was very poorly before; but he had a deal to do, and would not give in on no account. He was sitting by himself in the study after breakfast, and at last he rang the bell, and told them to send me up. When I went in, he was bolt upright in his chair, with a beautiful smile on his face, but so pale, white I ought to say, Miss, and so weak he could hardly move. 'John,' he says, 'Yes, Sir,' says I; 'John,' he says again, 'you are a most respectable man, and I can trust you with anything in the world, John. Take this letter for Miss Vaughan, and put it with your own hands into her own, directly the moment she comes back. I am rather uneasy about the poor girl,' he says, as it were to himself. 'Which Miss Vaughan, Sir?' says I. 'Your mistress, John. Can't you see what is written on it? And now help me upstairs; and if ever I spoke to you harshly, John Hoxton, I ask your pardon for it. You will find as I haven't forgotten you.' And with that I helped him upstairs, Miss, and I had almost to carry him; and then he says, 'Help me to bed, John. I would like to die in my bed, and it will save some trouble. And let me look out of the window; what a lovely day it is, it reminds me quite of the South. So I set him up in the bed, Miss, handy altogether, and beautiful, and he could see two larks on the lawn, and he asked me what they was. Then he says, 'Thank you, John, you have done it wonderful well, and I hope they won't speak evil of me round this place, after I am gone. I have tried to do my duty, John, as between man and man: though I would be softer with them, if I had my time over again. Now send my daughter to me, though I wish I had seen my son, John. But I ought to be very thankful, and what's more, I am. All of you likes Miss Lily, unless they tell me stories, John.' 'Sir,' says I, 'we wusships her, though not like our own Miss Vaughan.'"

Ah, John Hoxton, did you say that to him, I wonder, or interpolate, *ex post facto*?

"So he looked very pleased at that, Miss, and he says again, 'John, let all that love her know that she is the living image of her mother. Now go and send her quickly; but John, take care not to frighten my little darling.' So I went and found Miss Lily got along with the Shetland pony and giving it bits of clover, and I sent her up and Jane too, for I was dreadfully frightened, and you away, Miss, at the time. And what come afterwards I can't tell, only no luncheon went up, and there was orders not to ring the bell for the servants' dinner; and I heard poor Miss Lily crying terrible all along the corridor, and I did hear say that his last words was, and he trying to raise his arms toward the window, 'Blessed be God, I can see my own Lily,' but she warn't that side of the bed, Miss; so he must have made some mistake."

"No. He meant her mother. Where is my cousin now?"

"In your own room, Miss, lying down, they tell me. She did take on so awful, Jane thought she would have died. But at last she brought her round a little, and persuaded her to lie down. She calls for you, Miss, every time she comes to herself."

I went straightway to the poor little dear, without even stopping to read the letter placed in my hands. The room in which she lay was dark; for Jane, who was watching in my little parlour, whispered to me that the poor child could not bear the lamp-light, her eyes were so weak and sore.

At first Lily did not know me; and it went to my heart, after all my own great sorrows, to hear the sad low moaning. She lay on my own little bed, with her pale face turned to the wall, her thick hair all over her shoulders, and both hands pressed to her heart. Annie Franks had been many times to ask for her, but Lily would not let her come in. Bending over I laid my cheek on Lily's, and softly whispered her name. At last she knew me, and took my hand, and turned her sweet lips to kiss me. Then she sobbed and cried most bitterly; but I saw that it did her good. By and by she said, with her fingers among my hair:

"Oh, Clara, isn't it hard to find him at last, and love him so, and only for three days, and then, and then--"

"And then, my pet, to let him go where his heart has been nearly twenty years. Would you be so selfish as to rob your mother of him? And to go so happy. I am sure he has. Come with me and see."

"Oh no, oh no. I cannot." And her lovely young form trembled, at the thought of visiting death.

"Yes, you can, if you only try, and I am sure that he would wish it. That you and I should kneel hand in hand and bless him, as others shall kneel some day by us. What, Lily afraid of her father! Then I have no fear of my Uncle."

God knows that I spoke so, not from harshness, only in the hope to do her good.

"If you really think he would wish it, dear--"

"Yes. It is a duty I owe him. He would be disappointed in me, if I failed."

"Oh, how he longed to see you once more, dear Clara, But he felt that you were safe, and he said you would come to see him, though he could not see you. He talked of you quite to the last; you and darling Conny."

"Conny will be here to-night."

"No! Oh I am so glad!" and a bright flash of joy shone forth from the eyes that were red with weeping. Something cold pushed quietly in between us, and then gave a sniff and a sigh. It was darling Judy's nose. He had learned in the lower regions, where he always dwelled in my absence, that Miss Clara was come home; and knowing my name as well as his own, he had set off at once in quest of me. After offering me his best love and respects, with the tip of his tongue, as he always did, he looked from one to the other of us, with his eyebrows raised in surprise, and the deepest sorrow and sympathy in his beautiful soft-brown pupils. I declare it made us cry more than ever.

"Oh, Clara," sobbed Lily at length, "he did howl so last night. Do you think he could have known it?"

His eyes dropped, as she was telling me. They always did, when he thought he had been a bad dog.

"Now go down, Judy; good little Judy, go to Mrs. Fletcher. A great friend of mine is with her."

Away he trotted obediently, and his tail recovered its flourish before he had got to the corner.

"Now, darling, let us go there," said the poor child, trembling again. "I would go anywhere with you."

Hand in hand we walked into my Uncle's chamber. Young as I was, and still thoughtless in many ways, twice before now had I gazed on the solemn face of death; but never, not even in my mother's holy countenance, saw I such perfect peace and bliss as dwelt in and seemed to smile from my dearest Uncle's lineaments. The life, in youth puffed here and there by every captious breeze of pride, in its prime becalmed awhile on the halycon deep of love, then tempest-tossed through the lonely dark, and shattered of late by blows from God, that life whose flaw of misanthropy and waste of high abilities had been redeemed, ennobled even, by a pure and perfect love--now it had bidden farewell to all below the clouds, calmly, happily, best of all--in faith.

We knelt beside the bed and prayed--Lily as a Catholic, Clara as a Protestant--that we, and all we loved, might have so blest an end. Then we both sat peacefully, with a happy awe upon us, in the dark recess behind the velvet curtains. Two wax candles were burning on the table towards the door, and by their light the face we loved, looked not wan, but glorious, as with a silver glory.

Clasping each the other's waist, and kissing away each other's tranquil tears, how long we sat there I know not, neither what high fluttering thoughts, thoughts or angels, which be they--stealthily a door was opened, not the door of heaven, not even the main door of the room we sat in, but a narrow side-door. Through it crept, with crawling caution, he whom most of all men I now despised and pitied. Lily did not hear his entrance, neither did she see him; but my eyes and ears were keen from many a call of danger. Stunned for a while by the heavy blow, that met me on my return, I had forgotten all about him; I mean, at least, all about his present design. I had indeed told the farmer, for it was only fair to do so, my object in bringing him down; and how I relied on his wonderful strength and courage, having then no other to help me; but since I got home, and heard the sad tidings, it seemed a mere thing for contempt. Not even Lepardo Della Croce could catch a departed spirit. So, and in the landslip of the mind, sapped by its own, and sliding swiftly into another's sorrow, I had not even ordered that the house should be watched at all; I had not even posted Giudice, who had a vendetta of his own, anywhere on guard.

With a stiletto still concealed, all but the handle on which the light fell, he approached the bed, wriggling along and crouching, as a cat or leopard would. Then he rose and stood upright at the side of the bed, not our side but the other, and glared upon his intended victim's face. I pushed Lily back behind the curtain as if with the weight of my bosom, while I watched the whole. Never in all my tempestuous life, of all the horrible things I have seen, and heard, and shuddered at, saw I anything so awful, so utterly beyond not only description, but conception, as that disdainful, arrogant face, when the truth burst on him. Not the body only, but the mind and soul--if God had cursed him with one--were smitten back all of a lump, as if he had leaped from a train at full speed into a firing cannon's mouth. Before he had time to recover, I advanced and faced him. All dressed in white I was, with my black hair below my waist, for I had thrown off my travelling frock, and taken what first came to hand. They tell me I look best in white, it shows my hair and eyes so.

He believed that it was a spirit, the Vendetta spirit of the other side; and he cowered from me. I was the first to speak. "Lepardo Della Croce, it is the rebuke of heaven. Dust upon ashes; such is man's revenge. I have nursed, but scorn it now. Go in peace, and pray the Almighty that He be not like you. Stop; I will show you forth. You have a vindictive foe here, who would tear you to atoms."

I led the way, trembling at every corner lest we should meet Giudice; for I knew he would not obey me, if he once caught sight of this hated one. After standing silently, unable to take his eyes from the placid face of the dead, Lepardo began to follow me, walking as if in a dream. Meeting none, I led him forth along the corridor, down the end staircase, and out on the eastern terrace. There I waved him off, and pointed to the dark refuge of the shrubbery, beyond the mineral spring. The moonlight slept upon the black water narrowly threading the grass. Over our heads drooped the ivy, the creeper of oblivion. The murderer turned and looked at me; hitherto he had glided along with his head down, as in bewilderment. Oh that he had said one word of sorrow or repentance! He spoke not at all; but shuddered, as the ivy rustled above us. His face was pale as the moonlight. Did he see in me something higher than the spirit of Vendetta?

I pointed again to the trees, and urged him away from the house. He had two strong enemies there; a minute might make all the difference. Breaking as if from a spell, he waved his Italian cap, and his lithe strong figure was lost among the Portugal laurels. For a minute I stood there, wondering; then slowly went round the house-corner, and gazed at the grey stone mullions of the room which had been my father's.

I was still in the anguish of doubt and misgiving--what right had an ignorant girl like me to play judge and jury, or more, to absolve and release a crime against all humanity?-- when a mighty form stood beside me, and Giudice, all bristle and fire, dashed forth from the door in the gable. With command and entreaty I called him, but he heard me not, neither looked at me; but scoured the ground like a shadow, quartering it as a pointer does, only he carried his nose down.

"Dang my slow bones," said the farmer, "but I'll have him yet, Miss. I seed him go, I'll soon find him."

"No, no. I won't have him stopped. He shall go free, and repent."

"By your lave, Miss, it can't be. A man as have done what he have, us has no right to play buff with. Never before did I go again your will, Miss; but axing your pardon, I must now. Look, the girt dog know better."

As the dog found the track and gave tongue, the farmer rushed from me and followed him, dashing headlong into the shrubbery, after leaping the mineral spring, at the very spot where the footprints had been. Judy and Farmer Huxtable were fast friends already; for that dog always made up his mind in a moment on the question of like and dislike.

For a time I was so horror-struck, that no power of motion was left. I knew that the farmer was quite unarmed, he carried not even a stick. Even with the great dog to help him, what could he do against fire-arms, which Lepardo was sure to have? What should I say to his wife and children, what should I say to myself, if John Huxtable fell a victim to that wily and desperate criminal?

Resolved to be present, if possible, I rushed down the narrow path which led to the little park-gate, where probably they would pass. I was right: they had passed, and flung it wide open. Breathless I looked around, for hence several tracks diverged. No living thing could I see or hear, but the beating of my heart, which seemed to be in my throat, and the hooting of an owl from the hollow elm at the corner. I flung myself down on the dewy grass, and strained my eyes in vain; until by some silver birch-trees on which the moonlight was glancing, I saw first a gliding figure that looked like a deer in the distance, then a tall man running rapidly. Away I made by a short cut for the "Witches' grave," as the end of the lake was called, for I knew that the path they were on led thither. Quite out of breath I was, for I had run more than half a mile, when I came full upon a scene, which would have robbed me of breath if I had any. At the end of a little dingle, under a willow-tree, and within a few feet of the water, stood Lepardo Della Croce, brought to bay at last. A few yards from him, Giudice was struggling furiously to escape the farmer's grasp; perhaps no other hand in England could have held him. His eyes kindled in the moonlight, like the red stars of a rocket, and a deep roar of baffled rage came from the surge of his chest, as he champed his monstrous fangs, and volleyed all the spring of his loins. The farmer leaned backward to hold him, and stayed himself by a tree-stump.

"Sharp now, surrender, wull e, man. In the name of of the Quane and the Lord Chafe Justice, and the High Shariff of Devon, I tell e surrender--dang this here dog--surrender, and I 'ont hoort e; and I 'ont let the girt dog."

Lepardo answered calmly, in a voice that made my blood cold:

"Do you value your life? If so, stand out of my way. I have death here for you, and five other dogs."

I saw the barrel of a large revolver, with a stream of light upon it. He held it steadily as a tobacco-pipe. I am glad he owned some courage. For my life, I could not stir. All the breath in my body was gone.

"Dear heart alaive. Thiccy man must be a fule," said the farmer quite contemplatively. "Don't e know who I be? Do e reckon they peppermint twistesses can hurt Jan Uxtable? I seed ever so many in a smarl shop window to Lunnon. Surrender now wull e, thou shalt have fair traial to Hexeter, as a Davonshire man have took e, and a dale more nor e desarves. Sharp now: I be afeared of the girt dog getting loose. Dang you dog. Ston up a bit." And the farmer approached him coolly, trailing the dog along; as if what the murderer held in his hand was a stick of Spanish liquorice.

"Fool, if you pass that stump, your great carcase shall lie on it."

"Fire away," said the farmer, "I knowed you was a coward, and I be glad it be so. Now mind, if so be you shuts, I lets the dog go, honour braight, because e dunno what fair play be. But if e harken to rason, I'll give e one chance more. I'll tie up the dog with my braces to thiccy tree--allers wear cart rope I does--and I'll tak e Quane's prisoner, with my left hond, and t'other never out of my breeches pocket; look e, zee, laike thiccy."

And the farmer buried his right hand in his capacious trowsery. The Corsican seemed astonished.

"Fool-hardy clown, worthy son of a bull-headed country, stop at the stump--then, take that."

Out blazed the pistol with a loud ring, and I saw that the farmer was struck. He let go the dog, and leaped up; his right hand fell on Lepardo's temple, and seemed to crush the skull in,--another shot at the same instant and down fell the farmer heavily. "Great God," I screamed, and leaped forward. But Giudice was loose to avenge him, though I could swear that it was on a corpse. Corpse or living body, over and over it rolled, with the dog's fangs in its throat. I heard a gurgle, a tearing, and grinding, and then a loud splash in the water. The dog, and the murderer, both of man and dog, sunk in the lake together. Twenty feet out from the shore rose above water one moment, drawn ghastly white in the moonbeams, the last view seen till the judgment-day of the face of Lepardo Della Croce.

Almost drowned himself--for he would not release his father's murderer, while a gasp was in him--staggered at last to the shore my noble and true dog Giudice. He fell down awhile, to recover his breath, then shook himself gratefully, tottered to me, where I knelt at the farmer's side, and wagged his tail for approval. The water from his chest and stomach dripped on the farmer's upturned face, and for a moment revived him.

"No belt, no tino lad, I 'ont tak' it. Zimth laike a ticket for chating. I dunno as I'd tak' the mony, if it warn't for the poor chillers, naine chillers now, and anither a-coomin. Mustn't drink no more beer, but Beany shall have his'n." And his head fell back on my lap, and I felt sure that he was dead. How I screamed and shrieked, till I lay beside him, with Judy licking my face, none can tell but the gamekeepers, who had heard the shots, and came hurrying.

Of this lower end of the lake they happened to be most jealous; for a brood of pintail ducks, very rare I believe in England, had been hatched here this summer, and no one was allowed to go near them. Poor Judy kept all the men aloof, till I was able to speak to him. Then I perceived that he as well was bleeding, wounded perhaps by the poniard as he leaped on his enemy's breast. It had entered just under the shoulder, and narrowly missed the heart.

They took us at once towards the house, carrying the farmer and Judy on the wooden floodgates of the stream called the "Witches' brook," which here fell into the lake. As we entered the avenue, being obliged to take the broad way, though much further round, we heard a carriage coming. It was the one I had sent for Conrad, with a hurried note to break the sad news of his father's death. He had been detained in London by a challenge he found from Lepardo; which was of course a stratagem to keep him out of the way. How delighted I was to see his calm brave face again, as he leaped down, and took my tottering form in his arms. In a minute he understood everything, and knew what was best to be done. He would not allow them to place the poor farmer in the carriage, as they foolishly wanted to do; but laid the rude litter down, examined the wounds by the lamplight, and bound them up most cleverly with the appliances of the moment.

"Oh, Conrad, will he die?"

"No, my darling, I hope not; but he must if they had let him bleed so much longer."

"I never heard that you were a surgeon, Conny."

"Could I call myself a sculptor, without having studied anatomy? My dearest one, how you tremble! Go home in the carriage, and give directions for us. A room downstairs, with a wide doorway, and plenty of air. I will stay with them, and see that they bear him gently. Poor Judy may go with you."

Thus Conrad saw for the first time the hearth and home of his ancestors, with his father lying dead there, and his avenger carried helpless. But I met him at the door. Did that comfort you just a little, my darling?

CHAPTER XII.

The lake was dragged that night, and all the following day, in spite of the gamekeeper's strong remonstrance for the sake of the tender pintails. But nothing whatever was found, except the Italian cap. The "Witches' grave," invisible I am glad to say from the house, is more than forty feet deep, when the water is at its lowest. Three or four years afterwards young William Hiatt caught a monstrous pike in the lake, and sent him, with our permission, to be stuffed at Gloucester. Like the famous fish of Samos, this pike had swallowed a ring, which was sent to Conrad by the Gloucester gun-maker. It was Lepardo's seal-ring, the cross of the family engraved on a bloodstone, with L.D.C. below it.

Whether the midnight stabber died by the blow of an English fist, or suffered vivisection through a dog's vendetta--an institution more excusable and dignified than man's--is known to Him, and Him alone, who holds the scales of retribution, and laughs in scorn as well as wrath at our attempts to swing them. For are we not therein ourselves; and how shall the best and strongest of us carry the thing he is carried in? Right glad I am, and ever shall be, that I moved not in the awful scene, which closed my father's tragedy.

Through Conrad's skill and presence of mind, the dear farmer's life was saved. We sent to Gloucester immediately for the cleverest surgeon there; and he owned that he could not have fixed the ligatures better, though he did what Conny durst not attempt, he extracted the murderer's bullet. It was the first shot that did all the mischief, being aimed deliberately at the large and tender heart. Thanks to the waving of the willow-tree, for Lepardo was a known marksman, it had missed by about two inches. The second shot, fired quite close and wildly, had grooved the left temple, and stricken the farmer senseless.

For six weeks now our dear friend, whose patience amazed all but me, was kept from his Devonshire home. To London I sent at once for the two children and Mr. Dawe, and would have sent to Devon as well, for kind and good Mrs. Huxtable, but her husband would not hear of it. By Ann Maples, who had left Lady Cranberry "shockingly," on hearing from Mrs. Fletcher that I would take her again, he sent to his wife "kind love and best duty, and for goodness' sake, stop at home now. No call to make a fule of yourself, and the farm go to rack and ruin. There be fuss enough 'bout I already, and never I brag no more, when a pill like thiccy upsot me. But Miss Clara, God bless her bootiful eyes, she nurse me, just as if she wor my own darter, with the apron on as you give her. And you should see the kitchen, Honor, you loves a kitchen so; they be a bilin and roastin arl day, and they be vorced to swape the chimbley three times in a vortnight"--the rest of this glorious message, about three pages long, I am "vorced" to suppress; I only hope Ann Maples remembered a quarter of it.

But his wonderful Miss Clara did not nurse him long. Hearing from the surgeon that all the danger was over by the end of the following week--so strong was the constitution-- Conrad, Lily, and I set sail for Corsica on our melancholy errand. In that letter, which seemed to come to me from the grave, my poor Uncle after expressing his joy and deep gratitude at so happy a close to his life, continued thus:--

"Yes, my dear child, the close of my wasted and weary life. You may be surprised and perplexed at what I am about to tell you; but you are not one of those low-minded ones, who condemn as superstition all beyond their philosophy. The very night after you brought me my new Lily, a sweet thing just like her mother, I lay for some hours awake, broad awake as I am now. I was thinking of my two Lilies, the lovely and loving creatures. I was not in the least excited, but calm, reflective, and happy. Soon after the clock struck two, at the time when our life burns lowest, I heard a soft voice, sweet as the music of heaven, call me by name three times. Of course I knew whose it was: too often that voice had murmured upon my bosom, for me not to know it now. Not rashly, but with a mind long since resolved, I answered: 'Sweetest mine'--her own artless and young endearment--'Sweetest mine, no longer will I keep you lonely.' No answer came in words; but the light, the golden light of my own love's smile, as I had seen it in Corsica, when she came from the grave to comfort me. And now, as after that visit, I fell into deep and perfect rest, such rest as comes but rarely until the sleep of all. No wonder you and Lily thought me so strong next day. In the morning I knew and rejoiced in my quick departure. This cold obstruction was to be cast aside, this palsied frame to release the winged soul. On the third day I was to find and dwell with my Lily for ever. So on the first day I enjoyed the harmless pleasures of life, and could not bear you to leave me, because that would have turned them to pain. The second day I got through all the business that still remained, refreshing its dryness often with my sweet child's society. On this, the third, I write to you, and am, through the grace of God, as calm and content, nay more content than if I were going to bed.

"Beloved daughters both, and my dear son as well, I implore you not to grieve painfully for me. Too well I know the weight of excessive sorrow, and how it oppresses the lost one, even more than the loser. Since the parting is so brief, the reunion so eternal, why make the interval long and dreary by counting every footstep?

Alas, it is easy to talk and think so, but very hard to feel it. Time demands his walk with sorrow, and will not have his arm dispensed with. Then think of my happiness, darlings, and how your own will increase it.

Only one more request, which after Ciceronian sentiments--which Cicero could not practise--you are all too young not to wonder at. If you, my three children, can manage it, without any heavy expense, or much trouble to yourselves, it is my last wish as regards the body, that it should lie by the side of my wife's. The name of the little church, St. Katharine's on the Cliff, can scarcely have escaped my Clara's excellent memory. Lily lies beside her father, in the right-hand corner towards the sea. Each of them has a cross of the Signor's alabaster, made from my own design. Lily's is enough for me: put my name with hers."

Not only did we look upon his last fond wish as sacred, but we accomplished it in the manner that was likely to please him most. We put his own "Lilyflower," the little love-boat as they called it, into commission again, engaged a good captain and crew, and taking old Cora with us, set sail from Gloucester for the Mediterranean. Poor Cora was now all devotion to Conrad and Lily, ever since she had found that they were lawful blood and direct heirs of the Della Croce. The more recent part of the family story she had known only from her master's version, and had set little store by the children as bearing the stamp of disgrace; though she could not help loving sweet Lily. Now, by her evidence, coupled with my dear Uncle's deposition, his relics, and documents, and my own testimony, confirmed by Balaam and Balak, we established very easily the birth and the claims of my Uncle Edgar's children; and the old Count Gaffori, most venerable of signors, would have kept us a month at least to go through all his accounts. He was entreated to retain his position as the guardian of our Lily.

So far as our recent sorrow permitted enjoyment of scenery, we were all enchanted with the Balagna. At the funeral of "Signor Valentine," whose name was still remembered and loved, nearly all the commune was present; and many a dignified matron shed tears, who had smiled as a graceful girl, and strown flowers, at his wedding. They were burning with curiosity to see our beautiful Lily, for the tender tale had moved them, as Southern natures are moved; and many of them had loved and gloried in her mother.

But in spite of all this desire, not a prying glance fell on her, as she bowed in the hooded robe, and wept to the mournful vocero. Foremost of all stood old Petro and Marcantonia, who had found out and kissed with sobs of delight their beloved master's daughter. For my part, I loved the Corsicans; there is something so noble and simple about the men, so graceful, warm-hearted, and lady-like in the women; and in a very short time I could understand more than half they said. The black Vendetta, they told me, was dying out among them, and in a few years would be but a wonder of the past. God in His mercy grant it.

There must have been something surely in my Uncle Edgar's nature, which won the Southern hearts, as my father won British affections. Such things I cannot explain, or account for. I only know and feel them.

We were all back at Vaughan St. Mary before the end of August, and found the farmer, the two chillers, and Beany Dawe as happy as if they were born and reared there. Old Cora was left at Veduta Tower; and having obtained Mr. Dawe's permission I presented her once and for all with the whole treasure of the gordit. She intends, however, to bequeath it to me in her will. Soon afterwards Conrad gave her a more substantial blessing; for he sold the things left in Lucas Street, under letters of administration, as being the next of kin. All the proceeds he handed over to Cora, except one-tenth, which he presented to the Society for the Prevention of Cruelty to Animals. As many of the specimens, iguanodon, and other monsters, fetched prices as hard to explain away as themselves, poor Cora was amply provided for: all which of course she attributed to the holy Madonna's heart. And now at last I understood how 19, Grove Street had become No. 37, Lucas Street. The change of number I have already explained; the change of name was on this wise:--The builder, a rising man, who had bought the old part of the street, and built thereto the new one, had a son, a fine undergraduate, better skilled in the boats than in the books of Oxford. Reading hard one day, after his third pluck, this young man discovered that lucus was the Latin for grove. He smote his hand on his forehead, and a great idea presented itself. Had there not been both nymphs and philosophers of the grove? The street that was his inheritance should be distinguished by nomenclature from the thousand groves of London, wherein the nightingale pipeth not, neither--but I am getting poetical, and don't understand the Gradus. Enough, that he wrote at once and earnestly to his father, forgetting the vivid description, which was now growing stale, of his pluck--a result secured, as the Winchester gentlemen tell me, by learning too solid to carry--but begging that his Oxford career might at least be commemorated in and by the street that paid his bills there. "Lucus" he wrote plainly enough, and in very large letters, but the father read it "Lucks." No, said the mother, she was sure Alexander never meant such a low thing as that, it was "Lucas" of course; why the Lucases were her own cousins, and Rosa such a nice girl, she saw how it was, that she did, and Alexander might have done worse. And so it was painted most bravely "Lucas Street," and the builder wasn't going to make a fool of himself, when Alexander protested.

When John Huxtable set off for home, just in time to see to his harvest, which is always late round Exmoor, I kissed him--ay, Conny, you saw it--and thrust, during his amazement, something far down into his mighty pocket, which something he was not upon any account to look at until he got home. It was a deed, prepared by our solicitors, presenting him with the fee simple of Tossil's Barton farm. True, I was not of age, but I signed it as if I had been, and Conny and I again signed it, when we paid our first visit there. Perhaps, in strict law, it binds not my interest even now; but if ever any one claiming "by, from, through, under, or in trust for" me, forgets the Vaughan honour and dares to dream of that farm, I'll be at him as sure as a ghost; and I trust before that time comes, the farmer will have sound title by immemorial years of possession. He is now a prosperous man; and has never found it necessary to give up his beer, as he threatened Young John, who is just like his father, cleaves fast to Tabby Badcock, now a blooming maiden; but my Sally has more than balanced that imminent loss of caste, by fixing the eyes and transfixing the heart of George Tamlin, the son of our principal tenant, and himself of Devonshire origin. The young lady comes to and fro every six weeks, and is to be married from our house, when her father considers her "zober enough." Beany Dawe, who does not like work, still lives at Tossil's Barton, and is in receipt of a pension of sixpence a day from Government, as a bard at last appreciated.

As for me, Clara Vaughan, on the very day after that which released me from my teens (counting forward, as we do, till we count receding years), to wit on the 31st of December, 1851, I did not change my name, but wrote it in the old church register, half an inch below a better and firmer hand. There was no fuss or frippery; no four clergymen and ten bridesmaids simpering at one another. Our good vicar represented the one class, dear Lily and Annie Franks the other. My godfather, newly disclosed for the purpose, gave me away very gracefully, and young Peter Green helped Conrad. Lily Vaughan looked so exquisite, so deliciously lovely, that nobody in the whole world--Now Conny, hold your tongue, I never fish for compliments, don't degrade yourself so for a kiss, of course I know all my perfections, but how can I care about them, when you say they belong to you?--Lily Vaughan, I say once more, was such a sunrise of loveliness, that young Peter Green, just new from his Oxford honours, collapsed, and fell over the railings, and wedged his head in the "piscina," or whatever those nice young gentlemen, who see the duty of wearing strait waistcoats, are pleased to denominate it.

Ah, Little Distaff Lane, most unconnubial title, ah firm of Green, Vowler, and Green, your Hercules holds the distaff, and holds it, alas, in his heart! From that shock he never recovered, until we had at Vaughan Park a really merry wedding; and I, ah me, I could not dance just then, but I showered roses upon them, for the shadow of death was past. Old Mr. Green,--nay, nay, not fifty yet, by our Lady,--Mr. Peter Green the elder, came down here for the occasion, and I hardly ever took such a fancy to any man before. He seemed to know almost everything, not by the skin, as Dr. Ross seemed to hold things, but by the marrow and fibrine of their alimentary part. And withal such a perfect gentleman: he kept in the horns of his knowledge, instead of exalting them, and making us wish for hay on them, while tossed in headlong ignorance.

Scant as I am of space, I must tell how he behaved, when his son revealed his attachment. "Is it a lady, Peter?" "I should rather think she is, father." "Do you love her with all your heart?" "Of course I do, every bit. I am tough, but I know I shall die, unless--" "That will do, my son. You have my full consent, and your mother's is sure to follow. Most likely you got it beforehand. You young fellows are so deep. Let me kiss your forehead, my boy, although I am not dramatic."

Having behaved so nobly, for this boy was his only hope, he deserved to find, as he did, that if he had searched the world he could not have hit upon any other so desirable for his son, as the daughter of his old friend. The only mistake he has made is that he so adores her, he cannot bear her to be in Corsica; though the trade they conduct is worth at least fifty thousand a year. When Lily fell in love, I told her that it was because she had an eye for the olives; and olives enough the darling has, I trow, and olive branches too. The eldest is called Clara. "Clara Green!" I don't like the sound altogether; but the substance is something beautiful, and the freshest of all Spring verdure. Nevertheless, my Clara is an inch larger round the calf, and I think her eyelashes are longer. Her hair weighs more, that is certain. We compare them very often; for they live only half the year at Veduta Tower. In the summer heats they are here, and the children between them, my own every bit as bad, leave dear Annie Elton (Annie Franks of old), uncommonly few British Queens. It is all Mr. Shelfer's fault. What is the use of a gardener, if he allows dessert all the day long?

Every autumn we go to Corsica to help at the olive harvest, and rarely we enjoy it. The Old Veduta Tower is like a nest in the ivy, chirruping with young voices; and the happy sleep of the two who loved so well is dreaming, if dream it can or care to do, of the fairest flowers in Europe, scattered there by little soft hands. Conny is wild every time about the Rogliano and Luri; and if Peter Green listens to him--which every one does, except me--he will introduce, very slowly of course, those fine-bodied yet aerial wines to the noble British public, that loves not even intoxication, unless it be adulterated.

Oh, queer Mrs. Shelfer, oh Balaam and Balak, shall I pretermit your annals? The two Sheriff's officers, having secured their reward, set up therewith a public-house called the "Posse-Comitatus," which soon became the head quarters of all who are agents or patients in the machinery of levying. As at such times all people drink and pay more than double, the public-house has already a Queensbench-ful of good-will.

Poor Mrs. Shelfer and Charley did not invest the 325*l.* altogether judiciously: at least, it went mainly to purchase "eternal gratitude," whose time does not begin to run till the purchaser's is over. But Patty, I am glad to say, has still that 30*l.* a year of her own, left to her in the funds by good and grateful Miss Minto. "Can't touch it, my good friend, not the Queen, the Lord Mayor, and all the royal family. Government give their bond for it, on parchment made of their skins, and the ink come out of their gall." Be this as it may, what is much more to the purpose is that Mr. Shelfer cannot touch it. And now I have pride in announcing, for I never expected such glory, that all the cats and birds, squirrels, mice, and monkeys, live, like the happy family, in our northern lodge, where Patty is most useful and happy as the Queen of the poultry. In a word, they keep the gate, not of their enemies, but of old and grateful friends. I expected to see at least a leading article in the "Times," when Mr. Shelfer left the metropolis; but they let him go very easily for the sake of the discount market. They gave him only two-and-twenty dinners; but when he first came to Vaughan Park, how he wanted country air! Now he attends to the wall-trees, and the avenue, and I hope finds harmony there. At any rate, he never breaks it by any undue exertion. Nevertheless, his very long pipe is of some account with the green fly, which has been very bad on our peaches, ever since they repealed the corn laws. Mr. Shelfer, accordingly, is compelled to spend half his time in smoking them. "Wonderful nice they do taste, Miss Clara; you'd be quite surprised, you know. Wonderful good, Miss, and werry high-flavoured you know, when they begins to fry."

"Come, come, Mr. Shelfer, I fear you cultivate them for their flavour. There are ten times as many of them, I see, as of peaches on the trees. And you charge me every week five shillings for tobacco."

"To be sure, Miss Clara. Shows a fine constitooshun, you know. And dreadful hard work it is to have to smoke so much, you know. And then the sun will come on the wall, and only a quart of beer allowed all the afternoon. And sometimes they makes me go for it myself, you know! Indeed they does, Miss, they has such cheek here in Gloucestershire!"

Patty brought all her sticks of course, in spite of the twenty-five bills of sale, which by this time had grown upon them. One whole roomful was packed in the duplicate inventories. The law on this subject she contemplated from a peculiar point of view.

"Lor, Miss, I never grudges 'em. They do cost a bit at the time; but see how safe they makes them. If it wasn't for them I should be frightened out of my wits of thieves, down here where the trees and all the green grocery is, worse than the Regency Park. Bless me, I never should have gone out of doors, Miss, if you hadn't pulled me. And to see the flowers here all a-growing with their heads up as bootiful as a bonnet. Pray, my good friend, is that what they was made for, if I may be so bold?"

"No, Patty, not for bonnets. They were made for the bees and the butterflies, and for us to enjoy them, while they enjoy themselves."

"Well, I never. Pray, Miss, did I tell you Uncle John's come home, and they only ate a piece of his shoulder for they found his belt was tenderer; and he put the glazing on it the same as they wears on their hats, and three cork pins to hold it, and he find it werry convenient, it save so much rheumatism: and he'll be here next week to convict the man that made his wife swallow the tea-pot. Dear, dear, what things they does do in the country. Not a bit like Christians. And so, Miss Clara, the old man won't drop off after all; and Uncle John a-coming, how nice it would have been."

The old man was poor Whitehead, whose lodge Mrs. Shelfer coveted, as it was larger and livelier than her own.

"No, Mrs. Shelfer, I think he will get over it. Surely you would not wish to hurry him."

"To be sure, my good friend; no, no: let him have his time, I say. But he would have had it long ago, if he had any reason in him. What good can he do now, holding on with his eyebrows? Please God to let him go in peace; and so much happier for us all."

When Uncle John appeared, he scolded me for my want of intelligence on the night when I was blinded. Of the four men in that room, the one whom I had noticed least was the very one whom he had meant me especially to observe. At least, so he said; but I fully believed, and did not scruple to tell him, that he had discovered little beyond the information and description given at the time by Mr. Edgar Vaughan. These he had disinterred from the archives of Bow Street and Whitehall, and was then trying to apply them. However, I forgave him freely; inasmuch as, but for my blindness, even blind love would have known me as an objectionable being.

And now I come to a real grievance. When there is another Miss Clara--such a beauty! I can't tell you--and a little Harry, for whose sake this tale is told--why will every one on these premises, even the under-gardener's boy, persist in calling me "Miss Clara?" It makes me stamp sometimes, and such a bad example that is for my children. Dear me, if either of my ducklings were to carry on as I did at their age, I would cut down immediately the largest birch-tree on the property, and order a hogshead of salt. But, to return to that contumely--is it to be suspected that I was more forcible and pronounced, in the days of my trial and misery, than now when I am the happiest of all the young mothers of England? "Come, Conny, tell the truth now, don't I keep you in order?"

"My own delight, I should think you did. I am nearly as much afraid of you as I am of little Clary. Clary ride on Judy now, and Harry on pup Sampiero, and come and see papa go chip, chip, chip?"

"No, Clary stop and see mamma go scratch, scratch, scratch, like Cooky at the pie-crust. Clary love mamma to-day, and papa to-morrow."

And the lovely dear jumps on the stool, to pull the top of my pen. Harry pops out from under the table, and prepares himself for onset. My husband comes and lifts my hair, and throws his arm around me. It is all up now with writing.

"Darlings, I love all three of you, to-day, to-morrow, and for ever. Only don't pull me to pieces."

THE END.

CPSIA information can be obtained
at www.ICGtesting.com
Printed in the USA
BVHW011326131221
623931BV00011B/388